CHILD WELFARE

CHILD WELFARE

England 1872–1989

Harry Hendrick

London and New York

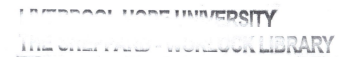

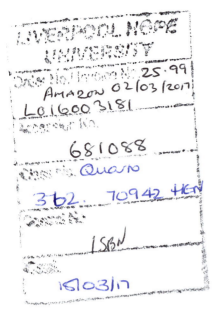
First published 1994
by Routledge
2 Park Square. Milton Park, Abingdon, Oxon OX14 4RN

Simultaneously published in the USA and Canada
by Routledge
711 Third Avenue, New York, NY 10017

Reprinted 1996 (twice)

First published in paperback 2011

© 1994 Harry Hendrick

Phototypeset in Garamond

British Library Cataloguing in Publication Data
A catalogue record for this book is available from the British
Library

Library of Congress Cataloguing in Publication Data
Hendrick, Harry.
Child welfare: England: 1872–1989 / Harry Hendrick.
p.   cm.
Includes bibliographical references and index.
1. Child welfare – England – History – 19th century. 2. Child welfare –
England – History – 20th century.   I. Title.
HV751.A7E55   1994
362.7'0942'0904—dc20   93–22964

ISBN13: 978-0-415-00773-3 (hbk)
ISBN13: 978-0-415-51313-5 (pbk)

Once again to Josie and Eve,
my daughters,
who make everything worthwhile

CONTENTS

Preface   xi
Acknowledgements   xiv

INTRODUCTION: BODIES AND MINDS, VICTIMS
AND THREATS, AND INVESTMENTS   1
The narrative of Bodies/Minds: BODIES   1
The narrative of Bodies/Minds: MINDS (and Bodies)   4
The narrative of Victims/Threats   7
The relationship between Bodies and Minds/Victims and
   Threats   12
Investments   14

Part I The emergence of the child, *c.*1800–94

Introduction

1 IDENTITIES AND DEFINITIONS   21
Preliminary definitions of childhood: the 'natural', the Romantic
   and the evangelical   21
The factory child   24
The delinquent child   27
The school child   29
The Child Study movement   33

Conclusion   37

Part II From rescue and reform to 'children of the nation',
*c.*1872–1918

Introduction   41

2 THE MORALLY REFORMING STATE: RESCUE,
RECLAMATION AND PROTECTION, 1872–1908   43
The infant life protection movement   43

CONTENTS

Child cruelty and the NSPCC   49
The age of consent and punishment of incest   60
Reforming child labour   67
Children in care: the Poor Law, voluntary societies and child
    emigration   74

3 THE SOCIAL SERVICES STATE: PROVIDING
  FOR THE CHILDREN OF THE NATION, 1889–1918   84
The blind, the deaf and the 'feeble-minded'   85
The infant welfare movement   93
The School Meals Service   103
School medical inspection and treatment   111
The Children Act, 1908   121

Conclusion   127

Part III Minds and bodies: contradiction, tension and
              integration, 1918–45

Introduction   131

4 HEALTH AND WELFARE BETWEEN THE WARS   133
Nutrition   133
Medical treatment   141
The handicapped child   145

5 PSYCHOLOGISING THE CHILD   149
Psychology and progressive education   150
Educational psychology and mental testing   153
The child guidance movement   162

6 THE CHILDREN AND YOUNG PERSONS ACT, 1933   177
Changing perspectives on juvenile delinquency   177
The Juvenile Offenders Committee, 1927   178
The scope of the Act   183
The meaning of the legislation   186
Young people's institutional experiences   188

7 THE WAR YEARS   194
Evacuation   194
School meals   199
Health and welfare under the Education Act, 1944   200

Conclusion   203

CONTENTS

Part IV Children of the Welfare State, 1945–89

Introduction   211

8 CHILD CARE POLICY   214
The Curtis Report, 1946   214
The Children Act, 1948   217
The Children Act, the family and the State   220
Deprivation and depravation: Ingleby and the family   222
The Children and Young Persons Acts, 1963 and 1969   227
The 'family service' in the community, 1970–5   235
Fostering, adoption and the Children Act, 1975   237

9 THE REDISCOVERY OF CHILD ABUSE   242
The discovery of the 'battered baby'   243
Maria Colwell: child abuse comes of age   246
The hiatus of concern for abused children between 1908 and
*   the 1960s*   249
The rediscovery of child abuse   253

10 HOSPITAL WELFARE, HEALTH AND POVERTY   258
The welfare of children in hospital   258
'Fit for the future': the child health services   263
The Black Report and 'The Health Divide'   267

11 'CHILDREN ARE PEOPLE, TOO': CHILD CARE
   POLICY IN THE 1980s   272
Child care policy in the 1980s   272
The Children Act, 1989   276
An assessment of the Act   281

Conclusion   285

JUSTIFICATIONS AND EXPLANATIONS   289

Notes and references   293
Bibliography   331
Index   347

PREFACE

This is a textbook about the history of social policies for children. It has been said that much of the history of childhood is really the history of what adults have thought about and done to children. The area of social policy exemplifies this bias. I would like to be able to claim that the following pages present a history from below – informed by children's views and by their responses to the various policies. Alas, the writing of such a history, even if it were possible at this historiographical moment, which I doubt, is beyond my talents. Instead I hope to provide readers with a text which, though written from 'above', is overtly sympathetic to children (and young adolescents) and their perspectives. In my view, historians and sociologists devote far too much time to understanding the class and gender (and, recently, the racial) biases in social policy, at the expense of according proper recognition to the influence of ageism, that is, the repression and oppression of young people, principally through political and economic forces.

Although there are numerous historical accounts of social policy which have either references to or even chapters on children, as well as several important studies of specific social policies involving young people, there is nevertheless a shortage of general and comprehensive texts focusing on their welfare. Furthermore, and broadly speaking, the critical history of relevant legislation, the motives of reformers, the development of the social services and the manner in which they affected children's lives tend to be ignored, or at best are subsumed within apparently more prestigious political analyses. Nor can the history of child welfare be written simply as progressive narrative. The danger remains, however, that the enormous volume of protective legislation involving children can obscure its meaning. It can make interrogative questions appear ungracious. They seem like messengers of discontent. But this should not deter us. In such circumstances good manners are always of secondary importance.

My intention here is to bring together writings that have previously appeared in article, thesis and book form, in order to produce an integrated text on children and social policy in England since the 1870s.* The follow-ing pages will cover a range of topics, including infant protection and welfare, health, delinquency, care procedures, abuse, mental testing, child guidance, and provision for children with special needs. And, while the book proceeds along a narrative course, the emphasis throughout is on issues and controversies. With this in mind, the subject-matter is rarely treated in isolation from either the history of social policy in general or those political, economic, social and cultural influences which impinge themselves on the formation, implementation and development of all social policies. Indeed, it is central to the interpretation offered in this study that decisions concerning children's welfare were (and are) dependent on these influences.

This account will attempt to identify the consequences of various policies for children, not simply in terms of their health or welfare, but also with respect to their happiness and their anxieties. Another aim will be to ask to what extent were children exploited by adults in pursuit of social, economic and political ends? For example, were their needs and wishes made subservient to disciplining parents and ordering the working-class family? How often was the imposition of middle-class norms of social order in the streets and the schools the determining objective of welfare innovation? And, in matters of health and hygiene, to what extent was the full physical, mental and emotional development of children sacrificed to political and economic goals? But this is not meant to suggest that the oppression of children is always class-based, for *ageism*, in the form of a prejudice against young people shared by adults of all social classes, may well be shown to have been an active force. The consideration of *ageism* as an influence on the design and practice of social policy for children is an innovatory feature of this study. It can hardly be doubted that ageism is closely related to, if not entirely dependent upon, the social and political status of children and, therefore, the politics of childhood is implicitly considered through examinations of the ways in which different social policies exemplify the relationships between children and parents, edu-cators, social workers, doctors and the law.

In the following pages several conclusions are reached. First, the history of children and childhood is inescapably inseparable from the history of social policy. We cannot hope to understand the former without an appreci-ation of the latter. No other sector of the population has been so closely identified with the expansion and multiplication of these policies since the 1870s, and with the growth of the State and its 'expert' agencies. Second, the general effect of social policies has been to create a perception of children which sees them as predominantly ignorant, dependent, vulner-able, untutored and very often threatening. Of course, there is no denying

* Legislation applies throughout only to England and Wales. A separate jurisdiction and practice apply in Scotland.

PREFACE

that at different stages in their lives children do inhabit each of these conditions, and often more than one simultaneously. The important issue, however, is what adults do to children on the basis of these conditions. Third, while many of the policies have ensured that children have (i) a degree of medical attention (the extent depending upon the child's social class), (ii) some protection from the arbitrary exercise of parental power, (iii) the provision of adequate meals, and (iv) a number of safeguards, legal and otherwise, for their physical and mental health, certain features of these policies have also pursued other objectives. For example, the Edwardian concern with 'national efficiency', and the perennial interest in social discipline, the stability of the family, and an appropriately educated labour force. Neither can we overlook concerns of a metaphorical nature involving the child as a symbol of progress, purity, innocence and redemption. Fourth, the manner in which policies were created and implemented revealed the inability of children to influence their own treatment. In some circumstances this was inevitable, if only for biological reasons, but not in every respect, and therefore children's powerlessness needs to be recognised and critically examined rather than passively accepted. Finally, though it is not unusual to say that childhood is a social construction, this is one of the first attempts to show the process of construction in any historical detail and, more specifically, to show the role played by social policy in that process.

ACKNOWLEDGEMENTS

A general textbook calls upon the work of numerous scholars, the majority of whom have laboured for years in the archives of one sort or another, doggedly researching their specialist monographs. I hope that the authors upon whose work I rely heavily in certain chapters will not feel abused, betrayed or exploited. I have put their studies to different uses. In many instances standard texts have been used as a take-off point; sometimes I have paraphrased several pages of a work, often of a specialist nature, in order to fill in the gaps in my own knowledge and to complete the narrative or the argument of a particular chapter. Occasionally I have taken extracts as the opening for a counter-interpretation or speculation; and where appropriate I have drawn upon well-known scholars in support of my own views.

In some respects it is invidious to single out those authors who have been of special assistance to me. On the other hand, so many have been sources of stimulation, information and instruction that I feel the need to acknowledge them: David Armstrong, Victor Bailey, Peter Boss, George Behlmer, R. Dingwall, J. M. Eekelaar and T. Murray, Jacques Donzelot, Deborah Dwork, Michael Freeman, Nick Frost and Mike Stein, Deborah Gorham, Bernard Harris, David Hirst, Jean Heywood, John Hurt, Jane Lewis, John Macnicol, Nigel Middleton, Jean Packman, Nigel Parton, David Pritchard, Lionel Rose, Nikolas Rose, Brian Simon, Gillian Sutherland, John Stewart, Deborah Thom, Charles Webster, John Welshman and Adrian Wooldridge.

I am also very grateful to Michael Hill, John Macnicol, Nigel Parton and John Stewart for their comments and criticisms of draft chapters. I am especially grateful to Anne Digby and John Stewart for the encouragement they have given me over the years. It has been much appreciated.

Several of the governing themes of this book first saw the light of day in papers presented to seminars at Oxford Brookes University, and the universities of Oxford, London, and Linkoping, Sweden. My thanks to participants for their helpful comments. I would like to thank Professor Bengt Sandin for inviting me to speak in the stimulating environment of the Department of Child Studies at Linkoping, and for his kindness and hospitality.

Parts of the book have appeared in the following: 'Constructions and Reconstructions of British Childhood: An Interpretative Survey, 1800 to the Present', in Alison James and Alan Prout (eds), *Constructing and Reconstructing Childhood: Contemporary Issues in the Sociological Study of Childhood*, Basingstoke: The Falmer Press, 1990; 'Child Labour, Medical Capital, and the School Medical Service, c.1880–1918', in Roger Cooter (ed.), *In the Name of the Child: Health and Welfare, 1880–1940*, London: Routledge, 1992; and 'Changing Attitudes to Children, 1800–1914', *Genealogists' Magazine*, June 1992. I am grateful for permission to use this material here.

I also wish to thank the Nuffield Foundation for a small grant and the staff of the Bodleian Library for their friendly service.

I am indebted to Judith Hendrick for looking after the domestic welfare of our daughters.

By way of the usual disclaimer, I alone am responsible for the arguments presented in this book.

INTRODUCTION
Bodies and Minds, Victims and Threats, and Investments

This introduction has two objectives. First, to propose the use of two dualisms – mind/body and victim/threat – in order to provide a compass, in the sense of taking measurements, with which to navigate a way through the various histories of social policy in search of attitudes towards and treatment of children. Second, to suggest that these dualisms have tended to encapsulate children in an entity of investment. Bodies and Minds and Victims and Threats, well-known images in historical and contemporary legal literature, are deployed here as a means of revealing and examining different and yet overlapping policies concerning children.[1] Each of these images involves both a dualism and an opposition or contradiction: Bodies as opposed to Minds; perhaps in contradiction to Minds, and yet philosophically speaking representing the theory that 'in any domain of reality there are two independent underlying principles, e.g. mind and matter' (OED). Although Victims/Threats cannot be underpinned by the same philosophical theory, where children are concerned, as a dualism it represents a similar kind of relationship as Bodies/Minds, i.e. it constitutes a specific 'domain of reality' – in this case one that was primarily located in law, and which usually expressed itself through concepts of 'delinquency' and what came to be known as childcare proceedings.

We begin with two narratives: Bodies/Minds and Victims/Threats. These will provide the basis for an understanding of the character of child welfare in the period as it will be defined later on.

THE NARRATIVE OF BODIES/MINDS

BODIES

First, some general remarks concerning bodies. The history and sociology of the body is currently an academically fashionable area of research. However, to be fashionable is not necessarily a disabling characteristic. So, what can be said in favour of using the notion of 'the body' in a history of children's welfare? Bryan Turner, the sociologist, has written that a

1

sociology of the body 'involves a discussion of social control and any discussion of social control must consider the control of women's bodies by men under a system of patriarchy'.[2] Leaving aside the reference to 'social control', which is of dubious analytical value, these words could just as easily have been written in respect of children (indeed, it is surprising that Turner completely ignores children). For his observation that 'the body is a location for the exercise of will over desire'[3] is especially true of the age relationship between children and adults, which allows adults to impose their will on the child's body irrespective of the child's desire. Much of the history of social policy, as will be shown, is in fact the history of the imposition of adult will upon children's bodies. This imposition took four primary forms: food and feeding, medical inspection and treatment, the ordering of the body in movement and of the tongue in speech, and the infliction of physical pain on the body in elementary and industrial schools, reformatories, orphanages and Poor Law institutions.

When we look at the body in relation to children during our period, we have to remember that it has been 'experienced and expressed' within a particular cultural system, 'both private and public', which has itself 'changed over time'.[4] The body, then, does not exist as a timeless entity, forever the same from the perspective of itself and from that of the observer. The body in relation to mind (defined as 'will, self, soul') 'differs notably according to century, class, circumstances and culture, and societies often possess a plurality of competing meanings'.[5] This will certainly be shown to be the case in this study. For example, the working-class child came to be 'known' primarily through observation of its body in the classroom after the introduction of compulsory education in the 1870s and 1880s. Such an identification of the child through its physicality was both temporally and class specific, and it was by no means an uncontested process between middle-class experts and working-class parents. It is argued here that the disciplining of the *school* child's body through its physical ordering and through 'silence', corporal punishment, medical inspection and treatment and, for the children of the poor, school meals was in accordance with the view of the body as 'a lord of misrule'.[6]

One particularly helpful way of looking at 'the body' is to see it in terms of what has been called 'political anatomy'.[7] Michel Foucault has referred to the human body as defining 'a space whose lines, volumes, surfaces, and routes are laid down . . . by the anatomical atlas'. In effect the atlas became 'a means of interpreting the body'.[8] And no group of people were more eager to use this atlas than those with medical interests. Medicine 'analysed and investigated bodies'.[9] This had particular reference to children when towards the end of the nineteenth century medicine began to 'fabricate' the child's body (in common with 'various moral and educational concerns'), which meant that it entered medical discourse as 'a discrete object with attendant pathologies'.[10]

2

Broadly speaking, when social scientists, philanthropists, doctors, and educationalists and reformers looked at children in the period, say, 1870–1914, they saw 'bodies' – that is to say, they saw children who were homeless and ragged; infants who were starved, neglected and sometimes murdered by paid carers; children who were hungry; children who were were ill; children who suffered from mental and physical disabilities; children who were cruelly treated by parents; and delinquent children who were put into close proximity to adult criminals. Even when these working-class children were in schools, it was their sick, undernourished and otherwise defective bodies rather than their minds (emotions) which imposed themselves on the educational system.[11] This history is well known through the work of Dr Barnardo's, the Infant Life Protection Society, the reform of the education of the deaf and the blind, the NSPCC, the campaigns for free school meals and medical inspection and treatment of school children, and the establishment of a juvenile court system – all of which focused on the body. However, it needs to be stressed that for social reformers and educationalists such as Margaret McMillan, after 1895, with her close reading of works on psychology, neurology and physiology, there always existed a relationship of some kind between body and mind, although for her 'the body came first'.[12]

This is not to say that Victorian intellectuals had no interest in the Mind, or in the mind–body as sharing the same functioning principles. Nevertheless, 'they all thought physiologically: they adopted the well-knit body as their model for the well-formed mind'.[13] After all, the healthy body had a special place in nineteenth-century thought, if only through the development of physiology, which promised to reveal the 'laws of life'. There was also the emergence of physiological psychology, which promoted the interdependence of body and mind; and, third, there was a belief in physical education as a path to personal culture, which was necessary if the whole person was to be fostered. In this context, the 'healthy man' was he who displayed the influence of Carlyle's healthy hero, Spencer's biologically perfect man, Newman's gentleman-Christian, and especially Kingsley's muscular Christian. Apart from specialist medical interest in psychophysiology, the mind–body relationship was not pursued.[14]

For the Victorian intellectual, then, there were two kinds of health: bodily and spiritual. Both were seen to have a similar effect on the mind in that they imported a sense of belonging, of being in harmony (however, there were disagreements as to the priority of body over mind). The place where bodily and spiritual health came together, perhaps most perfectly, was on the playing-field in games. The reformed public schools, while concerned with the morality of the mind, none the less emphasised the health of the body. For the schools, and for those who believed in their ethos, the game embodied a set of moral imperatives in which the healthy man was an athlete – physical but with moral definitions: 'strong body and strong character'. It was in this sense that the Victorian's Manly Ideal equated health and manliness.[15] Such an ideal had little room for the mind as the guarantor of the emotions; 'character' was what mattered, and this was part of *bodily* health. While this ideal had little direct application to working-class children, it remained influential – as a motif – in terms of the ways in which these children were perceived in class relations.

THE NARRATIVE OF BODIES/MINDS

MINDS (and Bodies)

In emphasising the importance of the body in the identification of children during the late-Victorian and Edwardian periods, I do not mean to deny the existence of mind in the scientific perception of them, in particular of infants. It is well known that from at least the 1880s the Child Study movement focused attention in part on the mental characteristics of young children, on the 'brain power' of school children, and on identifying 'feeble-minded' pupils. However, at this time the interest in mind was as a feature of development, of evolution in terms of distinguishing man from animals, in support of the theory of recapitulation, and as showing how far certain human traits were innate or learned. Medical and psychological developments meant that the mind could no longer be considered as entirely separate from the body, so that the progress of identifying the child's mind was also in part a continuation of the more complex under-standing of its body. All the same, there is a distinction to be made between the notion of the child's mind in the late nineteenth century as opposed to the inter-war period and thereafter. On the one hand, psycholo-gists in the latter period rejected the work of their predecessors as 'idiosyn-cratic', 'anecdotal', 'unsystematic', neglectful of all the relevant factors, and so methodologically variable as to lack comparability.[16] On the other hand, having noted that the nineteenth-century interest was with evolutionary aspects of mind, the inter-war interest (which had been developing since the early 1900s) was more concerned with the emotions and with individual adjustment to, and integration within, the community, and with the mass assessment of IQ through mental testing. In the later period, the manage-ment of minds, as will be shown below, was an objective of welfare.

The new interest can be seen developing in the pre-1914 practice of Dr David Eder at Margaret McMillan's Deptford Clinic, where he made notes on 'the nervous traumas hidden in the starved little bodies of his child patients', through to the inter-war years when children were increasingly described as 'nervous', 'delicate', 'unstable', 'maladjusted', 'over-sensitive', and so on. Eder's focus was one consequence of the 'invention of the neuroses' towards the end of the nineteenth century when it was realised that some people suffered not from madness, but from 'mental instability'. By 1920 this new awareness had led to what has been called the 'medicalisation of the mind'. Children were now important in the 'observation and surveillance' of the mind because of the potential for change: children's 'abnormalities are as unshaped as their normalities and they can often be modelled to what shape we please'.[17]

In the inter-war period, the 'mental welfare' of children was attended to by educational psychology in schools, the British Paediatric Association (1928), the National Institute of Child Psychology (1931), the Children's Clinic for the Treatment and Study of Nervous and Delicate Children (1928), the Tavistock Clinic (1920) and the Child Guidance Council (1927). However, by this time the perception involved body and mind in a new complex. Influential doctors, such as Hector Cameron in his classic text *The Nervous Child* (1919), advocated seeing childhood within the remit of preventive medicine, and urged his profession to 'busy itself in nurseries and schools, seeking to apply there the teachings of Psychology, Physiology, Heredity and Hygiene'. Arguments of this kind sought to unite body and mind with the social and material environment, and they found their institutional expression in the increasing number of child guidance clinics. Thus Cameron wrote that the child's body was 'moulded and shaped by the environment in which he grows. Pure air, a rational diet and free movement give strength and symmetry to every part.'[18] Clearly, then, there was a shift from a 'hygienist emphasis on children's bodies and physical health to an emphasis on children's minds and emotions'.[19]

By 1940 social, medical and psychiatric knowledge of children was such that the mind–body unity in common with environmental and familial influences gave children (and childhood) a greater sense of depth than at any other time in their history. Indeed, the excavation of their minds, through child guidance and the growing influence of psychiatry, together with the presence and surveillance of their bodies through the collective experiences of doctors, dentists and nutritionists since the introduction of medical inspection and school feeding in the early 1900s, had given children detailed individual and group histories. Besides the growth of the child guidance movement during the inter-war years, the British Paediatric Association helped the medical interest in children to move away from the manifestation of 'adult diseases' in their bodies to diseases peculiar to them alone, so that by 1940 children's diseases had become a speciality for physicians. [20]

Nevertheless, when wartime evacuation occurred nearly 900,000 children produced largely unanticipated social and psychological problems, notably the thousands who arrived in reception areas in a dirty condition, the many other thousands with head lice, and those experiencing enuresis (bed-wetting), in addition to a variety of other physical and mental ailments. During the course of the war some 15,000–20,000 evacuees were classed as 'unbilletable' owing to temperamental and behavioural problems. Throughout the periods of evacuation much attention was given to both the physical and the emotional condition of the children (and also to those who experienced the Blitz and others who were in special war nurseries). Under the influence of psychologists and psycho-analysts such as Susan Isaacs, Anna Freud, Melanie Klein and John Bowlby, these groups of children were seen as being of both body *and* mind. In legislative terms nothing was done to alleviate either the physical or the mental suffering of the children, though numerous departmental circulars tried to attend to local problems. To a large extent, however, evacuation provided contemporaries with a dramatic illustration of the proximity of body and mind in children in relation to environment. Apart from the social significance of the evacuation process, it was the evidence produced of mental disorientation and emotional turmoil (both of which were felt to have serious social consequences), caused in part by separation of children from their parents (mothers), that proved to be one of the formative influences on early post-war childcare policy.

The first public initiative in this policy came with the Curtis Report (1946), which indicted the conditions in local-authority and charitable homes, and the organisation and personnel of the childcare system as it had existed. The report led to a major piece of legislation, the Children Act, 1948, which established a centralised and coherent child care structure, with trained personnel and local-authority children's officers. The Act heralded, as many child care officers were later to testify, 'a new dawn' in the community care and protection of children. These were to be not only children of the Welfare State, cared for both in body and in mind, but also children of 'the family' – soon to be the recurring dominant theme in virtually all aspects of child care policy.[21]

Of equal significance for the future of children's welfare was the critical refocusing of perspective in medicine with paediatricians increasingly looking at the 'normal child' as the source for the creation of the 'sick child'. In fact, interest was slowly moving away from notions of 'normal' and 'abnormal' towards that of 'development'. The decisive point was the publication in 1953 of Illingworth's *The Normal Child*, which sought to describe both physical and psychological normality. This approach removed the child from its isolation and put it – body and mind – into the community. Where once the child had been delicate, nervous or solitary, it became battered, deprived and neglected. By this time, the 1950s, paediatricians had also discovered the mind of the child. In 1943 a committee of the BPA suggested closer working relations between child guidance clinics and children's hospitals. A special Child Psychology Sub-committee was formed which warned that paediatricians should acquaint themselves with child psychology, pointing out that no hard-and-fast line could be drawn between physical and psychological disabilities. Thus, by the end of the

1940s, children's minds and bodies, and their social identity, were regarded as indivisible if only in terms of the mental consequences of bodily sickness and discomfort.[22]

However, the rediscovery of child abuse in the 1960s and 1970s re-emphasised the importance of the body, in both the physical and the sexual senses, for perceptions of children as specifically victims and more generally as vulnerable beings. This is especially true where sexual abuse is concerned. It is well known that the abused child, primarily through its body, was portrayed as the 'victim' of a disturbed national culture in which, according to its critics, conventional family and moral values, respect for authority and the rule of law were all cast into doubt by the social, sexual and political 'permissiveness' of the post-war years. The abused child took on a metaphorical role while providing the physical evidence of moral decay. The political meaning invested in *abused* children was one of the principal reasons why the 1970s and 1980s saw a shift back to a relatively straightforward interest in bodies as opposed either to minds or the mind–body unity.

This brief outline of the significance of the mind–body dualism has attempted to show that during the period *circa* 1880s–1940s the emphasis among professionals and social-welfare reformers moved from (*a*) focusing on the child's *body* (1880s–1914) – mainly as an object of psychological observation, as a receptacle of medical inspection and treatment, school feeding and clothing, and as the object of school discipline – to (*b*) that of the *mind* as evidenced by the increasing interest in children's neurosis and their emotional stability, the psycho-social interpretation of delinquency (interests which were institutionalised through the growth of child guidance clinics), and the spread of mental testing in schools. Of course – and this needs to be stressed – there remained a concern with the body (and the mind–body unity), which continued to be of medical, social, political and disciplinary relevance, notably in the debate on inter-war living standards and as illustrating urban poverty among evacuees. However, I hope that an awareness of the mind–body dualism will help to elucidate the different meanings of social policy for children throughout the period. But this dualism alone cannot fully explicate the policies. A successful understanding also requires the incorporation of a second dualism, that of victims/threats, and it is to this that we now turn.[23]

THE NARRATIVE OF VICTIMS/THREATS

In one respect there is no difficulty in identifying periods or occasions when children have been presented as victims: of cruelty, neglect, hunger, homelessness, war, illness, indifference, and so on. Much of the social legislation from the early nineteenth-century Factory Acts through to the Prevention of Cruelty to Children Act, 1889, the school meals and medical inspection legislation of 1906–7, the Children Act, 1948, and beyond to the Children Act, 1989, has been, in part at least, concerned with protecting children from forms of neglect and abuse in the widest sense of these words. In nearly all of the legislation the rhetoric has been that of the child as helpless, as being acted upon, usually in some kind of damaging manner. However, it is one of the arguments of this book that despite numerous advantages accruing from the ostensibly protective Acts the victims were rarely allowed to reap the benefits of sympathy for their condition without the suspicion of what they might become if, in the nineteenth century, they were left unprotected by charitable organisations such as Dr Barnardo's or, in the twentieth century, by the State. The child victim was nearly always seen as harbouring the possibility of another condition, one that was sensed to be threatening: to moral fibre, sexual propriety, the sanctity of the family, the preservation of the race, law and order, and the wider reaches of citizenship. It is important for a proper understanding of social policy in relation to children (and adolescents) that we recognise just how much of so-called protective legislation has been concerned with their presence as *threats* rather than their suffering as *victims*. Indeed, more often than not, the image of young people as threats has undermined their reality as victims.

We can best see this dualism at work from the early nineteenth century onwards in attitudes and in legislation. The full extent of the overlapping between 'victim' and 'threat' status will become evident throughout the following chapters. In this introduction four examples must suffice. First, the charitable effort of the nineteenth century as epitomised in the evangelical concern for children and exemplified in the persons of Hannah More, one of the founders of the Sunday-school movement, and Lord Shaftesbury, the great Tory social reformer. The evangelicals, who from the late eighteenth century set out to reform the manners and morals of society, were foremost in an appreciation of the importance of childhood, and of the need, as they saw it, to protect society from the children of the poor, for which purpose they established Sunday schools. Hannah More, looking back on the apparent success of the schools, asked:

> Where are the half-naked, poor, forlorn, wretched, ignorant creatures we used to find lying about on Sunday . . . swearing, gaming, reprobates, vagabonds, flying as it were in the face of the Almighty, a disgrace to their parents, a scandal to their country, a dishonour to their God, and a prey to the devil – where are they now to be found? At school, at prayer, at church – serving the Lord, keeping his Commandments.[24]

The presence of children as representing a threat here is obvious – be it social, religious or moral. Unsurprisingly, given the evangelical view of children as inherently possessed of Original Sin, believers had little alternative but to view them as being in need of discipline and education in order to provide the necessary salvation, and to protect not only their souls but also Christian society itself.

Lord Shaftesbury, 'the Moses who led the children of bondage into their Promised Land', was without doubt the foremost social reformer of the nineteenth century. He was active in campaigns to save climbing boys, factory children, and mineworkers, and in getting street-children into Ragged Schools. Street-children, in particular, ever growing in number, were cast in the role of 'savages', threatening to the continued development of Victorian civilisation. For Shaftesbury the task of social reform, of 'saving' children, rescuing them from the ravages of industrialism and the iniquities of the city, was made all the more urgent by his belief in the Second Coming. 'There is very little seeming, and no real, hope for mankind', he wrote in his diary, 'but in the Second Advent.' He regarded evil as more powerful and lasting than good: 'evil is natural, good is unnatural; evil requires nothing but as he is, good must find the soil prepared by the grace of God'. This was an Augustinian view of the world: doom-laden, propelled by the Fall and governed by Original Sin.

There was another related and equally potent threat in Shaftesbury's mind, linking politics to religion. In an article on 'Infant Labour' he observed that 'the two great demons in morals and politics, Socialism and Chartism' were 'stalking through the land', while at the same time 'the vast and inflammable mass [lay] waiting . . . for the spark to explode it into mischief'. If this were not to occur, then children must not be neglected, particularly if it were to come to pass that 'God's good providence has yet in store for us some high and arduous calling'.[25] In such a philosophy, the threat posed by the child is both literal and symbolic. On the one hand, the street-child challenges civilisation through its threat to political order and, on the other, the child figure embodies a 'natural evil'.

The second example covers the spectrum of legislation concerning infant welfare, the age of consent, cruelty to children, school meals, and school medical and treatment programmes. Numerous studies have shown that this legislation was in part at least an attempt to sustain the racial purity of Britain, to counter infant mortality, to protect the integrity of the Empire, and to maintain a stable social structure. For instance, one – among several – of the principal reasons why it was deemed to be important to legislate against cruelty to children was the fear that such children could grow up to be cruel and ineffectual citizens themselves. It was believed that in their cruel treatment lay the seeds of a threatening citizenry. Similarly with respect to hungry and sick children, and improperly reared infants. It was John Gorst, a leading Tory social reformer, who wrote that the object of his book *Children of the Nation* (1906) was 'to bring home to the people of Great Britain a sense of the danger of neglecting the physical condition of the nation's children'. There is no doubt that in many instances humanitarianism and legitimate indignation played important roles in bringing about reform, but it is very unlikely that ameliorating Acts would have reached the statute books without the element of fear.[26]

Third, from the time of the 1861 Industrial Schools Act children could be sent to these schools for begging, wandering or frequenting the company of known thieves. In other words, these children could be sent to the schools for reasons other than criminal guilt. They were in the schools because they were thought to constitute a risk to society as much as a risk to themselves. There were also 'reformatories', which were intended for those found guilty of a criminal offence. By 1913 there was a clear call in a government report for the amalgamation of the two types of institution, since both were aimed at preventing children from falling into what was described as 'criminal courses'. In the Report of the Young Offenders Committee, 1927, the position of the deprived child was revealingly clarified in relation to the depraved child: 'there is little or no difference in character and needs between the neglected and the delinquent child. It is often a mere accident whether he is brought before the court because he is wandering or beyond control or because he has committed some offence. Neglect leads to delinquency and delinquency is often the direct outcome of neglect.'[27] In some respects this was an expression of the desire for social stability at a time of regional social distress in the inter-war economic depression. But it was also a reflection of a prejudice that can best be described as ageist in that the legitimacy of the deduction was inherently dependent upon its applicability to young people. If it had been uttered with respect to adults, it would have been ridiculed as nonsensical.

The terms of reference for the Young Offenders Committee asked it to 'enquire into the treatment of young offenders and young people who, owing to bad associations or surroundings require protection and training'. The committee also considered itself free to look at 'the neglected boy or girl who has not yet committed offences but who, owing to want of parental control, bad associations or other reasons needs protection and training'. This language, and the thinking behind it, served to bracket neglected and indeed cruelly treated children together with criminally liable children and, therefore, it fused notions of depravity and deprivation. Thus 'protection and training' was a carefully chosen combination of notions, designed to accomplish a particular task, namely to turn the threatening victim into the self-supporting individual; into the citizen of the community. Protection, then, never existed simply within its own confines; it usually dwelt within a policy which had extra-territorial objectives. The outcome of this construction in the form of the Children and Young Persons Act, 1933, which abolished the distinction between reformatory and industrial schools, renaming them approved schools, was to emphasise the potential for delinquency among neglected children, rather than attempt to ameloriate the non-delinquent consequences of neglect.[28] The fact is that

10

children were seen first and foremost as threats – as law-breakers, rather than as victims of law-breakers.

Fourth, a brief consideration of post-1940s social legislation suggests that there is an overtly political framework influencing the direction in which the dualism proceeds at any one time. The issues of the post-war period can be categorised as professionalising public childcare practice, rehabilitating the 'problem family', responding to the rise in juvenile crime, the recognition of child physical and sexual abuse, and the creation of strategies for coping with the problem. The political influences are usually described as being Labour's social democracy 1945–51, Conservatism and consensus 1951–74, social democracy and dissent 1974–9, and the emergence of the New Right from 1979.

The first period witnessed a liberal humanitarianism in welfare work with children, through which they were to be restored to the family. On one level, there is no denying that the children who were in public care were looked upon as victims rather than as threats. On the other hand, their social and political significance arose not from being victims but because of the relationship of children *per se* to *families*. Children outside families, argued John Bowlby in his profoundly influential theory of 'maternal deprivation', were in danger of becoming either emotionally disturbed and/or criminally delinquent. Consequently, children as victims reappear (indirectly) yet again in the 1950s and 1960s as potential threats to the civic body – society. This view attained legislative authority with the Ingleby Report and the subsequent Children and Young Persons Act, 1969, which united deprivation and depravation through delinquency and neglect, both of which were seen as products of the disturbed family.[29]

The figure of the child as an overt threat was much less in evidence during the period in the 1970s, which was noted for the evaporation of the consensus and the rise of anti-psychiatry, deviance theory, Marxism, and welfare rights practice. The social deprivation approach tended to dominate social work during its 'radical hour'. However, in the midst of the political debates concerning the family, there was little in the way of a recognition of children as victims. Issues of class and gender dominated the radical agenda. Nor did the rise of the New Right affect this recognition. Instead the slowly emerging interest in child abuse was transformed into a 'moral panic' after the murder of seven-year-old Maria Colwell by her step-father, which culminated in the 'anti-natural family' provisions of the Children Act, 1975. Sections of the Left criticised this Act, not because of its attitude to children, but because it offered no economic or social assistance to poor families.[30] Not for the first time, the status of the child as victim was overshadowed by traditional left-wing concern for the economic status of the working-class family. Of course, these two status conditions were intimately related, but they were also distinct.

The most perplexing, revealing and distressing type of victim is the child

11

who has been deliberately abused, physically and sexually. A clue to the ambiguous status of this child can be found in the question asked by two contemporary social-policy analysts. Given that in 1987 alone approximately 15 million children died throughout the world, many of 'predictable and preventable causes', and that millions of children were experiencing the effects of poverty in Britain, why does the death of one child – such as Jasmine Beckford in Brent in 1985 – result in widespread media interest? Was the public expression of concern directed at the child as a victim or as a symbol, a representative of what was felt to be a more disturbing and widespread phenomenon than its own death? Perhaps the answer is to be found in the remarks of an MP who asked in the House of Commons in 1986 whether the Church had a role to play in helping to save the nation from 'the so-called permissive society and the slackening of moral constraints that have resulted in people being given less support by the bonds and discipline of family life'. Another Member responded by saying that he hoped the prophets of the permissive society 'should now be able to recognise the social wreckage they have helped to encourage'. Obviously, the significance of this exchange is that it immediately connects the child abuse issue with a much wider range of problems symbolised by the 'permissive society'.[31] It is in this way that we can speak of the dualism of children as victims and as threats.

THE RELATIONSHIP BETWEEN BODIES AND MINDS/ VICTIMS AND THREATS

Let us now look at children as *Victims* and *Threats* in relation to children as *Bodies* and *Minds*. The relationships can be expressed as follows:

VICTIMS: their *Bodies* are sick, malnourished and abused; their *Minds* are tormented, frightened, anxious, diseased and abused.

THREATS: their *Bodies* are also sick, malnourished and abused; and their *Minds* are also tormented, frightened, anxious, diseased and abused.

In other words, the 'objective' condition of the children is more or less the same, irrespective of whether or not they are labelled as victims or as threats. It is the social construction inherent in the labelling process which determines their definition as either victims or threats. It is important to keep this in mind, for it will help to shape an understanding of how and why social policy for child welfare appeared as it did during the period *c.*1870–1989.

Turning to *Bodies* and *Minds* in relation to *Victims* and *Threats*:

BODIES of *Victims*: sick, malnourished and abused. BODIES of *Threats*: sick, malnourished and abused.

MINDS of *Victims*: tormented, frightened, anxious, diseased and abused.

MINDS of *Threats*: also tormented, frightened, anxious, diseased and abused.

Once again the condition of the Bodies and Minds does not vary between Victims and Threats. The 'body' of the Victim and of the Threat share the same condition (varying only according to particular circumstances). Similarly, the 'mind' of the Victim and of the Threat share the same condition. In this respect there is no difference between any combination. Neither the physical nor the mental condition of the child determines its identification as either victim or threat. However, the very existence of these dualisms, and the common understanding as to their meanings, meant that children could easily be categorised without reference to their individuality since what was deemed to be relevant for the formation and implementation of policy was their designated category. Nevertheless, there is an important distinction at work throughout the period, and throughout all the investigations and the legislation. In the early period, 1870–1914, the child, whether as victim or as threat, is seen to be constituted far more by its body than by its mind, albeit that the recognition of the latter was increasingly of interest to psychologists and educationalists (though neither bothered much about the child's *emotional* geography in relation to the development of personality).

With the growing familiarity of Mind (emotions) which, as was shown above, became a significant dimension of childcare in the inter-war period, a much more complex understanding of childhood developed. It was one that began to appreciate the interplay between body and mind, prompting mind to occupy a special place of its own in the hierarchy of cause and effect in physical and mental development. One crucially important consequence of this more or less new and certainly more widespread appreciation was the beginning of the erosion of the distinction between victim and threat status. Perhaps this is better-expressed as the enveloping of the former by the latter. The terminology begins to be almost anachronistic since children who were *victims* posed a variety of *threats* to public health, social stability, family cohesion, and educational progress – to name but four areas. Similarly, children who were seen as *threats* were so primarily by virtue of their *victim* status, that is, their neglect or cruel treatment led them into situations or forms of behaviour that in some way or another were deemed to be threatening to the social order. While this was recognised in a simplified form in the nineteenth century, the introduction of Mind into the equation allowed for a 'scientific' understanding (which made for more effective treatment), and also for a deeper appreciation of the variety of threats posed by the child.

INVESTMENTS

The two dualisms described here served as ordering categories by which child welfare could be justified and organised. It is not intended to suggest that these were the only portrayals of children. Far from it. But they were the principal identities, or what I call the informing identities used by contemporaries; though in different ways at different times. However, the dualisms were not ends in themselves. They achieved meaningful political existence only when they had completed their task of transforming children into investments. Not that the transformation always worked easily or successfully or in the same manner. But in one way or another some sort of transformation usually occurred leading to investments of a racial, educational, familial, medical, social or political nature. As Nikolas Rose has observed: 'In different ways, at different times, and by many different routes varying from one section of society to another, the health, welfare, and rearing of children have been linked in thought and practice to the destiny of the nation and the responsibilities of the state.'[32] Let us look at a few examples.

In Part Two below we shall focus on a number of state and philanthropic social policies whose objective was either in some general sense to safeguard the nation's future, as with the infant welfare movement, or to inculcate responsible parenthood, as with the work of the NSPCC. Similarly, the motives behind the punishment-of-incest legislation and the care of the 'feeble-minded' had more to do with a combination of racial and hygienic considerations than with an uncluttered concern for child welfare, just as the school meals service and school medical inspection and treatment aspired to express in part a commitment to new understandings of public health while also securing a sound return on educational provision. This was of particular importance from 1901 onwards with the political birth of the 'national efficiency' movement. However, the most popular focus was on the sustenance of the British race since 'An Empire such as ours . . . requires a race vigorous and industrious and intrepid'. According to Bentley Gilbert, after the Boer War ended in 1902, influential opinion believed that 'an unhealthy schoolchild was a danger to all society, [and] that it was in society's selfish, non-humanitarian interest to see that the child was [medically] treated'.[33]

The range of investment interests between 1918 and 1945 was more diverse and less easy to classify. The inter-war debates involving nutrition and health say less about investing children in the future and more about the relative unimportance of child welfare in a period of economic depression and financial retrenchment. The reason being that those children suffering malnutrition and ill-health were not deemed to be of sufficient investment significance to warrant the necessary expenditure. The expansion of the child guidance movement, however, was a far more popular

14

source of protecting the future since it promised to regulate families, harmonise individuals and, in so doing, enhance national mental health. In attempting to deal with the emotional life of children, the clinics looked to their growth to maturity. But a healthy maturity could only be reached by properly adjusted children. In order to produce such children it was necessary to understand their wishes and anxieties. Dr Emmanuel Miller, one of the leading figures in the movement, explained the significance of the task: 'Understanding produces tolerance, and tolerance gives us the power to guide.'[34]

In Part Four the nature of children as investments is more straight-forward. The post-1945 society was marked, for a time at least, by a sense of confidence in democracy, in the potential for progress, and by a faith in the family as the ideal humanitarian and disciplinary environment. In more cynical mood, children were also of value with regard to older concerns such as national and racial hegemony. The Royal Commission on Population (1949) warned of the effects of a low and declining birth rate on 'the security and influence of Great Britain' and on 'the maintenance and extension of Western values'.[35] Not even the rediscovery of child abuse can be said to have lacked characteristics of investment. It has already been argued that in their role as victims/threats these children became figures in 'moral panics' arising out of political struggles involving fundamental questions of liberal government. The solutions to child abuse were usually in part investments in social and political consensus, most recently in the Children Act, 1989.

Hopefully sufficient explanation has now been given to indicate the emphasis of the arguments to be encountered in the following chapters. Many of the issues raised in this introduction are taken up and developed throughout the book, though without continually referring to what I have described here as the governing themes. I do not want to be accused of leading the reader by the nose. And I am not suggesting that the entire range of social policies for children can be neatly fitted into my schema; indeed, some readers may well find it too schematic. I do, however, want to avoid presenting the history of children and social policy simply as either narrative or a series of disconnected pragmatic responses. Perhaps I have erred too far in the opposite direction. At least I hope that readers who reject the dualisms and/or their relationship with the concept of investment will be forced to think through their own interpretation. My intention here has been to point towards a set of understandings which may act as avenues down which it is possible to travel so as to arrive at hitherto undisclosed destinations, secret places, obscured from the public gaze.

Part I

THE EMERGENCE OF THE CHILD
*c.*1800–94

INTRODUCTION

The purpose here is to survey some of the most important social constructions of British childhood since the end of the eighteenth century, in order to illustrate the historical variability of the concept, and to show that by the 1890s the emergence of a clear notion of 'the child' was beginning to be formulated. Such a brief account is unable to do more than suggest the principal identities and the attributable 'prime movers of social change'.[1] The hope is that a familiarity with these perceptions, as held in the first instance by dominant interests, professional, religious and political, will both help to explain the tenacity and the self-confidence of our 'modern' interpretations of 'childhood', and unravel those understandings of childhood held by reformers, politicians and administrators throughout our period.

The focus is on four related themes: First, the gradual shift away from an idea of childhood fragmented by geography – urban/rural – and by class life-experiences, to one that was much more uniform and coherent; second, the rise and development of what historians refer to as the 'domestic ideal' among the early nineteenth-century middle class, which helped to present the family as the principal institutional influence; third, the evolution of the compulsory relationship between the State, the family and welfare services; and, fourth, the political and cultural struggle to extend the developing concept of childhood through all social classes, to universalise it.

But what is the meaning of 'social construction'? The term has nothing to do with 'the cultures which children construct for and between themselves'.[2] During our period, 'childhood' was composed by adults, usually those of the professional middle class. This is not meant to sound conspiratorial. No attempt is made here to suggest that children's condition is entirely devoid of a biological dimension, nor to deny the effects of physical being, though the nature of the consanguinity between the social, the psychological and the biological is extraordinarily problematic. All the same, 'ideas like parenthood and childhood are socially constructed and thus can be put together in [a] diverse set of ways'.[3] We know also that, whatever its historical mutability, there is always a relationship between conceptual thought and social action and the process of category construction and, therefore, definitions of childhood to some extent must of necessity be dependent upon the society from which they emerge.

Consequently, the supporting premiss of what follows is that the numerous perceptions of childhood, which have been produced over the last two hundred years or so, can only be fully comprehended within the context of how different generations (and, no less significant, social classes) responded to the social, economic, religious and political challenges of their respective eras. Throughout the nineteenth century, the influence of evangelicalism, the impact of the Industrial Revolution, and the combined effects of urban growth, class politics, and the 'rediscovery' of poverty, all made necessary new understandings, together with new procedures, intentions and ambitions. Since these changes involved no less than the building of an industrial state and, later on, a liberal industrial democracy, no part of the societal fabric was left unattended, unreconstructed. Similarly, since the early 1900s, war, welfare, a changing social fabric and psycho-analysis and medicine, have profoundly affected the ways in which childhood has been 'put together'.

1

IDENTITIES AND DEFINITIONS

PRELIMINARY DEFINITIONS OF CHILDHOOD: THE 'NATURAL', THE ROMANTIC AND THE EVANGELICAL

Although the history of the family and parent–child relations is shrouded in controversy, there is general agreement that from the late seventeenth century a new attitude towards children began to manifest itself, so much so that the eighteenth century has been claimed as a 'new world' for them.[1] The extent to which the treatment of children prior to this time had been either 'autocratic' or even 'ferocious' is disputed, but there is no doubt that they were held to be the inheritors of Original Sin, which justified a near-universal corporal punishment. However, in some respects, this was probably countered by the more benign influence of the humanists, who believed in 'the child's capacity for good and the moral neutrality of its impulses'. Here was an optimism which acted as a corrective against the more dour Protestantism.[2]

Nevertheless, the eighteenth-century social construction of childhood emerged fragmented and ambiguous, torn as it was between the notion of 'innocence' and a pessimism born of evangelical and political anxieties. In the 1680s the Cambridge Neoplatonist philosophers asserted an innate goodness in the child, and in 1693 Locke published *Some Thoughts Concerning Education* (the first of twenty-six British editions alone before 1800). This attacked the idea of infant depravity, and portrayed children as *tabula rasa*. In effect the eighteenth and early nineteenth centuries heard a debate on the child's nature. At one extreme stood the famous statement of John Wesley, the Methodist leader, which urged parents to 'break the will of your child', to 'bring his will into subjection to yours that it may be afterward subject to the will of God'. At the other extreme stood Rousseau, author of the seminal *Émile* (1762), and all those who, under his influence, invested their children with a new affection.

In *Émile* Rousseau captured the imagination of Europe with his validation of Nature, which espoused the notion of the natural goodness of children and the corrupting effects of certain kinds of education: 'Let us lay it down as an incontestable maxim that the first promptings of nature are always right.' In Rousseau's thought, which drew on ideas from the Renaissance, Comenius and Locke, the natural growth of children was of paramount importance. He was not alone in his attachment, for the age was one of a wider change in social beliefs, many of which manifested themselves in more 'sensitive' responses to the natural world, animals, women and slaves.[3] Rousseau's view of childhood was Pelagian, that is, he denied the doctrine of Original Sin. Childhood was important for him because it represented the human potential for fulfilment. The originality of the educational theory found in *Émile* lay partly in the claim that from both the physiological and the psychological perspectives the educator was to treat the child as 'a little human animal destined for the spiritual and moral life' who developed 'according to certain laws whose natural progression must be respected above all'.[4] No less significant in inspiring a new outlook was the book's philosophical emphasis on the child as *child*: 'Nature wants children to be children before they are men.' This is why the focus of *Émile* lay in the assertion that the primary objective of education should be 'the identity and peculiar nature of the child itself', and that the 'original nature' of the child was 'innocence'. Rousseau can be credited with two seminal accomplishments with respect to childhood: he made it important for itself, not merely as a diminutive adulthood and, in rejecting the Christian 'fallen state' and emphasising natural goodness, he freed it from the burden of Original Sin. Rousseau took children from the gates of damnation to the doorway of trust in human capacity.[5]

The construction of childhood propagated by Rousseau hardly had an independent existence before it met up with the influences of the Romantic and evangelical revivals. In the works of Blake, Coleridge and Wordsworth, which were at the heart of the 'Romantic revival', the child stood centrally in the search of poets and novelists to investigate 'the Self' and to express their romantic protest against 'the Experience of Society'. The Wordsworthian child (though varying between Wordsworth's early and late writing) endorsed Rousseau in its original innocence except unlike Rousseau's childhood, which human beings pass through towards a rich adulthood, it is a state that is lost as soon as it is completed. In the ode 'Intimations of Immortality' (1807), Wordsworth is closest to Rousseau, for here childhood is not only good in itself but, if properly cared for, yields up useful and fulfilled adults. It is 'the seed-time of the soul'. In this poem the child figure shuns the lost Eden, and looks forward to the future. Whatever the differences between Wordsworth and Rousseau over the concept of 'original virtue', the former adopted the latter's tone of reverence towards the child.[6]

While Wordsworth and Blake had different understandings of the child, they used the child figure to make their readers *feel* a truth, rather than simply to *understand* it. For Blake, the symbol of the innocent child stood at the centre of his testimony against the tradition of English rationalism of Bacon, Newton and Locke. In his *Songs of Innocence*, he affirmed the joy of human life in children, and throughout his writings he constantly attacked the inhumanity of society, especially with respect to children. Coleridge shared much of this outlook, seeing in children what has been called an 'intuitive, imaginative quality of the soul'. The 'feelings' of childhood, he wrote, should be carried into 'the powers of manhood'. In Coleridge, the emphasis on the child derives not so much from its capacity for joy, as from its integrity.[7]

What was happening here was the construction of a particular childhood, narrowly confined to an élite, as a literary, social and educational theme in order to combat much of the century's materialism and rationalism or what Mill described as 'the revolt of the human mind against the philosophy of the eighteenth century'. The new child was a figure in the 'Cult of Sensibility' associated with Rousseau; it was a feature of the 'reinstatement of Feeling'. The Romantics turned to children because they were in search of new awareness and psychological insights.[8] All in all this was a search which helped to assign a new importance to childhood, and one that saw the condition as optimistic and life-enhancing. At the most basic level, therefore, this construction related to the contest for a particular kind of society – for a particular set of beliefs – which was to stand between eighteenth-century rationalism and nineteenth-century industrialism.

In many respects the 'Romantic Child' was short-lived; the assertion of the Romantics never rose far above a protest, albeit one of great influence and longevity. But poets are no match for political economy. Both the reaction to the French Revolution – the suppression of liberties – and the impact of the Industrial Revolution – the demand for free labour – pushed adult–child relations in the opposite direction to that promised by Romantic aspirations. But the idea – at least, certain versions of it – was not so easily displaced, and continued to assert itself until at least the end of the nineteenth century. However, between 1789 and 1848 various insurrectionary threats in Britain brought forth a programme of coercion from the State. Notions of freedom were barely tolerated as democrats, trade unionists, labourers, women, reformers and others fought for food, work, political representation, and the right to free opinion.

Besides the reactionary political climate of the period, optimistic notions of childhood had to struggle against the influence of religious evangelicalism with its belief in Original Sin and the need for redemption. In evangelical hands, human nature, having been tarnished in the fall from grace, was no longer 'pleasing to the author of our Being'. It goes without saying that evangelicals rejected Rousseauism. The *Evangelical Magazine* advised parents to teach their children that 'they are sinful polluted creatures'.[9] There was no more typical counter-revolutionary than Hannah More, a

23

leading evangelical intellectual and pamphleteer, who denounced 'the rights of man' and of women, and warned that in future society would be subject to 'grave descants on the rights of youth, the rights of children, the rights of babies'.[10] By the 1820s More had overtaken Maria Edgeworth, a disciple of Rousseau, and author of *Practical Education* (1801) in popularity, which suggests the drowning-out of the optimistic view of childhood with its faith in natural goodness. More's message, convenient for the age, was written in its fears. 'Is it not', she wrote, 'a fundamental error to consider children as innocent beings, whose little weaknesses may, perhaps, want some correction, rather than as beings who bring into the world a corrupt nature and evil dispositions, which it should be the great end of education to rectify?'[11] This found a ready audience among evangelicals and the upper classes who were unsettled by the French Revolution, the Napoleonic Wars, and by domestic political and social unrest. More was popular because she articulated their desire for a settled society, characterised by religious observation, order, obedience and authority.

While More opposed both Rousseau and the Romantics, along with other evangelicals, she never underestimated the importance of educating and rearing children. In part her conviction was rooted in a tradition born during the Reformation, which sought to register childhood as the age in which it was appropriate for adults to invest time, concern, thought and money. Nevertheless, the nineteenth-century discussion on the meaning of childhood in an industrialising and urbanising nation was very much the work of evangelicals who produced their own agenda for reform, largely through the promulgation of a Domestic Ideal which emphasised home, family, duty, love and respect.[12] During the course of the debate, the purity of the Romantic view of the child gave way to the alarmism and pessimism of counter-revolutionaries. The loss occurred despite the continued (though limited) influence of the Romantic idea in portraying childhood as fundamentally different from adulthood; different, that is, in the sense of having its own nature, and not simply being an immature condition, apprenticed to adulthood. More and her followers grasped this difference, and used it for their own purposes.

THE FACTORY CHILD

This is probably one of the best-known of all historical stories: the struggle to rescue 'little children' from long hours and cruel conditions in factories, mines and workshops. The early Factory Acts, those of 1802, 1819 and 1833, prohibited children under the age of nine from employment in a variety of mills. The 1833 Act gave children aged between 9 and 13 an eight-hour day with two hours for schooling. A further Act in 1844 lowered the minimum age to 8 but introduced daily schooling and reduced children's working hours to six and a half or seven per day. There were additional reductions in hours in the Acts of 1850 and 1853, and those of 1864 and 1867 extended the regulations to non-textile factories and workshops. Where agricultural labour was concerned, two of the most important Acts were those of 1867 and 1873, which forbade employment of children under 8. In 1875 the minimum age for all half-time employment was raised to 10, and for full-timers to 14, unless the child obtained an early school-leaving certificate.

There are at least two important points to note about this legislation. First, it introduced and later confirmed the view that children were not 'free' to make contracts – they needed the protection of the State; and, second, it marked a turning point in the perception of children as 'workers' – which they had always been. We see the emergence of the view that children should not work at all (or do only the minimum necessary for 'educational' purposes); that childhood should be quite separate from wage-earning.[13] This was to have profound repercussions. To all intents and purposes it began to set children aside from wage labour – one of the most important forms of social activity.

There was nothing new about children working in the Industrial Revolution, for it had long been established that they should contribute to the family economy. By the early decades of the nineteenth century they were widely employed in textiles, dress, mining, agriculture, domestic service, docks and navigation, metals, and machinery and tools. However, it was their work in textile mills, mines and as chimney-sweeps which most dramatically captured the imagination of reformers and philanthropists who campaigned against this form of exploitation. Many contemporaries were appalled, not only by the scale and intensity of the exploitation, but also by the brutalisation of the young workers, and the violence which it was felt was being done to the 'nature' of childhood itself. Others were equally appalled by the scale and intensity of the industrialisation process, and for these critics the plight of the factory child seemed to symbolise profound and often little-understood changes in British society, changes which appeared to threaten an imagined natural order. In campaigning to restrain this form of child labour, reformers were in effect arguing about the direction of industrialisation, the meaning of progress, and the kind of childhood necessary for a civilised and Christian community.

In opposition to *laissez-faire* capitalism, there was of course the Romantic image of childhood which opposed the unremitting debasement of children through long hours, unhealthy conditions, corporal punishment, and sexual harassment (of girls by employers, foremen and fellow-workers). Similarly, the evangelical attitude to children, though in conflict with the Romantic, also opposed their economic activity. This attitude emanated from the combined (and often contradictory) influences of evangelical opinion about human nature, the gathering pace of the bourgeois 'domestic ideal', and fears about the social and political behaviour of

25

the working class. It saw the brutalisation of children (including alleged precocious sexual awareness) as contributing to the dehumanisation of a social class and, therefore, was to be avoided. Many upper-class commentators felt that Chartism (the first mass working-class movement for parliamentary reform) was a perfect example of the social and moral instabilty which, in common with wide-ranging economic distress during the 1830s and 1840s, turned issues relating to public order into matters of national security.[14]

The first Factory Act, 1802, against child labour, proved ineffective with the expansion of industry and the introduction of steam power. But thereafter the reform campaign grew in vociferousness, assisted as it was by government investigative committees and numerous publications. There were several grounds on which reformers attacked child labour, especially where it involved factories. Reformers focused on the moral and physical consequences, with the former often deemed to be the more important. Hugh Cunningham has perceptively argued that these objections led to the 'utilitarian' argument that child labour threatened the reproduction of society. This, he continues, implied that 'there was a proper way to rear children, one . . . which would recognise that childhood had its own special characteristics'.[15] In effect, the argument led to the view that all children shared a common nature.

The campaign to reclaim the factory child for civilisation was one of the first steps in what might be described as the creation of a *universal* childhood. Where the 'natural', Romantic and evangelical constructions were always partially in the arena of cultural and symbolic figures, the withdrawal of large numbers of children from factories had a *practical* effect on the definition of childhood *per se*. Since the arguments against children's labour focused very much on what was thought to be their 'nature', it is worth noting that in important respects the understanding of that nature was influenced by the Romantic tradition in so far as the rhetoric of reform stressed innocence, childlike happiness and the child's affinity with the natural world. This was perfectly compatible with the evangelical understanding of childhood for, as Shaftesbury and others warned, industrialism was exploiting children and in the process leading the nation into damnation.

In the debates of the 1830s, the 'fundamental categories' of analysis were 'childhood-adulthood'.[16] The substance of the 'nature' in question was that it differed in kind from that of the adult. The age at which adulthood began was undecided, but in 1833 a Royal Commission declared that at the age of 13 'the period of childhood . . . ceases'. This was not a completely new view since, as we have seen, Rousseau had also sought to distinguish between the child and the adult. It was, however, the issue of labour – free and unfree – which gave meaning to the 'fundamental categories'. As one of the spokesmen for the mill-owners admitted, children were not free.[17] This was the principal success of the reformers' campaign: to establish the distinctive quality of child labour and, thereby, of all children.

THE DELINQUENT CHILD

The mid-nineteenth-century debate on juvenile delinquency had much to do with what Margaret May has called 'Innocence and Experience'.[18] The clue to the new attitudes being proclaimed by reformers can be found in this quotation from M. D. Hill, the Recorder of Birmingham:

> The latter [the delinquent] is a little stunted man already – he knows much and a great deal too much of what is called life – he can take care of his own immediate interests. He is self-reliant, he has so long directed or mis-directed his own actions and has so little trust in those about him, that he submits to no control and asks for no protection. He has consequently much to unlearn – he has to be turned again into a child.[19]

The campaign for reform produced the Youthful Offenders Act, 1854, which, together with further Acts in 1857, 1861 and 1866, was important for four reasons. First, it provided the initial recognition in legislative terms of juvenile delinquency as a separate category. Children coming before the courts were seen as beings with their own special characteristics, and not always responsible for their actions, rather than as small adults (prior to the Act only children under 7 were presumed to be incapable of criminal intent). Second, it introduced 'care and protection' features, which referred to potentially delinquent children; and, third, it established 'reformatory' schools with the intention of 'treating' and 'reclaiming' delinquents, rather than merely 'punishing' them. Fourth, the cumulative effect of these changes was to extend 'childhood' beyond the customary first seven years. Accordingly the legislation defined children as 'different'; reinforced the view that they were not 'free' agents; drew attention to the child–parent relationship with the latter expected to exercise control and discipline; and emphasised the danger of those in need of 'care and protection' becoming delinquents: neglect and delinquency were seen to stand side-by-side. One of the most important consequences of the Act (and of the debate which preceded it) was the perception of working-class children as 'precocious', sexually and otherwise. The Act was intended to 'save' such children who had a too detailed knowledge of 'the adult world and its pleasures'. Needless to say, the question asked by Micaiah Hill in his prize winning essay of 1853, 'Can these be children?', implied that he (and his society) already had a concept of childhood.[20] Clearly, the intention was to make working-class children conform to the reformers' middle-class notion of what constituted childhood – a constitution characterised by dependency.

27

Indeed, the mid-nineteenth-century construction of juvenile delinquency sought not only to deal with law-breakers, but also implicitly to universalise childhood (within Britain and between classes). From the outset there was a determination to remould the working-class child who was in the process of being freed from the factory. The Reverend Henry Worsley, another prize-winning essayist, indicted the factory system, describing it as 'a school of iniquity'.[21] To counter this and other malign influences, reformers sought to deposit the child in what Mary Carpenter, the leading activist, called '*the family*', by which she had in mind the kind of home being generated through the 'domestic ideal'. Micaiah Hill voiced a common theme throughout the literature when he wrote that understandings of middle- or upper-class childhood were 'utterly inapplicable to that of a child brought up to vagrant habits'.[22]

In order to understand the significance of developments in the concept of juvenile delinquency, it has to be remembered that the movement to create the beginnings of a separate order of juvenile justice emerged from three sources: the debate on child labour, the economic and political upheavals of the 1830s and 1840s, and the increasing popularity of the school as a means of class control. Consequently, the writings of reformers were rarely spontaneous. They were the products of deeply held and widely debated convictions, the main objective of which was to resolve what most commentators saw as an extremely dangerous tension in the life of the working-class child between innocence, which was desirable (not the innocence of Romantic 'feeling', but rather a form of ignorance leading to dependency), and experience, which was undesirable.

Here was a critical turning-point in the history of age relations, second only in significance to compulsory mass schooling. For under construction was a carefully defined 'nature', which also posed a return to an earlier mythical condition of childhood. Hence the phrase 'he has to be turned again . . .'. The clue to the success of the reformers, and those who succeeded them, lay in the 'care and protection' clauses of the Acts. These took the concept of the Romantic child as it was being popularised (debased) by nineteenth-century literature and, with the help of religious conviction, produced an image of the 'innocent' child, who needed to have the protection, guidance, discipline and love of a family. Given the widespread criticisms of working-class family life, in particular that of the poor, in their failure to conform to middle-class standards, Carpenter and others determined that, where necessary, parental discipline for delinquent children should be provided by the reformatory schools.[23]

At the core of this reconstruction, and the reason why it was so important, lay the desire of reformers to make children 'unlearn' what they knew and to substitute a new conception of childhood, derived from middle-class domesticity. Thus, urged Carpenter, 'a child is to be *treated as a child*'.[24] What physiologists tell us, she wrote, justifies representing 'the

28

child in a perfectly different condition from the man'. The problem was believed to be that young delinquents – and, by implication, the majority of working-class children – exhibited qualities which were the reverse of 'what we desire to see in childhood'. Children were 'independent, self-reliant, advanced in knowledge of evil, but not of good, devoid of reverence for God or man, utterly destitute of any sound guiding principle of action . . .'. In a revealing passage Carpenter continued, 'That faith or trust so characteristic of childhood, which springs from a sense of utter helplessness, from a confidence in the superior power and wisdom of those around', scarcely existed in the child in need of proper parental care. Such children had to be restored to 'the true position of childhood'. The child 'must be brought to a sense of dependence by re-awakening in him new and healthy desires which he cannot himself gratify, and by finding that there is a power far greater than his own to which he is endebted for the gratification of these desires'.[25]

In no way were these idle sentiments plucked from the air; they were thoughtful expressions of a developing social and political philosophy (extending well beyond a concern with children), which was finding an audience among a class anxious about what it deemed to be the rebellious and aggressive attitudes and behaviour of young people (and of their parents).[26] Juvenile lawlessness, then, was seen as one of the heralds of a possible political insurrection. The question facing reformers and politicians was how to build an organic society, which would have a cohesive social and moral fabric, to replace the chaos and immorality which substantial sections of the upper and middle classes felt to be the consequences of urban industrial capitalism.[27] The conception of juvenile delinquency, with its implication for the universalisation of an ideal childhood, was part of the answer.

THE SCHOOL CHILD

Children had received a schoolroom education through state and voluntary provision since the early nineteenth century. However, the Elementary Education Act of 1870 made possible free and compulsory education, which came with the Acts of 1876 and 1880, although it was not free for the majority of elementary children until 1891. During these years the minimum leaving age was raised from 10 in 1876 to 11 in 1893, to 12 in 1899.

The immediate impact of compulsory schooling was theoretically to prohibit wage-labour by children of school age. Since only a small minority of young children were so employed, those most affected were older children, aged 10 and over. However, schooling affected not only wage-earning children, but also those who were unpaid domestic workers in

29

their own homes. The size of the child labour force at this time is very difficult to estimate.[28] An approximate account suggests the following:

Table 1.1 Percentage of children aged 10–14 in England and Wales in employment

1851	36.6 (Boys)	19.9 (Girls)
1861	36.9	20.2
1871	32.1	20.4
1881	22.9	15.1
1891	26.0	16.3
1901	21.9	12.0
1911	18.3	10.4

Source: *Census Papers, England and Wales*, PP, 1913, Vol. LXXVIII, pp. 461–9. See also Nardinelli, *Child Labour and the Industrial Revolution*: 106, 110, 119

These figures are almost certainly an underestimate. Parents and employers evading the school-attendance laws no doubt lied to the census enumerators; many children were casually employed and so would have missed the census; and it would have been difficult to gauge the true size of the child workforce in the sweated trades and in rural areas. Of even greater significance in terms of child labour, the census took no account of unpaid labour performed in and around the home for parents, where the child's labour contributed either directly or indirectly to the family economy: for example, the children of women who took in washing, or the sons and daughters of small farmers.[29] It is, therefore, difficult to know exactly how many older children were compelled to leave their employment to become school pupils.

Whatever the 'educational' benefits, in prohibiting full-time wage-labour, schooling probably reduced older children's sense of their own value, especially those who were conscious of the significance of their contributions to the family economy. They were now no longer included in the assumptions covered by the moral belief that a fair day's work should be met by a fair day's wage (though no doubt they were always at the margin of this assumption). In working-class communities, where money mattered, schoolwork, in common with housework, lacked the wage factor, so that while both were necessary to social reproduction they were ideologically counterposed to waged employment in the labour market. To this extent children were removed from what has been called 'socially significant activity', with its 'major human values', which is essential 'for the development of a sense of individual worth'.[30]

In terms of the developing emergence of 'the child' (and of the development of age relations) compulsory schooling made its impact in five significant respects. Education, though not in itself new to working-class children, served to emphasise their *ignorance*: school was the place where 'knowledge' could be – indeed, had to be – 'learned'. The working-class cultural knowledge that children possessed was deemed to be both useless and harmful in that it encouraged precocious behaviour. Second, the allegedly precocious behaviour of working children – not least the ability of many of them apparently to survive independently of their parents – was taken to be evidence of their moral weakness and, therefore, they could only be made 'innocent' again by being made incapable of such 'adult' behaviour, and the school was the institutional means of achieving this end. Third, children were compelled by law to submit themselves to the discipline of the school whose teachers were given the legal right to subject them to corporal punishment. This was a conspicuous example of how, in the process of *emerging*, the child's body helped to define its status in so far as it could be legally assaulted by virtue of its age. Fourth, education was a decisive point in separating and segregating the child from adult society; in portraying childhood as a properly distinct world from that of adults. The child's proper place was the school (middle-class children had long been kept separate from adults through nurseries, nannies and boarding schools); the adult's proper place, the workplace and, for women, the home (the middle-class domestic ideal always had difficulty incorporating the working-class wife and mother in her wage-earning role). In accordance with the ideal of domesticity (which included the public and the private spheres), everything and everyone was to have its place. Education helped further to order society in this respect: the child was in the school, learning; the male adult was in the workplace, working; and the female adult in the home, mothering. Finally, through compulsory schooling, children began to be seen as valuable in relation to investment, in numerous forms (economic, occupational, military, demographic and emotional) for the future.[31]

In their construction of juvenile delinquency, many of the social and criminological investigators of the 1840s and 1850s made the implicit assumption that, in the long run, only education would prevent the 'dangerous classes' from continually reproducing their malevolent characteristics. The work of reform of 'habits of order, punctuality, industry and self-respect', advised one enquirer, must 'begin with the young... They are the depositories of our hopes and expectations.' While a Justice of the Peace warned: 'I have no other conception of any other means of forcing civilisation downwards in society, except by education.' According to a government report, there was a need to produce educated men who 'can be reasoned with'. Mary Carpenter had these sentiments in mind when she referred to reformation as the necessary step towards 'willing obedience' which, she warned, in the coming age of industrial democracy, was an essential condition of 'rule by consent'.[32]

The evolution of the concept of juvenile delinquency and the compulsory introduction of the school child, while not exactly chronologically hand-

31

in-hand, were certainly ideologically related. Thus there was nothing coincidental in mid-century penologists and social investigators seeking to return children to their 'true position' (to their nature), which also involved making them more amenable to the classroom. The fact that it was a minority of children who were either delinquent or vagrant was irrelevant to the basic restructuring process which was as much concerned with images and concepts and establishing norms as with rates of delinquency. For the reformers, precocity and effective schooling were irreconcilable. The reconstruction of the 'factory child', as representative of working-class children, through the prism of dependency and ignorance, was a necessary precursor to mass education in that it helped to prepare public opinion for shifts in the child's identity (from wage-labourer to school pupil); for a reduction in income of working-class families, as a result of the loss of children's earnings; and for the introduction of the State into child-rearing practices.

There is no doubt that in the last quarter of the nineteenth century the school played a pivotal role in the making of a new kind of childhood. It was not alone in this process, for as the century came to a close other agencies and philosophies were also reconceptualising the child's condition. But the classroom and the ideological apparatus of education were crucial because they demanded – indeed, could not do without – a truly *national* childhood, which ignored (certainly in theory) rural/urban distinctions, as well as those of social class. This construction directly involved *all* children and was intended to be inescapable. Schooling, however, did more than merely declare a particular definition of childhood. By virtue of its legal authority, and on a daily basis through the school attendance officer, it was able to impose its vision on unwilling pupils and their parents.[33] And, though the perception was portrayed as classless, the school child was always available for a political end, usually the reformation of working-class morals:

> the greatest influence in our parish outside the home is beyond doubt the school ... For good or for evil the rising generation is there receiving instruction and discipline which cannot fail to leave its mark upon the whole life of the nation ... in face of all criticism the solid fact remains, that in our schools the children are being firmly and gently brought into line ... I do not think we attach nearly sufficient weight to this fact in estimating the advance that has been made towards reclaiming the 'submerged' classes of the community[34]

Clearly, though schooling foregrounded children as pupils, its role in the universalisation of childhood was one that subjected them to overtly political agendas which had nothing to do with their welfare. Whatever the compensations (and in the long term these were numerous), the school put

32

many children into the servitude of a repressive innocence and an ignoble ignorance.

THE CHILD STUDY MOVEMENT

Child Study developed into a movement during the 1890s, but its provenance dates back to German scientific works throughout the nineteenth century. However, it was Darwin who authored the most widely known English study, 'A Biographical Sketch of an Infant', published in *Mind* in 1877, while earlier in the year the same journal had published Hippolyte Taine's 'On the Acquisition of Language by Children'. Both men, in common with many upper-middle-class observers (usually women), confined their studies to their own children. Taine's observations, in looking at a child's innate creativeness in the acquisition of speech, shared with those of Darwin a desire to classify human attributes and, in their human–animal comparisons, to identify that which was most unique to the human baby. In fact, as Cunningham has suggested, these articles were addressing 'some of the most funadamental issues in the study of human beings'. Within a few years the intelligent general public was being presented with the scientific importance of infants. In 1881, James Sully, Professor of Philosophy and Psychology at London University and later to be a critical figure in the psychological study of children, wrote a piece on 'Babies and Science' for the *Cornhill Magazine* in which he described the new scientific interest as seeing in the baby 'a biological specimen'. These early popular publications heralded a number of studies in the closing decades of the nineteenth century, the most important of which during the 1880s were, from Germany, Wilhelm Preyer's *The Mind of the Child* (1888) and, from the United States, Stanley Hall's article on 'The Content of Children's Minds'.[35]

The 1880s were an important decade in the history of children's welfare since they saw the beginning of 'a prolonged and unprecedented public discussion of the physical and mental condition of school children'.[36] Medical intervention in the general welfare of school children (other than their employment) emerged during the 1880s in the course of 'a sustained public discussion of the[ir] health and capacities . . . of quite a new kind'.[37] Doctors were interested in anthropometric studies, mental and physical defectiveness, and in the effects on children of what has been called the 'rediscovery of poverty'.[38] According to the historian of the 'people's health', 'The sheer amount of bodily infirmity in the common schools alarmed medical contemporaries, and drove them to make even larger, ever more gloomy – and self-fulfilling – investigations'.[39] One development above all turned children into attractive research-subjects, namely the opportunities offered to enquirers by compulsory mass attendance. In fact, compulsory schooling was crucial in making children 'visible' to the professions. The medical profession, in common with sociologists and philanthropic workers, soon recognised that the school could be used as a laboratory in which it hoped to produce 'scientific' (always an important adjective) surveys of the pupils.[40]

Earlier in the century the focus of attention had been on distinct groups of children such as factory workers, delinquents and those under the Poor Law, but now it was on the entire school-age population. The inauguration of the 'public discussion' began in 1884 with the publication of a report by the prestigious Dr (later Sir James) Crichton-Browne, on 'over-pressure' (mental strain) in elementary schools. The same year saw Francis Galton open an 'Anthropometric Laboratory' where parents could have their children's 'powers' measured. Four years later, after hearing Dr Francis Warner, Physician to the London Hospital, address its psychology section on 'Examining Children in Schools as to Their Development and Brain Condition', the British Medical Association (BMA) established an investigative committee which was led by Warner and supported by the Charity Organisation Society and the British Association for the Advancement of Science. Over the next few years other committees were formed to pursue similar inquiries in the classroom, and between 1889 and 1906 there were five large-scale inquiries in London alone.

Much of the inspiration for this research emanated from the Child Study movement which was formed in the 1890s.[41] The impetus behind the movement came from several sources. The extension of mass education after 1870 revealed the extent of mental and physical handicap among school children; second, biologists and natural historians saw a close affinity between racial development and that of the child; third, there was anxiety about racial degeneration, much of it inspired by urban growth; and fourth, sections of the professional middle class were interested in the work of Stanley Hall, the American pioneering child psychologist. Generally speaking, it was a movement that grew out of a concern about the quality of the child population and an interest in the details of natural human development. However, it was soon made redundant by the rapid growth of educational psychology as a specialist subject which itself emerged under three influences: how to deal with the mentally handicapped, the search for a science of education, and the struggle of psychology to achieve status in the academic world.[42]

In its early years child study was divided between the Child Study Association, founded in 1894, and the much more medically oriented Childhood Society, founded in 1896. The former owed its inspiration to Stanley Hall and argued for 'a scientific study of individual children by psychological, sociological and anthropometric methods' and for the examination of 'the normal as well as the abnormal'.[43] The Association's journal, the *Paidologist*, stated its objectives and identified its audience: it would help parents 'with observations of the periods and aspects of child life'; it would interest teachers by offering them 'guiding principles'; and it would prove of interest to those involved in 'education, psychology, biology and medicine'. The emphasis of the Association was on the individual child, rather than with the condition of the child population as a whole. It wished to gain 'insight into child nature', since 'it is only by a more precise unfolding of the human mind, and of the way in which this was modified by the environment' that further advance could be made in elucidating the principles of a natural and sound education.[44] The membership consisted of doctors, psychologists, biologists, teachers, school inspectors, and parents, usually mothers.

The Childhood Society owed its origins to two committees: one established by the BMA in 1888, and the other by the 7th International Congress on Hygiene and Demography in 1891. Members tended to come from medicine, education and statistics. Its main interest lay in the mental and physical condition of children, and it was always very anxious about the condition of the race, although members did not share the pessimism of the eugenists. Instead they sought to improve the environment and to train the 'unfit', which explains their concentration on abnormal children.

In 1904 the two groups began to co-operate with each other, and in 1907 the Childhood Society amalgamated with the London branch of the Association to form the Child Study Society (London). In practice this amounted to a takeover by the Association. The main success of the Society thereafter was in conducting scientific investigations, interesting parents, doctors and teachers in its work, in diffusing knowledge about the conditions of children, and in campaigning for improved child-centred education. By 1914, however, the movement was in decline, caused partly by the growth of educational psychology, partly by an exaggerated emphasis on physiology at the expense of psychology, and partly by its adherence to old theories of recapitulation and the inheritance of acquired characteristics.[45]

The movement was not without its critics, though it has been suggested that the professionals, especially the psychologists, were too harsh in condemning the movement for what was said to be its amateurishness. Child Study did much to spread the techniques of natural history to the study of children, leading to observation, classification and experiment. Through literature, lectures, and the practice of its influential members, it popularised the view that the child's conception of the world differed from that of adults, that there were marked stages in normal development, and that there were similarities between the mental worlds of the child and what in anthropological terms were primitive peoples. Moreover, we should note that it helped to create an audience for educational and child psychology, just as it helped to establish links between educational practice and scientific research which informed educational psychology for nearly fifty years.[46]

In effect the movement served to position the social, educational and psychological importance of understanding the child. By the 1890s 'the child' had been discovered. It was not merely a kind of theoretical construct, it was defined in Body and was beginning to be defined in Mind. Just as the eighteenth century had turned from Original Sin to the cult of the innocent child, so the nineteenth century turned from a belief in innocence and sentiment and moved towards the Freudian investigation of infant and child consciousness.[47] In common with sociological research into social welfare and the development of educational psychology (which was also becoming more influential), medical psychologists and doctors were defining children in an apparently 'scientific' manner thereby making it difficult for lay persons to dispute their findings. It was especially significant that Child Study endorsed the idea of recapitulation (the growing child goes through the same evolutionary stages as does the species) which presented children as threats in that they stood at the beginning of evolution – they were 'savages'.[48] This period marks the beginning of the psycho-medical construction of childhood, one whose foundations were in child development and evolutionary studies. The psycho-medical approach was to remain a thread running through twentieth-century definitions.

CONCLUSION

This impressionistic chapter has shown that understandings of what constituted a proper and 'natural' childhood were subject to development during the nineteenth century. In other words the concept of childhood in 1800 was not that of 1900. In 1800 its meaning was ambiguous; nor was there a popular demand for an unproblematic conception. By 1900 the uncertainty had been more or less resolved and the identity of childhood determined – to the satisfaction of the middle class and the respectable working class. At the risk of appearing anachronistic, it could be argued that a recognisably 'modern' notion was being put into place: childhood was being legally, legislatively, socially, medically, psychologically, educationally and politically institutionalised. During the nineteenth century the making of childhood into a very specific kind of age-graded and age-related condition went through several stages, involving several different processes. Each new construction, one often overlapping with the other, has been described here in approximate chronological order as: the natural child, the Romantic child, the evangelical child, the factory child, the delinquent child, the schooled child and the psycho-medical child.

Limitations of space prevent a more detailed account of these developments being offered. However, my intention has not been to provide an analysis of developing concepts of childhood, but rather to show that by the beginning of this study, the 1870s, a working definition of childhood was well in place. The introduction and gradual consolidation of compulsory schooling confirmed the trend towards the creation of the child as a distinctive being characterised by ignorance, incapacity and innocence. This understanding of the 'nature' of childhood was then subjected to scientific scrutiny and elaborated upon through further description and explanation by the Child Study movement. In other words, by the end of the century reformers of all hues had a fairly clear perception of what they felt was the nature of childhood, of the constitutive parts of that nature, and where it stood in evolutionary narrative. Consequently, reformers also knew what they expected of children in terms of behaviour, performance and development. These expectations, and the apprehensions on which they were based, would be broadened and deepened well into the twentieth century, but many of the fundamental stereotypes were in place around the early 1900s, and they were derived almost entirely from middle-class patriarchal and domestic ideals. In relation to children as victims and threats they would figure prominently in the construction of relevant social policies, and they would serve to illustrate the need to use children as investments.

Part II

FROM RESCUE AND REFORM TO 'CHILDREN OF THE NATION'

*c.*1872–1918

INTRODUCTION

The thesis in this second part of the book is that social policy moved from a concern with the rescue, reclamation and reform of children, mainly through philanthropic and Poor Law action, to the involvement of children in a consciously designed pursuit of the national interest, which included all-round efficiency, public health, education, racial hygiene, responsible parenthood, and social purity. These children were given a new social and political identity as belonging to 'the nation'. This is not to say that there had been no self-evident national interest governing the campaigns of Mary Carpenter and other penal reformers in their reconception of juvenile delinquency in the mid-nineteenth century, or that Dr Barnardo was motivated merely by an evangelical desire to save souls. Such figures obviously strove to accomplish goals of national importance with respect to incorporating the 'dangerous classes' within the boundaries of civil society. Similarly, the NSPCC did not confine its objectives to punishing and preventing parental cruelty; it repeatedly claimed to be primarily concerned with improving standards of parental care among the poor in order to make their behaviour more 'respectable'. However, it is argued here that the policies and interests of politicians, social reformers, and what would later be termed the caring professions, in the late-Victorian and Edwardian periods, were more comprehensive, more universal and more specific in their perception of all working-class children as members of the population.

Briefly, the following chapters describe the change of emphasis from 'children of the state' to 'children of the nation'. The different agendas of concern between these two categories can be gauged from the contents of a few standard social texts. Florence Davenport Hill's *Children of the State*, first published in 1868 and revised in 1889, dealt with the workhouse school; state aid and individual self-help – emigration; boarding out; and outdoor paupers. The interests were broader in Gertrude Tuckwell's *The State and Its Children*, published in 1894: reformatories and industrial schools; truancy; workhouse schools; voluntary schools; hospitals and lunatic asylums; canal and van children; homes for the blind, deaf and dumb; circus and theatre children; prevention of cruelty; and half-timers. However, compare these topics with the range listed in Sir John Gorst's *Children of the Nation*, published in 1906: infant mortality; medical inspection in schools; children under school age; underfed children; overworked children; children's ailments; medical aid; infant schools; school hygiene; physical training; child labour in factories and mines; state children in care; hereditary disease; and the home. Not only is the range of concerns more comprehensive, but interest is no longer focused mainly on the child in institutional care.

To what extent are our dualisms (see Introduction) reflected in this shift of emphasis? The presence of Bodies, and the relative absence of Minds, is more or less self-evident. Almost every area of concern mentioned by Sir John Gorst referred to the child's body: medical inspection; hunger; labour; hygiene; physical training; and infant mortality and welfare. It has already been suggested that the way in which we can know social policy for children in this period is through their bodily presence, albeit that there was a sectional interest developing in their minds. Thus the chapters here show not only the development of an increasing state welfare provision for children, but also that this was overwhelmingly concerned with attending to their bodily needs.

In many respects the children were victims of cruelty, poverty, sickness, sexual abuse, neglect and insensitivity. Yet they were also seen to be threats, either indirectly or directly. It is difficult and sometimes misleading to make clear distinctions between those conditions posing a threat and those determining the child as a victim. However, if 'feeble-minded' and other groups of handicapped children were neglected, they might grow up to be the indigent citizens, promiscuous, exploited, and a drain on society's resources. Underfed school children not only might fail to take advantage of educational opportunities, which were therefore wasted, but also they threatened to grow up physically and mentally malnourished, passing on defects to the next generation. Similarly, those children subjected to what adult contemporaries felt to be cruel treatment could easily develop into either insensitive and brutal adults, or even become criminally delinquent.

The condition of children as either victims or threats, bodies or minds, was increasingly seen within the parameters of investments. Children were regarded as a national asset; a source of raw material. Dr T. N. Kelynack, active in promoting social health, wrote that 'the world of childhood has been an undiscovered or at least unexplored land. The child is a new discovery. Realizing at last the wealth, power, and requirements of this long-neglected treasury, minds and hearts everywhere are awakening to a realization of opportunities and responsibilities, and in all sections of society eagerness is being manifested to understand and serve the child.'[1] The understanding and serving of children did not develop from unblemished altruistic motives. In an age of fierce imperial, political, military and economic national rivalries, in addition to domestic anxieties regarding class politics, urban hygiene, and social stability, children were indeed promises of wealth, power and opportunities.

2

THE MORALLY REFORMING STATE
Rescue, Reclamation and Protection 1872–1908

THE INFANT LIFE PROTECTION MOVEMENT

There is no doubt that baby-farming, as it is commonly called, is carried on to a large extent in London ... as well as in other great towns ... In its criminal character ... in those cases where the children are put out for block sums of money, or small weekly payments, with an utter disregard as to what shall become of them, and possibly with the intention that their lives should be criminally soon brought to an end ... There are ... a large number of private houses, used as lying-in establishments, where women are confined. When the infants are born, some few of them may be taken away by their mothers; but if they are to be 'adopted', as is usually the case, the owner of the establishment receives for this adoption a block sum of money ... The infant is then removed ... to the worst class of baby-farming houses, under an arrangement with the lying-in establishments, by which the owners of the baby-farming houses are remunerated, either by a small round sum, which is totally inadequate to the permanent maintenance of the child, or by a small weekly payment ... which is supposed to cover all expenses. In the former case, there is obviously every inducement to get rid of the child, and, even in the latter case ... improper and insufficient food, opiates, drugs, crowded rooms, bad air, want of cleanliness, and wilful neglect, are sure to be followed in a few months by diarrhoea, convulsions and wasting away ... The children born in the lying-in establishments are usually illegitimate, and so are the children taken from elsewhere to the worst class of baby-farming houses ... Nobody except the owners of these houses knows anything more about them ... some are buried as still-born children, some are secretly disposed of, many are dropped about the streets ... the number of children found dead in the metropolitan and city police

43

districts during the year 1870 was 276 . . . a very large number of these infants were less than a week old.[1]

The history of infanticide is sparse, in part probably because the sources are extremely problematic. No doubt another reason is the diffidence of historians in writing about such a difficult subject. Writing and thinking about infanticide seems to force upon the writer a choice between parents (nearly always mothers) and babies. Sometimes it is argued that infanticide and abandonment were untypical; on other occasions the historian becomes a participant in the mother's struggle as exchequer of the family economy. Shedding a child, so the argument goes, was the only way in which the family, including other children, could survive. A third form of explanation is to attempt to offer an interpretation couched in the values of the time. It is difficult to avoid concluding that the topic involves us in 'a genuine problem of imagination'.[2]

Much of the initial interest in infant welfare came from the wider ramifications of the public health movement, especially the impact of the cholera epidemics of 1832, 1848 and 1854. Once the sanitarians had established programmes for public cleansing, drainage and water-supply by the 1860s, attention came to focus on infant survival. This explains why the early reformers were medical figures. However, the more immediate cause of child abuse and infanticide was in part the poor provision given to unmarried mothers under the bastardy laws and the refusal of the Poor Law authorities to give outdoor relief to mothers with illegitimate children. Indeed, neither the movement for infant life protection nor the legislative Acts of 1872 and 1890 can be understood without reference to bastardy and infanticide. Prior to the Poor Law Amendment Act, 1834, there was little concern over infanticide. But under the Act unmarried mothers were given little sympathy and, while they could secure outdoor relief in the early days, after the 'Hungry Forties', when there was more space available in the workhouses, indoor relief became the rule.[3]

In 1844 an Act was passed giving mothers power to apply to the courts for a maintenance order against the putative father. But the mothers were often either reluctant or unable to bring proceedings and so were left in dire financial circumstances. Consequently, the practice of placing children with 'professional' foster mothers for payment, known as 'baby-farming', flourished. One of the obstacles to infant protection was the absence of any strict enforcement of the Registration of Births and Deaths Act, 1836, so that very often the births and deaths of fostered or 'nurse' children were unrecorded. No verifiable figures were produced for infant mortality resulting from professional fostering, but estimates (probably exaggerated by reformers) varied between 40 per cent and 60 per cent in rural areas, and between 70 per cent and 90 per cent in large towns where insanitary conditions made infant life particularly dangerous.[4]

By the 1860s the sanitarians had begun to focus on the question of infant deaths, and the period witnessed the beginnings of the new spirit of concern about infanticide. Indeed, many reformers referred to what they described as 'the slaughter of the innocents'. The growth of the popular press, following repeal of the Stamp Duty in 1855, did much to disseminate awareness of the reporting of inquests. In 1861 *The Times* had cited the Registrar-General's report that in the previous five years 278 infants had been murdered in the Metropolitan district alone. It is difficult to make a correct assessment about the extent and nature of infant deaths. Violence accounted for only 1.5 per cent of these deaths. On the other hand, of the 5,314 homicides during the years 1863–87, 63 per cent were of infants under 1 year old (in 1977 the figure was 6.1 per cent). It seems that babies were more likely to be killed than any other age group.[5]

In 1862 the Association for the Preservation of Infant Life called for the repeal of the Poor Law Amendment Act, 1844. The intention was to make the social stigma of bastardy the joint responsibility of both mothers and fathers and, therefore, relieve mothers of the burden which often led them into criminal activity. A similar call came from another group, the National Society and Asylum for the Prevention of Infanticide. In 1864 the Health Department of the Social Science Association passed a number of resolutions recommending compulsory registration of all births and deaths. During the same year the Royal Commission on Capital Punishment (1864–5) looked at the matter. But it seemed from legal inquiries that child-murder had ceased *de facto* to be a capital offence: the popular view was that a newborn baby should not have the same rights as other people; and, second, murder presupposed 'malice and malignity', but public opinion declined to believe this of mothers killing their babies. Attempts to change the law and introduce a non-capital offence for infanticide failed. Nevertheless, in 1865 the famous trial of Charlotte Windsor illustrated the general situation. Windsor, it emerged, ran a business looking after illegitimate babies and disposing of them for a fee. This seemed to many observers to be clear evidence of the existence of 'professional infanticide'.[6]

Doctors and baby-farmers

In the mid-1860s, a group of London doctors (no doubt conscious of the enhanced self-image of the medical profession, certainly in respect of public health matters), together with the *British Medical Journal* (*BMJ*), began their campaign. In May 1866, London's prestigious medical association, the Harveian Society, acting on a proposal from Dr John Curgenven, formed a special committee to investigate child-murder. Within a year the committee had a list of twenty recommendations and it sought a meeting with Walpole, the Home Secretary, to discuss legislation. But he offered no prospects, arguing that such domestic legislation would prove much too controversial. In 1868, another reforming doctor, Ernest Hart, editor of the *BMJ*, commissioned an inquiry into baby-farming and abortion, and published several articles in the first quarter of the year. Though the articles were widely reported in the press, and Lord Shaftesbury raised the matter with the Government, nothing happened. Even the vivid description of baby-farming given by the popular investigative journalist James Greenwood had little effect. In Hart's words, the baby-farming question 'went to sleep'.[7]

The campaign struggled along until the discovery of two infant bodies in Brixton in June 1870, which eventually led to the conviction of sisters Margaret Walters and Sarah Ellis, professional baby-farmers. The case stimulated a new interest in infanticide with a determined effort among reformers to produce remedial legislation. The most important immediate development was the formation of the Infant Life Protection Society (ILPS), whose membership was open to laymen as well as to doctors, so long as they were 'gentlemen'. The society soon prepared the first Infant Life Protection Bill, which focused on the registration and licensing of child-carers, for presentation to Parliament. The Bill met with strenuous opposition from the champions of 'individual liberty' and most effectively by the National Society for Women's Suffrage, which formed a committee to fight it. In a propagandist pamphlet the Society argued that the Bill was hostile to women and ignored the real causes of child-murder, which were: prejudice against employing unwed mothers, the inequitable bastardy laws, and maternal ignorance. Feminists also saw the proposed legislation as a threat to employment opportunities for self-supporting women. The ILPS replied to the criticisms but without success.[8]

The Bill was abandoned when the Government made clear its opposition but agreed to a Select Committee on the subject. The Committee gave the matter a national forum and within a few months it issued a report, with four recommendations, which was favourable to legislation. The recommendations were that there should be compulsory registration of all births and deaths, compulsory registration of all lying-in establishments, registration of board-nurses who took for payment two or more infants under 1 year of age for a period longer than a day, and that those nurses who were not required compulsorily to register should be encouraged to do so on a voluntary basis. The ILPS accepted the guidelines of the report and presented a new Bill which became law in 1872.[9]

The Infant Life Protection Acts, 1872 and 1897

The Act was a failure both in conception and in practice. It provided that paid carers taking in *more than one* infant under 1 year of age for longer than twenty-four hours had to register with their local authority. Carers had to keep records and report infant deaths in their houses directly to the coroner. It made no mention of any kind of stringent inspection of private homes; it ignored day nurseries; and those who cared for only one child at a time were exempted from registration. Its sponsor, W. T. Charley, a Conservative MP, defended the Act, arguing that together with reform of the bastardy and birth- and death-registration laws it would allow local authorities to protect infant life. In practice, however, few local authorities pursued even their limited powers with any enthusiasm so that by the end of the 1870s very little had been achieved.[10]

Nevertheless, George Behlmer believes that if the infant life protection movement is considered more broadly there were two important results. First, the ILPS, through Charley, introduced a Bill to amend the bastardy laws. Three important amendments were proposed: courts were to be given more latitude in assessing putative fathers for child support; women were to be assisted by the Poor Law board of guardians in the recovery of maintenance costs; and fathers were to continue to be liable for child-support until the child reached 16 years of age. The Bill was successfully passed as the Bastardy Laws Amendment Act with little opposition in June 1872, and it remained the basis for the financial maintenance of illegitimate children until 1957.[11]

Second, in addition to the Bastardy Act, the ILPS, in common with the British Medical Association and the Obstetrical Society of London, forced the Government to enact another recommendation of the 1871 Select Committee: the Birth and Death Registration Act, 1874. Under this Act failure to report a birth within forty-two days and a death within eight days incurred a forty-shilling fine. But this still gave plenty of time to those mothers who wished to conceal the birth. Failure to inform registrars within a week of finding an abandoned child alive was also punishable with a forty-shilling fine. Graveyard officials were only allowed to bury stillborn infants with written confirmation from a 'registered medical practitioner' that the child had been born dead; and not more than a single body, without a written explanation, could be put in a single coffin. However, these death certificates could be signed by either midwives or herbalists. Moreover, medical certificates for these infants were notoriously unreliable since the doctors most likely to be called upon were those who were overworked and poorly paid in the slums where the infant death rate often reached 20 or 30 per cent. Furthermore, stillbirths continued to be left unregistered, so that the likelihood that live-borns would be buried as still-borns continued to exist.

In some respects the legislation did point towards more effective safeguards for infant life. But direction is one thing, achievement another. For example, besides the failure of the Infant Life Protection Act, 1872, and despite Behlmer's claim about the broader consequences, it seems much more likely that, as Lionel Rose argued, 'Victorian registration processes were riddled with loopholes and widely abused'.[12] The Select Committee

47

on Death Certification, 1893, which made a number of recommendations, confirmed the frequency with which babies were either secretly or falsely buried in cemeteries, and not until the Registration Act, 1926, were the Select Committee's recommendations passed into law.

From the time of its enactment, critics had attempted to strengthen the 1872 Act. The *British Medical Journal* regularly reported inquests held on infant deaths from unregistered baby-farms, and the Waifs and Strays Society expressed concern at newspaper advertisements for so-called adoption. There were also several grisly scandals, and in August 1879 an Exeter woman, Annie Took, was executed for infanticide. Further evidence of the inadequacy of the Act came a few months later when a married couple from Merseyside received life sentences for the manslaughter of a baby girl in their care. In 1888 three more notorious cases attracted national attention, with one of those convicted being hanged in March 1889. These events persuaded the Home Secretary at the time to circularise all local authorities asking them to suggest further reforms, the outcome of which was the government Bill of 1890.[13]

The principal intention of the Bill was to extend registration to foster homes which took in only one child. However, its critics claimed that such an extension would jeopardise 'neighbourly arrangement'. The matter was referred to a Select Committee which recommended that such registration be confined to illegitimate children, which were felt to be those most at risk from the professional baby-farmers. But there was dissatisfaction with the wording of the final draft and the Bill was dropped. In the mid-1890s there were three further attempts to introduce new legislation and once again the matter was referred to a Select Committee. As the Committee debated, a Mrs Dyer, who had first been convicted seventeen years previously, was the subject of a sensational trial which led to her execution in 1896. With an eye on popular feeling, the House of Commons passed the Infant Life Protection Act, 1897.[14]

While the new Act exempted the single-child minder, it did raise the protected age to 5, and 'obliged' the minder to notify the local authority, and any transfer of a child had also be to notified. Local authorities could, if they wished, appoint inspectors who might apply for a magistrate's warrant in cases where they were refused entry to premises where children were housed. Workhouses could no longer refuse to take in children removed from baby-farmers, as had been so previously. One of the most contentious clauses was the '£20 rule' which allowed adoptions of children up to 2 years old to go unnotified by the local authority if the sum paid was more than £20. The intention was to control cheap, low-class and therefore potentially dangerous adoptions. (Formalised legal adoption, with transfer of parental rights, was unknown until the 1926 Adoption Act.) Leaving aside the class-discriminatory nature of this clause, the rule could obviously be evaded with ease.[15]

This Act, like the others, was persistently criticised, especially the exemption of the one-child house which meant in effect that the majority of child-minders were beyond regulation and inspection. By now there was a formidable division of opinion on the matter. On the one side stood the National Society for the Prevention of Cruelty to Children, Miss Zanetti, the Manchester appointed infant protection visitor, the Poor Law Unions Association, and the Infant Mortality Conference, 1906. On the other side were the charitable organisations, such as the Charity Organisation Society, the Waifs and Strays Society and the London Foundling Hospital, each of which made their own arrangements for the fostering of (single) children in their care and who were fearful that further inspection from local authorities would frighten away respectable foster parents. Both sides, however, opposed the £20 clause.[16]

Infant life protection in the Children Act, 1908

It is probable that there was a decline in infanticide between the 1860s and 1900, though between 1900 and 1907 three baby-farmers were executed. During this period, in each parliamentary session, Private Members' amending Bills had been unsuccessfully introduced to extend regulation to one-child minders and to abolish the £20 clause. In 1908, while the Children Bill was in passage, another Select Committee on Infant Life Protection was appointed, and its recommendations were incorporated into the Bill. These recommendations were that the £20 rule was to be abolished; the protected age was raised to 7; and 'one-child' houses were to be inspected, though local authorities could make exemptions where they saw fit. Where charities were concerned, the authorities could delegate the responsibility to the inspectorate of individual charities. Finally, local authorities, which outside London meant Poor Law Unions, were now obliged to appoint inspectors.[17]

CHILD CRUELTY AND THE NSPCC

In the closing decades of the nineteenth century parental authority was substantially reduced as it found itself in conflict with that of the State. According to George Behlmer, the historian of the NSPCC, the reasons for this change lay not simply in 'the slow spread of humane sentiment', but in the creation of 'a new moral vision in which justice for the young took precedence over the claims of parenthood'. However, as Behlmer continues, those who created this vision did so 'by arguing that the security of the home demanded it. The Englishman's castle was to be breached for the good of the castle, and, ultimately, for the good of the Englishman as well. Thus, child savers labored also to save parents.' Another and equally important motivation lay in the offence all forms of sadistic behaviour gave to middle-class culture; it threatened not only to undermine the declared belief in humanity and toleration, but also to spread moral degeneration.[18]

The founding of the NSPCC

In April 1881 the *Liverpool Mercury* published a letter from the Reverend George Staite calling for the formation of a society for the protection of children in the city. The society would use volunteers to investigate rumours of cruelty; attempt to educate parents and guardians in their proper responsibilities through lecturing, preaching and the distribution of appropriate literature; and 'aim generally at doing works for children in their homes, and to influence public opinion on the subject'.[19] In the summer of 1881, Staite wrote to Lord Shaftesbury, England's premier philanthropist, hoping for legislative support. While Shaftesbury agreed that the evils of child abuse were 'enormous' and 'indisputable', they were, he opined in oft-quoted words, 'of so private, internal and domestic a character as to be beyond the reach of legislation'.[20] Perhaps he had in mind the occasion in 1873 when A. J. Mundella, MP, introduced a Bill for the better defence of children, which failed to reach the debate stage. It expressed a concern that looked far beyond the issue of 'baby-farming' and, therefore, was seen to threaten parents' rights. Speaking of children at risk, Mundella lamented that 'the state neglects these children because, forsooth, it respects the "liberty of the parents" '. Unlike Infant Life Protection legislation, which related to a minority of poor, Mundella's Bill promised a more universal form of intervention and supervision.[21]

By the 1880s, child abuse was being seen as a major social disease. Why was this? Among the numerous reasons, the most influential were, first, the protests over teachers' mistreatment of school children, especially in the *Lancet* which drew attention to the 'evils and injuries likely to result from the boxing of ears and the smacking of faces'. Second, and in similar vein, there was the 'overpressure' controversy, whereby it was claimed that children were being overworked by teachers whose salaries depended upon exam results. Third, and much the most influential, there was the 'condition of England' question, first raised in the 1830s and 1840s, and rediscovered in the 1880s. This had particular relevance to the urban slums, where informed opinion held that the poor – a race apart – needed to be civilised.[22] Indeed, there can be no proper understanding of the NSPCC (nor of any of the social legislation affecting children) without an appreciation of the social, economic and political nature of the society from which it emerged, and of the significance of social class in the creation of that nature.

Shaftesbury's reply was indicative of a certain approach to domestic matters, namely that, except in exceptional circumstances, the home was sacrosanct. By the early 1880s, however, it was not the only approach since social distress, economic depression of a kind, and political developments involving working-class consciousness were causing a shift in opinion among those involved in dealing with social problems. In such a climate many influential commentators were coming to believe that the poor – at least, those within reach of 'respectability' – needed assistance in living up to the principles of the domestic ideal. These observers saw that conditions in the urban slums were having adverse effects not only on the poor, but also on the respectable working class, whose resolve to practise individual responsibility looked like being undermined. Not for nothing did Samuel Smith, one of the founders of the NSPCC, stress the 'culpability and responsibility of the individual family units'.[23] Thus it seemed that the ideal of the bourgeois family – self-contained, private, patriarchal, loving, religious, hierarchical and civilised – was at risk, especially from those families of Irish extraction who made up a large proportion of the urban poor. Child cruelty was one of the specific threats, exemplifying as it did irresponsibility, callousness and brutality.

While it was widely believed that the poor in particular were thriftless and morally bankrupt, it was also recognised that the circumstances of their lives, especially their housing, made it difficult for them to aspire to personal purity. Andrew Mearns, author of perhaps the most famous pamphlet of the period, *The Bitter Cry of Outcast London*, identified 'child misery' as the most serious problem. And Samuel Smith, referring to city life in London, warned: 'It is impossible to conceive that children brought up thus can fail to become unhealthy in body and depraved in mind and morals ... *Our only hope lies in rescuing the children.*'[24] 'Saving' children, then, was necessary because it would break the cycle of poverty with all its dire consequences.

This explains why in the atmosphere of the 1880s, regardless of Shaftesbury's reply, there was a willingness among Liverpool philanthropists to consider Staite's proposal. The credit for turning an idea into an organisation belongs to Thomas F. A. Agnew, a Liverpool merchant and banker, and Samuel Smith, Liberal MP for the city. On a visit to New York, Agnew had been impressed with the work of the city's Society for the Prevention of Cruelty to Children and went on to visit similar groups throughout America, before returning to Liverpool in 1882 with the annual reports of these societies. On his return he first interested the Central Relief Society before approaching Samuel Smith, who was an active worker on behalf of the YMCA, the Council of Education, and various organisations involved in child emigration schemes to Canada. Soon afterwards Smith attended a meeting of the RSPCA where he converted a proposal for a dog's home into a call for the defence of children, and on 19 April, 1883 the Liverpool SPCC was established.[25]

From the beginning the Society was conscious of the delicacy of its task and of the need to proceed with caution. At its inaugural meeting it was suggested that it should emulate the RSPCA in giving priority to education rather than to prosecution. What emerged was a conservative body, both in policy and in membership, which was dedicated to moral suasion rather than to active initiation. Unlike much early nineteenth-century child protection, these philanthropists put the emphasis not on removing the child from the home, but on compelling parents to be humane. The London Society for the Prevention of Cruelty to Children had no intention of separating children from their parents. 'Your committee would have this widely and thoroughly understood.'[26] The Reverend Benjamin Waugh, Secretary of the Society and editor of its journal, was always at pains to stress that 'we are not a prosecuting society'.[27] The intention was 'to deal directly with the parents, and to reform the home rather than to punish the culprits'.[28]

This emphasis on not taking the child away from the home was part of a comprehensive strategy to secure public approval for the movement as a whole in order to maximise the Society's influence. However, this was only one factor. The other, and a much more important one, concerned the desire on the part of these new 'child-savers' to educate parents and redeem the non-respectable working-class home, which could hardly be done without the presence of the child in the offending home – it was the child who transformed the household into 'a family'. The Liverpool SPCC was not unaware of its innovatory strategy. Samuel Smith boasted that 'new principles of legislation will be introduced, and fresh powers will be asked and obtained to stem the tide of misery'. The objective was 'the more strict enforcement of parental obligations . . . we wish to make it obligatory on a parent to feed, clothe, and bring up his child in a decent manner'.[29] So the York SPCC declared in 1899 that its aim was 'not to relieve parents of their responsibilities, but to enforce them by making idle, neglectful, drunken and cruel parents do their duty to their children'.[30]

There then began a campaign for the better legal protection of children. *The Times*, the *Pall Mall Gazette*, Baroness Angela Burdett-Coutts, the country's most influential philanthropist (second only to Lord Shaftesbury), Florence Davenport-Hill, author of *Children of the State*, and Hesba Stretton, a well-known children's writer, all argued for further action.[31] But everyone knew that it would be necessary to establish the Society in London if headway were to be made. Bristol and Birmingham had already followed Liverpool in establishing societies. The decision to promote a London Society in 1884 was taken at a major public meeting with Shaftesbury, Burdett-Coutts, Dr Barnardo and Cardinal Manning among the platform speakers. In having the support of some of the most influential journals and philanthropists, the Society was obviously addressing itself to what was deemed to be a major social problem.

The passing of the Children's Charter

... each division of the kingdom will be at least morally bound to
see that its infant citizens are neither tortured nor neglected, or
physically or morally incapacitated. The empire of childhood is one
which the nation cannot ignore. It is the Empire within the Empire.
If it cannot now command our sympathy it must some day command
our fear.[32]

The credit for the passing of the Prevention of Cruelty to Children Act,
1889, is given to the London Society with its three-pronged campaign of
'legislative analysis, wrenching propaganda, and organisational growth'.
From their beginnings both the Liverpool and the London Societies recognised the need for statutory reform. Their early experiences suggested that
child abuse included a range of categories, involving several different causes,
few of which were adequately covered within the existing law. The movement's leaders knew that it had to fight against the reluctance of Poor Law
guardians to punish parents for wilful neglect; the inability of women to
give evidence against the husbands; and the father's 'absolute right' to
custody of his children. There was also opposition from schoolteachers
who feared that the prospective Act would outlaw corporal punishment in
classrooms; from the liquor trade who objected to fines on the sale of
alcohol to children; and the Band of Hope temperance movement who
feared that the clauses prohibiting employment of children in public places
would restrict their use of juveniles in their penny readings, parades and
choir gatherings. The Home Office was lukewarm, although it did have
an interest in prohibiting child street-trading and in the prosecution of
neglectful parents.[33]

Both these issues were of interest to others outside SPCC circles. Street-
trading had long been frowned upon by educators, childcare workers and
chief constables as an avenue into juvenile delinquency and because the
children were said to be supporting lazy and irresponsible parents. It was
also seen as possibly putting young girls at moral risk, and definitely as a
civic nuisance. For some time Parliament had been aware of the need to
deal with neglectful parents. It was known that Poor Law guardians often
failed to prosecute such parents (which they were empowered to do by
section 37 of the Poor Law Amendment Act, 1868). In 1888 a Lords Select
Comittee examined the problem, in particular how to prevent neglectful
parents from having custody, and in December of that year the Local
Government Board issued a circular to Poor Law districts reminding guardians of their duty to prosecute parents who were neglecting their children.
To this extent there was a certain sympathy for legislative action which
no doubt assisted the SPCC in its objective.

By 1888 the London SPCC (which now had several provincial 'aid
committees'), together with independent groups in Liverpool, Hull and

Birmingham, had made child protection a significant social issue. Moreover, in May 1889 the Society became a national organisation with thirty-one aid committees spread throughout the country. The mood of the period, as has already been shown, was responsive to social unrest and, therefore, amenable to social reform. It was in this climate that the Society's Bill was first sponsored by John Morley, a famous and influential Gladstonian Liberal, and then by A. J. Mundella, President of the Board of Trade. The struggle inside Parliament was strenuous, even though Benjamin Waugh, Secretary of the Society, thought the Bill very weak, nothing more than 'statutory hypocrisy'. Critics argued that the penalties were too severe for various groups of offenders. Consequently, Mundella dropped his original Bill and after much consultation between different parties presented a revised version which secured a second reading on 4 April 1889. So it was that after an extremely skilful campaign involving meetings, publications, legal representation and the involvement of important public and religious figures the Act was passed on 26 August 1889.[34]

The Children's Charter, as it came to be called, was England's first attempt to consider the parent–child relationship on anything like a comprehensive scale. Until the Act, prosecutions could only be undertaken for offences (which had actually occurred) listed in the Offences against the Person Act, 1861. Furthermore, prior to 1889, parents and guardians could not be charged with cruelty and neglect unless the prosecution was brought by the Poor Law. Previous ill-defined restrictions on parents' rights were now more clearly stated. The new Act set out to prevent cruelty before it occurred; to inhibit overwork in employment not regulated by Factory Acts; to allow courts to treat a spouse as a competent witness, to receive the evidence of children, and to take a child into care if the parent were convicted of ill-treatment or neglect; to provide magistrates with various powers of search; to make the ill-treatment of boys up to 14 and girls up to 16 a punishable offence; to broaden the definition of cruelty to include assault, and 'suffering' and 'injury', which were more clearly defined; and further to restrict child-employment. The Act not only created new crimes; it also made specific the means for fighting them.[35]

Although the NSPCC would go through difficult times during the 1890s, the existence of the new legislation marked a turning-point in legal and social attitudes towards children, the whole idea of parental rights and – in many respects the most influential development, the new interventionist relationship between parents and the State. The problems of the Society, largely of its own making, were twofold: an extremely controversial critique of child-life assurance as practised by the working class, and allegations of administrative inefficiency. The first involved the fear on the part of those concerned about child welfare that unscrupulous parents were encouraged to take out multiple policies which provided sums far in excess of what was needed to pay for the child's burial. Despite limitations set on the amounts involved by the Friendly Societies Act of 1875, the practice was seen as a possible encouragement to infanticide. Throughout the late 1880s and the 1890s the Society sponsored several Bills to amend the insurance law with regard to children, but none was successful. The administrative difficulties arose in part from the Society's growth, and partly from the refusal of the leadership to allow any kind of policy autonomy to provincial branches.[36]

Nevertheless, undaunted by controversy and public hostility from certain quarters, near the end of 1893 the NSPCC prepared a new Bill intended to consolidate the 1889 Act. The Society wanted to raise the age limit for male children from 14 to 16 and under, as it was for girls under the 1889 Act. In addition there were to be stiffer penalties, revisions in search and arrest procedures, new restrictions on juvenile street-traders, and poor parents were to be compelled to seek parish assistance for their sick children. This particular Bill never gained a third reading. However, a year later a similar Bill was presented and with the aid of powerful parliamentary support it was enacted in late 1894.

If the 1889 Act made cruelty to children a crime, the new Act, in the words of Behlmer, 'established it as a positively hazardous practice'.[37] Intentional ill-treatment or neglect was punishable by up to six months imprisonment; policemen were empowered to take suspected child victims from their homes without a court order; workhouses were compelled to accept children of parents who were too poor to care for them; parents were made responsible for calling a doctor when needed by a sick child; courts could impose higher maximum fines (from five to twenty shillings) on parents whose behaviour made it necessary for their children to be given new homes; drunken parents had to consent to the 'alternative sentence'.[38]

Further NSPCC-inspired child protection legislation came in 1904 and 1908. The Prevention of Cruelty to Children Amendment Act, 1904, allowed for the enforcement of maintenance orders against parents, made it easier to prosecute in cases of alleged carnal assaults on the young by adults, and provided that courts no longer required the attendance of an injured child. The Act also dealt with the employment of children, and evidence and procedure. Society inspectors were now allowed to remove a child without being accompanied by a policeman or a relieving officer. The Children Act, 1908, was a consolidating Act in six parts with 134 clauses covering numerous aspects of child welfare from infant life protection to the exclusion of children from public bars. Part Two dealt specifically with the prevention of cruelty and covered a variety of circumstances: assault, ill-treatment, neglect, abandonment, suffocation of infants, allowing children to beg, exposing children to risk of burning, allowing children or young people to be in brothels, causing or encouraging or favouring seduction or prostitution of a young girl. However, 'nothing in this part of the Act shall be construed to take away or affect the right of any parent, teacher or other person having the lawful control or charge of a child or young person to administer punishment to such child or young person'. In general the Act strengthened the law of prevention of cruelty to children and in particular it imposed penalties for neglect as well as for wilful cruelty.[39]

'Practice and experience'

Now that we have some idea as to the early legislative history of the Society, it will be useful to pose three questions: What did the Society understand by 'cruelty'? What kind of parents did it pursue? And what punishments did it seek for offenders? The Society's definition of cruelty was as follows:

1 All treatment or conduct by which physical pain is wrongfully, needlessly, or excessively inflicted, or
2 By which life or limb or health is wrongfully endangered or sacrificed, or
3 By which morals are imperilled or depraved;
4 All neglect to provide such reasonable food, clothing, shelter, protection, and care, as the life and well-being of a child require;
5 The exposure of children during unreasonable hours or inclement weather, as pedlars or hawkers, or otherwise;
6 Their employment in unwholesome, degrading, unlawful, or immoral callings;
7 Or any employment by which the powers of children are overtaxed, or the hours of labour unreasonably prolonged; and
8 The employment of children as mendicants, or the failure to restrain them from vagrancy or begging.[40]

As the Society gained experience, so its early character and emphases changed. In the first four and a half years the London branch investigated over 1,100 cases, of which approximately 200 were dismissed. Of the remainder, 800 were warned and 180 brought to trial. Prison sentences ranged from 1–6 months (76), 6 months to a year (11), 1–5 years (20), 5–15 years (5), with fines being imposed in a further twenty-one cases. The kinds of offence included 'starving' (112), 'assault' (523), 'dangerous neglect' (219), 'desertion' (66), insufficient clothing (87), 'cruel immoralities and other wrongs' (112).[41]

The figures from the Liverpool Society for the year ending March 1885 show a different pattern. It investigated 844 cases, but here the offences were categorised as 'violence' (61), 'cruel neglect' (407), 'begging, vagrancy, and exposure' (307), and 'immorality' (69).[42] It is noticeable that 'violence' accounts for approximately 7 per cent of cases, whereas in London the proportion was over 50 per cent. The Liverpool statistics represented the future trend. By 1900, what had become the National Society inquired into 222,536 complaints, of which 206,388 were found to be true, affecting 573,325 children and involving 285,636 offenders; 159,172 cases were warned and 22,934 prosecuted, of whom 96 per cent were convicted. Of the 573,325 children, 446,722 were 'neglected and starved', 77,098 were 'assaulted and ill-treated', 27,907 were beggars and hawkers, 12,798 were 'morally outraged', and 8,800 were 'sufferers in other ways'.[43] Clearly, neglect was by far the major offence, with violence accounting for approximately 16 per cent of cases. By 1910 the proportion was further reduced to 7 per cent.[44]

How can this be explained? Behlmer suggests that the increasing emphasis on 'neglect', rather than on 'assault' or 'cruelty', reflected the increasing professionalism of the Society as it grew more sophisticated in discovering less observable and less dramatic forms of abuse.[45] There is another possible though not exclusive explanation, namely that neglect was easier to 'treat' as a social problem than was cruelty. The Society came to feel that neglect, which referred to an absence of adequate food, shelter, health, clothes and supervision, could best be dealt with through the inculcation of a sense of personal responsibility on the part of parents. It was also a more urgent problem given that the prevailing middle-class critique of working-class life charged parents, especially the mother, with ignorance and incompetence, and with having habits which could lead the family into poverty. Thus neglect was seen as more important because it signified the social failure of the poor, and it was deemed to be far more widespread than cruelty. This accounts for the emphasis on neglect in the Acts of 1889 and 1894 and in the prevention-of-cruelty sections of the Children Act of 1908. Cruelty, it was soon realised, was a difficult notion to interpret, whereas neglect was far more amenable to a consensus view – at least, among middle-class welfare workers.[46]

So cruelty remained an issue only within limited parameters. Its existence was real, but it raised more issues than reformers felt they could contend with, since *it* spread beyond the behaviour of the poor. Cruelty posed questions not only about criminal assault, but also about 'reasonable' corporal punishment. To investigate corporal punishment would have meant looking at the power relations between adults and children (and possibly between husbands and wives), and, more precisely, at methods of maintaining discipline and authority within the family. The nature of family discipline by this time had become the subject of some debate between what Behlmer refers to as democrats and autocrats – the latter giving approval to the infliction of physical pain on children while the former, much the minority, advocated restraint. Unsurprisingly, therefore, in its efforts to avoid unnecessary conflict, the Society 'routinely dismissed complaints about mild beatings administered "to intensify the child's hatred of wrong" '.[47] It was not concerned with 'what is properly known as punishment' but with 'inflictions . . . exceeding the limits of sound reason'.[48]

The attitude of the NSPCC has to be understood within the context of the Victorian idealisation of the family. This was the starting-point for the Society's perception of the protection of children. A crucial feature of this ideal was the interdependence of notions of masculinity and authority. These proclaimed the 'natural' superiority of male over female, and of the need for this to be recognised and legitimised within the family circle. Such an ideological belief necessitated a hierarchy of power relations between husbands, wives and children, which taught valuable social and political lessons in authority, deference, obedience and discipline. But, beyond this, the family stood square in the framework of national politics and security. As commentators never tired of saying, the family was the fundamental unit of national stability; it was the barometer of moral health; in fact, at any one time, its condition was testament to the state of progress, to the very process of civilisation itself. Consequently, the Society was proud to be one of those agencies enforcing traditional ideas about family duties and obligations.[49]

Given these beliefs, the threat to the family came not from 'normal' and 'reasonable' physical chastisement, around which many middle-class writers imposed 'civilised' restraints, but from uncivilised behaviour, which was always defined as 'brutality', that is, anything considered to be outside the norm defined by the middle-class. The Society claimed that brutal and cruel treatment of children was classless – it was perpetrated by 'unnatural and callous persons' who 'lacked human nature' and were motivated by 'moral hideousness'.[50] However, by the 1890s this could no longer be sustained either by reference to Charles Booth's social survey of the people of London, in which he spoke of neighbourhoods marked by 'brutality within the circle of family life', or by the Society's own statistics which suggested that its rescue work was most needed in the lowest-class districts. In York, 42 per cent of families visited by the inspector were 'chronically ill housed, ill clothed, and underfed'. The corollary of this, as the social surveys and Society statistics confirmed, was the significance of poverty in the aetiology of child abuse.[51]

The Society also changed its stance on the influence of drink. Originally it denied the connection between drink and child abuse, preferring to see cruelty as the result of callous and calculating behaviour. However, as early as 1884–5 the Liverpool SPCC made the connection and provided statistics which showed that the consequences of alcohol were the 'apparent cause of trouble'.[52] The York records also indicated that 53 per cent of alleged offenders were regularly drunk. In the amending Act of 1894, the Society secured a clause which, as an alternative to prison, allowed for the detention for twelve months in an inebriates' retreat of parents convicted of cruelty while under the influence of drink. There is little doubt, then,

58

that by 1900 the relationship between drunkenness and cruelty was firmly established.

The NSPCC, it has been argued, represents a classic example of the transformation in 'punishment, social practices, and welfare ideologies' which occurred during the years 1890–1914.[53] Prison ceased to be the principal sanction in social practice, becoming instead just one of many sanctions. The Society could always use the threat of prison and criminal prosecution in its dealings with parents, even though it preferred to reform them through warnings and advice; through what has been referred to as the 'positive incentives of "hope" '.[54] Furthermore, cruel parents were seen as temporarily deviant and subject to the 'rehabilitative' ideal. This is why the Society constantly reiterated that it did not seek to prosecute them, but to make them acknowledge their responsibilities to their children.

It is within the paradigm of 'hope' that we should see the prevention of cruelty to children, or, as Harry Ferguson describes it, 'the birth of child protection practice', as being concerned with much more than the protection of children. The NSPCC was of vital importance in reshaping public opinion away from the view that the family was inviolate, towards a view which recognised that if the ideal of the family were to be realised, then a certain amount of interference by outside bodies was essential for the purposes of education and, occasionally, prosecution. This meant persuading the public to accept that there were limits to parental power, even if these were ambiguous. The work of the NSPCC, then, was directed at the reformulation of responsibilities and codes of behaviour. It was no idle remark on the part of Samuel Smith when he referred to the neglect of children as part of 'the horrible corruption of public morals'.[55] Clearly, child welfare was seen in relation to wider social disciplinary concerns.

The Society gave itself the task of correcting that corruption. It saw itself as 'contributing to an elevated moral tone by making crimes seem crimes, both in the culprit's mind and in the mind, too, of his nobler neighbours'. It sought to re-educate working-class neighbourhoods into a new moral sensibility. In this respect, the Society represented the supreme confidence of the Victorian middle class to refashion the world in its own image, and in so doing to 'raise children to the rank and right of citizens'.[56] The giving of limited 'rights' to children was an important part of the general strategy to discipline the family through the application of selected liberal democratic principles, while simultaneously avoiding economic reform – in effect to liberalise authority within the family in keeping with the slowly emerging tendency towards self-regulation.[57] By 1910, the Society was well pleased with its successes. Robert Parr, the Secretary, judged that since 1885 'a phenomenonal change has taken place' in both conditions and the state of public opinion with respect to children.[58] This was more or less a correct judgement, although the extent to which the welfare of children was enhanced is another matter.

By the early 1900s the health and welfare of children was a subject of major importance and was clearly one of the significant issues of the period. In fact between 1885 and 1913 there were fifty-two Acts affecting child welfare. Child protection had become inseparable from major political issues. In this climate the NSPCC was just one agency, albeit an important one, at work in the developing relationship between voluntary effort and collectivism. The principal business of agencies such as the NSPCC was 'to patrol family life' and encourage better parenting. It would be wrong to assume that the reformation of parents was the child-savers' only objective. The work of the Society also expressed a belief in the child as a figure, within the family, in the onward march of progress and civilisation. 'Civilised' parenting was testimony to Progress, and the child stood centre-stage in this relationship.

THE AGE OF CONSENT AND PUNISHMENT OF INCEST

The Criminal Law Amendment Act, 1885

If we are looking for an example of children whose moral corruption is manifested and made visible by their bodily experiences, which then presents them both as victims of 'evil' men and as a threat to public hygiene, we need look no further than those described by the social purity campaigners in the 1880s. The ostensible issues were the age of consent and child prostitution. However, as with so much of the apparently protective legislation affecting children, these issues were themselves part of larger agendas, in this instance involving purity, feminism, state medicine and the law. In order to understand the sequence of events and to facilitate an interpretation of them, it is necessary to look more generally at the 'medico-moral politics' of the period.[59]

The politics of sexuality entered a particularly anxious and controversial stage during the 1880s. Attention has already been drawn to the importance of social class relations, the economic depression, the debate on working-class housing, and the condition of the poor. Middle-class contemporaries were also anxious about the possibility of national decline following the defeat of General Gordon, the continuing consequences of extending the franchise since 1867, the revival of socialism and growing trade unionism. In this atmosphere calls for social purity were couched in the language of national salvation: '. . . for the good of your nation and your country . . . Rome fell; other nations are falling.' The family alone, it was said, could halt degeneration: 'In all countries the purity of the family must be the surest strength of a nation.'[60]

Broadly speaking, the closing decades of the nineteenth century saw the coming-together of a number of those different strands of thought and influence concerned with the regulation of public and private morality.

Jeffrey Weeks has called them 'sexual discourses', comprising 'class pride and evangelism, moral certainty and social anxiety, the double standard [a restrictive code of sexual behaviour for women and a permissive one for that of men] and "respectability", prurience and moral purity'. He reminds us that Victorian culture and morality was premised on what he calls 'ideological separations: between family and society . . . the restraint of the domestic circle and the temptations of promiscuity . . . the privacy, leisure and comforts of home and the tensions and competitiveness of work'. These tensions reflected themselves in sexual attitudes, especially where 'decency and morality of the home confronted the danger and pollution of the public sphere'. In the minds of the purity campaigners, the private home sphere embodied domestic integrity, while the public stood for prostitution and vice. Thus, in their pursuit of a single sexual standard, they sought to erase all public displays of sexual immorality.[61] The public sphere was to be reformed in the manner of the private through adherence to the principles of social purity, which meant a policy of social regulation.

The immediate origin of the campaign in the 1880s was the controversy surrounding the Contagious Diseases Acts (1864, 1866, 1869) which were designed to control prostitution through registration and medical inspection of the girls and women involved. These Acts were fiercely contested by feminists and social purity supporters (both of whom saw the Acts as legitimising the double standard), and a long battle ensued until their successful repeal in 1886.[62] The debates over prostitution, the double standard, social purity, and the struggle to repeal the Acts need not concern us here. It is sufficient to appreciate that these themes included the concern about the level of juvenile prostitution and the sale of British girls to Continental brothels and, therefore, were inextricably bound together in the campaign leading to the passing of the Criminal Law Amendment Act of 1885.

From its earliest days the London SPCC had been interested in this problem, and both it and Lord Shaftesbury, among others, urged the Government to pass appropriate legislation. Pamphlets were published and meetings held, and the London Committee for Suppressing the Traffic in British Girls was formed. Under its influence, the House of Lords appointed a Select Committee in 1881 to inquire into the protection of young girls. Although the Committee found evidence of a small foreign traffic in girls, most of the testimony focused on juvenile prostitution in Britain so that one of the recommendations of the Committee was to raise the age of consent to 16. Further evidence came from an investigation carried out by a barrister appointed by the Home Office, Thomas Snagge, who found evidence of young girls being bought and sold to Continental brothels. Parliament, however, refused to pass any legislation when it was asked to do so in 1884. Faced with this reluctance, purity campaigners, who were now focusing their energies on child prostituion in London, turned to W. T. Stead, editor of the *Pall Mall Gazette*, for help, and a sensational series of articles on 'The Maiden Tribute of Modern Babylon' soon followed.[63]

Stead linked juvenile prostitution to the white slave trade, while emphasising the former, and warned his readers that he was about to print details of 'a serious social evil'. In his articles, with such titles as 'The Violation of Virgins' and 'Strapping Girls Down', he described in graphic detail the sale of 'five-pound' virgins to old men. He even procured a girl himself (for which he was later imprisoned) in order to collect evidence. The girls were all working-class, and the men who bought them were described as 'evil'. Three days after the third article was published, the Home Secretary put the Criminal Law Amendment Bill through its second reading. Soon meetings and popular demonstrations (one in Hyde Park) were held demanding legislation; local 'vigilance' committees were formed, as was a new organisation, the National Vigilance Association; and a massive campaign ensued to make certain the Act contained the required provisions.[64]

In the event, the campaign was successful. The Criminal Law Amendment Act (1885) raised the age of consent to 16 for girls (the Act did not apply to boys); it became an offence to procure a girl younger than 21 years of age, and – what was a very important clause – the oath for girl victims of sexual assault was abolished. There were also new penalties for white slavery, and brothels where girls were thought to be kept against their will could be searched and the imprisoned girls taken to a refuge. (The Act also outlawed all forms of male homosexual activity.) But it would be a mistake to see the Act simply in terms of the protection of young girls. Instead it 'signalled a new, more coercive system of state intervention into the domain of sexuality', and 'many of the provisions . . . were designed to protect a guardian's right to control a girl's sexuality, rather than to prevent harm to the girl'.[65]

The reform rhetoric portrayed the young prostitutes as 'sexually innocent, passive victims of individual evil men'. This was convenient since it retained the notion of 'innocence' for children and young adolescents, while defining the problem as one of individual sexuality, rather than in social and economic terms such as the poverty and destitution of young girls and their families. The crusade was a means of assuaging middle-class guilt without involving the class as a whole in a consideration of the economics of working-class life. Furthermore, reformers assumed not only that all working-class female adolescents needed protection, but also that they were unable to protect themselves. This ignored the fact that the majority of the girls were not 'entrapped'; many were semi-professional prostitutes. Equally significant, a large number of adolescent girls other than prostitutes, perhaps the majority, had illicit sex because they liked it, and not for financial gain. The truth was that the reformers understood little about the reality of working-class childhood, and even less about what was coming to be known as 'adolescence'.[66]

Furthermore the Act illustrated the uncertainties in reformers' minds about differences between male and female sexuality – the former was ignored by the legislation, while the latter was seen as requiring careful monitoring and supervision. It comes as no surprise to learn that reformers brought to the child prostitution question, and by extension to that of all kinds of female sexuality, middle-class assumptions on a whole range of age, class and gender issues. All in all, the legislation and the movement behind it were engaged in a symbolic crusade, and though it touched on domestic sexual abuse it was indeed a 'touch' rather than a meaningful intrusion. Deborah Gorham has written that many of those involved in the passing of the Act, and in the wider purity movement, 'did not fully understand either their own motives or the nature of the problem they were attempting to confront'.[67] Her examination of their motives, which is briefly summarised below, provides an example of the difficulty reformers had in understanding young people and their relationship to the wider society. It shows how definitions of 'victims' and 'threats' are often dependent on each other, and how class and gender, as well as age, can serve to create genuine contradictions and confusions in the creation and implementation of social policies.

According to Gorham, age-of-consent legislation 'has a special significance because it is an important example of the way in which society's conception of sex differences has been incorporated into the notions of majority and of full citizenship'. Thus it is relevant to note that the age of 16 represented a consensus between those who argued for the original age of 12 and those who wanted it to be 21. Those who wished to raise the age spoke in terms of protecting the defenceless 'young girls from the evil lusts of wicked men'. Of course, this act of defence also involved coercion since such legislation explicitly denies the adolescent the right to decide her own sexual behaviour. Moreover, it is important to appreciate that the purity movement was using the law to enforce its moral vision.[68]

Turning to those who wished to retain the lower age of 12, many upper-class men saw nothing objectionable in prostitution. In a famous passage from the House of Lords debate in 1884, one Member expressed the view that 'very few of their Lordships . . . had not, when young men, been guilty of immorality. He hoped they would pause before passing a clause within the range of which their sons might come.' Others objected to the proposed legislation on the grounds that it was repressive. These voices, however, were drowned in the hysterical agitation of 1885 which led on to the passing of the Act.[69]

Part of the reason for the confusion in the minds of reformers lay in their ignorance of adolescence as a definite stage of life. Victorians in the 1870s and 1880s had little or no clear understanding of the psychology of

63

what came to be termed 'adolescence'.[70] The arguments, says Gorham, were based not on notions of psycho-sexual development but on an older conception of youth which viewed 'the status of the individual in relation to other groups in society'. Childhood, especially for girls, was seen to continue until the verge of adulthood. This led reformers to argue that working-class girls should be given protection, whether they wanted it or not, since they were little more than children and not yet adult. Others in the debate alleged that working-class morality differed from that of their social superiors and any attempt to enforce a moral code was more likely to lead to the prosecution of middle-class male youths, who were essentially 'innocent'.[71]

But it was not simply a matter of the psychological definition of age groups. Much of the confusion arose out of Victorian images of childhood – in particular the continuing influence, however sentimentalised, of the Romantics, which throughout the century was engaged in a somewhat uneven contest with the evangelical view, with its emphasis on the child's wickedness and need for discipline. If the child could be seen as burdened by Original Sin, it could also be regarded as the redeemer of Man from the Fall. In this imagery female children played a special role. Where adult women were concerned, the ideological 'angel in the home' had her counterpart in 'the fallen woman', so the girl-child as redeemer had her counterpart in the 'wayward, evil girl' who lured the innocent male into vice and corruption. The logic of the thinking seemed to be that if the sexuality were removed, then so would be the 'evil' – the girl-child would be restored to a state of purity in which she could exhibit a comforting and non-threatening self-sacrificing love.[72]

And yet the reality of early adolescence for working-class girls was wage-earning, often in morally dangerous situations as field-hands and as servants in houses, hotels and inns. Quite apart from the difficulty of parental supervision for these girls, their age was making them more independent and, therefore, less susceptible to parental guidance – this was thought to be particularly true of the poor.[73] Nevertheless, the age-of-consent legislation was in many respects a formal denial of adolescent female sexuality. It expressed a fear of sexual precocity among the female children of the non-respectable poor and of working-class childhood itself – a childhood so different from that of the middle class. The objectives of purity campaigners, like their anxieties, were mixed and confused: protection of individual children and young adolescents, together with a coercive moral reform which was intended to counter threats to public health, family harmony, and stable age and gender relations.

The Punishment of Incest Act, 1908

Historically the law had little interest in incest, which was an ecclesiastical rather than a criminal offence. In 1650 the Puritan Commonwealth declared incest a felony which carried the death sentence, but it was rarely invoked. In 1661 incest was again left to what Blackstone called 'the feeble coercion of the spiritual court'; and in 1883, in his history of the criminal law, Stephen referred to incest as the 'only form of immorality which in the case of the laity is still punished by ecclesiastical courts on the general ground of its sinfulness'. These courts, however, rarely functioned. The lack of official interest could hardly be said to be caused by ignorance. The House of Lords Select Commmittee on the Protection of Young Girls and the Royal Commission on Housing of the Working Classes heard evidence concerning the prevalence of incest without recommending any reform of the law. Similarly, Andrew Mearns claimed in *The Bitter Cry of Outcast London* that 'incest is common'; and William Booth, the Salvationist, also stated that 'Incest is so familiar as hardly to call for remark'. A lack of knowledge was clearly not the issue, and yet secular law displayed little concern with this particular sexual offence.[74]

Why was this? A. S. Wohl has suggested three reasons. First, incest was very much a subject Victorians preferred not to acknowledge. Even the medical journal the *Lancet*, wrote euphemistically of 'things done in secret'; while in Parliament, as late as 1903, a Bill to punish incest was introduced as a 'rather . . . unpleasant subject'. One of the best-known post-Victorian comments is that of Beatrice Webb, the Fabian social scientist, who recalled that in her article on workgirls, published in the 1880s, 'I omitted references . . . to the prevalence of incest in one-room tenements. The fact that some of my workmates . . . could chaff each other about having babies by their fathers and brothers, was a gruesome example of the effect of debased social environment on personal character and family life . . . The violation of little children was another not infrequent result.'[75]

Second, to admit its existence would have undermined the bourgeois domestic ideal. Wohl reminds us that incest, unlike prostitution, was a domestic vice and so 'evoked the nightmare of exploitation and animal sexuality within the most sacred of institutions, the home and family'.[76] The problem for those middle- and upper-class Victorians who were involved in public affairs was how to reconcile their undoubted sincerely held belief in the almost sacred nature of domesticity with some of the realities of working-class life in the slums. To have exposed the family – what G. M. Young called one of 'only two articles' of a 'common Victorian faith' – to the potentially destructive truth about the human propensity for sexual abuse (certainly among fathers and daughters) would have created unbearable contradictions in the logic of the ideal.

Third, the strength of *laissez-faire* kept the State out of private life unless there was good reason to become involved. No one knew the extent of incest and, therefore, it seemed reasonable to leave the matter alone, especially since it would have involved legislating for the home. It was the kind of matter referred to by Shaftesbury in respect of cruelty to children as 'so private, internal and domestic a character as to be beyond the reach of legislation'. There was also the view that much of the sexuality of the working class resembled that of degenerates. One medical officer wrote with more than a hint of resignation that 'In a great city there must and always will be produced a number of degraded forms deficient in intellect . . . possessing all . . . the moral obliquity . . . of savages'.[77]

Why, then, were reformers successful in 1908? The Act was the result of a campaign dating back to the early 1890s during which time there had been unsuccessful attempts to pass legislation in 1899–1900, 1903 and 1907. The movement for reform of the law originated in the mid-1880s with 'the rediscovery of incest' through revelations of working-class housing conditions. However much the State may have been reluctant to interfere in what it regarded as a difficult area, the National Vigilance Association (NVA), women's organisations, the NSPCC and, by the 1890s, increasingly the police were all pushing for legislative action.[78]

The NVA emerged in the campaign for the Criminal Law Amendment Act (CLA), 1885, ostensibly to protect children, but it was increasingly concerned with all aspects of public morality. The list of prominent NVA activists reflected the close relationship between child rescue and sexual purity: W. T. Stead conceived the Association; the Reverend Benjamin Waugh, Secretary of the NSPCC, was a council member; Samuel Smith, MP, founding father of the Liverpool SPCC, acted as chief spokesman on obscenity; and Donald Maclean, MP, acted as solicitor for both the Society and the Association. Both the NVA and the NSPCC made use of the Criminal Law Amendment Act wherever possible to prosecute fathers for unlawful sexual intercourse with their daughters under 16 years of age. Moreover, both organisations also complained to the Home Office of the difficulties in using that law, which they claimed was inadequate, mainly because under the law prosecution had to occur within three months of the offence being committed. In 1893 the NSPCC had drafted an Incest Bill which it put before the Home Office in an unsuccessful attempt to persuade it to take up the matter, and in 1896 the NVA had also tried unsuccessfully to introduce a Bill. A new Bill was then drafted, and to assist in its parliamentary passage the NVA started a 'national purity crusade' in 1901 with meetings and resolutions which were forwarded to selected MPs.[79]

It seems that the Home Office 'was definitely influenced by the evidence submitted to them of the inadequacy of the existing law to cover all cases, and of the frequency with which incest was being committed'. The Home Office was unhappy that in the absence of a law specifically making incest a crime it was the law on rape – with its focus on consent – which was used to prosecute. The department was further moved by evidence of the extent of incest brought before it, especially among the working class, which in 1906 led it to state that 'Incest is very common among the working classes in the big towns'. Even so, parliamentary opposition continued and influenced the final shape of the new Act.[80]

When the Act was passed 'it made sexual intercourse between persons within a certain degree of consanguinity a misdemeanour' – the punishment for which was penal servitude for three to seven years or imprisonment for up to two years. Incest by a man with a girl under 13 was a felony punishable with penal servitude for life. In looking for ways in which to explain the Act, it has been suggested that the legislation can be seen as 'a product of a distinctive social movement which combined preventative work in the cause of child protection with a demand for social purity'. Bearing in mind the sparsity of reported cases of incest, the Act was 'symbolic' of public and legal disapproval rather than an effective instrument of law. There was little expectation that it would more than nominally protect children. In effect, it was 'less an act of rational social policy than a manifestation of the strength and status of the social purity movement'.[81]

As with so much of the legislation concerning the sexual and physical welfare of children and young adolescents, the CLA Act, 1885, and the Punishment of Incest Act, 1908, involved several overlapping concerns, not the least important of which were attitudes to sexual freedom, notions of social regulation, family ideology, concepts of childhood and adolescence, and visions of public morality. Neither of these Acts was exclusively or even mainly concerned with protecting children from sexual abuse. The earlier Act was equally concerned with safeguarding parental ownership, and suppressing prostitution and homosexuality, and it also shared with the later Act a desire to regulate public morals. Both Acts were strong on symbolism in that they were declarations of reformers' ideals (nearly always middle-class in origin) of sexual, family, gender and age relations. They were attempts to legislate a public and a private morality in a period of intense anxiety, unrest and historical discontinuity. Together they aptly illustrate the ways in which children's welfare is always dependent upon national social, political, economic and cultural concerns, and on the perception of their nature by influential interests in society.

REFORMING CHILD LABOUR

The introduction of compulsory schooling in the 1880s did not put an end to all forms of wage-earning employment for children. Instead a wide-ranging debate developed over the continued use of half-timers, that is, those who combined wage-labour with school attendance, and over those children who worked for wages before and after school for long hours and in conditions damaging to their health and morals. Effectively, the debate on child labour was a product of two fairly comprehensive anxieties. One emphasised the general welfare of children considering virtually every aspect of their lives from paediatrics through education and nutrition to protection from parental cruelty. The other took a more limited view, seeing child health in terms of individual physical and mental development, but within the context of imperialism, eugenics, social reform and 'national efficiency'.[82]

Many reformers, perhaps the majority, viewed the employment of children as essentially a nineteenth-century issue which, so it seemed, had been more or less resolved through factory legislation and compulsory education. With this in mind, in one sense the worries expressed in the debate can be seen simply as those of unfinished business. However, they were also uncomfortable reminders of the continuing failure of sections of the working class to conform to approved notions of family responsibility: child labour detracted from home-centredness; it confused dependent relationships between adult and child; it posed moral dangers to the children; it interfered with schooling; and it was unhealthy.

The reformers' critique

There were mixed views as to the best course of action. While doctors and social reformers tended to oppose 'excessive' (always the important qualifying adjective) labour, there remained differences of opinion over what constituted conditions 'prejudicial' to health. By and large, observers viewed *some* degree of child labour, either paid or unpaid, as 'positively beneficial' in terms of moral and social teaching; and, given that the alternative often meant spending time in 'public thoroughfares or in the penny music-hall', it was 'a useful part of a boy's education', if only because it taught 'habits of industry'.[83] Reformers also had to confront the economic necessity of child wage-earning among the poor, as shown by numerous investigators, including Booth and Rowntree. Booth, for example, had revealed that 30 per cent of the population in London were unable to survive on a man's wage alone.[84] The use of children by various groups of employers as a convenient and cheap form of labour was equally influential in conditioning attitudes and strategies. Furthermore, in the case of the half-time system, this had the support not only of employers, but of parents, municipal officials and trade unions, too. The young workers themselves were not always so enthusiastic, especially those who worked as piecers in spinning factories where they feared being caught in the machinery if they slipped on the oily wooden floors.[85] Nevertheless, complete abolition was rarely seriously canvassed; instead there were calls for greater controls, raising the minimum age and limiting hours of employment.[86]

The first formal public pronouncement on wage-earning school children in this period came from the government committee on Conditions of School Attendance and Child Labour, 1893–4, which was primarily concerned with the use of half-timers.[87] The principal criticisms of the system were that it was damaging to the health of the young workers; that after work the pupils were difficult to teach in the classroom since they were so fatigued; and that they were inclined to become precocious – 'they lose their childish habits'. The Committee also found that thousands of parents, after obtaining half-time status for their children, were then sending them to jobs other than those in the textile mills for which they had received the exemption order. It went on to question whether the employment of children street-selling, or working as shop assistants, milk boys, errand boys, office boys and domestics, could be termed either 'necessary' or 'beneficial'.[88]

The continuing interest in child labour was no doubt responsible for an inquiry conducted by the Women's Industrial Council which resulted in Edith Hogg, one of its members, publishing her influential article on wage-earning school children.[89] The upshot was a Parliamentary Return in 1899, purporting to show that 144,000 pupils were working for wages in England and Wales. Unfortunately for the reformers, the usefulness of the Return was limited by its narrow focus on children in regular out-of-school employment, thereby excluding seasonal and casual workers, those in occupations not deemed 'prejudicial' to health, those whose wages were paid directly to parents, and those who worked illegally during school hours. In the same year, however, the London School Board published a report on child labour, emphasising the danger of 'physical incapacity', and this helped to consolidate opinion in favour of a more searching inquiry.[90]

The Government's response

Within a few months of the Parliamentary Return, an Interdepartmental Committee on the Employment of School Children was appointed to consider the whole matter and to advise on legislation. In its Report (1902), the Committee found that the largest numbers of working children were in shops, agriculture and domestic service, with half-timers in factories and workshops, followed by street-trading, home industries, and miscellaneous employment. The size of the child labour force was said to be in the region of 300,000 (a more detailed survey, by the Fabian labour-exchange manager Frederic Keeling, published in 1914, suggested a United Kingdom total of 'possibly considerably over 600,000'). The great variety of jobs available in shops and agriculture is fairly obvious: serving, delivering and packing in the former, and bird-scaring, tending animals, and picking vegetables and potatoes in the latter. The home industries included, among others, lace-making in Nottingham, metal trades in Birmingham, the matchbox trade in London and handkerchief-hemming in Manchester. Street-employment referred to selling newspapers and matches, delivering milk and parcels, hawking various goods, running errands, taking dinners and 'knocking up'. Domestic work, nearly always employing girls, tended to be divided between baby-minding, helping with the laundry, and cleaning. The half-timers were to be found overwhelmingly in the textile districts of Lancashire and Yorkshire, with others in a motley collection of trades such as the manufacture of ropes, bread and confectionery, paper bags, cigars, fire-lighters and machinery. These were just a fraction of the jobs done by children. In reality the labour market was riddled with child wage-earners, especially in irregular and seasonal employment. And as for the extent of unpaid domestic work, which was undertaken primarily by female children, this was simply incalculable. Girls were the hidden drudges of the working- and lower-middle-class family economies.[91]

Although the Committee agreed that the danger of particular employments to health and to education was hardly 'in question', its refusal to abrogate part-time labour put a premium on identifying a reasonable number of hours, which was deemed to be about twenty a week. But the important consideration was not so much the total number of hours worked as the *length* of each shift – witnesses agreed that a thirteen-hour shift, for example, was 'excessive' and, therefore, damaging to the child's development.[92] The hours of children working in domestic environments were difficult to calculate, though there was little doubt that they were subject to 'the longest hours and the hardest conditions'. Keeling found that different groups of young workers worked different hours. Children aged 13, who through exemptions were employed full-time under the Factory Acts, worked a maximum of sixty hours; those who worked part-time, also under the protection of the Acts, could be employed for up to thirty-four hours. The limit for other groups of children outside the Acts was set by local bye-laws. The average appears to have been between ten and twenty per week, although a substantial number probably worked in excess of this figure. In Liverpool it was reported that 60 per cent of working children were employed for more than twenty hours, and 17 per cent in excess of thirty hours. Moreover, many of those who worked less than twenty hours did so on a Saturday in an excessive thirteen-to-seventeen-hour shift.[93]

What were the legal restrictions on children working for wages? The Education Act of 1876 prevented children under 10 from being employed at all, while the Factory and Workshops Act, 1878, only allowed those between the ages of 10 and 14 to work as 'half-timers' in certain trades, mainly textile mills, provided they were 'necessarily and beneficially employed'.[94] The minimum age was raised to 11 in 1891 and to 12 in 1899 (except for children in agricultural districts, who could start a year earlier).[95] Although the school-leaving age was 14, on reaching a certain standard of proficiency a 13-year-old could become a full-timer. But there was no legislation to prevent children from working either before or after school, or at the weekends, and they had little protection against long hours and poor conditions. However, several provincial cities possessed special powers obtained from private Acts in the 1880s to restrict street-trading, and others would do so under the terms of legislation passed in 1903.

The Employment of Children Act, 1903, allowed, but did not compel, local authorities to make bye-laws prescribing a limited number of daily and weekly working hours, and the age below which employment was illegal. It also permitted the prohibition of their employment in any specified occupation, and the curtailment of street-trading. It was the first and only comprehensive attempt to regulate child labour during the late-Victorian and Edwardian eras. Even so, the Act hardly pacified those who had been most vociferous in calling for further legislation. Its permissive nature, and its focus on street-trading at the expense of employment in home industries, was disappointing to reformers. No effort at all was made to regulate the half-time system, which was not abolished until the passing of the Education Act, 1918, when the school-leaving age was raised to 14. By 1915 only ninety-eight out of 320 authorities had made bye-laws affecting general employment, and only 131 had issued regulations governing street-trading, despite the widespread belief that this was the most morally dangerous form of child employment. Obviously the issue of child labour, including that of young adolescent half-timers, was far more complex than reformers either believed or wished to believe.

Child labour and medical opinion

Nevertheless, the medical dimension of child labour became increasingly important in the early 1900s. Broadly speaking, the physical condition of children did not become a *popular* public issue until the beginning of the twentieth century, though of course reformers had been campaigning for improvements for years. While the major cause of ill-health was seen to be malnutrition, next in importance was the 'excessive' work done out of school hours. The claim, put simply by one of the leading propagandists, was that *all* forms of *overwork* were damaging to school children. They were employed for long hours and deprived of rest and sleep and, therefore, they arrived at school tired and unfit to cope with either the physical or the intellectual efforts demanded of them. This condition, it was asserted, then tended to 'the serious deterioration of public health'.[96]

One of the principal medical contributions to the debate on child labour concerned the half-timers. A large and frequently quoted survey on the subject claimed that not only was there a relative decline in the physique of children in half-time towns, but also they showed defects of eye, nose and throat, were 'not so bright or responsive in appearance' and were 'less clean and tidy'.[97] On the other hand, a government Report Committee concluded that the alleged deterioration of the health of these children was 'a too wide generalisation'.[98] Despite this view, there was general agreement that they suffered ill-effects brought on by too much 'strain'. Furthermore, apart from physical stress, young workers in textile mills suffered from a variety of additional ailments: they were prone to skin disease and poor eyesight; dust and fluff caused asthma; the heated atmosphere of the sheds brought on a low fever known as 'mill sickness'; and the weavers sucked up weft which rotted their teeth, while the noise of the machines affected their hearing.[99] Even when it was admitted that these children owed their physique more to the poverty of their families than to the effects of half-time, the point was made that this only reinforced the need to protect such children from overstrain, since they were already 'anaemic, tired, dull and listless, and often with muscular tremor', all of which were made worse by the long hours, lack of sleep, monotony and an unhygienic environment.[100]

However much disagreement there may have been as to how their health could best be improved, the extensive amount of morbidity among working children was evident from contemporary surveys and from the conclusions of the Chief Medical Officer at the Board of Education. The report for 1911, for instance, quoted with apparent approval the views of government and local-authority inquiries, all of which showed the deleterious effect of child labour.[101] One of the investigations, carried out among 2,000 children, found 384 wage-earning boys, of whom 233 had signs of fatigue, 140 were anaemic, 131 had severe strain, 64 were deformed through carrying heavy weights and 51 had severe heart signs. Heart strain in children was a particular concern and was 'apt to follow prolonged exertion'.[102] Observers also emphasised the long hours involved in child labour, resulting in lack of sleep. One of the reasons behind this particular criticism was the 'keen and growing anxiety' of psychologists and physiologists 'on the subject of the deficient sleep' which 'directly conduces to mental instability, physical inefficiency and emotional excitability'. Sleep was essential for the needs of the nervous system and for the regeneration of the organism as a whole. Thus there could be no doubt that 'premature employment' was 'physiologically detrimental'.[103]

The danger from all forms of child labour, as the Lancet observed, was one of 'physical incapacity', which was an important consideration given the journal's warning that the future was one in which the safety of a 'large section of the community' would depend upon making labouring children's lives 'healthier and better'. It seemed obvious that working school children, and not just the half-timers, were prone to numerous ills, including 'fatigue' and 'restlessness', and – at least, as far as home workers were concerned – that these were likely to be related to 'miserable physique' and the spread of 'infectious diseases'. The Lancet concluded, therefore, that reform would be 'of benefit to the race in the next generation'. The *British Medical Journal* made a similar observation, but emphasised that the crisis was in the present rather than in the future.[104]

Assessing the debates

How can we understand the debates on child labour during the period 1880–1918? The attitude of reformers towards young wage-earners derived in part from the peculiar contemporary importance of labour as a moral good, as an educative process, and as one that ought to be experienced from a young age. It was widely held that labour, performed in the proper manner, taught thrift, perseverence and individual responsibility. While the importance of these virtues was often reinterpreted, they remained the starting-point for most of those who involved themselves with social and economic problems (except for the socialists and the Marxists). For example, the Report of the Inter-departmental Committee (1902) argued that for a boy of 12 or 13 from a respectable home, 'quite irrespective of anything he may earn, it is better for him mentally, morally and physically to be engaged for a few hours a day in regulated labour rather than to spend his whole leisure in the public thoroughfares or in the penny music-hall'. 'All children', it claimed, 'should have the liberty to work as much and in such ways as is good for them and no more'.[105]

One reinterpretation of the value of labour, which was firmly in place by 1900, involved the exemption of children from the logic of the free labour market, so that their labour was regulated, often in accordance with the demands of education. At first this had created a certain tension in the theoretical framework of classical political economy until the difficulty was resolved through the development of mass schooling as the classroom offered numerous possibilities not only for a particular form of labour, now translated into schoolwork, but also for instruction in relevant virtues, including those of obedience, punctuality, silence and concentration. However, it is true that up to 1918, and beyond, a few vested interests remained free to exploit child wage-earners, especially in agricultural and textile areas. And this is not without significance since it shows that in the face of specific economic demands the exact relationship of children to labour, while remaining unclear, could be accommodated in favour of employers and parents.

Notwithstanding the medical evidence against the half-time system and so many other areas of child labour, there remained a conflict between the child as school pupil, the child as the wage-earning employee learning occupational discipline, the child of the poor, indispensable to the economic security of his or her family, and the child as damaged in its physical and moral development through 'excessive' labour. Which of these conditions most accurately reflected a 'natural' childhood? And how natural could the working-class child ever be? Few contemporaries had a convincing answer. In effect the moral lessons to be derived from working, and the economic advantage to parents and employers, were set against the likely physical and mental injury to children. Ideological conviction seemed to conflict with medically demonstrable impairment, thereby allowing a number of different interests to continue to call for the availability of some form of child labour. These were ranged against those reformers who campaigned for stricter controls, or even for the prohibition of all forms of child labour. The former group were confident in their arguments and had the force of custom and law on their side. The latter group were hesitant and uncertain of the role of 'labour' in the 'nature' of childhood – at least, as far as working-class children were concerned. Hence the conflicts over child labour remained unresolved.

CHILDREN IN CARE: THE POOR LAW, VOLUNTARY SOCIETIES AND CHILD EMIGRATION

Poor Law children

Poor Law children occupied a transitional position between the State as the arbiter of rescue, reclamation and protection, and as the provider of services for children as publicly recognised citizens of the future. The welfare of Poor Law children represents an area of social policy that saw the free flowing of ideas on the treatment of deprivation, as reformers and administrators looked, often unwittingly, for ways in which to conceptualise institutional child care in a changing environment. In attempting to reconcile the often conflicting demands of administrative efficiency, low cost, educational value and moral tuition, while simultaneously avoiding undue exploitation or inhuman treatment, different forms of care were practised.[106]

Social policy for deprived children began seriously in the sixteenth century with the inauguration of the 'boarding-out' system whereby Poor Law children were apprenticed to whomsoever would take them. The children were usually either orphans or those who had been deserted by their parents or guardians. This type of boarding-out lasted until the Poor Law Amendment Act, 1834, when the Poor Law guardians rejected outside apprenticeships in favour of their own forms of industrial training and education to be given in buildings separate from the workhouse. Reformers felt that the old system helped to perpetuate pauperism and to create nurseries for crime. The proclaimed aim of the new system was to educate the children for independence, employment and Christian adulthood (in reality this hardly differed from the old system, which had also sought to reduce the poor rate and guarantee against future civil disorder through training and educating pauper children). However, as most workhouses were too small to provide this education, Poor Law Unions began to combine to form large district schools, many of which came to have over 1,000 pupils in each by the 1850s. But the practice of bringing so many children together in such large institutions soon fell into disrepute as critics argued that it was detrimental to their development in terms of character formation and academic performance. The trend towards these schools, such as it was, was halted by the passing of the Education Act, 1870, though many continued to exist. By this time, a new type of boarding-out began to be proposed which aimed to obtain for the children a 'more healthy and beneficial training than is believed to be obtainable in either the workhouse or district school itself'.[107]

From the late 1870s onwards some Unions began to board out their children in 'cottage homes' (already being used by several voluntary societies). These homes became increasingly popular, being seen as providing an ideal 'family' environment. But soon they, too, were criticised as it was found that the 'villages' into which groups of cottages were formed were too large and were isolated from the outside world. In an attempt to reproduce an ordinary domestic environment, the Sheffield Board of Guardians tried to pioneer a 'scattered Home system', and other schemes followed in Leeds and Cardiff, but as a system it never became widespread.[108].

Although the cottage homes continued, increasing attention was paid to the Scottish experience which showed that it was possible to board out or 'foster' children in an area outside the Poor Law Union, in ordinary homes in the community, and that this was a cheap form of care. Between 1870 and 1900 more and more local committees were appointed by the Local Government Board (LGB) to implement the boarding-out policy. The children involved were usually orphans, illegitimate and motherless, deserted, and those whose parents were convicts, insane, or had left the country. These groups were chosen because they were without a family since it was officially stated in the Poor Law Board Order, 1870, which sanctioned boarding out children beyond their own union, that 'it is most important on all grounds to avoid severing or weakening in any way the ties of the family'.[109] Once boarded out, however, the severance of the child from any connection with its natural family was regarded as crucial for the success of the policy.

Boarding-out, or 'fostering', was described in a Local Government Board Report (the Mundella Report, 1896) as advantageous, for 'it provides home training and allows the development of personal affections'. The Report knowingly commented, 'Of course, the home training is what has made the English working class as good as they are,' and it continued by listing the qualities of the home as self-dependence, resourcefulness, thriftiness, and the example of the parents: self-denial, forethought, industrious habits, value of money.[110] None the less, despite the social and political importance

75

of what we would now call fostering, it never accounted for the majority of Poor Law children. One of the main explanations being the care demanded by the LGB of local boarding-out committees in choosing foster parents and in maintaining supervision of the child in the home. In addition there were the administrative difficulties in placing individual children with individual sets of parents. Consequently fostering was a much slower process than placement in either cottage homes or district schools.[111]

It is difficult to give precise figures as to how many Poor Law children there were at any one time. Between 1900 and 1914, the figure was probably between 70,000 and 80,000 in residential care. The main groups of these children were in the general wards of workhouses (20,000–24,000), which all passed through on their way to specialist institutions. The larger of these institutions were the district and separate schools which housed approximately 12,000 children; in addition there were 5,000 in scattered homes and 8,500 in grouped homes. The latter two categories were attempts at creating family environments. (The district and separate schools, together with a number of cottage homes, were known as 'barrack schools' owing to the barrack-like rooms in which the children were housed and the oppressive discipline under which they were forced to live.) Between 10,000 and 15,000 children were also placed in voluntary society homes, paid for by the Poor Law guardians. Boarding-out arrangements accounted for another 10,000 children.[112].

In her standard text, Jean Heywood claimed that the systems of childcare administered by the Poor Law during the last quarter of the nineteenth century 'were a developing experiment to meet the individual needs of deprived children in care'. These systems, she wrote, were attempts to substitute personal care for that of the institution. Moreover, the men and women who reported on the systems showed 'an enlightened understanding of the child's emotional needs', but they were hampered by 'the social conditions of the time'.[113] All this is true, but it is only a part of the truth.

There are three objections to such a straightforward interpretation. First, it leaves out the *political* considerations of childcare policy (both Poor Law and philanthropic). There were no doubt several overlapping political objectives which included keeping down costs, maintaining the deterrent features of the Poor Law, and the long-standing and widely discussed desire to rear children under the influence of Christianity and domestic respectability. The intention here was a cluster of concerns that had to do with morality, piety, thrift, obedience, and political stability in its broadest sense. Hence the call of the Mundella Report for the emancipation of the children from their pauper associations and for their lives to be more closely assimilated with those of the respectable working class. Second, Heywood's interpretation divorces contemporary 'social conditions' from the objectives of those who formulated childcare policy. The 'social conditions of the time' were not divinely ordained; they were made by people who possessed the power to change them had they so wished. While Poor Law administrators were searching for the most appropriate form for a public child care policy, little or no thought was given to the idea that, with sufficient public funds available, poor parents may well have been the best people to care for their own children.[114] This was an option – at least, in part; it was simply not politically acceptable.

Third, such an interpretation says nothing about the experiences of Poor Law children. The act of rescuing children from destitution appears to carry within it a clause that precludes further investigation of the meaning of rescue for the children concerned. However, Mrs Elizabeth Senior, reporting for the LGB in 1873 on the education of girls in large 'District Schools', was critical of their clothing, their food and the lack of personal attention. What they needed, she wrote, was 'mothering'. In later years there were numerous scandals at different schools, including the serving of soup made from maggot-ridden meat (the fresh meat being eaten by the staff) and physical cruelty. Twenty years later, in the Mundella Report, it was freely admitted that the child's experience in Poor Law 'barrack schools' in London was one of 'the dull monotony of institutional life and its weary routine . . . [which] reduces everything to the dead level of a colourless experience'.[115] This is unsurprising given that everything was done to numbers, from sitting down at meal-times to undressing for bed. The children had little in the way of culture except for a few books and meetings of the religious 'Band of Hope'. While several homes had swimming-pools, recreational activities generally seem to have been limited to football; nor was there much opportunity for free and informal play. In about half the schools underclothing was held in common; in the majority the Poor Law uniform was compulsory, and visits outside the institution were limited to a weekly walk on Sunday afternoons, except in a minority of schools which organised trips to places of interest. When Dr Macnamara, Parliamentary Secretary to the LGB, conducted a survey of institutionalised Poor Law children in 1908, he found that they 'spoke in half-whispers and lacked the spontaneity of youth'.[116]

We must also remember the sheer scale of the legal violence to which the children were subjected as a matter of routine. All total institutions are infamous for their discipline, and where young people are the inmates this nearly always means corporal punishment (and sexual abuse). In his autobiography, Charlie Chaplin recounts the formal beatings with a four-foot cane every Friday in the Lambeth Union Institution for Boys. Girls were less often beaten, though it was by no means unknown. For a hundred years or more critics of corporal punishment had tried to have it banned. In 1841, Kay-Shuttleworth, a progressive Poor Law inspector, advocated instead 'confinement in a warm room . . . where in solitude the pupil may be left to calm his passions and reflect on the consequences of his faults'. Perhaps the most violent regimes were those in Poor Law army and navy establishments. In 1904, for example, 4,300 naval boys received over 8,000 canings a year, each one being of six or twelve strokes, and in addition there were 241 birchings of up to twenty-four strokes. The Secretary to the Admiralty made no attempt to deny the facts during a House of Commons debate, preferring instead to protest that nothing of an excessive nature had occurred.[117]

The truth was that Poor Law children were viewed with distaste; they were subjects for reclamation. As one official unwittingly revealed in a testimony before the Royal Commission on the Poor Laws (1909), the children 'have as a rule been neglected and subjected to bad example in such moral faults as dishonesty, intemperance, idleness, lying and the like, and the re-shaping of their character needs expert handling'.[118] There could hardly be a clearer expression of a perception of child victims being treated as threats.

The voluntary societies

Poor Law childcare was profoundly affected by the development of the religious voluntary childcare societies for which the nineteenth century, especially the second half, is so well known. The Poor Law sometimes collaborated with voluntary societies, for under the Poor Law Certified Schools Act, 1862, its children could be sent to voluntary institutions approved by the Poor Law Board. However, by 1878 there were fifty philanthropic institutions for children in London alone, and by the end of the century the voluntary organisations were set to leave almost as much of an indelible mark on childcare policy as the Poor Law itself. The best-known of the societies were: Dr Barnardo's, 1870 (which had 11,277 children in its care in 1905); the National Children's Home, founded a year earlier by the young Wesleyan, Thomas Bowen Stephenson; the Church of England's Waifs and Strays Society, 1881, which arose out of the Sunday-school work of two brothers, Edward and Robert de Montjoie Rudolf (with 3,071 children in its care in 1902); and the Catholic Crusade of Rescue, founded by Cardinal Vaughan in 1899.[119]

Each of the societies housed its children through a combination of institutional homes and experiments with boarding-out (or fostering), cottage homes and emigration schemes. Barnardo, for example, besides his boarding-out system, more or less brought the principle of the cottage homes into the voluntary sector by opening thirteen cottages in July 1876, later known as 'village homes'. He shared with the Poor Law the desire to remove children from the institutional atmosphere which was felt to be counterproductive in inculcating the values of Christian domesticity. The family homes were intended to cultivate a certain individuality, through allowing the children to wear their own clothes, promoting respect for parent figures, and the 'performance of commonplace duties'. 'Surely', wrote Barnardo, without fear of contradiction, 'the family is God's way.'

The names of the societies inform us that it is impossible to understand the history of British child care policy without an appreciation of the influence of religious organisations. They illustrate the importance which religiously motivated individuals attached to 'rescuing' and 'saving' the children of the poor. The histories of these individuals tend to be presented as if it were by chance that they fell upon the founding of their organisations. This can hardly have been so. Each of them devoted their lives to moralising the poor; to providing a Christian education for the children in their care; and to advancing a conservative vision of responsible social order. The point of departure for each of them was a critique of Poor Law provision for children, coupled with a sense of personal destiny and denominational competitiveness. Barnardo saw two limitations with the Poor Law: it depended on people approaching it, and yet it operated under the principle of deterrence. The result was that, rather than face the break-up of the family on entering the workhouse, many families tried to survive but found that their children ended up on the streets. He also saw that the standard of care was oppressive, stamping children with the brand of pauperism.[120]

However much the societies differed in approach, they agreed on the central task of 'rescue'. And it is important to understand that children were to be rescued not only from bad conditions, but also, as one of the aims of the Crusade of Rescue proclaimed, from 'dissolute and degenerate parents'. Barnardo wrote that if slum children 'can be removed from their surroundings early enough, and can be kept sufficiently long under training, heredity counts for little, environment counts for everything'.[121] It is hard to disagree with Robert Holman's verdict that while many of the children taken into homes did in fact have parents, 'in the eyes of the voluntary societies that was a hindrance. They were better off without parents.' Barnardo remarked of parents that they 'are my chief difficulty everywhere; so are relatives . . . because I have to take from a very low class'. Barnardo's foster parents had to sign a contract undertaking that they would not permit visits from the child's relatives or friends without official authorisation, and similar contracts were used by the Waifs and Strays Society. At the same time, the Waifs and Strays Society tried 'to avoid encouraging natural guardians in idleness, or evil courses, and every legal step was taken to compel parents to discharge their responsibilities'. But once the child became the responsibility of the Society, then contact between it and its natural parents was discouraged.[122]

It has been observed that, while the Poor Law and the philanthropic systems of child care are held up as contrasts, it is not sufficiently recognised that 'in their attitudes towards preventing children having to leave their own homes, and towards encouraging rehabilitation between children and parents, the two systems reinforced each other with few dissenting voices'. It was never policy to rehabilitate children to their parents. Thus, the principle was established that *'needy children were best brought up outside the influence of parents'*.[123] Other historians have argued that it is wrong to assume that 'abused' children were taken out of parental custody and placed in institutional care. In Cleveland only 1 per cent of children dealt with by the NSPCC during the period 1891–1903 were not returned home.[124] But this refers only to NSPCC cases, and not to children involved with voluntary societies whose desire to separate children from undesirable parents and families reached its apotheosis in emigration schemes.

Child emigration

Rescuing the child was one thing; providing it with a 'fresh start' was another. Children had been sent to the colonies since the early seventeenth century and, though little is known about them, the reasons seem to have been the desire of local authorities to reduce their poor rates and the threats posed by vagrants, beggars and juvenile delinquents. One of the first nineteenth-century emigration schemes was organised by the Society for the Suppression of Juvenile Vagrancy. However, in 1840 the conditions of 440 children who had been sent to the Cape were the subject of an inquiry which eventually led to the demise of the Society. Eight years later Lord Shaftesbury argued without success for a coherent policy of sending slum children abroad. It was not until the late 1860s that emigration began on a large scale under the control of Annie Macpherson and Maria Rye, both of whom were staunch evangelicals, and whose activities represented one of the strands of philanthropic activity associated with the evangelical revival of the time. Both women occasionally worked in collaboration with Boards of Guardians, and were soon sending hundreds of children to Canada. But it was Barnardo who did so much to perfect emigration as a solution for the human consequences of social distress. He began by using the services of Macpherson, and by 1882 was operating his own emigration organisation which quickly overshadowed all others. Between 1867 and 1914 he alone sent 24,346 young people overseas, more than twice the number sent by Macpherson over the same period, and seven times the number of the Waifs and Strays Society. Thus the late-Victorian and Edwardian years saw more than 40,000 children leave Britain through these emigration schemes, in addition to the thousands sent by Quarrier Homes, the Salvation Army, the Boys' and Girls' Refuges and other smaller organisations, to Canada, South Africa, Australia and New Zealand.[125]

Who were these emigrant children? Some were orphans, others were from reformatory and industrial schools, and many were 'street arabs' who had been taken into one of the many voluntary homes. Older children were often sent direct from Poor Law workhouses, after making a sworn declaration before two Justices of the Peace that they were willing to go. The majority, however, had no protection against the arbitrary manner in which the societies took their decisions. Less than one-third of the children in the philanthropic homes were orphans. It was usually the case that the children had been brought by destitute parents (often widows), in preference to the workhouse, others referred themselves, and others were referred by third parties such as the NSPCC. Although often not without one or more parents, or relatives, no attempt was made by the societies to ensure that once abroad the children maintained contact with their roots back home, despite the efforts of many of the parents and the young emigrants to keep in touch with each other. The youngsters were not entirely without advocates, though these were ineffectual. Nevertheless, history should remind us of those contemporaries who opposed acts of inhumanity. One such figure was George Cruikshank, illustrator of Dickens and Harriet Beech Stowe, who proclaimed 'such transportation of innocent . . . children a disgrace to the Christian world'.[126]

We can only speculate as to the misery endured by these boys and girls, taken from their parents, brothers and sisters, families, communities and friends, and put to work in often Spartan environments where they were subjected to exploitation and violence. Historians agree that there was a large demand overseas for boys to work as farm labourers and for girls to drudge, usually as rural domestics. The government investigator sent to inquire about conditions in Canada later wrote that the children were exploited. 'In no other way can one account for the eagerness of Canadian employers to get them, and the unwillingness of the working people of Canada to send their own children into service upon the same terms.'[127]

There were four principal reasons for child emigration: economic, religious, political and, by the early 1900s, social imperialistic. It was an economic fact, of which Barnardo was well aware, that it cost only ten pounds to send a child to Canada, while to keep a child in a home cost sixteen pounds a year. Barnardo found that, although his revenue was increasing by the 1880s, so was the number of children coming into his care. The housing crisis of the 1880s, with its various social and economic repercussions, was having an effect on increasing the number of child paupers, so that Barnardo found himself faced with a shortage of funds. The solution came in the form of a donation given by Samuel Smith, the Liverpool MP and founder member of the NSPCC, to be used solely for emigration. Barnardo accepted the offer. Writing in 1885, Smith made clear the political reasoning behind all the child-saving societies, as well as emigration schemes: '. . . the time is approaching when this seething mass of human misery will shake the social fabric unless we grapple more earnestly with it than we have yet done.' Children were obviously threatening as part of this 'seething mass', especially given that at this time there were perhaps 30,000 street children in London alone. These children were the raw material from which the 'dangerous classes' were formed. Emigration, then, was to act as a 'safety valve to tide over the troubles at home'. It would help to reduce the numbers of the degenerate poor who posed moral, economic and political dangers to respectable society. Far from being an expression of humanitarianism, emigration was part of a political strategy for dealing with unwanted slum children.[128]

Closely associated with the notion of the 'safety valve' was the religious concern to 'save' the individual slum child from the immorality of his or her environment. Children with irreligious parents would 'grow in evil'; they would prize 'the fruits of evil' as 'the best things in the world'. For the evangelicals in particular, with their pre-millenarian beliefs, saving the souls of the children could only be accomplished by rescuing them from the damnation in which they were cast by economic, social and moral circumstance, and putting them on the path to conversion. By the turn of the century, the influence of evangelicalism gave way to imperial sentiment. The philanthropist became the 'imperial philanthropist', and emigration was a way of populating the largely deserted lands of the Dominions. In Gillian Wagner's words, 'Children were now no longer merely to be rescued and given new opportunities, they were seen as the bricks with which the Empire would be built . . . the young colonists of the future . . . would help to consolidate the Empire and form a living link between the Dominions and the mother country'. Child emigration was presented as 'an investment in Empire.'[129] In the age of imperialism, then, children were seen as investments – human capital in its most elemental form.

In trying to understand the nature of the philanthropic societies, it would be a mistake to imagine that they were simply Christian (mainly evangelical) institutions, innocent of wily political ambitions with respect to instilling social discipline in their charges. However much certain historians may shy away from the uncomfortable implications of class, the societies knew what it meant – and it meant trouble of one sort or another: financial, political, social, religious. The sight of hungry barefooted children no doubt touched the hearts of the philanthropic workers, but their heads fully understood the social and political necessity of 'rescuing' the children from what they regarded as the awful potential of their condition, not the least dreadful feature of which, certainly from the evangelicals' perspective, was the failure of poor families to provide moral and religious tuition. It was an act of charity dictated by self-interest at a time when Britain was ceasing to be an agricultural society, so that the full impact of urban conditions was making itself felt in terms of crime, disease, slums and urban poverty – all under the shadow of a rapidly changing political culture.

Nor should it be forgotten that this brief institutional account is only one part of the history of emigration. Another, and possibly one of far more importance for the children concerned, was the objectification of the child, no matter how old and responsible, in order to mould its character according to religious and political principles, and often to exploit its labour power. The children of the poor, as well as those who were orphans, found themselves living experiments in the cultivation of environmentalism. It was a tradition that would linger long in British child care policy.

3

THE SOCIAL SERVICES STATE
Providing for the children of the nation, 1889–1918

After a history of neglect, the children of the poor were to be among the first 'children of the nation'. The term comes from Sir John Gorst's *The Children of the Nation: How Their Health and Vigour Should Be Promoted by the State* (1906), which was representative of the new thinking in Edwardian Britain about social problems in general, and in particular about child welfare. Important political, professional and business interests were undecided about priorities for the new century, and it was by no means agreed that all working-class children were in fact 'of the nation'. However, this was certainly the view of left-wing Liberals, radical Tories, of which Gorst was the leading example, orthodox philanthropists and social theorists, such as those affiliated to the Charity Organisation Society and, of course, the socialists. On the other hand, agreeing that children were of the nation was one thing; a common understanding as to what this meant in terms of social policy was something quite different.

Part of the problem for all those involved was the rapidly changing nature of the State, given the influences of new industrial and labour-management techniques, the continuing intensification of foreign competition, the demands of the Empire, the growth of an organised working class, and the enormity of the problem of poverty, despite rising living standards for the majority of the population. It is no exaggeration to say that the nature of the State was once again in the process of being reformulated (as it had been in during the Industrial Revolution, and in the course of the great nineteenth-century debates on the franchise, public health and the Poor Law); but, more than this, there was an uncertainty, which had been growing since the 1870s, as to the role of Britain in what was clearly a newly emerging world economic, social and political order. One area, one of many, of this uncertainty concerned children (and by implication the family): their role in society, their significance in the social fabric, and the degree of responsibility for them on the part of parents and the State.

A particularly popular framework for discussing many of the issues was that of Social Darwinism, a social theory of some considerable complexity, which was popularised along the lines of the 'survival of the fittest'.

This was often to be found mixing with another popular socio-scentific programme, which also called on the racial dimension, namely eugenics, sometimes known as the philosophy of 'proper parenthood', pointing as it did to the belief of eugenicists in the need to breed a healthy race. Eugenics manifested itself in two main approaches to social life: one emphasised heredity and the other environmentalism. Both eugenics and Social Darwinism congregated around issues relating to infant mortality, mental defectiveness, the differential birth rate between the classes (the middle-class rate was declining in proportion to that of the working class), and the fear (never proved) that urban living was somehow leading to the deterioration of the race, by which reformers usually meant slum-dwellers. These theories tended to provide a set of common references for politicians and reformers, many of whom, perhaps the majority, were in no way card-carrying followers of any particular belief. Instead they used the language, of race, parenthood and survival as part of a general political vocabulary.[1]

THE BLIND, THE DEAF, AND THE 'FEEBLE-MINDED'

The early history of handicapped children is very much bound up with the development of education. It was not until after 1750 that schools for the blind and the deaf first appeared in Britain. Around 1776 the first school was opened for the deaf by Thomas Braidwood in Edinburgh; and, in 1791, Henry Dannett opened a school for blind adults and children in Liverpool. When the National Society and the British and Foreign School Society began to build their schools to promote elementary and religious education in the early nineteenth century, neither bothered about the handicapped. By 1830 no more than a further six schools had been established, mainly for the deaf. During the following decade nine new schools were founded, including one in Wales, some of which began to cater for the blind as well as for the deaf and dumb. A more prolific expansion occurred in the 1840s, while the 1850s saw the opening of only one new school. The position was similar with respect to the physically handicapped. The first educative institution in England was the Cripples' Home and Industrial School for Girls which opened in 1851 in Marylebone, followed in 1865 by a school for boys in Kensington. The objective of the schools was to provide a rudimentary education and to teach a trade to their mainly poor pupils. Virtually nothing more was done for these children until 1890.

Care for the mentally defective, as opposed to the mentally unbalanced, began proper in 1847 with the Asylum for Idiots (of all ages) at Park House, Highgate. In the 1850s and 1860s other asylums opened in Colchester, Devon, Lancaster and Birmingham. Mentally defective pauper children, however, were without any provision at all. The Metropolitan Poor Act, 1867, gave powers to the Poor Law Board to establish asylums for pauper imbeciles, and in 1870 the newly established Metropolitan Asylum Board opened institutions in Caterham, Leavesden, Hertfordshire, and Hampstead. These were soon followed by separate buildings for the housing and education of mentally defective pauper children.[2]

By the mid-1870s the Charity Organisation Society (COS) had begun to interest itself in the matter. Sir Charles Trevelyan, one of its council members, coined the term 'feeble-minded' to distinguish between 'idiot' and 'imbecile', which together with 'mentally defective' were used interchangeably until the 1890s. In 1877 the Society appointed a sub-committee to investigate the education and care of mentally handicapped adults and children. The subsequent report recommended that the difference between lunatics and the feeble-minded should be given greater recognition, and that the State should give financial assistance towards the building of large institutions together with schools for the children.[3] But, since the Government had no interest in legislating in this area, there was little education available for the children until the twentieth century.

None the less, the decade 1865 to 1875 saw several important developments in the history of special education. In addition to the establishments of the Metropolitan Asylum Board, a college for the preparation of blind boys for the universities and the professions was established, as was the first training college for blind teachers. The British and Foreign Blind Association for Promoting the Education and Employment of the Blind was founded and made the important decision to recommend Braille as the educational system for all blind children. The London School Board appointed a special teacher for the blind together with special classes for the deaf. And the first of several abortive Bills calling for state intervention on behalf of education for the deaf was introduced.[4]

The Education Act (1870) made no mention of special provision for handicapped children. They were neither specifically excluded nor specifically included. However, the London School Board, which began in 1872, did initially exclude blind, deaf and mentally defective children from its responsibility, describing them as 'permanently disabled', thereby making them ineligible for classes. Within a couple of years there was a change of mind, and a superintendent of instruction for the deaf was appointed. By 1888 there were fourteen centres with 373 children in ordinary elementary schools. Blind children fared little better. In 1875 the London School Board secured the help of the Home Teaching Society to teach blind children in its schools. Progress was slow, so that as late as 1888 only 133 children were being taught at twenty-three centres attached to ordinary schools. Despite this limited provision, in its early days the Board had more success with education for the blind than for the deaf, though the level and nature of the education were basic and unimaginative and often repressive. No doubt it was not much better in those areas which followed the London example, notably Sunderland, Bradford, Cardiff, Sheffield, Leeds, Nottingham, Bristol, Leicester and Oldham.[5]

In 1882 the Conference of Headmasters of Deaf and Dumb Schools passed a resolution allowing individual schools to ask for state aid. Within a few years it was rumoured that government assistance was about to be forthcoming for the education of the blind. This spurred on deaf educators to ask the Government for a comprehensive form of financial assistance. But before any final decision could be made Gladstone's second ministry fell. The new government appointed a Royal Commission on the Blind and the Deaf whose terms of reference also included 'such other cases as from special circumstances would seem to require exceptional methods of education'. This referred to the physically and mentally handicapped.

The tone of the Report of the Royal Commission suggested that the education of all groups of handicapped people was 'an economic expedient' rather than 'an ethical duty'.[6] 'Indigence' was found to exist among the 'great majority' of the people so afflicted, though not by any fault of their own. Unsurprisingly the Report concluded that 'The blind, deaf and dumb, and the educable class of imbeciles form a distinct group, which, if left uneducated, become not only a burden to themselves, but a weighty burden to the State. It is the interest of the State to educate them, so as to dry up as far as possible the main streams which ultimately swell the great torrent of pauperism.'[7] With reference to elementary and technical education for the blind, for example, the Commissioners asserted that it was better to use state funds for a few years 'than to have to support them through life in idleness, or to allow them to obtain their livelihood from public or private charity'.[8] The basic recommendations for blind children, of which there were reckoned to be 1,710 between the ages of 5 and 15, were elementary education until the age of 12, to be followed by a technical instruction course until the compulsory leaving age of 16.[9]

One of the main difficulties contemporaries faced in discussions concerning deaf children was that, unlike the blind, there were no firm estimates of their number, though the census of 1881 gave a figure of 5,129. It was thought, however, that little over half of those of school age were in receipt of any academic instruction. Another problem was the different methods of teaching, each of which had its own vociferous advocates. The three main methods were sign and manual, oral, and combined. The recommendation avoided taking sides, except to say that all children should be taught to speak and lip-read, and be compulsorily educated from the age of 7 in separate schools (usually residential institutions), rather than in ordinary classes as was possible with the blind, until they were 16.[10]

When the Commissioners came to the third class of handicapped, their main difficulty was to distinguish between feeble-minded, idiots and imbeciles. They resolved this by agreeing that the difference was one of degree rather than of kind. In many respects the Report was enlightened in its attitude towards imbecile children. It not only identified them as 'educable', but also advocated that school authorities be responsible for them and that they be taught by properly trained teachers.[11] However, the Report had almost nothing to say about the feeble-minded, except to recommend their separation from normal children in pursuit of special education.

In September 1893, three years after its first introduction, the Bill based on the recommendations of the Report became the Elementary Education (Blind and Deaf Children) Act. This made it a duty for local authorities to ensure that blind and deaf children received 'efficient and suitable' education in either one of their own schools or an institution. The system of grants whereby school authorities only received a grant if the child was educated in a local school (and not sent to an institution) meant that some problems remained, especially in rural areas where poor authorities desired the grant but provided minimal provision. Despite these drawbacks the Act improved the overall situation since after 1894 almost all blind and deaf children were legally entitled to an elementary education.

The situation for physically handicapped children was much less enviable. Prior to the COS-sponsored report *The Epilectic and Crippled Child and Adult*, published in 1893, there had been no serious investigation into their condition. The COS was especially interested in their education and industrial training, as were several London Settlements and the Victoria Settlement in Liverpool. Probably under these influences, by early 1900 both the London and the Liverpool School Boards had each opened one special school for the physically handicapped.[12] Nevertheless, the main effort on behalf of physically defective and epileptic children continued to be philanthropic until the Education Act 1918 made it compulsory for local education authorities to make provision for them.[13]

Legislation for the 'defective' child

The introduction of compulsory education in the 1870s brought into classrooms thousands of 'dull' pupils and others with various kinds of learning difficulty. They could not be taught in ordinary schools, yet were not sufficiently defective to be certified as either idiots or imbeciles.[14] The majority of them were stuck in the lower classes so that, while in theory all aged 10 and upwards should have been in the upper standards, in practice the figure in 1880 was less than 50 per cent. In some schools either a standard 0 was created, or groups of children (the feeble-minded, the physically handicapped, the partially sighted and the delicate) were confined to standard 1.[15]

In the late 1880s and early 1890s, as part of the general interest in the condition of the child population (and in response to concerns about urban degeneration), there were extensive inquiries made into the educational needs of mentally handicapped children. By 1890, under the auspices of

88

the Royal Society and the British Association, Francis Warner, a well-known paediatrician, had made a visual examination of 50,000 London school children and concluded that 1 per cent needed special education in separate schools. Two years later, a report from the COS supported Warner's findings.[16] These reports, in conjunction with the recommendation of a Royal Commission (Egerton, 1889) which recommended special schools for the feeble-minded, presented a strong argument for further legislative action and encouraged the London and Leicester School Boards to establish such schools. By 1897 London had twenty-four special schools, and other schools or classes were to be found in several other towns and cities, with a grand total of 1,300 pupils.[17]

Under a growing pressure for action from the COS, its affiliated organisation, the National Association for Promoting the Welfare of the Feeble-Minded (NAPWFM), and the London School Board, in December 1896 the Department of Education appointed the Committee on Defective and Epileptic Children. As with the earlier inquiry, the Committee had difficulty in defining terms. Medical members suggested that 'imbecile' should refer to those mentally deficient children who were incapable of being educated to the point where they could become self-supporting. Those who were feeble-minded, while not imbeciles, were to be taught in ordinary elementary schools by ordinary methods, and henceforth they were to be known as defective. Originally 'defective' had applied to the physically handicapped. But defining 'defective' proved too difficult, and all attempts to reach a satisfactory definition failed. The result of the Committee's deliberations was that 'defective' referred to mentally *and* physically handicapped children who could not be taught in ordinary schools, and this remained the case until the Education Act, 1944.[18] A related problem lay in establishing the criterion for admission to a special school. This involved not only the problem of measuring defectiveness, but also the professional rivalry between doctors and teachers as to who was best-qualified to undertake the task.

At issue here in the problem of definition was a construction of a classificatory system which would allow for the identification of different sections of the child and adult population in order to know better how to allocate resources and to plan educational and social policies. But it was not simply a matter of planning. The Committee was faced with the task of formulating concepts of feeble-mindedness, imbecility and idiocy which would be used to 'know' the mental structure of the population at a time when racial considerations were of increasing importance. Part of the significance of the Committee's task was that it *asked* the question: it posed the problem concerning identification of the three different groups. Posing questions is one of the foremost prerequisites for the advancement of all forms of knowledge. Once the question began to be answered, the correctness of any single answer was initially of secondary importance. The political anatomy of abnormality had begun to be drawn.

In January 1898 the Committee presented its report to Parliament, and on 9 August 1899 the Elementary Education (Defective and Epileptic Children) Act received its royal assent. The weakness of the Act (unlike the report) was that, rather than compelling local authorities to make educational provision for the children, it was permissive. As a result, by 1909 only 133 out of 228 authorities had exercised their powers.[19] While it is true that very little progress was made during the 1890s in either the aetiology or the treatment of mentally handicapped pupils, the decade did witness the legislative recognition of a class of children which hitherto had been neglected.[20] These children now mattered not only in terms of provision of appropriate social and educational policy, but also as figures in the process of defining 'normal' behaviour.

Feeble-mindedness as an issue

If public and official attention to the physically handicapped was marginal prior to 1918, clearly this was not so where the mentally defective were concerned. For the racial, social and political reasons already mentioned, interest in mental handicap assumed a major importance. The debate on the care and education of the feeble-minded was one of the first occasions on which issues relating to both Body and Mind were raised, albeit tangentially. The leading organisation in this area was the Charity Organisation Society, with its mixed and overlapping membership of evangelicals and subscribers to the principles of classical political economy. The Society had been founded to organise charitable relief among the innumerable agencies, and to this end it investigated individual applications for relief through systematised social casework. By the 1890s, among its many interests, it was involved in campaigns for special education and the treatment of the feeble-minded, primarily through its affiliated organisation the NAPWFM; and, as we have seen, it was instrumental in persuading the government to appoint the Departmental Committee on Defective and Epileptic Children.

After the passing of the 1899 Act, the next step was to create a policy for the mentally defective child, and from then on it was this area of special education which received maximum attention up to 1914. But it is important to understand that the concern with special education was part of a wider campaign to create a social policy for feeble-minded adults, which eventually led to the Mental Deficiency Act of 1913. It was during this campaign that the different vocabularies of 'social waste', Social Darwinism and eugenics came together, very often to form a single demand for government action, usually of a custodial nature. The COS took a leading role, partly because of its interest in all aspects of poverty and partly in pursuit of its belief in the rationalisation of social welfare. The principal reason why the Society was concerned with feeble-mindedness in general was its desire for economy in terms of reducing the rates, maximising resources in relation to the tenets of political economy, unburdening the families of the feeble-minded, and protecting society against the consequences of their exploitation by criminal, commercial or immoral elements.[21] As early as 1875 it had established a committee for investigating provision for all classes of mental welfare. However, the rediscovery of poverty in the 1880s and the social crisis of which it was a feature not only altered the scope and nature of all debates involving economic and social welfare, but also made them more urgent.

One of the first actions of the COS in the new climate, undertaken out of a fear of sexual promiscuity and procreation, was to work with other organisations to establish homes for feeble-minded adolescent girls. It was in this circumstance that the NAPWFM was formed, bringing to the fore the influential presence of Mary Dendy, who worked in Manchester, and Ellen Pinsent, who worked in Birmingham. Both women were active in establishing special residential schools, and both looked on the feeble-minded as presenting a threat to the well-ordered society and, therefore, 'care' was always to be custodial. Mary Dendy wrote: 'children . . . are to be detained for the whole of their lives . . . only permanent care could be really efficacious in stemming the great evil of feebleness of the mind in our country.' Pinsent shared this view, referring to children's 'own degradation' and that of 'the society in which they live'.[22] For these women and like-minded supporters, the feeble-minded child, through its imperfect mind, which was seen to affect its bodily behaviour, was more obviously a threat than a victim.

By the beginning of this century, influential opinion focused not on special schools as such, but on the segregation of the feeble-minded of all ages. In 1903 a petition, signed by 104 prestigious persons, called for a Royal Commission on the subject, which was appointed in 1904. The Commission, under the chairmanship of the Earl of Radnor, heard evidence on the relationship between mental defect and crime, drunkenness, prostitution, poverty and illegitimacy. With reference to special schools for children, witnesses agreed on the desirability of residential care and of the necessity for vocational instruction.[23] The Radnor Report, which proved to be extremely controversial when it was presented to Parliament in 1908, not only concurred with this view, but also went further in advocating the amendment of the 1899 Act, so that mentally defective children could be excluded. Responsibility for the children was to be given over to local mental deficiency committees who would be charged with providing for their manual, industrial and other training. Furthermore, where local education authorities had established special schools, these were also to be transferred to the control of the local committees.[24]

It was five uncertain years before legislative action was taken, by which time there were 177 LEA special schools catering for 12,000 children. Much of the experience gained from these schools pointed to the opposite conclusion to that of the Radnor Commission in terms of the value of non-residential education.[25] The experience seems to have been convincing, for when the Bill on mental deficiency finally received the royal assent in 1913, contrary to Radnor's recommendation, the education of feeble-minded children was left with the LEAs, who were now compelled to identify such children and to decide whether or not they were capable of benefiting from special schools. Only those who were incapable were to become the responsibility of the local mental deficiency committees. Even so, it was another year before the Elementary Education (Defective and Epileptic Children) Act, 1914, made the 1899 Act obligatory on LEAs with respect to providing educational classes for the feeble-minded, and it would be another four years before it was made obligatory to provide for physically defective and epileptic pupils.[26] In effect the emphasis of the Act with regard to children remained on education rather than on custody. This can be explained by reference to the cost of permanent incarceration over that of day-time education. Costs were a major consideration at a time when expenditure on defence and the new social services was rising. Furthermore, there was a deeply ingrained hostility to the curtailment of individual freedom, which should not be underestimated.

The historian of education for the handicapped child has suggested three reasons why the optimistic work of Montessori with mentally defective children was not followed up in Britain. First, the influence of the eugenics movement, through the researches of Francis Galton, published between 1869 and 1907, which, broadly speaking, claimed that mental ability and physical characteristics were transmitted from parents to children. This argument found support in a number of American family studies which were well known in British eugenic circles, and these gave credence to theories about racial degeneration, especially from the 1880s onwards, which led to calls for the segregation (and sterilisation) of mentally handicapped people. Second, the practice of mental testing was an attempt to solve a number of different problems involving the measurement of intelligence and the process of discrimination, one of which focused on the feasibility of educating the feeble-minded child. The eugenicists tended to argue that normal education was pointless and that mental defectives should be educated along vocational lines in order that they might contribute to their own livelihood. Third, as it proved difficult for defective adolescents to find employment, so they became a financial burden on their families, risking the threat of being economically and sexually exploited. For these reasons a policy of permanent incarceration was advocated.[27]

The extent to which Social Darwinism and the eugenics movement influenced policy for mentally handicapped children has been disputed.[28]

The emphasis in what might be termed purely eugenic sentiments and literature was on custody, while the emphasis of the Education Act, 1914, as we have seen, was on education. Nevertheless, it is possible to see a movement of opinion between the 1890s and the early 1900s, which was certainly influenced by eugenic opinion. The COS Report in 1893, while acknowledging the major role of heredity in mental defect, was less sure about custodial remedies. Similarly, the first edition of Shuttleworth's influential *Mentally Deficient Children* (1895) made no mention of detention and was even hesitant about attributing sole responsibility to heredity. The emphasis in the second edition was very different: inheritance was given more prominence, and legal custody was advocated for adults. Three years later Ellen Pinsent's paper, calling for a national system of compulsory residential schools, was published in the *Lancet*. The Radnor Report on Feeble-Mindedness (1908) also emphasized the importance of heredity and proposed custodial care for adults. Mental defectives, it argued, often bred prolifically and, moreover, the problems of delinquency, alcoholism and illegitimacy were aggravated by the freedom of these defectives to move around in the community.[29]

Clearly there had been a change of mood on the question of feeble-mindedness. Opinion had moved in favour of the hereditarians. By 1908 the debate on 'national efficiency' was well in progress, having developed in the debates on Britain's performance during the Boer War (1899-1902), with particular reference to the physical condition of the urban working class. Thus the vocabulary of national efficiency was added to those of Social Darwinism and eugenics. It was in this climate that the shift in favour of the hereditarian argument had occurred.

THE INFANT WELFARE MOVEMENT

While the debate on the care and education of the feeble-minded projected children as being of both mind and body, the infant welfare movement focused almost entirely on stressing the physical aspects of child development. In some respects infants were much less obviously threats than were feeble-minded children. Of course, by virtue of their early death or failure to grow according to expectations, they could have been classed as victims, but this was rarely the case. The dominant theme of the movement was public health, with all its social, economic and political ramifications. However, given that the ultimate focus of public health was on the future of the race, infant mortality posed a threat in relation to the strength of the population *vis-à-vis* long-term national security, which was of major political significance in a period of strident European imperialism.[30]

The infant welfare movement derived from three separate groups of activities. The agitation for the protection of the foster child, which began in the late 1860s with the formation of the Infant Life Protection Society

93

(ILPS), has already been discussed. The second influence arose from the decline of the birth rate, as it fell from 35.5 in 1871–5 to 29.3 in 1896–1900. Imperialists in particular were anxious about the implications for the defence and administration of the Empire. The *British Medical Journal* solemnly noted in May 1901: 'There has been for some years a steadily declining birth-rate, which requires the consideration of all who have the well-being of the country and of the empire at heart.' Furthermore, confused ideas of evolution and biology, together with middle-class apprehension in the face of the rise of an industrially and increasingly politically organised working class, made the question of *quality* of population as important as quantity. It was felt to be essential that the respectable working class remain numerically superior to those of a degenerate tendency. Third, and of major significance as a social and health problem in the context of concern over national physical efficiency, was the knowledge that, though the death rate had fallen from the 1850s (from 22.6 per 1,000 of the population to 16.9 in 1901), the infant mortality rate had risen since the 1880s (from 145 to 151 deaths under 1 year per 1,000 births, 1891–5).[31]

Understanding the problem

By the early years of the century it was obvious that infant mortality was a difficult and complex problem, with several causes, not all of which were fully understood. Between 1900 and 1910 there were numerous medical, sanitary and statistical investigations and publications, in addition to two national conferences and the five reports issued by the Local Government Board (LGB) between 1910 and 1916. In the search for solutions, the focus of attention fell almost simultaneously on two areas: the feeding of infants and what soon came to be called 'mothercraft', with the former being the most important element in the latter. For many medical, social and political figures, infant mortality became 'a matter not so much of environmental hygiene but of personal hygiene'.[32]

In the first phase of the movement, the infant mortality rate was judged to be between 'preventable' and 'non-preventable'. It was believed that deaths in the first month (the neonatal period) from 'developmental and wasting diseases' owed more to inherited weakness than to any other factor. Not until after 1914 was the artificiality of this distinction recognised as neonatal deaths were found to be related to antenatal sources involving maternal health. The causes of the high rate in general were classified into four main groups: (i) developmental or wasting conditions, including premature birth, atrophy, debility and marasmus, and congenital defects: (ii) diarrhoeal diseases; (iii) bronchitis and pneumonia; and (iv) 'convulsions', but this was often a misnomer for conditions more appropriate to one or more of the other main groups.[33]

Diarrhoea, known as the 'recurring tragedy', usually became something of an epidemic in the summer months. During the record year of 1899, diarrhoeal diseases accounted for one-quarter of the mortality rate for children under 1 year old. In an influential paper, Dr Arthur Newsholme (later to be Chief Medical Officer at the LGB) defined epidemic diarrhoea as a disease of urban life relating to the lower working class, to the absence of water-carriage system of sanitation, and to inadequate scavenging arrangements. The disease, he wrote, was favoured by 'unclean soil, the particular poison from which infests the air and is swallowed, most commonly in food, especially milk . . . [it is] a "filth disease" '.[34] Such views ensured that much attention was paid not only to proper feeding in the early months of life, with an emphasis on breast-feeding and personal hygiene standards in feeding practices, but also to the mother's responsibility for the domestic environment in which the infant was reared.[35]

Premature birth was a significant cause of infant mortality, being responsible for 12.8 deaths per 1,000 in 1876, rising to 19.9 out of a total mortality of 154 in 1900, though the increase was never properly explained. However, it served to remind observers that the health of mothers during pregnancy affected the health of the unborn, and Dr Ballantyne's *Manual of Ante-Natal Pathology and Hygiene* (1902) exerted a cumulative influence on those concerned with the problem. Three years later, a report by Dr Sykes the MOH at St Pancras, drew attention to the different mortality rates *within* the first year of an infant's life, further emphasising the importance of antenatal care. Sykes showed that it was during the first three months of life that the baby was at greatest risk and that the mortality rate had risen from 68.1 in 1876 to 76.5 in 1901, rather than in months nine to twelve which had seen a decline in mortality during the same period from 26.8 to 20.8. Sykes further showed that the first month of life was more dangerous than the second and third. In order to reduce infant mortality, he recommended the amelioration of pre-natal and post-natal conditions, and that during both periods 'the mother should receive primary care before confining attention to the infant'.[36]

Responding to the problem

The first and largely unsuccessful response to the problem was the establishment of 'milk depots' which followed the examples of the French (and Belgian) Consultations de Nourrissons and Gouttes de Lait and the American milk depots. These provided mothers who had difficulties with breast-feeding with milk in 'sterilised' bottles at a reduced price. Each bottle contained sufficient milk for one meal and no more, and each child received between six and nine bottles each day. The first British depot opened in St Helens in 1899 and by the end of its first year was feeding 140 babies. Within several years similar municipal depots were opened in Battersea, Liverpool, Ashton-under-Lyne, Dukenfeld, Leith, Bradford,

Burnley, Glasgow, Dundee, Leicester, Lambeth, Woolwich and Dublin. In order to obtain the milk, mothers had to explain why they were not breast-feeding, and allow health visitors to keep a check on the progress of their infants and report to the local MOH.[37]

The English milk depots proved to be unlike the Consultations de Nourrissons and the Gouttes de Lait in France where the clinics had three clear functions: to weigh infants; to give a medical consultation to the mother on the infant's care; and to provide milk. In England, with one or two exceptions, the milk depots tended to emphasise the provision of milk supplies and generally failed to accustom mothers to accept baby-weighing and medical supervision of their infants. But the milk depot movement never became widespread. They were expensive to run, and the price charged for the milk was usually too high for those mothers who were most in need. The depots were also inconvenient for mothers, some of whom were accused of apathy, who often could not afford the time for the daily visits, especially when caring for several children. Furthermore, doctors argued (correctly) against boiling the milk, saying that it reduced its nutritive quality. The depots were also accused of discouraging breast-feeding, though their defenders maintained that they were fully aware of its importance.

As the depots faded from favour, so the emphasis among health workers and reformers shifted increasingly to a focus on the competence of the mother and to the philosophy of 'mothercraft'. This had been evident in several of the depots which sent health visitors to advise mothers in their homes. Thus these depots provided not only milk but also 'advice' and, through the health visitor (who was essential to the success of the movement), monitored domestic conditions and the wider features of 'mothercraft'. In this way the seeds of the philosophy of mothercraft were sown. Despite their overall failure, then, the depots were instrumental – as one of their propagandists, G. F. McCleary, claimed – in helping to stimulate public interest in infant mortality – to show that it was too high and that it was preventable.[38]

Health visitors

The wider features of 'mothercraft' in the infant welfare centres are discussed below, but the nature of health visiting should be clarified since, to quote Jane Lewis, it was 'the bedrock of infant welfare work'.[39] The practice had started in the Manchester area in 1862 with the formation of the Ladies' Sanitary Reform Association, later renamed the Ladies' Health Society. The declared aim of the Society was 'to popularise sanitary knowledge, and to elevate the people physically, socially, morally, and religiously'. Over the years the work of the Society increased, as did the number of visitors; and, in addition to home visiting, mothers' musical afternoons were arranged, as were annual trips to the country, and meetings with such topics as 'personal and household cleanliness, thrift, ventilation, the prevention of infection, care of children, the feeding, washing, and dressing of babies, cutting out clothing, patching, etc.'.[40]

There is nothing surprising about all this since it was in the long-established tradition of philanthropic provision for the social education of the working-class family. Health visiting reflected the long-cherished view that *individual* efficiency, morality and responsibility underlay true social welfare. Hence the importance of seeing people in their own homes in order to give them advice and to exercise supervision and influence. What *was* new was the developing emphasis on infant care as a specialism. Whether health visiting had a beneficial effect on reducing the infant mortality rate is uncertain. It was, however, promoted in the first health visitor's manual, through the language of investment, which explained the importance of efficient care of infants who were 'the nation's asset and England's future working men and future mothers'. In order to counter racial deterioration 'we want not only to keep babies *alive*, but we want them to be healthy young animals'.[41]

The high infant mortality and morbidity rates encouraged an interest in health visiting, especially as the increasingly popular view in some professional circles held that one of the main causes was maternal ignorance of the best baby-rearing practices. Accordingly, lady visitors were attached to the different varieties of infant welfare centres where, through home visiting, they were to supervise the health of expectant and nursing mothers, and children under school age. By 1905 there were about fifty towns, with Huddersfield in the vanguard, in which the local authorities had appointed women as paid health visitors (increasingly from the middle class), in addition to voluntary visitors, to do educational work among working-class mothers. There was often a problem in visiting new births, however, as prior to the Notification of Births Acts, 1907 and 1915, births could be registered up to six weeks after the baby had been born, by which time death had often occurred. In London, the County Council arranged for midwives to notify MOHs of the births they had attended so that visits could be made to the homes of newly born babies when the mothers would be given an instruction card on the feeding and general care of infants. The expansion of health visiting was not entirely a haphazard affair since many authorities decided that as the depots had failed to make influential contact with mothers and their babies they would expand what Dwork calls their 'out-reach activities'. The interest of the authorities in this matter reflected that of probably the bulk of the medical profession, who were moving towards the view of the *Lancet* that 'instructions should be given to women as to the proper management of children'. This was the beginning of the campaign to educate the mothers.[42]

Infant welfare schemes

At the core of the infant welfare movement stood the network of facilities, variously named as 'schools for mothers' (usually run by voluntary societies with the support of the local Medical Officer of Health), 'Babies Welcomes' (similarly run by voluntary societies), clinics and welfare centres. It is worth recording some of the details of the Huddersfield scheme, devised by Dr S. G. Moore, the MOH, and operating from 1905, not only because as the first self-conscious institutional exponent of 'mothercraft' it was an important example for the welfare movement, but also to show the extent and precise nature of the growing official and medical surveillance of, and intervention in, infant care. The primary objective was to 'help the mother to nurse her infant herself in her own home' after an initial visit from a woman doctor immediately subsequent to the birth, followed by visits from voluntary workers. The births were notified to the MOH under a voluntary system with the incentive of one shilling paid for every one notified within twenty-four hours. After the initial visit by the doctor (one of two assistant female MOHs), the list of babies was distributed to the Lady Superintendent of the health districts. She then divided up the list among her volunteers, so that each baby was under the supervision of a Lady Helper:

> In all cases where the child is not thriving and where no medical practitioner is in attendance she is expected to send to the Public Health Department for aid ... it is a rule that no dole shall be given in any shape. In cases of need the various official, religious, and philanthropic agencies of the town are communicated with ... In cases of sanitary defects information is given to the proper Health Authorities. The visits of the Lady Helpers ... are entirely optional on the part of the visited ... in some cases only a very occasional visit is required, but in others more frequent visits are necessary. Where a case seems to require help, and no doctor is in attendance, the Lady Helper asks the Assistant Medical Officer of Health to pay a visit. A free use is made of printed matter, and in every available way general interest is aroused in the welfare of babies, as well as individual attention being given to each one.[43]

Dr More claimed that the infant mortality rate fell during the first nine months of 1907 from 138 per 1,000 in the same period in 1906 to 85 per 1,000. The basic reason for the success was a special Act of Parliament which from November 1906 allowed the Huddersfield corporation to make notification of births to the MOH compulsory within forty-eight hours of delivery and, therefore, enabled the health visitor to be of assistance at the start of the most at-risk period for the infant. It had an immediate impact in that within the first year 94 per cent of births were notified. This led to the passing of the permissive but widely adopted Notification of Births Act, 1907 (made compulsory in 1915), which required that the MOH be informed of every birth within thirty-six hours of the baby being born. These Acts were considered important because it was believed that they 'will prove invaluable to the Medical Officer of Health in obtaining information as to the circumstances of the birth of each child, and will form the starting point for the helpful home visitation and guidance which many of these cases require'.[44] The 'guidance' referred not only to the home visits but also to the distribution of instructional leaflets and record cards. In other words, the legislation helped to create procedures of observation and intervention on a national scale. Similarly with the Midwives Act, 1902, which made it an offence for any woman without a medical qualification to assist in childbirth for gain. The Act was working extensively by 1910 and served as a further means of controlling the childbirth process and the immediate post-natal period by bringing them under the supervision and attendance of local authorities.[45]

Other influential local and originally voluntary attempts to counter high infant mortality and morbidity rates, principally through educational methods promoted at the centres themselves and by health visiting, included the St Marylebone Health Society, 1905, and the St Pancras School for Mothers, 1907. The former established a medical centre where infants could be examined and mothers receive medical advice. The latter attracted far more attention, probably because it combined a number of features from other schemes. Among the more important of these was the provision of charged dinners for nursing mothers and, following the example of 'The Ghent School for Mothers', a medical dispensary, a provident club, a milk supply, a bureau for fathers, and lectures and classes in childcare and domestic management, including sewing and cookery. The St Pancras School also sold banana-crates at a shilling each for use as cots. As the schools developed and increased in number, they always emphasised personal hygiene for the mother and general cleanliness for baby and home, as well as the benefits of fresh air. One school, representative of many, reported in 1916 that 'our workers can tell you of homes where the windows are now always open, where the babies take regular rests in the tiny garden, where the mother's appearance and outlook on life has changed'. All these infant welfare services were characterised by the *educational* nature of their work. No treatment was given, and where maternal welfare was concerned the emphasis was on improving medical care at parturition. Medical treatment was available for babies at only a few centres. General practitioners objected to anything other than preventive care for fear of threatening their private practice. Instead mothers were referred to a doctor where necessary.[46]

Influential figures in the movement tended to stress the importance of educating the mothers. Sir George Newman, Chief Medical Officer at the

Ministry of Health, declared that 'this practical and continuous training of the mother goes to the root of the whole matter'. Similar views were expressed at the Third National Conference on Infant Mortality, 1914, and by Eric Pritchard, the eminent paediatrician, who held 'mothercraft' responsible for the decrease in infant mortality between 1904 and 1914. However, not everyone agreed that the solution lay solely or even mainly in educating mothers. Robert Hutchison, an expert on the problems of infant feeding, while in favour of health visiting, maintained that besides ignorance of mothers the main cause 'of infantile mortality [was] poverty in the home'. Poverty, he said, 'was part of the social problem and as the condition of the working class improved infantile mortality would decrease'.[47]

Several commentators were aware that the underlying cause (or at least one group of causes) of infant mortality lay in poverty, unemployment and insanitary housing. In the opinion of Dr E. W. Hope, MOH for Liverpool, 'no tried and approved measure of general sanitary improvement . . . should be neglected as of no influence on infant and maternal welfare. If the general sanitation of the area is good, it becomes a far easier task to bring into effective operation measures directed more precisely to domestic necessities and the rearing of infants.'[48] Others, while acknowledging the importance of poor sanitation and poverty, nevertheless proposed programmes of education for mothers as the principal solution, thereby overshadowing the more fundamental reforms necessary to raise the working-class standard of living and so improve child health and welfare.[49]

One small gesture towards a more comprehensive (and ultimately more expensive) solution to infant and child morbidity was the provision of a maternity benefit under the National Insurance Act, 1911. It had long been recognised that infant health was closely associated with maternal health, in particular during and immediately after pregnancy. The benefit was a cash payment only, originally thirty shillings, beginning with confinement and paid to insured women or the wives of insured men. By the mid-1930s annual payments for England and Wales amounted to approximately £1½ million.[50]

Infant welfare as a state social service

By 1908 the infant welfare movement had finished its pioneering phase and had become part of the social services system, with the approval of the LGB.[51] By 1911 there were approximately a hundred centres operating under various names throughout the United Kingdom, and in order to provide a central organisation for these the National League for Physical Education and Improvement formed the Association of Mothers and Infant Consultations, under the chairmanship of Dr Pritchard. The Association acted as a publishing house for advisory pamphlets and organised 'National Parentcraft Competitions'. In July 1912 another organisation, the National Association for the Prevention of Infant Mortality, was formed to co-ordinate the work of a number of different agencies working to combat the problem.

Of far more significance for the development of infant and maternity care was the lead taken by the LGB with its circular to local authorities in 1914 explaining that a grant would be available in aid of their expenditure (and that of voluntary agencies) 'in respect of institutions or other provision for maternity and child welfare'. This made it possible for local authority public health committees to take over voluntary centres. The grant (50 per cent of the cost) was to cover 'clinics, dispensaries or other institutions primarily concerned with the provision of medical and surgical advice and treatment, as well as in respect of the salaries of health visitors and other officers engaged for this work'. The circular also advised expansion in two areas. First, that ante- and post-natal care should be improved; and, second, that provision should be made for the care of infants beyond their first year of life. Attached to the circular was a memorandum from the Chief Medical Officer which outlined the elements in the proposed maternity and child welfare scheme. After specifying arrangements for local supervision of midwives, it was divided into three main sections: (i) ante-natal – requiring a clinic for expectant mothers; the home visiting of these mothers; and a maternity hospital or beds in a local hospital for complicated pregnancies; (ii) natal – assistance for mothers during home confinement, and confinement of sick women (and those suffering from any condition liable to endanger either themselves or their babies) at a hospital; and (iii) post-natal – arrangements were to be made for hospital treatment for problems arising after parturition, provision of treatment and advice at infant clinics; the continued availability of the clinics for older pre-school children, and home visitation for these children. Many centres also began to provide milk and foods for children and expectant and nursing mothers, and beginnings were made to provide them with dental care.[52]

The war years

The development of infant and what was by now also maternity care continued during the First World War. These years witnessed a greater appreciation of the association between foetal and neonatal deaths and maternal welfare and, as a result, infant welfare facilities were extended to the ante-natal period. In 1915, with the help of a gift, six experimental clinics admitted their first expectant mothers, and within three years there were 120 such clinics, mainly within urban areas (by 1933 the number had risen to 1,417). The Notification of Births Act, 1915, besides extending the 1907 Act, gave county councils statutory powers to care for not only young children but also expectant and nursing mothers. In a subsequent circular the LGB encouraged all local authorities to use their full powers to promote infant and maternal welfare. By this time the infant welfare movement was receiving financial support from central government through the LGB and exchequer grant system.

Throughout the war years the movement developed with the main progress being an increase in the number of local-authority health visitors from 600 in 1914 to 2,577 in 1918 (including 1,044 district nurses acting as part-time health visitors). The number of qualified midwives also rose, from 37,000 in 1914 to 43,000 in 1918, at a time when the birth rate was falling. (The Midwives Act of 1916 had made their training more demanding.) And the maternity and child welfare centres (philanthropic and local-authority) grew from 650 in 1915 to 1,278 in 1918 (local-authority centres increased from 300 in 1915 to 700 in 1918).[53]

The passing of the Maternity and Child Welfare Act in 1918 (which was only superseded by the National Health Service Act, 1946) confirmed the importance of maternal and child welfare in the sphere of public health policy, at least from the perspective of central government, and helped to accelerate the trend towards provision of ante-natal clinics. One reason for this concern was the fear of population decline following the huge loss of military life at the front, hence the inclusion of unmarried mothers in the welfare schemes. The Act gave power to local authorities to provide a range of services, but they were prevented from establishing a general domiciliary service which would require the attendance of GPs. Under the Act local authorities had to establish a maternity and child welfare committee in order to exercise its powers. The LGB issued a circular itemising the services which could be sanctioned with a grant of up to 50 per cent of expenditure. These were: health visiting; maternity and child welfare centres; provision of milk and foods; trained midwives; making arrangements for attendance of a doctor in connection with pregnancy and confinement; nurses for pregnancy, confinement and a number of infant illnesses; hospitalisation for acute illness in connection with pregnancy, confinement and infancy; maternity homes and homes for infants suffering from conditions not normally treated in hospitals; convalescent homes for women, infants and young children; homes for attending to the health of widowed, deserted or unmarried mothers; provision of day nurseries and crèches for working mothers; and home helps for mothers during confinement.[54]

Alas, it was left to local authorities to decide that such services were necessary. In 1916 an inquiry into infant and maternal welfare in England, Wales and Scotland found an embryonic and poorly staffed service.[55] This was borne out by a memorandum from Dr Arthur Newsholme, CMO at the LGB, written in 1914 to one of his officials. Writing of local authorities, he thought they were 'not likely at the present time to be willing to pay much attention to the Board's recent circular on Maternal and Child Welfare'.[56] Indeed, between 1914 and 1918, Newsholme and his office repeatedly urged reluctant local authorities and doctors to take advantage of the opportunities to provide a developed range of services for the mother and child. Nevertheless, it remains true that the passing of the 1918 Act formalised an infant welfare system which had been developing since the early 1900s. It was one more response on the part of central government signifying the responsibility of the State for public health, albeit a partial responibility and one confined to children.

It has been claimed that the infant welfare movement, together with 'enlightened public opinion', was largely responsible for the decline in infant mortality which fell during the period 1891–1917 from 149:1,000 to 96:1,000. J. M. Winter, who has made a special study of infant mortality, argues that, taking 1901–3 as the basis for comparison, the rate dropped by 17 per cent between 1903 and 1914–18.[57] But it has to be remembered that the downward turn began *before* these services could have had much effect. While improved ante-natal care in the home contributed towards the decline in the wartime death rate, only 60,000 of the 700,000 annual births were attended to at health centres by 1918. Moreover, the services on offer at the infant welfare centres were educational rather than of a kind involving medical treatment. Other explanations, while not denying the importance of health visiting and 'mothercraft', also emphasise the availability of cheap pasteurised milk and, especially during the war, improvements in the standard of living and the domestic environment. From 1891 there was a period of increasing real wages which in helping to improve nutrition may have contributed to a generation of mothers born after 1880 being freer of TB and able to give birth to stronger and heavier babies, and to breast-feed them. And yet this would have been a very slow improvement. In general the war is said to have had a beneficial impact on infant welfare in that it led to a greater awareness of the need to preserve infant life through the education of mothers and the provision of maternity services.[58]

THE SCHOOL MEALS SERVICE

In the history of children few institutions can equal the school for its impact on their lives and on shaping perceptions of them throughout society, and in its influence on the development of child welfare policy. The school stands like a colossus whose gaze extends far beyond the horizon. The importance of the classroom, and of pedagogy in general, in making visible blind, deaf, dumb and feeble-minded children has been described. The school has also been shown to have functioned within a political framework which was designed to accommodate a rapidly changing social system as it confronted a number of problems. The school, in

103

the form of 'education', lurched forward, prepared to cut its way through doubt and hesitation, confident of its own authority and ability to discipline the child population.

The Education (Provision of Meals) Act, 1906, was a permissive Act giving local education authorities powers to 'take such steps as they think fit for the provision of meals for children in attendance at any public elementary school in their area'. It may be tempting to see this legislation as simply a 'social reform'. However, the feeding of school children, like infant welfare before it and the medical inspection service that was to follow, needs to be interpreted on several levels. To describe it as a social reform, especially as marking one of the foundations of the Welfare State, would be at best analytically facile and at worst grossly misleading. In order fully to understand the service we need to know something of its origins; to be aware of the early efforts at school feeding. Only then can it be seen how the revelations of the Boer War and the physical-deterioration scare turned the issue into a serious political question.[59]

Early efforts

Since at least the earliest days of the Ragged School movement teachers had observed large numbers of children who were underfed and poorly clothed. Their presence became even more obvious when the educational legislation of 1870 and 1876 made schooling compulsory, thereby bringing hundreds of thousands of children into classrooms for several hours a day, five days a week, week after week. Never before had so many children been brought together for such sustained periods. Thus, compulsory schooling not only made visible the distress of children on a scale hitherto unknown; it also illustrated the difficulties of trying to educate them without first alleviating their hunger. Many reformers and educationalists believed that to ignore their distress made education useless in the sense that not only were its objectives unattainable but also that it became detrimental to children's physical and mental development, and wasteful of resources.[60]

From the 1860s numerous voluntary agencies, including those in Edinburgh, Glasgow, Manchester, Newcastle-upon-Tyne and Birmingham, had attempted to provide some sort of nourishment. In London the Destitute Children's Dinner Society began work in February 1864 and had opened fifty-eight dining-rooms by 1870. During the winter it provided meals, usually hot meat, once or twice a week. As a matter of principle, the Society tried to charge parents a penny a meal, but this was not always forthcoming. On the other hand, from 1876, Sir Henry Peek successfully ran a self-supporting society in Rousden, Devon. By mid-1885 thirteen London districts were providing penny dinners; and in 1889, as a result of an inquiry by the London School Board, the London School Dinner

Association was founded. But the Association received little or no assistance from the Board, or from the Poor Law guardians. In 1895, a majority report of the Special Committee on Underfed Children (established by the London School Board) concluded that feeding was necessary, but the Board rejected this finding, preferring instead to accept the minority view that voluntary societies could cope if they were properly organised. Five years later the Board established a Joint Committee on Underfed Children to co-operate with voluntary societies. Unfortunately, it had limited functions and did little to feed necessitous children on its own initiative. By 1905 many, perhaps the majority, of the voluntary feeding agencies, in one way or another, were working in collaboration with local education authorities. Such agencies existed in 55 out of 71 county boroughs, in 38 out of 137 boroughs, in 22 out of 55 urban districts, and a much smaller number in county council areas.[61] But the feeding was sporadic and seasonal, and rarely for five days at a time.

Despite the revelation made by Charles Booth in his poverty survey, that in London alone 10 per cent of school children were underfed, there were many criticisms of charitable feeding, especially where the charity failed to compel parents either to pay for or contribute towards the meal, which was usually the case. In fact, by the mid-1890s only 10 per cent of agencies were still attempting to collect a fee. The Charity Oraganisation Society, however, continuously opposed 'free' meals, claiming that they would pauperise families who instead should be assisted to maintain themselves and carry out parental responsibilities. This was always the objection, widely aired in the press, both to charity and to state provision, namely that it would undermine the duty of parents to care for their own children.[62]

The debate

Those who opposed 'free' meals increasingly fought a rearguard action against a growing concern over the relationship of proper nourishment to effective learning. In the early 1880s the 'overpressure controversy' raised the issue when it was claimed that 'overpressure' was really only another word for 'underfeeding', while the report of the inquiry drew attention to the effect of malnutrition on children's physical and mental ability to learn. The point was reinforced by the *Lancet* when it argued that underfeeding was '*the* cause of the educational difficulty throughout the country'. From this time onwards, the connection between education and proper feeding figured in virtually all accounts of the malnourishment of school children. Twenty years later, for example, Sir John Gorst remarked how, without care of bodies, education in all its forms was 'an impossibility'. A particular criticism, as Gorst and other reformers expressed it in the Commons, was that money spent on the education of underfed children was largely wasted.[63]

105

In political terms an equally significant development was the growing pressure on the Government from socialist and Marxist groups and the Trades Union Congress (TUC). In 1893 the Bristol Emancipation League was campaigning for free school meals, and in Manchester the Independent Labour Party (ILP) campaigned for school meals and clothes for needy children. *Justice*, the paper of the Social Democratic Federation (SDF), called for free school meals in 1884; and Mrs Henry Hydman, the wife of the leader of the SDF, helped to pioneer feeding programmes in London. The Fabians were also active, emphatic in their objection to the wastefulness of trying to educate underfed children. In 1898 socialist school board members (mainly ILP-ers) argued for free meals and physical training; and, at the TUC in 1896, Ben Tillett, a prominent left-wing dockers' leader, called for children's stomachs to be filled 'in order to make their heads more effective'. Many similar calls were made at the TUC over the next ten years. The principal area of ILP activity was Bradford, where throughout the 1890s and early 1900s various schemes were run to feed and clothe poor children. In 1903 the Bradford ILP put school feeding in the forefront of its municipal programme and was largely responsible for making the city the leader in the provision of child welfare.[64]

We can see that the late nineteenth-century interest in school feeding was motivated by socialist–Marxist sentiments, philanthropic concerns with urban degeneration and its physical and moral consequences, and by the thought that money spent on educational provision was wasted on classes of hungry children. By the beginning of the twentieth century there had grown up a body of opinion, encompassing a range of ideological positions, advocating that welfare legislation be enacted to 'save' children. In the early Edwardian era this interest continued, but the emphasis changed. Effective education remained a vital consideration, if only to justify the growing expenditure upon it.[65] However, in the aftermath of the Boer War, there was the additional and pervasive worry over racial deterioration (which proved to be nonexistent), and the more comprehensive concern with 'national efficiency', which referred to all aspects of British life. In effect there was a perceived bond between physical deficiency, intellectual inefficiency and inadequate nutrition. Where formerly 'the tendency had been to sacrifice the needs of the child to the supposed moral welfare of the family, now the child was regarded primarily as the raw material for a nation of healthy citizens'.[66]

Among the most influential contemporary publications were the reports and evidence of two government inquiries. The Report of the Royal Commission on Physical Training (1903), despite being uncertain as to whether the State should assume responsibility for the welfare of young people, agreed that it 'is evident that among the causes which tell against the physical welfare of the population, the lack of proper nourishment is one of the most serious'. The lack of adequate nutrition, it said, resulted in a poor physical condition. This was the problem with school children, rather than the absence of physical training. In fact, such training could only have a beneficial effect on properly nourished children.[67] Similarly, the Report of the Inter-departmental Committee on Physical Deterioration (1904) concluded that the 'evils' arising from underfeeding 'were so widespread, and in certain localities so pressing, that some authoritative intervention is called for at the earliest possible moment to secure that the education of the children . . . shall not be hampered or retarded by the physical conditions thereby engendered'. It continued to warn that 'with scarcely an exception there was a general consensus of opinion that the time has come when the State should realize the necessity of ensuring adequate nourishment to children in attendance at school', since 'no purely voluntary association could cope with the full extent of the evil'.[68] Despite these semi-official calls for a new policy, there was always the tendency to hold parents partly responsible for the malnutrition of their children, as well as a governmental reluctance to support state action.[69]

Following the Reports, considerable agitation developed in Parliament and throughout the country for relevant legislation. Several articles in the *British Medical Journal* suggested that respectable medical opinion was moving towards acceptance of the idea of state intervention in this area: '. . . if the State insists on compulsorily educating children, it is also the duty of the State to see that the children . . . are physically equal to the training they have to undergo.' This appeared to follow naturally from the journal's view that 'From the highest to the lowest our children are badly fed as compared with those of other nations . . . [and] . . . in the race of life the well-nourished will generally beat the half-starved'. Thus the 'degeneracy in physique of the rising generation . . . is best to be combated . . . by an intelligent employment of the food factor'.[70] It was in this climate that the National Union of Schoolteachers (NUT) and the School Attendance Officers' Association called for legislation, and Gorst and his allies spoke in the Commons about the waste of education on ill-fed children.

In March 1905, in order to stave off further demands, the Government appointed the Inter-departmental Committee on Medical Inspection and School Feeding, with a brief to focus on the better organisation of voluntary agencies. Meanwhile, Gorst organised a spectacular stunt, in which he took a group of prominent reformers to a poor London school where one of them, Dr Robert Hutchison, Physician to the Great Ormond Street Hospital for Sick Children, selected twenty hungry boys. The party then went to the Lambeth Board of Guardians, and successfully demanded that they go directly to the school and provide food for the boys. Gorst next persuaded the Commons to pass a resolution calling for local education authorities to make provision for children to be fed, and for the cost to be recovered either from parents or from Poor Law guardians. The

Government, in another futile attempt to avoid legislative action, tried to deal with the problem through the Poor Law by passing the Relief (School Children) Order, April 1905. The intention was that relief would be offered as a loan and proceedings were to be instituted against parents who refused to repay costs. But from the beginning the Order, with a few exceptions, was more or less ignored by local authorities and Poor Law guardians. It was soon officially declared a 'relative failure'.[71] In hindsight the principal outcome from the Order was finally to put to rest any possibility that children's welfare could be looked after by the Poor Law. By now the issue was not whether local charities should be left to feed undernourished children, but whether the cost should come from the education rate or the poor rate.[72]

The Education (Provision of Meals) Act, 1906, and its administration

Within a matter of months, early in 1906, the Government felt compelled to acquiesce when a Private Member (W. T. Wilson, a Labour MP) introduced the Education (Provision of Meals) Bill which transferred the responsibility for providing meals away from the Poor Law to the local education authority.[73] The Act became law on 21 December 1906 and permitted LEAs in England and Wales (Scotland was excluded until 1908) to 'take such steps as they think fit for the provision of meals for children' attending elementary schools in their area. The Act, which was 'purely permissive' (i.e non-compulsory) allowed LEAs to associate themselves with 'canteen committees', with LEA representation, which would undertake to provide food. The authority might assist the committee by providing furnished buildings, and apparatus and personnel necessary for the preparation, organisation and service of the meals. In addition it could help private organisations to gather funds. While it could charge parents for their children's meals, in default of payment the amount was recoverable only as a civil debt. This meant that parents who failed to pay were not to be disfranchised. This provision separated the legislation from the Poor Law. Finally, if the LEA decided that the children required feeding in order to take advantage of the schooling, it might, with Board of Education approval, provide the food out of a maximum halfpenny-in-the-pound rate.[74]

The permissive nature of the Act meant that by 1911–12, no more than 131 out of 322 LEAs in England and Wales had established the service. Of these, ninety-five used rate money for food, nineteen used rate money just for administrative purposes, and seventeen depended entirely upon voluntary contributions.[75] Looking back on the years between 1906 and 1914, Newman, the Chief Medical Officer at the Board of Education, estimated that between one-third and one-half of LEAs made some provision, but it was difficult to tell how many used rate money and how many relied on other means of financial support. Moreover, 'in practice the Act has been a dead letter over the whole rural area of England and Wales'. By 1913–14 the number of children fed at school was 85,000 in London and 225,000 in the rest of the country. Although no details for the period of feeding for each child were available, it appeared that 310,000 received meals for fourteen weeks. Further estimates suggested that at least 600,000 children were suffering from malnutrition. 'The real facts', admitted Newman, were 'probably less favourable than the figures indicate.'[76].

The administration of the Act varied between authorities. The selection of children, for example, was based either on the physical condition of the child or on the economic circumstances of the family. The Board of Education recommended that both tests be used, but this advice was ignored and the majority of authorities selected primarily through the poverty test. Some authorities even imposed a 'food test' – the plainest food given under disagreeable conditions – to reduce the number of applicants. A nice example here of children's bodies being used in an attempt to compel allegedly neglectful parents to fulfil their responsibilities. The Board also advocated administering the Act in co-operation with the newly established School Medical Service, where it existed. The School Medical Officer (SMO) was to approve the diet and supervise the quality, quantity and cooking and service of the food, and inspect the feeding centres. But in practice the SMO played a negligible role.[77]

The initial selection procedure was carried out by teachers or on request from parents. Many authorities, such as those in Manchester, Leicester, Birmingham and West Ham, demanded a personal application from parents before taking any further action. Once selection had been made the family would be investigated, usually by the School Attendance Officer, to determine its economic viability and to see whether help was needed in other areas. Where meals were provided, as in Bradford, a poverty test was usually applied if the weekly earnings were less than three shillings after deducting rent. Furthermore, 'friendly advice' was offered with respect to improving the conditions of the home. The final decision on whether or not to give meals would be taken by either the central committee for the area or a smaller sub-committee. Although in some LEAs teachers could issue 'urgency tickets', the normal time between application and the child receiving a meal was between two-to-three and ten days.

The lack of uniformity among LEAs extended to whether breakfast or dinner should be given. Twenty-seven per cent of LEAs gave breakfast, 45 per cent gave dinner, and 28 per cent gave both meals. There was general agreement that body growth required proteins and that the best diet should concentrate on these and fats. With this in mind the diet was intended to compensate for ingredients lacking in home meals. However, it proved to be too expensive for the majority of LEAs. Nor did the menu vary very often. Meals were variously described as soup, stew or hash, but 'it is really almost precisely the same'. In some areas porridge was given for breakfast, but it was normally either cocoa or coffee with bread and butter, margarine, dripping, jam or syrup.[78]

Food is often the bearer of much more than physical nourishment. It comes to us laden with aesthetic and moral imperatives. In their ideal form, school meals were no exception. The meals, and the serving of them, were intended to have 'a directly educational effect' upon the children 'in respect of manners and conduct'. This may have simply been a means of broadening the appeal of the service to critics of state intervention but, allowing for the almost universal desire to improve the manners and habits of the working-class child, it was more likely to have been a matter of principle. There is no doubt that it was constantly repeated as one of the objectives of school feeding – the official view being that the meal was to serve 'as a valuable object-lesson', while reinforcing the practical instruction of hygiene, cookery and domestic economy. The tables were to be 'nicely laid, regard being paid to the aesthetic side of the meal, and table manners should be taught'. Many authorities also tried to impose standards of cleanliness of face and hands. Besides manners, administrators and reformers saw in the Act 'One great merit', which was 'the teaching and training of the child in the matter of taste'. Slum children were too accustomed to 'tasty' rather than 'nourishing' food, so that 'a pure and simple taste will be cultivated'. Of course, these were the ideals. And though it was claimed that there had been an 'improvement' in the behaviour of children receiving the food in Bradford, Derby and Kettering, for the most part much of the advice from the Board of Education was quietly ignored. Once again financial considerations outweighed ideological aspirations since to have attained such objectives would have necessitated a far higher investment in staff and supervision than most authorities were prepared to spend.[79]

Consequences

The Education (Provision of Meals) Act by no means solved the problem of malnutrition among working-class children. In his report for 1910, Newman noted: 'Defective nutrition stands in the forefront as the most important of all physical defects from which school children suffer.' Malnutrition, debility, and other physical defects in childhood, he continued, 'are the ancestry of tuberculosis in the adult. They predispose to disease, and are, in a sense, both its seed and its soil.'[80] While the President of the Board of Education estimated that 10 per cent of all elementary pupils in England and Wales were malnourished, one of the most widely quoted private investigators put the figure at 20 per cent.[81] Nevertheless, the effect on those children who were receiving school meals was claimed to be beneficial. Inquiries in Bradford, Northampton, Sheffield, Brighton and

Bethnal Green pointed towards an improvement in physique. Similarly London teachers reported that 'Physical progress is most marked' and that 'chronic headaches, sores on faces, gatherings on fingers, pains in chest' seem to have disappeared. 'Their eyes have become brighter, their cheeks rounded.' There was also said to be an improvement in the mental capacities of the children.[82] The official medical view at the Board of Education was that feeding not only helped to sustain school children's health, but also diminished the likelihood of diseased adults, thereby improving the condition of the people.[83]

The principal difficulty in assessing the impact of school meals on the health of the children lay in the absence of agreed criteria throughout the School Medical Officers' (SMOs) reports. During the inspections, school doctors noted only the appearance of the children. Nutritional standards were merely described as 'A' good, 'B' normal, 'C' below normal, and 'D' bad. The rates for each category varied enormously. In 1912, for example, the variation in rural areas ranged from 2.2 per cent malnourished in Anglesey to 18.6 per cent in Dorset, and in urban areas from 0.8 per cent in Walthamstow to 31.2 per cent in Todmorden.[84]

Since the original Act of 1906 there had been several attempts to introduce compulsion, but not until the Education (Provision of Meals) Act received the Royal Assent on 7 August 1914 were LEAs compelled to make provision for school feeding. The Act also legalised provision of meals during school holidays and repealed the halfpenny limit on the rate, providing in its place a 50 per cent Exchequer grant-in-aid. Newman claimed that the summer of 1914 saw 'the beginning of a new stage in the evolution of the movement for providing meals for children in Public Elementary Schools'. However promising this may have appeared on paper, the start of the First World War soon curtailed the effective expansion of the service. Moreover, so meagre was the regional spread that *half* the meals given in 1917 were to London school children, leaving the other for the rest of England and Wales. The Board of Education ensured that demand for meals did not outpace supply through its system of parental incomes scales, just as it would do in the 1920s.[85]

SCHOOL MEDICAL INSPECTION AND TREATMENT

In the introduction to a textbook on school hygiene, published in 1910, the author remarked that 'the centre of responsibility has shifted from the adult to the child'.[86] This shift had begun in the 1890s and received legislative confirmation in the Education (Administrative Provisions) Act, 1907, which began to establish the school medical service on a national basis. Although the Act excited little of the controversy associated with the school meals legislation, medical inspection had an equally long paternity. There has been some dispute as to whether the whole issue of inspection

111

and treatment was slipped through the House of Commons 'buried among more than a dozen other clauses dealing with uninteresting and involved housekeeping details of State school administration'. It has been claimed that 'the medical service grew unnoticed and quietly from ministerial order'.[87] However, recent research has convincingly demonstrated that the issue of treatment was clearly spelled out in the original Private Member's Bill.[88]

The real issue was not the principle of treatment, which was virtually non-controversial, but who should pay for it. Treatment was to be given provided it could be shown to be relevant to the needs of the child at school – in other words, for educational purposes.[89] The majority of those involved with child welfare knew that once medical inspection was formalised, *treatment* would not be far behind since it made no sense to identify ill-health and then take no remedial action; nor did it make sense to ignore the preventive side of public health.

Origins

The origins of the service were in five sources: foreign examples; sanitation reform and public health concerns; the 'overpressure' debate of the mid-1880s; administrative and legislative developments since the 1890s; and fears of racial deterioration and urban degeneration. There had been forms of medical inspection on the Continent since around the 1840s, but from the early 1870s schemes developed rapidly in particular regions or towns in France, Belgium, Germany, Hungary, Norway, Switzerland and the United States. Thus when in 1890 the London School Board appointed the first School Medical Officer in Britain it was following a well-trodden path. Between 1870 and 1885 the sanitary influence and 'over pressure' both played a part in creating a public awareness of the importance of public health in relation to elementary-school children. Edwin Chadwick, the great public health reformer, stressed the sanitary importance of schools and looked on them as centres from which infectious diseases might spread, as did the LGB. By 1870 Medical Officers of Health were discussing the physical education of school children, and barely a decade later were publishing texts on school sanitation relating public health to school life. The first thought that 'overpressure' in schools might have an effect on child health came in 1867 from the work of the Prussian doctor H. Cohn. But it was the controversy around 'overpressure' in the mid-1880s that made the connections with child health and nutritional standards, principally through the report of the inquiry. Indeed, it is probably true to say that the report marked the beginning of real interest in the health of the school child.[90]

Since the 1880s there had been a growing understanding of the relationship between the school and the wider society, just as there was of that between child health and public health. In the early days the medical interest had been with the adverse effects of poor light, inadequate ventilation, cramped desks, and mental 'overpressure'. Other influences came from the sanitary experiences of residential and special education schools, which gave rise to concern about the fitness of certain categories of children for schooling, such as the blind and the deaf. A similar anxiety about pupils with poor eyesight led to eye testing in selected schools by the 1890s. Often MOHs had their own specialist interests. J. H. Crocker, MOH for Richmond, warned of the need to identify those children who were suspected of 'suffering from an infectious or contagious complaint whilst attending school'. The latter concern was very much the province of the sanitarians, MOHs – some of whom would be appointed as School Medical Officers – who were anxious to incorporate school hygiene into public health administration. In a letter to the *British Medical Journal*, early in 1904, F. G. Haworth, a former medical officer to an education committee, described his experience in discovering the 'prevalence of adenoids' and argued that medical inspection was necessary in order to chart child development as revealed by 'the weight and height of the children, the teeth, eyesight, hearing, skin in regard to diseases, and mental condition'.[91]

From 1896 with the formation of the Society for the Promotion of Hygiene in School Life, the school was increasingly seen in terms of greater significance. The Society was part of the movement towards a recognition that the school was inseparable from an organic conception of health. In a broader view, which also illustrated the relevance of the school for the creation of public health policy, Dr W. Leslie Mackenzie stressed that it was a 'functional environment' in which the child was the focus of attention because in being 'easily seen, easily examined, easily described' (in other words, having such a clearly defined bodily presence) it has allowed 'us to crystallise the conception of personal hygiene and to test the possibilities of remedial measures'.[92]

The passing of the Education Act, 1902, which reorganised the education system, provided MOHs with greater access to the classroom (even though their role was limited) and so contributed towards a greater awareness of the extent of poor health. Considered together, the Education Acts of 1893, 1899 and 1902, which encouraged LEAs to provide for the needs of deaf, blind, mentally and physically handicapped and epileptic children, served to highlight how little was done for other groups, such as those suffering from adenoids, TB or skin disease. Thus an increasing number of LEAs began to involve themselves in medical inspection, and appointed SMOs. By 1906, sixty-five authorities had some sort of system of medical inspection. There was, then, a certain amount of local initiative in medical inspection which owed its inspiration to administrative and legislative developments since the 1880s.[93]

The usual explanation for the development of the school medical service focuses on the physical-deterioration scare (subsequent to the anxieties over urban degeneration in the 1880s), especially during the Boer War and the years immediately thereafter.[94] No one can dispute the rash of publications detailing the alleged physical deterioration of the urban working class, and in particular of army recruits. In the wake of the war, government inquiries were undertaken and, though their reports failed to find evidence of deterioration, they underlined the need for better welfare provision for children and adolescents. Without underestimating the importance of the sanitarians and developments since the 1880s, it remains the case that 'the rather casual public interest in the health of schoolchildren suddenly became a widespread fear over the apparent physical deterioration of the British working class'.[95] But clearly it would oversimplify the origins of the service if the racial consideration, following the impact of the Boer War, were seen as overshadowing all other influences. The mistake is to look for a single source. Undoubtedly school medical inspection was progressing both formally and informally throughout the 1890s. However this should not obscure the impact of the writings and inquiries highlighting fears of, at worst, physical deterioration of the race and, at best, the physical inefficiency of the urban poor at a time of intense imperial, military and economic competition.[96]

By way of a summary we can say that by the end of the nineteenth century a growing body of opinion felt that the State should recognise children as an investment – as an asset requiring protection and development; that it was necessary to conduct a physical census of child health; and that a knowledge of child health was essential for a proper understanding of national health. This represented something of a change in the relationship of medicine to the school. The School Medical Service (SMS) was to be part of the reorganisation of public health with a special responsibility for preventing preventable diseases, inculcating a high standard of national physique, and contributing towards the rearing of a healthy race. School hygiene was to become a feature of state medicine, standing alongside lunacy, sanitation, Poor Law medicine, alien immigration, and public health.[97]

The Education (Administrative Provisions) Act, 1907

The Act stipulated that the powers and duties of LEAs 'shall include . . . the duty to provide for the medical inspection of children immediately before or at the time of or as soon as possible after their admission to a public elementary school, and on such occasions as the Board of Education direct, and the power to make such arrangements as may be sanctioned by the Board of Education for attending to the health and physical condition of the children educated in public elementary schools'. It was intended that in practice the School Medical Officer (SMO) should carry

114

out a number of different functions: examine all children on entry into school; reinspect at regular intervals; periodically visit schools to inquire into children's surroundings; visit schools during periods of outbreak of infectious disease; examine absentees who were said to be ill; be responsible for special schools; and be a 'pervading influence' in the school. However, in the words of circular 576, with its overtones of neo-hygienism, none of this would be effective unless the 'personal and home life of the child are also brought under systematic supervision. The home is the point at which health must be controlled ultimately.'[98]

SMOs were expected to combat common diseases and physical unfitness by 'effective public health administration, combined with the teaching of hygiene'. Communicable diseases needed to be checked; heads and bodies had to be cleaned; schoolrooms were to be properly lighted, cleaned, ventilated and not overcrowded. Within a year a further circular indicated the scope of legal powers for local authorities. The school nurse was to assist with inspection and to treat minor ailments; spectacles could be provided free with the permission of the Board; also with the Board's permission contributions could be made to hospitals, infirmaries and dispensaries; but the establishment of school clinics 'gives rise to questions of considerable difficulty'. By the end of 1909 medical inspection schemes had been established in 307 out of 328 authorities.[99]

There were diverse methods of carrying out the medical examination. The most detailed published account comes from Bradford where the examination proceeded as follows. If the mother was present, details of previous illness and any infectious disease were recorded. The child was first weighed and measured, and then notes were made with reference to condition of clothing and cleanliness. The health schedule was arranged in a seriate manner – 'a glance being often sufficient to establish negative points': eyes – squint; enlarged glands; defective teeth; enlarged tonsils. The doctor would proceed to listen to the heart and lungs (for which children were partially stripped or their clothes were loosened), and test vision. The examination rate was usually ten children per hour, with the assistance of nurse, health visitor or teacher. The attendance rate for mothers with young children and with girls was said to be 70–90 per cent, though it was lower the poorer the district. The objections to inspection tended to come from five groups: those middle-class or skilled working-class parents with their own doctor; neglectful parents; anti-vaccinationists; parents of older girls, and the girls themselves.[100]

The procedure subsequent to inspection divided the children into three groups. Those who had nothing wrong with them; the small proportion who needed more detailed examination; and those who needed either 'watching' or definite treatment. After inspection the health schedules were completed by the head teacher and sent to central office where the Medical Officer went through each one again, sending notices to parents in regard to treatment. Where parents ignored a notice, another would be sent and either the parent would be asked to attend at the office or the nurse would go to the home. The careful procedures were an essential part of the classification system which the Service permitted. Certain classes had been differentiated prior to 1907, such as deaf, blind and imbecile. But by 1910 nine main groups of disability had been identified: normal intelligence, but with some physical defect that made normal schooling unsuitable; backward; feeble-minded; imbecile; blind; deaf; crippled; epileptic; combination of defects.[101]

Although the annual reports of the CMO at the Board of Education were full of statistics and assessments, Newman admitted that meaningful comparisons between different towns and regions were almost impossible to establish. This was partly owing to the fact that inspection standards varied from area to area. Moreover, poorer children were often specially dressed up in borrowed clothes, which prevented inspectors from accurately gauging the condition of footwear and clothing. The statistics on defective eyesight, hearing, TB, ringworm showed wide variation between different areas. In rural areas, where there was a shortage of medical staff, statistics on dental caries, malnutrition and mental deficiency were all of dubious value. The CMO conceded that he could not do much more than 'indicate the trend of things'.[102]

Medical treatment and the school clinic

The 1907 Act did not oblige local authorities to provide medical treatment for school children. As schemes for treatment developed, they did so slowly and were regionally diversified. The development of the school clinic in particular always had to overcome the suspicion and hostility of the British Dental Association and the British Medical Association, who feared for their private practices in the face of what they saw as competition from the clinics. Prior to LEAs initiating their own clinics, there were five agencies through which specific ailments could be treated: private practitioners, provident dispensaries, voluntary hospitals, the Poor Law, and Children's Clubs. In addition, and in demand, were charities such the the Red Cross, the NSPCC, the Charity Organisation Society, and the County and District Nursing Association. Regional surveys, however, revealed that there were serious problems in obtaining treatment, particularly in rural areas. Even where treatment was available (see Table 3.1), not more than one third of parents notified by the SMO acted on his recommendation for their child's medical treatment. The explanation for this refusal was thought to be in part that parents did not believe the ailment sufficiently serious to warrant treatment, but more likely that there were financial, geographical, administrative and cultural objections. Further weaknesses arose from the lack of persistent treatment for some ailments, such as running ears and skin diseases. Many doctors were not in a position to treat the problems identified by examination, as in treatment of defective teeth, removal of adenoids, and X-ray for ringworm. Nor was there a satisfactory link between the inspecting doctor and the treating doctor.[103]

Table 3.1   LEA providing medical treatment

	Some	Clinics	Hospital treatment	Free spectacles
1908	55	7	8	24
1914	266	179	75	165
1917	279	231	95	223
1920	309	288	168	282

Source: Hirst, 'Growth of Treatment': 330

Another important factor in the gradual emergence of the school clinic involved children with infectious or contagious diseases. Exclusion of these children from the school meant a loss of grant income, and this forced LEAs to act. They had three options. Parents could be compelled to seek treatment for their children; parents could be persuaded to seek the necessary treatment, or the LEAs could provide the facilities themselves. Many authorities used their powers to summon parents for neglecting their children, which led to popular demonstrations in, for example, Willesden, Stroud and Tring. The majority of LEAs tried to persuade parents, through the use of either council nurses or school care committees. But neither persuasion nor summonses were successful, and so authorities came to consider using their optional power for 'attending to the health and physical condition' of the children – this meant the provision of treatment facilities.[104]

LEAs also experienced problems with hospital medical staff, many of whom did not want to treat children sent to them by the SMO. A particular objection was to what hospitals regarded as the abuse of charitable medical facilities by parents who they said could afford to pay. Although hospital treatment schemes continued to exist, and to grow, with LEAs becoming subscribers to hospitals and receiving in return 'tickets' which could be given to children, there was increasing dissatisfaction with the arrangements. The specific disadvantages of hospital treatment included inappropriate treatment for certain diseases, infrequency of treatment, difficulty in securing regular attendance, long waiting periods, long travelling distances, and lack of co-ordination between inspection and treatment. The hospital facilities often reflected an appalling insensitivity to children's feelings, as at Charing Cross where after tonsillectomies the children were laid on the anteroom floor to recover consciousness, where other children could see them.[105]

117

Within a couple of years of the passing of the Act there was a broadly based movement in support of school clinics. The socialist and trade union movement had long been pressing for LEAs to provide treatment. The British Medical Association also supported the idea of the clinic, staffed by local doctors, as more preferable than treatment in hospital for minor ailments. Within the Board of Education there was sympathy for the clinic concept; and the example of German school clinics, coupled with imperial rivalry, further encouraged the development of treatment centres for school children separate from hospitals.[106]

Of the 6 million elementary-school children, it was estimated in 1909 that 10 per cent suffered from serious defects in vision, 3–5 per cent had defective hearing, 1–3 per cent had suppurating ears, 8 per cent had adenoids or enlarged tonsils, 20–40 per cent had injurious and serious decay of the teeth, 40 per cent had dirty heads, 1 per cent suffered from ringworm, the same percentage from TB, and ½–2 per cent from heart disease. With this in mind, proponents of school clinics justified them on five grounds: (i) they ensured treatment of hitherto neglected forms of ill-health; (ii) they ensured regularity of attendance once treatment had started; (iii) they provided for daily attendance of nurses; (iv) they provided close co-operation between teachers and clinic staff; and (v) were likely to attract more capable doctors to the Service.

Newman, the CMO, thought that the clinic would be suitable for the prescription of spectacles, cleansing of vermin, treatment of ringworm, favus and other skin diseases, and minor ailments such as discharging ears. Children requiring specialist attention were to be referred to either the local hospital or dispensary, and those with defective teeth were to be treated at specialist clinics. Ear discharge required regular cleansing, ringworm was gradually being treated with X-rays which were replacing drugs. Other forms of 'treatment' included advice on diet and hygiene (adenoids and enlarged tonsils), cod-liver oil and advice on diet (enlarged glands), and advice on personal hygiene given by a health visitor in cases of defective teeth. The list of cases for the year 1912 at the Deptford clinic in London included defects of vision 534; eye disease 392; ears 304; throat 835; nose 22; skin 622, spine 62; anaemia and debility 95; acute diseases 92; injuries 185; various 365; operations for tonsils and adenoids 701. The schedule for a week at the Bradford clinic was as follows: Monday and Thursday – examination of defective vision and prescribing spectacles; Wednesday and Saturday morning – skin diseases; blind, deaf and mentally defective, open-air school admissions; Wednesday afternoon – ear clinic; Thursday and Friday – scarlet fever or diphtheria. Each day saw X-ray treatment of ringworm.[107]

Although LEAs had been given the power to make arrangements for the health and physical condition of the children, this had to be done with the approval of the Board of Education. Moreover, the authority had to 'encourage and assist the establishment or continuance of voluntary agencies'. Obviously, 'treatment' remained 'an uncertain area'. Treatment for minor ailments such as ringworm and superficial sores could be given by school nurses. By 1908, twenty-one LEAs had received sanction to provide 'free' spectacles to necessitous children. Small-scale arrangements had been established by LEAs in several towns, but Bradford had the only sanctioned fully equipped school clinic. By July 1909, however, some fifty-five LEAs had submitted plans for treatment schemes to the Board, and within two years thirty school clinics and three London County Council medical centres had been opened. A further twenty authorities made contributions out of the rates to local hospitals for the treatment of school children, and the LCC had its own hospital scheme. But hospital subsidies were not regarded as a satisfactory alternative to school clinics.[108]

In general, the school clinic was something of a new departure for most authorities, and consequently practices and premises varied. In the early years the majority operated from either school buildings or from municipal offices, while others were housed in a variety of establishments including council flats in Sheffield, a church room in Epping, a co-op storeroom in Hindhead, and a 'lady's' drawing-room and garden at Stanton. Expenses for equipment also varied widely. In the large municipal clinic in Nottingham there was £418 worth of equipment, while in Newport it was valued at £14. In some clinics the services were extensive, while in others they were basic; some employed specialist staff, others did not. Propagandists for the concept of the clinic argued strongly that clinics were to be welcomed because not only were they specifically designed with the needs of school children in mind, but also (and these were almost certainly the significant reasons) they were useful in building up relationships between parents, children, doctors and teachers, and in relating the local authority to educational hygiene. There remained, however, at least two problems. In rural areas access to clinics was often difficult and was only partially overcome by travelling clinics. Second, many parents distrusted clinics, although in a survey of forty-two centres it was claimed that parental attitudes were generally favourable.[109]

Payment

The 1907 Act did not specify who should pay for medical treatment, but the subsequent Local Education Authorities (Medical Treatment) Act, 1909, required parents to pay the cost, unless they were in necessitous circumstances. This made it difficult for those LEAs who were already offering forms of treatment and created a cumbersome bureaucracy for those authorities in the process of attempting to collect payment, as well as making many parents reluctant to seek treatment for their children. For example, the LCC's procedure involved a medical inspection, an advice

119

card, entrance on a register, interviews with parents, a voucher card, arrangement of hospital appointment, correspondence between secretary of school care committee and Education Officer, notification to Education Officer by hospital of discharge of child and number of attendances, further correspondence of proposed charge, notification of charge to parent and call to collect sum.[110]

Such assessments soon fell into arrears in London. In practice many councils did not even try to impose a charge and the legality of free treatment was not challenged, thereby giving almost all elementary pupils access to the clinics. General treatment under the SMS also tended to be free. In a survey carried out in 1919–20 it was found that 188 areas charged for spectacles, but 67 did not; 115 charged for operations for tonsils and adenoids, but 81 did not. A majority of areas gave free treament for minor ailments (217 against 51), dental care (113 against 107) and X-ray (63 against 52). Moreover, more than seventy of the councils claiming to charge had not received any parental payment during the financial year. This trend towards a free service was helped by the introduction in 1912 of an Exchequer grant-in-aid, at first for the provision of treatment, and from 1913–14 towards the cost of the Service as a whole.[111]

The School Medical Service, 1914–18

Broadly speaking, it seems that by 1914 the Service had been successfully established and was well on its way towards consolidation. However, Newman, the CMO, was opposed to a move compelling LEAs to provide medical treatment, arguing that the grant system should be used to exert pressure on reluctant authorities. During the early part of 1914, unaware of the consequences of the forthcoming war, he was optimistic, writing that everything pointed towards the year's work being 'marked by exceptional progress and increasing effectiveness'. The outbreak of hostilities in the following August soon brought about large-scale disruption of the Service, and curtailed its expansion. As a result of the priority given to soldiers for medical treatment, in little more than a year 12 per cent of school medical staff had been called up for military service. By 1916 there had been a 31 per cent decrease in inspections, which rose to 34 per cent by 1918, and Newman admitted that inspection was at an 'irreducible minimum'. In Manchester and Sheffield inspection was confined to ailing children, while school nurses performed the inspections in Lancashire and Wiltshire. The war also caused disruption to the 'following-up' procedures. The fear was that as the Service came increasingly to focus on 'ailing' children so it failed to act as 'an educational system of preventive medicine'. In an internal memorandum Newman confided that the less said about the matter the better, but warned that something must be said otherwise 'we shall have the authorities thinking that we mean to shut down the School Medical Service altogether'.[112]

At the same time, medical treatment was actually being extended during the war, since there was an increase in the number of authorities claiming the full Exchequer grant-in-aid. In 1914 nearly 180 LEAs were providing treatment at school clinics. By the end of 1919, 298 out of 318 LEAs had made arrangements of one sort or another for treatment; there were 692 school clinics, and during the year 180,060 children received some form of treatment. Similarly, the number of LEAs contributing to hospitals rose from 75 to 110, as did the number providing spectacles, from 165 to 235. Thus it seems that facilities for school children continued to expand at a time when their medical inspection was declining. When the Education Act, 1918, was passed it extended medical inspection to secondary schools, and gave LEAs the 'duty' to make suitable arrangements 'for attending to the health and physical condition of children educated in public elementary schools'.[113] Newman summed up the impact of the war for the Service:

> The European war has now given new emphasis to the importance of the child as a primary national asset. The future and strength of the nation unquestionably depend upon the vitality of the child, his health and development, and upon his education and equipment for citizenship.[114]

Perhaps Newman believed in his own rhetoric, perhaps not. In the event, the post-war period, marked as it was by economic and social depression, left him leading a chorus of strident complacency with regard to children's health. Throughout the inter-war period this chorus was gradually eased off centre stage by a cast of medical, sociological and political sceptics, so that by 1939 the accuracy of the annual reports was widely disputed, especially with respect to their plaintive cry that malnutrition was a minor problem, and that where it did exist it was caused by parental inefficiency.

THE CHILDREN ACT, 1908

> An Act to consolidate and amend the Law relating to the protection of Children and Young Persons, Reformatory and Industrial Schools, and Juvenile Offenders, and otherwise to amend the Law with respect to Children and Young Persons.

This piece of legislation has been described as 'a humanitarian measure', 'a great and fundamental step in child protection', and one that 'emphasized the social rights of children'; although the same author acknowledges that it was 'also a necessary step taken by the state to ensure its own economic well-being'.[115] We shall return to these comments later on. But, first, what were the contents of the Act?

121

The Act, in six parts, covered Infant Life Protection, the Prevention of Cruelty to Children and Young Persons, Juvenile Smoking, Reformatory and Industrial Schools, Juvenile Offenders (the establishment of a separate system of juvenile courts), and Miscellaneous and General (covering sale of intoxicating liquor and exclusion of children from bars, etc.). Prior to Herbert Samuel, Parliamentary Under-Secretary at the Home Office, introducing his consolidating Bill to deal with the protection of children and the treatment and training of juvenile offenders, the law spread over a large number of statutes, thirty-nine of which were in some way repealed when the Bill became the Children Act, 1908. Hence, although the Act included little that was new, it was a major piece of consolidation.

Part 1 repealed earlier legislation on infant life protection. Under the new Act registration of one-child homes, where fostering was for payment, became compulsory (previously only two-child homes had been covered). Second, the minimum age for children to be registered was raised from 5 to 7. Other provisions included the prohibition of foster or adoptive parents from insuring the child's life; disallowing individuals who had been convicted of child cruelty from fostering; and compelling Poor Law guardians and the LCC to appoint infant life protection inspectors.

Part 2 strengthened the law to prevent cruelty to children, and extended the legislation of 1904, principally by adding the crime of 'wilful cruelty' to that of 'negligence', which included accidents such as overlaying or suffocating infants, or children being burned or scalded. Cruelty included the failure 'to provide adequate food, clothing, medical aid or lodging' or, if parents or guardians were unable to do so, failure 'to take such steps to procure the same to be provided under the Acts relating to the relief of the Poor'. It was also an offence to allow a child to beg in a public place, or to be in a brothel. Courts were given powers to remove children from prostitute mothers, and from the care of dissolute or drunken partners or guardians. Such persons could be detained under the terms of the Inebriates Act, 1900.

These provisions obviously related to the NSPCC thrust towards making parents responsibile for their children – an objective inspired as much by evangelical belief in the morality of the family as by a yearning for social stability. The mechanism through which parents could be compelled to be more responsible was partly one of punishment, in the form of court action against them, and partly one of supervision by health visitors and NSPCC inspectors.[116] What we see here is the gradual broadening of the term 'cruelty' to include subtle understandings of neglect of children, who themselves figure, as they did under the Prevention of Cruelty Act of 1889, largely as barometers by which it was possible to measure, through their treatment, one of the advances of 'civilisation', namely the development of respectability among poor working-class families. This was especially the case with reference to overlaying and burning, which were deemed to be the results of carelessness, thoughtlessness and, where over-laying was concerned, the drunken state of the mother.[117]

The third part of the Act prohibited juvenile smoking in the streets and made it unlawful to sell tobacco to children under 16 years old. Herbert Samuel, who was responsible for the Act, argued that the importance of these sections lay in the connection between smoking and the national physique, which had been identified by government investigations. Smoking was also linked to drinking and to hooliganism. There was some opposition within the House of Commons to the prohibition, with several MPs denouncing it as 'class legislation', while others objected to the scope it gave for authorities to interfere with personal liberty and parental authority.[118]

Part 4 dealt with industrial and reformatory schools, and consolidated nineteen statutes. This part was of special importance for the future devel-opment of policy towards young people. First, it weakened the distinction between reformatory schools (for those who had committed an offence) and industrial schools (for those who were deemed to be either 'beyond parental control' – for example, persistent truants – or in some kind of moral or other danger). The Secretary of State was given powers to transfer offenders from the reformatories to the industrial schools.[119] At the same time the Act maintained the more overtly punitive punishments – whip-ping, fining and committal to reformatories – for offenders. The trend was clearly towards a more refined concept of not only juvenile delinquency, but also the care and protection of juveniles. It was this Act which con-firmed and extended what has been called the 'conceptual integration of delinquent and deprived children'.[120]

Second, the new juvenile courts (see below) were given not only criminal jurisdiction, but also jurisdiction over children under 14 who seemed to be in need of 'care and protection'. The categories of non-offender who could be brought before the court were: children found begging, 'wander-ing' or destitute, those in care of either drunken or criminal parents, the daughter of a father found guilty under the Criminal Law Amendment Act, 1885, children frequenting the company of a reputed thief or prostitute, or living in a house used by a prostitute for prostitution, or living in circum-stances calculated to seduce the child or lead it into prostitution. The intention, so it was claimed in the parliamentary debate, was that the courts 'should be agencies for the rescue as well as the punishment of children'.[121]

In order to understand the trend it is necessary to look at the develop-ment of 'care proceedings'. The origins of these proceedings go back to the mid-nineteenth century, with the Industrial Schools Acts, 1857, 1861 and 1866, which gave Justices of the Peace jurisdiction over certain groups of children, such as beggars, destitutes, those termed 'refractory' from Poor Law institutions, those said to be beyond parental control and, after

123

the Elementary Education Act, 1876, truants. These children were deemed to be 'at risk' and could be sent to the industrial schools for education and training in approved moral habits. Alternatively they could be placed on probation, committed to the care of a relative or other fit person, or the parents could be required to enter into a recognisance to provide proper care.[122] The important point, however, is that in extending the categories of non-offenders the 1908 Act considerably broadened the scope of the 'at risk' classification for children under 14.[123] Such legislation served to enlarge the role played by care proceedings, thereby making it possible for adults to further limit the freedom of young people, as when probation officers co-operated with school officials in persuading parents to send troublesome children to industrial schools.[124]

The best-known part of the Act is that which established juvenile courts (special sittings of magistrates' courts) to deal with offences (except murder) committed by juveniles aged between 7 and 16. The public were to be excluded from these courts, which had to sit at a different time or in a different place from the usual court sittings. The intention was that juveniles would be kept separate from adult criminals both before and after their trial, and ostensibly were to be treated according to their needs rather than punished according to the crime. Thus children under 16 could no longer be imprisoned and those awaiting trial were to be held in 'remand homes', financed by the Treasury.[125]

There are several reasons which explain the passing of the Act, and in particular the juvenile offenders section. Until this time the legal emphasis with respect to juveniles had been on enlarging the summary jurisdiction of JPs, and not on establishing a separate system of juvenile trial. The Summary Jurisdiction Act, 1879, had distinguished between children under 12 and young persons between 12 and 16. The former could be tried summarily for indictable offences with the exception of murder. Similarly, if they gave their consent, young persons could be tried summarily for certain indictable offences. It seems that contemporaries only began to consider the problem of separating juveniles from adult criminals when 'extended jurisdiction' was fully established. Second, a large number of bye-laws had developed which, while necessary for the proper government of large cities, brought juveniles before the courts for minor offences such as playing in the street, football, card-playing and disorderly conduct. Consequently, the legal framework for juveniles required modernising to keep pace with growing local legislation. Third, adding weight to the arguments of those reformers who cited experiments with separate juvenile procedures in Australia, Canada and the United States, were the examples of the separate juvenile courts already in existence in Dublin, Glasgow, Birmingham, Manchester, Bradford, Bury and Bolton. These local initiatives made some rationalisation of the legal system in this area seem necessary and sensible. Finally, reformers argued that since the mid-nineteenth century the trend had been to remove children from the adult criminal system. Not only were young people morally contaminated by their contact with adult offenders, but also unless they were separated off from them there were no opportunities to subject them to the full rigour of reformation; they could not be 'treated'.[126]

The Child Study movement, together with developments in education, medicine and psychology, was showing the distinctive characteristics of childhood and where it sat on the scale of individual human development. The study of the child showed that 'character' and 'personality' were by no means already formed. A system of social, moral and physical education was required to wean the young person away from corrupting influences which had brought or could bring him or her into conflict with authority and the law. This view informed penal reformers who wished to see greater use made of probation so that young people could be educated (transformed) in the community rather than in institutions. Child psychology seemed to suggest that such a transformation was possible.[127]

As with so much of the social legislation involving children, the State and its agents rarely ignored the parents, tending to cast them in an associate role in the treatment of their delinquent young. A rationalisation of the law allowed such contacts to occur within a carefully defined legal framework which encroached into the home. The powers of magistrates to compel parents to pay the fine imposed on the child (given under the Youthful Offenders Act, 1901) were extended. Similarly, parents or guardians could also be ordered to attend court proceedings. Herbert Samuel claimed that the act of juvenile delinquency 'is in itself an indictment of his upbringing by the parent'. And, therefore, fining and inconveniencing parents (through their court appearances) would 'strengthen the sense of parental responsibility, and conduce to a more careful and effective exercise of parental control'. The period in effect witnessed the proper behaviour of young people being redefined through bye-laws, care proceedings, and the enlarging of non-indictable offences in the Act, while parents themselves were made to police their children under threat of financial penalty.[128] In these circumstances, the child as a 'threat' was seen as the 'family' child of 'neglectful' parents.

The emphasis on parental responsibility was carried through to the final part of the Act, 'Miscellaneous and General', which gave the courts power to fine vagrants who kept their children from school, and gave LEAs the power to refuse entry to school of verminous children and, where necessary, to arrange for the cleansing of such children without parental consent. Children under the age of 5 were not to be given intoxicating liquor, nor were children under 14 to be allowed entry into a public house. All this was in keeping with the sentiments expressed by the Lord Bishop of Ripon, Vice-President of the Infantile Mortality Conferences 1906 and 1908:

... all children are the natural care of the State, and ... where
parental responsibility is not understood and not acted upon, we
must for the very sake of the preservation of the State, step in ...
We are bound at all costs to see that the children grow up in such a
fashion that they may become useful, serviceable and profitable citizens of this great Empire.[129]

Once again, this is the view of children as investments who were looked
on as the citizens of tomorrow; to be reared through a delicate and complex
balance of responsibility between the agencies of the State and their natural
parents. As the century progressed this balance would be the subject of
much debate and controversy.

It should be remembered that the Act was passed during the great soul-
searching dialogues which characterised the 'national efficiency' years. In
such a climate, the vocabulary of much of British politics was derived from
economics in its use of 'investment', 'waste', 'resources' and notions of
serviceability and profitability. The vocabulary sought to stride (often
unsuccessfully) across the divide between the home and business, Church
and State, Christian and atheist, political parties and, wherever possible,
social classes. This explains why, when Herbert Samuel began to steer the
Act through Parliament, he proposed a Bill 'so striking and important
that it would attract a wide public interest and crucial parliamentary
support'.[130] It was to be a national Bill, devoid (at least ostensibly) of
ideological conflict.

CONCLUSION

It is a commonplace assertion in the history of medicine that the end of
the nineteenth century witnessed the rise of preventive medicine, that is, a
medical commitment to the solution of social problems primarily (but not
entirely) through environmental reform, parental education, and the medical inspection and treatment of children (the programme was known as
'neo-hygienism'). This represented a fundamental shift in perceptions of
health and sickness in relation to their social contexts (and one that preceded the mood of introspection following the Boer War). Preventive
medicine viewed public health as much more than a narrow understanding
of the environment. In his first annual report as CMO, Newman put it
thus:

> Preventive medicine . . . has become an appropriate medium for the
> solution of the problems of hygiene in relation to the education of
> the child . . . the centre of gravity of our public health system is
> passing . . . from the environment to the individual and from prob-
> lems of outward sanitation to problems of personal hygiene.

Where children were concerned this included child-rearing, nutritional
standards, personal hygiene in cleanliness, clothes, food and habits (such
as coughing, spitting and sneezing), developmental progress (and, by the
1920s, emotional happiness). But, more than this, through its clinical and
its social 'persuasions' medicine took the child's body, in common with
educationalists and moral entrepreneurs, and fabricated it as a distinct
entity with its own peculiar dimensions and resonances.[1]

Initially the emphasis was on the body because children were easily
observed at the clinics, and as school pupils in the classroom, which was
the place where ill-health, revealed itself most clearly. As Newman wrote,
the school provided the opportunity for taking stock of the *physical*
character of the people', and he went on to describe several of the surveys
of school children.[2] The school not only served to identify the condition
of the body, but also offered the scope in which to treat it. However, the
infant welfare clinic and the home (by virtue of health visiting), as well as
the classroom, were all areas where 'neo-hygienism' could be practised. In
all three the focus was not simply on 'the child', but on the *body* of the
child. Nikolas Rose expresses it succinctly:

> A body which conformed to normal standards of development in
> terms of height, weight, muscular co-ordination and so forth. A
> body unmarked by caries, rickets or incipient tuberculosis. A body
> uninfested by lice, and free from the conditions in which infestations
> might flourish.

But it was not merely a body since the 'habits and conducts', which were to promote its physical welfare, were also moral:

> the child was to be trained up in cleanliness, regular habits, avoidance of excess and intemperance and so forth. Ignorance and fecklessness were to be turned into conscientiousness and responsibility.

Nevertheless, the incorporation of mental morality was not in pursuit of mind over matter but, as Rose says, 'of . . . bodily efficiency'.[3]

This is not to say that there was no interest at all in children's minds prior to the First World War, or that their emotional anatomy was completely uncharted.[4] It has been shown that psychology and the Child-Study movement were beginning to pursue the child's psyche, just as the search for objective criteria for the classification of children was encouraging developments in educational psychology. But these were little more than the early stages in a process which did not reach any kind of maturation until the 1920s, if not later. During the period of interest here, the focus of the reform strategies behind infant welfare, school meals, and the School Medical Service was the governance of the child's body.

The preceding sections have hopefully made clear the nature of the victim/threat dualism as it was threaded through the shift from a perception of children in terms of 'rescue and reform' to their being 'of the nation'. There should be no doubt that the dualism played a prominent role in the analysis and design of social policies for dealing with the range of problems considered in these chapters. Neither is there any doubt that in almost no instance in this period did children as victims in the straightforward sense provide the impetus for reform. These chapters have shown that children in different conditions of victimism – physically abused, hungry, neglected, exploited and sick – were usually portrayed as a threat of one sort or another: social, economic, moral, racial and sexual.

Part III

MINDS AND BODIES
Contradiction, tension, and integration, 1918–45

INTRODUCTION

There are two main observations to make about child welfare policy in this period. First, there is a pronounced emphasis on the child's mind in educational, medical and penological thinking, and in the implementation of numerous aspects of social policies. At the centre of this new awareness stood the child guidance movement, and the influence of psychology and psycho-analysis, exemplified in the establishment of the Child Guidance Council and the growth in the number of child guidance clinics. And yet, second, we can see that throughout most of the inter-war period there was a continuous debate on nutritional standards with respect to children's physical development, thereby emphasising their bodies. It is interesting that at no time does there appear to have been any significant overlap in these two areas of policy. Not until the experience of evacuation focused political attention on the condition of slum children was there a more comprehensive analysis made of the body–mind unity.

Charting a way through the 1920s and 1930s is made difficult by the effects of the economic depression which produced its own priorities, notably and controversially in matters of government financial retrenchment. The consequences of retrenchment were felt most severely in those areas of relatively high expenditure such as local education services, including school meals and medical inspection and treatment. It was by reason of the general discussion on economic strategy that children were frequently discussed in the critiques made by social reformers of government policy. Children appeared as victims, especially those who lived in areas suffering from high unemployment. This was so prominent a theme that the iconography of the threatening child could barely be seen. Both sides in the debate examined children's bodies in search of supporting evidence for their own argument.

The psychological interest in children was far less visible by virtue of the specialised nature of the medical discourse, and because of the small number of children who attended the guidance clinics. None the less, the influence of child guidance spread well beyond the conspicuously disturbed child. Moreover, it was here that the child as a threat did serve as one of the organising premisses, albeit one of considerable subtlety. The threat was posed in terms of national mental hygiene, family harmony, and the potential for maladjustment in adulthood. The evacuation process provided a vivid demonstration of anxieties resembling a *grand peur* as urban children were alleged to be bodily verminous and mentally unstable. Such children, it was thought, had been lurking in the slums for generations, doing untold harm and, therefore, reform was urgently needed.

By 1945 new and deeper understandings of the psycho-medical condition of children were beginning to be widely accepted in government departments and among care professionals. The following sections on the inter-

131

war period will show that it was during these years that the contradictions and tensions in existing social policies for children, and in the underpinning analyses, were recognised and through new policies attempts were made to create a culture of integration suitable for post-war democratic capitalism.

4

HEALTH AND WELFARE BETWEEN THE WARS

NUTRITION

The most accessible source for the history of school child health during the period is the annual reports of the School Medical Service (SMS) and the Ministry of Health (MH), all of which were optimistic in their recording of mortality and morbidity statistics, as were the majority of local reports submitted by Medical Officers of Health (MOH). In his report for 1932, for example, Newman (who was both Chief Medical Officer (CMO) to the Board of Education and, from 1920, Chief Medical Officer to the Ministry of Health) claimed that for the first time no English or Welsh county borough recorded an infant death rate of above 100. In later reports he wrote of the 'spectacular improvement' that had occurred over the years, so that the rate had reached its 'irreducible minimum'.[1]

Not everyone agreed with the CMO. Contemporary critics such as Dr M'Gonigle, a local MOH, Sir John Boyd-Orr, the dietician, and C. E. McNally, Honorary Treasurer to the left-wing Committee Against Malnutrition, forcibly queried the accuracy and reliability of official statistics. Several modern historians, notably Charles Webster and John Macnicol, have also written critically about the standard of health and nutrition during the period. In addition to questioning the contemporary interpretation of the statistics, Webster has argued that many of the 'progressive health services', such as developments in hospitals, school clinics, and health centres as well as local midwifery provision, diphtheria immunisation, school milk schemes, and physical education were not properly available until the years immediately preceding the Second World War, and that universally available school meals did not come until the early 1940s.[2]

The 1920s

The 1920s saw the beginnings of the Slump and the creation of the 'depressed' areas, but for a long time this was masked by statistical improvements in health care for all children. Under the influence of financial retrenchment which began in the early 1920s, all aspects of the SMS experienced cutbacks. In order to rationalise the apparent connection between services, poverty and child health, Newman began to argue that the remedy for nutritional deficiency lay in the education of parents rather than in higher wages: '... more often it is careless mothering, ignorance of upbringing and lack of nurture rather than actual shortage of food which results in a malnourished child.'[3] It seems obvious that he and the Board of Education were keen to ensure that the meals were not given as a method of poor relief. 'Need' was to be based on a medical examination by the SMO, usually a more rigorous procedure than the 'means test' administered by the teacher. In practice this effectively ensured that the proportion of children obtaining free meals, milk, teas and cod-liver oil rarely exceeded 8 per cent of average school attenders in England and Wales.[4] In the Edwardian years, the Service had been seen as integral to the 'health of the nation'; its aim was 'the physical ... mental and moral improvement of coming generations'. By 1922, however, Newman was declaring a much more modest aim, namely 'to fit the children to receive the education provided by the State', and by 1929 he admitted that the Sevice 'does not comprise the whole sphere of the health and well-being of the child'.[5]

It has been shown that throughout the First World War the Board of Education successfully controlled access to the school meals programme through its parental income scales, and it continued to do so throughout the Depression. Newman encouraged general economies, maintaining that there was 'a good deal of waste' in the availability of school dinners.[6] In an attempt to reduce the provision for school feeding after the 1921 Miners' Strike (which had increased the cost of school meals threefold) the Board tried to ration the financial allocation for this part of the Service to local education authorities (LEAs) by placing an arbitrary limit on the number of children eligible for free meals. This was revoked by the Labour government in 1924. However, the Board continued to refuse to sanction feeding schemes unless they included what it regarded as satisfactory income scales for parents, and co-operation between LEA and Poor Law guardians. Consequently, the number of children receiving school meals was reduced by 50 per cent and never really recovered during the inter-war period. Another example of official pettiness in the service of political ends occurred during the General Strike in 1926 when the Board used a combination of less rigorous medical examinations and severe means tests to exclude from school meals many children who had previously been eligible to receive them free of charge.[7]

Among those hardest hit by the economies of the 1920s were children in rural areas. The SMO for Devonshire referred to the decadent condition of the pupils who were pale, undersized, underfed, sad-faced, suffering from a combination of bad housing, large families and inadequate food. Often such children had to walk one, two or even three miles to school in all weathers, sometimes arriving cold, soaked and tired. Moreover, their condition was exacerbated by a bad diet. In Shropshire poor children lived mainly on bread, jam, cake and potatoes, and throughout rural areas in winter thousands were left without either a warm drink or warm food between breakfast and suppertime. A few prosperous districts bought Thermos flasks in an attempt to alleviate the children's situation, but this made little difference. The conditions in too many of the schools were too often appalling, with few proper facilities.[8] Nevertheless, Newman continually refused to acknowledge the depths of the despair in either rural or depressed urban areas, despite regional surveys pointing to serious defects in the Service. He even claimed that voluntary efforts were successfully maintaining child health.[9] Years later, however, Lord Eustace Percy, the President of the Board of Education, admitted to the 'insensitive' approach of his Board in the late 1920s.[10]

The 1930s

The situation in the 1930s was little better, and for the first few years was probably worse. Under the influence of the financial crisis of 1931, Board of Education officials told local authorities that children could not receive free meals unless they were both 'necessitous' *and* 'undernourished' (it had previously been assumed that meals might be given to those who were either in poverty *or* malnourished). This led the SMO for Smethwick sarcastically to paraphrase the Board's attitude:

> 'You must stop having free meals. You do not need them yet. When you have starved sufficiently to show signs of actual malnutrition, "however slight", come back for meals. Then you may have meals until malnutrition is cured, but only until then. After that you must have another period of trial starvation.'

This system, he said, was 'Brutal, inhuman and a relic of barbarism'. All this at a time when the number of school meals served had only just reached the peak number of 1914–15. In 1931, 300,000 children received meals (but more than half were 'milk meals') from just under half the LEAs. However, between 1931 and 1935, the worst years of the Depression, the number of children receiving free meals doubled, while those receiving free milk increased fivefold. Even so, these meals hardly compensated for the inadequate diet of many poor children whose main meals consisted of bread, potatoes, tinned food, tea, a few vegetables, and a little butter and milk.[11]

The main debates on health, nutrition, unemployment and welfare occurred in the 1930s, described by the poet W. H. Auden as 'the low, dishonest decade'. These years saw a growing volume of independent criticism of official reports which eventually forced government departments to pay more serious attention to the problem of the distressed areas, although from 1932 onwards the reports of the Ministry of Health and the Board of Education were reorganised to mount a propaganda counter-offensive. However, this could not disguise the fact many officials were increasingly apprehensive about the condition of children. There were also disputes between groups of experts as with the row over nutritional standards between the Ministry of Health Advisory Committee and a rival body established by the British Medical Association. In addition controversy arose over unpublished surveys whose findings contradicted official optimism, and the value and criteria of regional statistics.

There were three main criticisms of official statistics. First, that different medical officers used different systems of classification. Second, that there was little connection between the classification of nutrition and the process of identifying children as suffering from malnutrition. Third, that the standards adopted by different medical officers were subject to a wide range of variations.[12] Part of the difficulty lay in the increasing sophistication of the science of nutrition and the growing variety and complexity of the social survey. Prior to 1900 the study of nutrition was confined to energy requirements which focused on proteins, fats and carbohydrates. The discovery of vitamins, amino acids and mineral elements enriched the subject, and soon researchers were discussing the contributions of poor diet to 'deficiency diseases'. Further knowledge accrued from experiences during the First World War, as some of the consequences of malnutrition became apparent. These and other research findings continued to multiply throughout the inter-war period, adding to the twists and turns of the debate.

Unsurprisingly, much of the research pointed to a long-term improvement in the standard of living. A study of five towns (Northampton, Warrington, Bolton, Reading and Stanley) recorded the number of children in poverty as having halved between 1912–14 and 1923–4. Seebohm Rowntree's second survey of York in 1936 found that the proportion of people living in primary poverty was only 6.8 per cent, whereas in 1899 it had been 15.46 per cent. Boyd Orr, the dietician, estimated that in 1930 about one-half of British families were adequately fed, whereas by 1939 the figure was two-thirds.[13] On the other hand, between 1934 and 1941 there were more than half a dozen surveys showing that up to half the population was failing to receive a proper diet, and that a disproportionate number of those in poverty were under 14. The difficulty for the Government's critics lay in showing that inadequate diet was adversely affecting people's, especially children's, health and general physical condition.[14]

In order to understand the nature of the debate, it has to be appreciated that the problem of poverty in the inter-war period was not that of a general nature, widely distributed throughout the working class; rather the condition of poverty affected mainly mothers and children in large and low-waged families in areas with high unemployment. The study of five towns in 1924 (mentioned above) found that, while 8 per cent of working-class families were living below the poverty line, this included 11.3 per cent of all children under 14. If the survey had been extended over several years, the researchers calculated that the figure for the proportion of children experiencing poverty for *some period* in their lives would have risen to 16.6 per cent. An East London survey found 16 per cent of children to be in poverty; while in Southampton a figure of over 30 per cent of a sample of school children was discovered. In 1934 the Merseyside survey showed nearly 25 per cent of working-class children living in poverty; and in 1936 Boyd Orr estimated that between 20 and 25 per cent of children were undernourished. Other surveys such as those made in Bristol and York came to similar conclusions. The surveys were important because they showed children in their domestic environments rather than in the isolated context of the school clinic, which was of particular importance for the 400,000 growing up in households suffering long-term unemployment.[15]

The picture drawn by official reports was very different. According to their statistics, prior to 1914 between 15 and 20 per cent of the school population suffered from malnutrition, but by 1925 the figure had fallen to 5 per cent, largely as a result of developments in the School Meals Service and the Maternity and Child Welfare Service. Between 1925 and 1932 it fell to 1 per cent, and after 1932 it seemed that malnutrition among school children was virtually eliminated. In Wakefield the rate was said to have slumped from 9.4 per cent in 1928 to 1.5 per cent in 1932; while in Sheffield it was even claimed that the nutrition of children had shown some improvement. So optimistic were many local MOHs that fifty authorities, mainly in depressed areas, were actually claiming to have less than half the average incidence for the two categories of subnormal nutrition. In some depressed areas, it was asserted that not a single child was suffering from 'Bad Nutrition'.[16]

By the mid-1930s, however, there was concerted criticism of the SMS for its underestimation of malnutrition, and for its refusal to acknowledge that ill-health and inadequate nutrition were built into the lives of poor children, irrespective of the consequences of parental unemployment. In 1936, *The Times*, not ordinarily sympathetic to the Government's critics, was moved to admit that 'one half of the population is living on a diet insufficient or ill-designed to maintain health'. At the same time, the Board's senior MO acknowledged the exaggeratedly optimistic tone of the annual reports and previous responses to criticism. For example, the reports said nothing about Blackburn where the percentage of 'normal' nutrition declined more among school entrants than among school children as a whole. Nor did Newman cite the increase of malnutrition among school children in St Helens, or the increase in the provision of 'free' school meals in Rochdale, which suggested an increase in the number of necessitous children.[17]

One of the reasons why the malnutrition debate was so charged with political prevarication related to whether low wages and poverty or ignorance and inefficiency were responsible for malnutrition. The official reports always alleged that public health could be improved through better management of the household budget and education in the nutritional value of foods. Both the Government and the health and education departments attempted to deny the relevance of either low wages or poverty and unemployment to the welfare of children. The different views were well expressed in two newspaper headlines. *The Times* supported the Government with 'The National Health – Well Maintained', while the left-wing *Daily Herald* proclaimed 'The Toll of Unemployment – Malnutrition in Depressed Areas'. In practice official arguments held the day since only 2 per cent of school children received free meals by 1939, and a small number applied to join the scheme on a fee-paying basis.[18]

Several unpublished surveys of areas in South Wales between 1933 and 1935 suggested that the condition of children had deteriorated, and with this in mind the Board conceded that in some areas 'there are children in need of supplementary nourishment who do not receive it'.[19] Further protests, this time from Welsh clergy, led the Board to accept that the selection of children should be on medical grounds rather than on simply income scales. The Children's Minimum Council, a multi-party pressure group with several large affiliated organisations, also attacked the Government's complacency. It pointed out that in the twenty-six areas with the highest unemployment rates, in September 1935, only 2.7 per cent of children received free school meals and 12.2 per cent of children free school milk. Furthermore, in eight of these areas, the LEAs provided no school dinners at all. But the Council failed to make any impression. The Board's lame and reiterated response was that its responsibilities were educational and not for the relief of distress.[20]

One of the sources of dispute concerned the criteria for identifying malnourishment. A major problem for contemporaries in assessing the state of children's health was the absence of standard criteria for attributing malnutrition, as well as the local variations in income scales adopted for means-testing in depressed areas, and in standards of health between rich and poor districts.[21] In some areas the classification system was 'normal', 'sub-normal' and 'malnutrition'. In others it was 'normal', 'sub-normal', 'fair' and 'bad'. In yet others it was 'good', 'fairly good' and 'bad'. Furthermore, there was always a much smaller percentage of children who were finally designated as suffering from malnutrition than those appearing in the categories 'sub-normal' or 'bad'. In London, though 4.7 per cent were in these categories, only 0.6 per cent were said to require 'observation' for malnutrition. It was this latter set of statistics which Newman used as the basis in his reports.[22]

Variations in standards adopted by different MOs meant that even when they used the same classificatory system it was impossible to compare the results. In 1931 the figure for Bootle for those requiring treatment for malnutrition was an incredible thirty times greater than that for Birkenhead and twelve times greater than for Liverpool. In comparable areas throughout Northumberland, the percentage ranged between 7.5 and 0.54 per cent. R. M. Titmuss suggested that in the absence of accepted criteria local SMOs based their examination on the general average within their own area. This meant that SMOs in, say, the Rhondda had a different criterion from those in Bournemouth. However, even in the same area with the same group of children, investigations showed that different doctors produced different results.[23]

In March 1934 the Board of Education reclassified malnutrition and recommended that, instead of making a distinction between degrees of malnutrition which required treatment, all children should be divided into four separate groups: 'excellent', 'normal', 'slightly sub-normal' and 'bad'.[24] In February 1935 the Board issued a circular to the effect that meals should be given to all children showing signs of malnutrition, and that the meals should be given free if parents were unable to meet the cost. The Board also recommended that clinical observation 'of the general appearance, faeces, carriage, posture, condition of the mucous membranes, tone and functioning of the muscular system and the amount of subcutaneous fat be added to the more normal criteria of height and weight, age and sex'.[25] These measures, which were attempts to silence mounting criticism of the wide variation in local malnutrition rates, did little to satisfy the sceptics. In September 1935 the Secretary of the Medical Research Council attacked the terms used for measuring malnutrition, arguing that 'excellent' should be classed as 'normal' and everyone not 'excellent' should be classed as 'sub-normal'.[26]

Despite these setbacks, the Board continued to present a generally optimistic picture of children's health, partly through its aggregation of statistics, partly through commissioning its own inquiries, and partly through manipulation of emphases. Unfavourable reports were simply not published, and physical education was emphasised in the late 1920s and early 1930s to refocus attention away from problems such as dental caries and malnutrition. Hostile medical personnel were bullied and pressurised against speaking out and often persuaded to rewrite their original reports. G. C. M. M'Gonigle, the MOH for Stockton-on-Tees, was threatened with removal from the Medical Register. The main problem, however, was the uncertainty surrounding the science of nutrition and the consequent inability to define accurately 'malnutrition', which allowed the Government to undermine its critics. What the inter-war debate on malnutrition showed, especially the inability of the medical profession to prove malnutrition, was that the profession possessed insufficient physiological knowledge of healthy children to enable it to identify ill-health; neither nor did it know enough about the aetiology of nutrition-related diseases to be able to use them as 'indexes of nutritional efficiency'.[27]

School meals

A particular focus of the malnutrition question was the supply of milk meals. In 1930 the Education (Scotland) Act allowed LEAs to supply milk to school children. It seemed that milk might be a cheap nutritional source, and in South Wales it had already replaced meals by the late 1920s. But the fear of giving 'free' milk, and the need to ensure a safe supply, hindered its widespread extension to England and Wales. In 1933 a Board of Education official wrote:

> It is a well established and accepted principle that those parents who can afford it should pay for medical treatment and the feeding of their children. A general supply of free milk might well lead to demands for the free supply of medical treatment and school dinners.[28]

However, by the end of the year there were fears that the excess supply of milk over demand would destabilise the price structure of the market. The result was the passing of the Milk Act, 1934, in the interest of the farmers, and renewed until 1939, which incorporated a 'Milk in Schools Scheme'. The Scheme allowed for free milk to be given to children who showed signs of 'sub-normal malnutrition', though the selection was to be done for both meals and milk through medical inspection, and the MOHs were nearly always reluctant to admit malnutrition in their areas. Not until December 1935 did the Board give its approval for the introduction of means tests for the selection of hungry children.

Obviously the Scheme had less to do with concern for children's welfare than with a desire to assist the milk-producing industry. Moreover, the milk, one third of a pint, was usually given grudgingly and attempts were made to obtain parental repayment. Nevertheless, within two years, nearly 46 per cent of children were in the Scheme, though the Government continued to inhibit its expansion to mothers and young children. However by March 1939, 55.6 per cent of elementary-school children were receiving milk, and from the following July nursing mothers and pre-school children were also included.[29]

There seems little doubt that on the basis of the findings of most of the surveys of the period the provision of free meals and milk for poor children during the 1930s was inadequate. As late as 1938, forty-seven out of 315

LEAs were still not providing any form of free meals, and 121 provided only free milk. Four per cent of elementary-school children (160,000) took dinners at school, of which 110,000 received them free of charge mainly through attendance at 'feeding centres', and the remainder paid for meals in 'school canteens'. A much greater number of children were receiving milk – 2½ half million (half the school population), about 20 per cent of whom paid no charge.[30]

The relative cheapness of milk had much do to with this expansion of provision. Even so, in 1932 over 900,000 children paid the full price, while in 1938 over 2½ million were paying half-price. In contrast during the same period the number of free school meals served increased much more slowly from nearly 26½ million to nearly 27 million (the number of children receiving these meals was 176,767). The figures tend to be inflated because they refer to individual children. The true figures, representing the daily average number of children having free meals and free milk was closer to 110,000 for the former and 560,000 for the latter. This means that the meals were given only in particular circumstances rather than on a regular basis. Nor should their poor quality be overlooked. Newman recommended that necessitous children be given milk, eggs, butter, green vegetables and fruit. In practice the meals were rich in carbohydrates and poor in proteins and vitamins. They were of the soup-kitchen variety, that is, either soup, hash or stew (often cold), with bread and jam. Moreover, they were served in hired halls which were dark and poorly ventilated and without toilets or cloakrooms.[31]

MEDICAL TREATMENT

The health of the school child is obviously problematic. It is not easy to secure unanimity on its condition or on how to measure it. However, too often little or nothing is said about the children's school environment and its possible effect on their physical health and psychological contentment. No one doubts that throughout the inter-war period the condition of school premises and playgrounds deteriorated, especially after the financial crisis of 1931. As early as 1926, the President of the Board of Education, bemoaning the amount spent on providing school meals for the children of striking miners, had remarked that for the same cost schools could have been rebuilt for 25,000 children who were 'now taught in schools which were scarcely fit to house a pig'. The financial retrenchment of the period ensured that the building programme had to wait until the late 1930s. In hundreds of areas the school environment was unhygienic; the furniture was antiquated, with many of the desks without back-rests (which caused muscular fatigue and bad posture); they were often situated in places of poor lighting, which resulted in eye strain; the playgrounds were unpaved and badly designed; there was a lack of drinking and washing water; and the classrooms were generally badly ventilated, ill-lit, dusty, noisy and cold. The situation was usually far worse in rural areas. Village schools seem to have been particularly delapidated, being poorly lit, inadequately ventilated, and without proper heating. Sanitary arrangements in these and other schools were often foul, with insufficient water for flushing. In Herefordshire, sixty out of 174 schools were without proper heating, thirty-six had toilets so primitive that they contaminated the water-supply, while fifty-two had no water at all.[32] When evaluating the health of the school child, these environmental facts need to be borne in mind.

In general, treatment schemes, as with all aspects of the School Medical Service (SMS), suffered in the cutbacks of the early 1920s. The Board of Education was eager to treat only those ailments that led to absenteeism from school. Indeed, the success of treatment was always measured in terms of educational benefits in line with the view that this was the primary purpose of the Service, that is, it was not intended to be a system of poor relief. In pursuit of this policy, as we have seen, Newman, who was strongly in favour of preventive medicine, was looking to the education of parents and children rather than to higher wages to counter the effects of poverty.[33] Prior to 1921 parental payment for treatment had varied from one authority to another: some made no charge, some had a flat rate, and others a sliding scale. The 1921 Education Act, however, restricted free treatment and compelled parents to make contributions according to their means. This may well have been responsible for the fact that in the early 1920s, not more than 60 per cent of children referred for treatment were actually treated. In 1920 secondary-school pupils became eligible for medical inspection for the first time, though treatment was to be a parental responsibility. In many districts, however, there were no facilities for treating secondary pupils, and as late as 1935 20 per cent of authorities were still without such facilities.[34]

Despite the erratic provision of facilities and auxiliary services, the issue of medical treatment through the SMS received far less criticism than did provision of school meals. It has been shown that Newman, ever mindful of the financial cutbacks, was always anxious to trot out optimistic statistics in his reports, emphasising the numbers treated, rather than the range of treatments and their quality, and to deny the influence of unemployment on standards of child health.[35] He was not alone since many doctors agreed with his conclusions, as did *Public Health*, the journal of MOHs.[36] But this is not to say that criticism was nonexistent. In 1929 the executive of the NUT criticised provision of treatment and, more effectively, so did the Committee on Local Expenditure. Similarly the *Medical Officer*, a journal representative of SMOs and MOs in local government, was increasingly critical of the SMS. Local surveys also carried criticism of local treatment schemes. Opinion tended to agree that the Service was probably more effective in treating ringworm and infestation, but that it was failing to provide a proper dental service or comprehensively to treat visual and aural defects. In London and other major cities the treatment schemes were far more effective than in areas such as the North-East, South Wales and rural counties. However, as with the effects of poverty on child health, the official view remained that parental education was the most important factor in accounting for lack of treatment. The Board of Education, in its use of aggregate statistics, disguised the inadequacies of the Service.[37]

Nevertheless, the school dental service was subjected to particularly severe criticism. It was 'the one area of undisguised and conspicuous failure' since for most of the period there was fewer than one dentist to every 10,000 school children, and at the end of the thirties, less than three-quarters of school children were inspected each year.[38] The only glimmer of improvement occurred in the percentage of children treated, which rose from 55.5 per cent in 1925 to 65.5 per cent in 1938. As usual, rural children fared far worse than those in urban areas since only 42.1 percent of the rural population lived in areas with established dental schemes.

In both rural and urban areas very little was done in the way of conservation of teeth, which was the hallmark of progressive dental care. The average of only one tooth-filling per child of the school population was the same in 1938 as it had been in 1925. The emphasis was always on extraction, the cheaper form of treatment, which of course meant the loss of teeth. Here, too, parents were held responsible: 'The chief obstacle to success in school dentistry . . . is the reluctance of parents to consent to conservative treatment of their children's teeth.' An official report, from the 1950s, looking back on the inter-war years, rather disingenuously commented that the low rate of consent to treatment, especially fillings, 'enabled limited staff to cope, with superficial adequacy, with a large school population'. This ignored the practice in LEAs such as Liverpool to adopt a conscious policy of doing very little propaganda work in schools, for fear that the acceptance rate would be so high as to overburden the staff. No wonder the time, the Durham SMO observed with reference to dental treatment: 'The universal inadequacy of the staff and clinics requires no reiteration.'[39]

Infants and pre-school children

Soon after the ending of the First World War, it was realised that the health of pre-school children required urgent attention. In the early 1920s, between a quarter and a third of those just coming into school needed medical treatment; and this excluded those who were too ill to start school. In a survey of regions where 3- and 4-year-olds were admitted to schools, doctors found 'ample evidence of physical damage'. Additionally, there was a comparatively large number who were so disabled that they should never have been admitted at all. Newman agreed that there was no improvement in the conditions of those children entering school for the first time, either from year to year or even from decade to decade. Nor did the position appear to improve in the early 1930s. The PEP report concluded that pre-school children suffered from 'excessive morbidity', and called attention to 'a distinct gap in the medical services'. These children, who were especially susceptible to infectious diseases, were not covered by either the infant welfare clinics or the SMS, or by National Health Insurance, which did not include dependants. School medical reports showed that those 5-year-olds entering school suffered in the same numbers from the same defects as those found in 8- and 12-year-old groups of children. These defects tended to originate during the pre-school years, which reinforced the arguments of those who were calling for a greater emphasis on maternity and infant welfare provisions.[40]

All the same, it would be fair to say that the inter-war period saw the Ministry of Health make a major effort to extend the maternity and child welfare services, which by 1935 included 3,113 centres and 1,417 ante-natal clinics, though the number of attendances at the latter was well below the recommended figure. We should also recognise that, given the permissive nature of the governing legislation, the provision of services varied enormously, except that most authorities gave milk to children under 1 year old, and many raised the age limit to 3 during the 1930s. However, in the early thirties less than half the local authorities were taking advantage of their powers under the Maternity and Child Welfare Act, 1918, and then only to provide 50 per cent of the possible services. Some services were given free – ante-natal and post-natal and health visiting; others were charged through a means test. Moreover, ante-natal care was especially difficult to obtain in rural districts. And even where services were provided the important question concerned their effectiveness. A report published in the 1940s argued that official statistics were unreliable and overestimated the number of mothers using the clinics.[41]

Charles Webster has argued that diversity in the practice of maternity and child welfare provision in depressed areas can be seen in the different responses to what was known as nutritional supplementation, to which many MOHs were opposed. These MOHs favoured medical inspection and education and looked on food rations as the short cut to turning their centres into solely food stations. This was the view of MOHs in Liverpool, Whitehaven, Cumberland, Durham, Carlisle and Monmouth. It was easy enough to discourage mothers from seeking free milk for themselves and their young children. The procedure was riddled with bureaucracy. Six separate forms had to be completed; applicants had to be inspected by a health visitor; birth certificates and pay-packets of husbands were examined; and corroborating information was taken from Pensions and Public

Assistance offices. In addition there was also a means test and a medical inspection, and successful applicants had to have their cases reviewed each month.[42]

The position was not helped by the Ministry of Health, responsible for infant and maternal welfare and for liaising with the Board of Education over school children's health, which had few powers of compulsion when it came to dealing with local authorities, beyond issuing advisory circulars. The usual approach of the Ministry was 'to get a little new money, and then ginger them [the local authorities] up as much as we can by a circular and any other possible way'.[43] This approach hindered the proper implementation of policy while providing conservative civil servants with a convenient excuse for inaction over child poverty.

Where the infant mortality rate (IMR) was concerned, there were wide regional variations as well as within the same town. The IMR for England and Wales between 1931 and 1935 was 62, falling to 56 between 1936 and 1940. The comparative rates for Scotland, however, were 81 and 74. Variations within districts were equally revealing of differential health opportunities. In Oldham in 1931, seven out of twelve wards had IMRs of more than 140, and in four it was more than 170. In Burnley and Stockport the rates were 86 and 79 respectively, but in each town there were wards where the rate was above 100. In Manchester, the rates ranged between 44 and 143. Such regional and local differences were rarely cited by the Ministry of Health. It is true that between 1911 and 1939 the *national* aggregate IMR fell from 130 to 51. But when the IMR for a longer period is considered, then the relatively poor performance of the 1930s (and of the 1920s as a decade) becomes apparent: 1900 – 142; 1910 – 110; 1920 – 82.0; 1930 – 67.0; 1940 – 61; 1950 – 31.2.[44] As Charles Webster has observed, 'The most acute problem with respect to mortality rates relates to the fallacies inherent in averages'. Average rates 'understate the advances in health enjoyed by some sections of the community' just as they overstate 'the position with respect to a substantial minority'. Neither do they say anything about class differentials in the rate since, according to R. M. Titmuss, in 1943 'the range of inequality for total infant mortality [was] as great, if not greater than, in 1911'.[45]

THE HANDICAPPED CHILD

By 1939 the SMS was supervising 458 day and residential special schools with 58,000 places, and financially assisting 150 schools operated by voluntary societies. With the exception of open-air schools and those for the physically handicapped, the major phase of expansion occurred prior to 1920, that is, before the years of financial cutbacks brought the bulk of the building programmes to an end. The open-air schools, which catered for pulmonary and non-pulmonary TB sufferers, among other complaints, prospered because the movement they represented played a prominent role in preventive medicine, which was fashionable among Board of Education officials in the late 1920s and early 1930s.[46] In general, however, special schools suffered as the Board warned LEAs to trim their budgets wherever possible. Table 4.1 shows the rate of growth of different categories of special school:

Table 4.1 Special schools

Year	Blind	Deaf	Open-air	Cripples	Mental defectives
1908	33	20	6	53	159
1920	–	–	55	75	201
1930	–	–	141	125	171
1938	33	53	157	117	154

Source: Welshman, 'The School Medical Service': 255, 259–62, 269, 279, 297–8; Hurt, *Outside the Mainstream*: 154–8; Pritchard, *Education and the Handicapped*: 188–9

Over the period the number of pupils in 'provided' day schools rose from 17,610 to 36,000. Aside from special schools progress for the physically handicapped continued, with expanding provision of orthopaedic treatment, so that by 1935 324 school clinics offered this service. On the other hand, classes for those who were *partially* deaf or blind were meagre, with no real expansion until the late thirties, while the epileptic child was more or less ignored. Unsurprisingly, the most neglected of the handicapped group were rural children. The SMS was far less efficient and comprehensive in rural areas where services and special classes were far fewer, and residential schools were too expensive to be a realistic substitute, with only one residential place for every seven or eight children.[47]

For most of the pupils the emphasis was on vocational education. Blind and deaf boys were trained for cabinet-making, boot-making, tailoring and baking; and the girls were taught dress-making, corset-making and laundry work. Indeed, the educational potential of all categories of defective children was assessed in terms of their employability. This was of course in line with the perception of all 'defective' persons as being a burden – racial, moral or economic – on the community and, therefore, employment both kept them out of trouble and allowed them to contribute towards their upkeep.[48]

The largest single group of handicapped children were those designated mentally defective, and they had long posed a problem with respect to their 'education' and the difficulties of assessment. The Elementary Education (Defective and Epileptic Children) Act, 1899, had *permitted* school boards to provide for the education of these children. By 1909 only 133 out of 327 LEAs were taking advantage of their powers under the Act. Under the Mental Deficiency Act of 1913 local authorities were required to ascertain the number of defective children aged between 7 and 16 in their area, and those judged to be ineducable were to be passed over to local mental deficiency committees. A further Education Act in 1914 converted the permissive powers of the 1899 legislation into a *duty* on behalf of educable mentally defective children. In 1914 approximately 13,500 children were in special schools, and the number had risen to only 17,000 by 1939.[49]

Part of the reason for the slow progress was the appointment of the Wood Committee in 1924, to examine educational provision for feeble-minded children, and LEAs were unwilling to take any action until the Report was published in 1929. The major conclusion of the Report was that 105,000 feeble-minded children were eligible for special education under the terms of the 1914 Education Act, of whom nearly 90,000 were in ordinary schools. The Report also estimated that a further 10 per cent of children were 'dull' or 'backward'. The recommendations were for both groups of children to be dealt with under a single comprehensive educational scheme, whereby ordinary schools would have special classes, which would require the abolition of certification of mental defectiveness, so that all the children could be brought closer to the mainstream of education. But this was easier said than done, and in the event it was not until the Education Act of 1944 that certification was abolished and only then did the concept of a single comprehensive group of 'educationally sub-normal' children enter the educational vocabulary.[50]

Until the inquiry conducted into 'children in care' by the Curtis Committee (1946) there was little or no interest in the treatment of children in public homes and special schools, so very little is known about the children's experiences in them between the wars. However, speaking of the matron of his convalescent home in Dorset, John Osborne remembered that for her 'the war against malnutrition was not to be conducted against the disease, but its victims'. And Joe Jacobs, a well-known communist activist in the East End, who spent four years in a home with trachoma, remembered that 'I was always so very frightened'.[51] Something of the flavour of life in special schools can be seen from the rules of the Worcestershire residential open-air school:

> respect for order and food and sleep, love of sunny, moving air and pure water, dutiful habits, gentle manners, the power of keeping silent, the self-control of ordered play, the concrete practical lessons which really develop brain agility in a way that books *alone* never do.[52]

Obviously, these establishments were about much more than medical care. In the open-air schools, the children were to be taught to be 'health missionaries' who would carry the lessons they had learned back into their homes and communities.[53] Special schools, of all kinds, were educational

5

PSYCHOLOGISING THE CHILD

Now that we have described and examined the understanding and treatment of the 'bodies' of children, we can turn to do the same for their 'minds'. This is not to say that during our period minds and bodies were ever completely separate in the adult perception of children, and certainly not in the perceptions held by the medical, educational and sociological professions. It was inherent in the develoment of child psychology as it occurred through the Child Study groups and educational psychology, and later psychiatry and the child guidance movement, that there existed a relationship between the physical machinery of the child and its mental apparatus. The psycho-medical dynamic as it progressed after, say, 1918 was notable for the clarification it provided for the long-term recognition of this relationship. From about the 1880s, psychology was gradually introducing into child-study a host of features that were making the concept of childhood more complex, especially when coupled with developments in medical and environmental science. In many respects these refinements came to fruition in the child guidance movement and with the influence of psychology on the understanding of juvenile delinquency. In so doing a subtle and more profound dimension was added to the child as victim and threat.

From the end of the nineteenth century individual psychologists had been researching and writing on a number of themes and they had dominated the child-study movement. In between the wars, however, psychology established itself, rather slowly, as an academic subject. In 1914 there were eleven academic posts in British universities, which had grown by 1939 to a total of thirty lecturing staff in psychology departments and six university chairs, three of them in London, the others at Manchester, Cambridge and Edinburgh. In Scotland in 1917–18 four universities established a new B.Ed. degree which included a large psychological component. In the 1930s more than fifteen LEAs appointed psychologists, and others with a psychological training worked in teacher-training colleges and as educational administrators. In 1904 the *British Journal of Psychology* was founded, followed three years later by the British Psychological Society.

By 1921 there was a separate *British Journal of Medical Psychology*, and in 1930 the British Psychological Society took over *Forum for Education*, renaming it the *British Journal of Educational Psychology*. Aside from academic developments, the National Institute of Industrial Psychology was founded in 1922, and the subject influenced the development of theories and practices relating to mental health and to crime and delinquency.[1] This, then, was the science, ambitious and aggressive, which entered into children's lives through its successful claim to inquire into their minds.

PSYCHOLOGY AND PROGRESSIVE EDUCATION

We saw in Chapter 1 the growth and influence of the late-nineteenth-century Child Study movement and how educational psychology, mainly in the form of the psychology of individual differences, took root in that movement before moving out to claim an independent status. Although the focuses of this branch of psychology would be mental testing and working generally within the school educational service, textbooks on the psychology of education claimed the more specific influence of explaining the nature of mental development.[2] By the early 1920s there was no doubt that education and certain branches of psychology were inseparable in their daily practices. In 1912, Sir John Adams had proclaimed, correctly, that 'education has captured psychology', and some years later Raymond Cattell made a similar remark to the effect that 'it was under the wing of the educationalist that psychology was fostered in its earliest years'.[3] What Cattell had in mind was the extent to which 'science', in the form of 'psychology', provided education, an aspiring discipline claiming intellectual rigour, with credentials of legitimacy. Leaving aside the politics of professionalism, which figured prominently in the development of these two subjects, the effect of this imperialist adventure was twofold: the practice of *teaching* was made subject to psychological theories, and the profession became the architect (but not always the practitioner) of the measurement of intelligence, principally through the technology of mental testing.

Where the practice of teaching was concerned, psychological theory – directly and indirectly – informed both it and the content of the syllabus as new educational ideals, focusing on 'child-centredness' advanced in the otherwise chilled climate of the inter-war years. Many of the ideas which found campaigning support in psychology came from foreign educators. John Dewey, the American educationalist, stressed the need to look at children as children, rather than as future adults, and to regard growth in children as an end in itself, not as a preparation for adult life. However, his influence in Britain, as opposed to the United States, was far from being universal. A primary influence on progressive infant education here were the ideas of Mara Montessori, the Italian psychiatrist, who emphasised the 'exercises of practical life' and freedom for children in a prepared environment. Another important figure was Percy Nunn who, through his *Education: Its Data and First Principles* (1920, fourteen reprints by 1930), helped to pave the way among British educators with his focus on education as activity. Psychology, of varying varieties, also influenced the work of Margaret McMillan, A. S. Neill, Bertrand and Dora Russell, Susan Isaacs and Homer Lane, all of whom, though often following very different educational pathways and ideals, ran schools and wrote exhortatory texts arguing from psychological theory for new understandings of children and schooling. The psychologist Susan Isaacs was a particularly important figure who later became head of the influential London University Institute of Education. The progressive approaches, mainly confined to infant and nursery education, underpinned as they were by psychological theory, found confirmation in all the contemporary major government education reports with their concern for education as activity, and the need to relate the curriculum 'to the natural movement of children's minds'.[4]

Psychology proved to be a significant ally of the progressive movement in terms of providing and sustaining many of its claims, and in promoting its causes. By the early 1920s Freud was well known in educational circles, and psycho-analysis reinforced the emphasis on child study, especially of infancy and early childhood with reference to the importance of emotional development and factors leading to learning difficulties. Probably of more direct relevance, however, was the work of William McDougall who, through his theory of behaviour derived from instincts, exerted a profound influence on, among others, Percy Nunn, C. W. Valentine (Professor of Education at Birmingham), and the Hadow Report, 1926. McDougall's lectures to teaching students and educational administrators also helped to spread his ideas. Despite never writing specifically about education, he was taken to be in support of the progressive view that an education which focused excessively on the intellect neglected the emotions from which behaviour sprang. Many of the leading psychologists such as Burt, Thomson, Cattell, Wheeler and Rusk agreed with McDougall, as did the authors of the principal textbooks.[5] Thus from the 1920s there was a growing interest in 'adjusting' children to their environment, which necessitated dealing with their emotional development. This became a concern that extended beyond educational psychology into the child guidance movement.

Besides Percy Nunn, there were several other important British psychologists who, either directly or indirectly, promoted the psychological approach to children and their education. Among the group were the institutional founders of modern psychology such as Spearman, Thomson, Winch and Burt.[6] Other important pioneers were Olive Wheeler and James Drever, who sought a review of methods of punishment and forms of discipline on the basis of insights derived from psychology. C. W. Kimmins, Chief Inspector of London Schools, was not only instrumental in having Cyril Burt appointed to a part-time post with the LCC as the first official educational psychologist, but was also himself the author of several psychological studies. In addition to Kimmins, LCC inspectors P. B. Ballard, who popularised mental testing, and A. G. Hughes, part-author of a very successful textbook of educational psychology, *Learning and Teaching* (1937), also helped to propagate the new ideas and approaches.

The London Day Training College, reconstituted as the University of London Institute of Education in 1932, also assisted the rise of educational psychology. In addition to Susan Isaacs, members of the staff included Sir John Adams, Sir Percy Nunn, Cyril Burt and H. R. Hamley. In Scotland, where psychology secured a strong grip on the child guidance movement (unlike in England and Wales), Godfrey Thompson and William Boyd advanced the practice of mental testing and child guidance, and the Scottish Council for Research in Education was founded in 1930. The expanding psychological influence in education could also be seen at work in the gradual employment of psychologists by LEAs. Between 1930 and 1938 at least fifteen authorities were found to be employing psychologists who were advising on various problems, including mental defect, maladjustment, and streaming. No wonder Adams said that the 'intelligent, practical teacher . . . cannot but be affected by the prevailing discussion of psychology".[7]

These educationalists and psychologists established through their publications and papers, and their students, a network of research programmes, guiding precepts, and methodologies of practice by which the psychological dimension came to be seen as essential for a proper understanding of child education. This was perhaps most clearly demonstrated in the evidence presented by psychologists, in particular by Isaacs and Burt, to the inter-war inquiries into education conducted by the Consultative Committee at the Board of Education. The report on *The Primary School* (1931), for example, emphasised the view that child psychology differed from adult psychology; underlined the importance of the 7–11 age group if proper assessment were to occur; stressed the importance of 'emotional development'; and supported the classification of primary-school children, which encouraged streaming.[8]

The psychological testimony produced for the reports of 1926, 1931, 1933 and 1938 did much to secure official approval for child-centred methods, which insisted that the purpose of school was not to impart a body of knowledge but to introduce children to successive phases of experience as they became able to cope with them. (However, this did not mean abandoning either a certain amount of rote learning or 'matter of fact' teaching in the form of reading, writing, arithmetic and character training.) Educational psychology brought to education a 'scientific' vocabulary; so that educationalists and progressive teachers could speak of 'research work', 'findings', 'hypotheses', 'data', 'experiment', and so on. Psychology allowed educationalists to call on the support of science when pressed to defend or explain their philosophies. In some respects, however, the Norwood Report of 1943 marked the end of the psychologists' influence as traditional values in teaching methods, objectives and the curriculum were reasserted. All the same, despite Norwood, the White Paper, 1943, and the Education Act, 1944, still retained psychological echoes.[9]

The purpose here is not to write the history of 'progressive' education, but to note the influence of psychology on inter-war primary schools. While progressivism did not dramatically transform teaching practice, it did make gains, certainly in training colleges, and among theorists and textbook-writers. It is clear that the straightforward concern with children's bodies, institutionalised by the SMS through physical inspection and clinic treatment, ceased to be the only dominant focus. The minds of children were increasingly of interest to the medical and pedagogical professions and, through their personnel, to social workers, penal reformers, policy-makers and parents. Understandings of children and childhood were being broadened and deepened, primarily via specific problem areas such as defining and classifying mental retardation, the relationship between the environment and heredity, and teaching methods. One problem in particular received considerable attention, namely the measurement of intelligence and mental testing. The chronological roots of the test lay in the late-nineteenth-century desire to measure individual differences and to differentiate between different groups of children in order to identify and segregate those who were mentally retarded. Both objectives involved the discriminatory act. Thus the knowledge gained was not to be passively accepted, but was intended to be acted upon.

EDUCATIONAL PSYCHOLOGY AND MENTAL TESTING

Mental testing, or psychometrics as it was often called, provided teachers and educational administrators with what seemed like a scientifically validated technology. The ostensible purpose of the tests, as promoted in the 1920s and 1930s, was the selection of children for a meritocratic education. How did this come about, and to what extent was it the explicit expression of a number of implicit assumptions and goals?[10]

Prior to 1914 little had been done in Britain in the way of developments in this area, with the important exceptions of those made by Galton, Sully, Spearman and Cyril Burt who, broadly speaking, were attempting to measure intelligence. Their efforts were encouraged by the contemporary concern with alleged physical deterioration among the working-class and the apparent inefficiency of national institutions and their staff. The first use of the word 'test' came in a paper by James Cattell, published in 1890. Psychology, he wrote, could not attain the scientific status of the physical sciences without experiment and measurement. In order to move towards this position it was necessary to apply 'a series of mental tests and measurements to a large number of individuals. The results would be of considerable scientific value in discovering the consistency of mental processes, their interdependence, and their variation under differing conditions.'[11] This would identify individual differences, see how they were positioned in the population, and where individuals were within the identifiable range.

In 1905, Alfred Binet (an important member of the French Society for the Psychological Study of the Child) and Victor Simon published their first series of tests. These were revised in 1908, with an age-related scale for scoring the results, and again in 1911. The tests were widely regarded as a subtle instrument of classification since they assessed a wide range of mental abilities while combining them into a figure which referred to the child's mental age. Thus 7-year-olds who scored a performance matching that of the average 7-year-old were said to have a mental age of 7. A particular advantage of this test was that it allowed for the gap between mental and chronological age to be easily identified so as to gauge the severity of the defect. Furthermore, because the age-related tests were in a sequence, it was possible to measure development and growth.[12]

By 1911, Newman, the CMO at the Board of Education, was referring to the Binet and Simon tests, and in his next report he recommended 'psychological and educational tests' for the assessment of the intelligence of children thought to be mentally defective.[13] This marked the beginning of the use of tests as part of the campaign to integrate mentally defective children within the education system. The Education Act, 1921, had adopted a selection criterion for mentally defective children to assist in deciding who would benefit from instruction in normal schools. The criterion was reinforced by the Wood Report, 1929, which built testing into official policy towards the sub-normal. The Report warned that a 'worrying percentage of the "social problem group" was recruited from the ranks of the retarded'. Not for the first or the last time, mental testing was directly related to a social need – identifying the retarded, which on this occasion provided an impetus to the growth of the mental testing movement.[14]

The principal task for the mental test, however, became the measurement not so much of sub-normality but of normality itself.[15] The Education Act of 1902 had seen the expansion of secondary education through the newly created local education authorities. In 1907 the Board had issued what were known as Free Place regulations which offered grants to secondary schools on condition that 25 per cent of their places were free to children from public elementary schools, provided they passed an entrance examination. By 1912, 49,120 secondary-school children were former elementary-school pupils, and these represented 32 per cent of the maintained secondary school population. The emerging problem for educationalists, and politicians, was how to construct a satisfactory test for transition from elementary to secondary school which would satisfy both educational and political requirements without violating the basic assumption of all competitive examinations, namely that 'ability' was unequally distributed among school children.

In 1904, Charles Spearman, an army officer of independent means with interests in psychology and eugenics, had argued that human abilities consisted primarily of two factors – the general or 'g' and the residual or 's' factor, and that 'g' was the more important of the two. Although Binet was sceptical about the reliability of 'g', his test was easily incorporated by the proponents of general intelligence. The tranformation process received a boost in 1911 with the work of William Stern, the German psychologist, on the device of the Intelligence Quotient, or IQ. Stern described the abilities of children as a single number derived from a division of the mental age by the chronological age, multiplied by 100 and rounded off to remove fractions. However, during the inter-war years the usefulness of 'g' was queried and other issues achieved equal prominence, not least whether general ability, if it indeed existed, could be inherited. By 1939, the 'g' factor was no longer regarded as the principal means of interpreting data derived from mental measurement, though it remained *one* of the respectable interpretations.[16]

Our interest is not so much in the detailed history of mental testing as in the application of the tests to school children and the consequences for their social, mental and educational welfare. It is important, however, to appreciate that the movement fascinated the educational establishment and its press. In 1919, 'in response to a number of inquiries' *The Times Educational Supplement* (*TES*) published a reading-list on the subject, and a year later gave Burt's *The Distribution of Mental Abilities* a thorough review. Conference reports on the subject were also seriously treated. P. B. Ballard, the LCC schools' inspector, already the author of *Mental Tests* (1920), had his *The New Examiner* (1923) reprinted eight times before 1940. Mental testing also made converts among the educational bureaucracy at the Board of Education's Consultative Committee and among the HMI. The Committee's Report on *Psychological Tests of Educable Capacity* (1924), which was mainly written by Burt, justified their use 'for comparing children in respect of their inborn capacity . . . selecting the best candidates for higher instruction, and sifting out defectives and dull children for treatment by special educational methods'. The *Hadow Report* (1926), the *Report on the Primary School* (1931) and the *Spens Report* (1938) were equally enthusiastic. 'Psychological witnesses' appeared before these committees and none was more influential than Cyril Burt. The whole tenor of the reports and other government educational publications was on the need for a universal system of mental testing.[17]

The *Report on the Primary School* took 'intelligence' to be the most important quality in a child's life. Individual differences, it was claimed, were already present and expanded year by year and, therefore, the need for streaming was paramount. Moreover, by the age of 11, 'a still more radical classification is required'.[18] The reports in general have been described as 'hymns of praise to the "g" factor', and Burt was one of its main protagonists.[19] However, intelligence tests were not without their educational critics who 'discussed questions of motivation, of particular aptitudes and the whole issue of culture loading'.[20] Nevertheless, the issue of heritability, which was aired in a climate increasingly concerned about 'national intelligence', social class and demography, and eugenics, was very much the province of Burt and his supporters. While it has been suggested that the interest among educational circles was with 'the *idea* and *technology*' of mental measurement, others have argued that the theory of general intelligence as innate and unchangeable was a 'major political triumph in Britain of hereditarian theories of mental testing' resulting in the 11 plus.[21]

The rising demand for secondary education

In order to see how mental testing came to be so widespread, it is necessary to explain in further detail the rise of the demand for 'secondary' education. In 1900 the meaning of elementary education was straightforward: it was for working-class children, the great majority of whom left school at the age of 12. By 1914, however, there was a very slight movement towards the education of working-class adolescents. The Free Place Regulations of 1907, which opened the way for 25 per cent of places at secondary schools to be allocated on the basis of an examination to elementary-school pupils, meant that examinations for these places were added to those existing for scholarships and bursaries provided from charitable funds. It was beginning to look as if the end of the strict partition between elementary and secondary schooling as two separate forms of education was in sight.

The political discomfort caused by such a prospect was heightened by the fear that the slowly growing pressure of numbers among the working class for 'advanced instruction' would lead to a situation threatening to the position of the existing secondary schools as élite institutions. The Parliamentary Secretary to the Board of Education told the House of Commons: 'If no intermediate type of school between the elementary and the secondary is created, I fear it will lead to the lowering of the standards of the secondary schools.' With this in mind 'higher elementary schools' were created in 1905. These failed to secure popularity, and local authorities found various ways of trying to meet the demand for post-elementary education. The LCC pioneered 'central schools' of a vocational nature for those who would leave when they were 15 or 16; there were also 'junior technical schools' intended for the same sort of pupil. However, the war made these efforts seem largely redundant. Both the reconstruction programme of the Liberal government and the education policy of the Labour Party made the subject of adolescent education more urgent. Official reports and government ministers noted the rising demand for what one of them called 'equality of opportunity'. Thus the 1918 Education Act raised the school-leaving age to 14, and LEAs were advised to plan for the overall integration of their education systems.

In 1919 a Departmental Committee was appointed to review the system of free places and scholarships. The Committee, echoing the sentiments of the 1918 Act, discussed the matter not in conservative terms of the number of free places available, but radically in terms of the 'number of children capable of profiting', which they estimated to be 2.75 million. At the time, the current population of the grant-aided secondary schools was only 300,000. For a moment the prospect of a democratically available educational provision appeared on the horizon before quickly fading as the Committee finally recommended a medium-term target of 720,000 places, of which 40 per cent were to be free.[22]

Obviously, for the majority of those involved in the debate, including the Labour Party, 'Secondary Education for All' never meant providing a place for *every* child; instead it meant providing for those with academic capability, while the rest could go to central and junior technical schools. There were, as educators and policy-makers well understood, real distinctions to be drawn between 'secondary education for all' and 'post-primary – or post-elementary – education for all'. In the words of the *Hadow Report* (1926), 'all go forward, though along different paths. Selection by differentiation takes the place of selection by elimination.' Clearly, élitism and privilege were to continue. British education was to proceed under a new ranking system for different kinds of school. It is also important to bear in mind here that it was not simply a question of increasing demand. Equally important was the aim of 'catching the capacity', preventing 'educational waste' and reducing 'human maladjustment'. This means that the debate on the nature of primary and secondary education and who should profit from the latter was never merely one of numbers. There were usually other considerations of a social, economic, political and public health nature.[23]

The need for a 'pocket rule'

In the inter-war period elementary education followed what was known as 'Hadow reorganisation' which recommended a break between primary and secondary schooling at the age of 11.[24] The report had intended that there should be new kinds of secondary education for all, but things did not turn out this way. Instead there arose a new kind of distinction between two main types of secondary education: the academic and the other. Primary schools became preparation grounds for the 11 plus scholarship which took the fortunate minority on to the academic secondary school, and passed the majority into the 'modern' non-academic schools. And from the 1930s elementary schools began to grade their pupils into A, B and C streams by way of preparing for the 11 plus.[25] It followed, then, that throughout the primary sector children were being classified 'in relation to the objectives and curriculum of the single form of secondary schooling recognised, itself geared to the university in academic terms'. All streaming and testing produced the minority academically qualified to move from the primary to the secondary schools, which seemed to confirm the view that there was only a minority of working-class children who were academically suitable for further education. Cyril Burt's proposal that schools be organised along a 'treble track' system had contained the proviso that room should be left in the arrangements for a child's mental *development*, but this was ignored by administrators and psychologists.[26]

It was this need to differentiate between children, in response to pressure on the number of places in secondary schools and the possibility of even greater pressure in the future, that fuelled what was primarily a political demand for a means of selection for appropriate pupils while maintaining the fundamental élitist structure. Burt recognised this in 1921: 'No appeal', he wrote, 'is more often addressed to the psychologist than the demand for a mental footrule. Teachers, inspectors, school medical officers, care committee visitors, the officers of the juvenile criminal courts, all have long felt the need for some such instrument . . .'[27]

Under the need to measure and to discriminate, what began as group tests of 'educable capacity' quickly evolved into 'intelligence' tests.[28] However, it should not be thought that the psychologists, led by Burt, imposed their system of testing, with all its ideological baggage, on British educators and their political masters. Educational psychology expressed itself in relation to mental testing within a politically determined education system, which has been succinctly described by Brian Simon:

> The concept of differing 'ability' entails a concept of correspondingly differing 'needs' . . . in terms of intellectual levels . . . it was this conception that was transmitted . . . into a programme of differentiated classes . . . It was in the context of this system . . . that the psychological doctrines associated with mental testing evolved. From the outset tests were integrally related to the selection of a few children from among many at the age of 11, on the grounds of capacity to profit from the academic secondary course. Accordingly the relevant curriculum was taken as given and as the yardstick for diagnosing 'intelligence'; the children who could 'take it' were intelligent, those who could not lacked ability . . . The illusion that the whole process of classification, between and within schools, was devised to meet children's differing 'needs' completed the circle.[29]

Of course, the 'illusion' was man-made with the materials of political power. Thus the Board of Education *Handbook* (1937) advised teachers that in the children's interests they should provide courses of work 'of a differentiated kind which can be followed through uninterruptedly by each type of child'. Consequently, in schools with streaming, the 'A' child remained an 'A' child, and the 'C' child remained a 'C' child from the time they were first streamed.[30]

A similar theme, reiterating the cardinal significance of 'intelligence', reappeared in the *Spens Report* (1938), with reference to secondary education. It seemed that intellectual development during childhood progressed

> *as if it were governed by a single central factor, usually known as* 'general intelligence'. It . . . *seems on the whole to be the most important factor in determining [the child's] work in the classroom.* Our psychological witnesses assured us that it can be measured approximately by means of intelligence tests . . . *We were informed that . . . it is possible at a very early age to predict with some degree of accuracy the ultimate level of a child's intellectual powers.*[31]

The report advised that 'different children from the age of 11, if justice is to be done to their varying capacities, require types of education varying in certain important respects'. This meant translating Burt's 'treble track' system of school organisation into three different kinds of secondary school.[32]

The extent of testing and its significance

The question was how could the pupils for such a system be differentiated? The answer, as we have seen, provided by government reports recommended an 11 plus examination. Until the publication in 1984 of Gillian Sutherland's *Ability, Merit and Measurement*, it was thought that by 'the outbreak of war in 1939 the use of intelligence tests and standardised tests of English and Arithmetic . . . had been adopted by almost every local authority'.[33] Sutherland's researches present a more complex picture of the use of tests. She describes their take-up by LEAs as 'lukewarm'. Apparently out of the 146 LEAs in England and Wales with responsibility for secondary education 'at least eighty-one of these, at some point, used something they called an intelligence test . . . It is possible that as many as twenty seven more authorities also did so.' However, the use of the test could be intermittent, 'having tried a test or tests, they did not invariably go on using it, or necessarily try any other'. Nor, apparently, were the tests always 'technically respectable'. So while the 11 plus dominated the move from primary to post-primary schooling, mental testing did not dominate the examination process. For example, it seems that Welsh authorities ignored the tests between the wars.[34]

Sutherland's precision with the figures is laudable, but such an approach can mask the political ethos and objectives of examinations and testing during the period. After all, it can hardly be denied that 'the whole tenor' of government publications was on the need for universal testing and/or selection. Furthermore, while it is true that a substantial number of LEAs did not use the tests, at one time or another the majority probably did and, as Sutherland admits, the HMI did its best to persuade the remainder to conform, pointing out that 'The purpose of the examination is the selection at the age of 11 plus of children fit to profit by secondary education. The importance of accurate selection is vital and the main business is to get the right children.'[35] But we should not confine the discussion to a narrow understanding of 'testing' since, as we have seen, by the early 1930s elementary schools were increasingly grading their pupils into A, B and C streams, partly in preparation for the 11 plus. Streaming was also organisationally useful since it served to eliminate the Bs and Cs from even attempting the 11 plus.[36]

If we are looking at the extent of mental testing as an indicator of the influence of educational psychology in this particular context, then the fact that 'at least' eighty-one LEAs used such a test at one time or another, and a further twenty-seven possibly did so, suggests a widespread impact. The tests themselves may or may not have been successful in accomplishing their objectives, but the extent of their usage within a period of twenty years or so surely indicates the degree to which a psychological apparatus had penetrated the educational system. In those LEAs using the tests, for however long a period, thousands of children's lives were affected, usually for the better when they were successful, and almost certainly for the worse when they failed. For it is a fact that the overwhelming social effect of the 11 plus was to designate the 20 per cent of children who passed as 'successful', while the remaining 80 per cent were branded as 'failures'. All tests are disciplinary tools. Within élitist educational systems, given their intimacy with social, economic and political power, such a discipline serves to reinforce the exclusion of the majority of children and, therefore, is deliberately anti-democratic.

This, then, was by no means an incidental consequence. Cyril Burt, doyen of the psychological establishment and confident of educational administrators, was surely speaking for more than himself when he wrote in 1959: 'It should be an essential part of a child's education to teach him how to face a possible beating on the 11 plus . . . just as he should learn to take a beating in a half-mile race, or in a bout with boxing gloves, or a football match with a rival school.'[37] Perhaps Burt really believed that life is but a game. Perhaps it was a convenient piece of self-delusion. In the 1930s Burt had made clear the relationship between testing, general intelligence and occupations (and, therefore, social class). He divided children into five categories according to their school, ranging from the secondary through to the feeble-minded. Each group was given an IQ ranging from 130+ to 70−. This was said to match what vocational psychology said about occupational classification, moving from the professional down to the casual labourer. The function of the test was to make it possible to 'find the right place for every man, and the right man for every place'. So it is with some justice that the effect of Burt's table of IQs is seen as turning class into 'a biological phenomenon'.[38]

The meritocratic ideal

It has been claimed that the inter-war psychologists believed in the 'meritocratic ideal'; that they were meritocrats rather than conservatives; reformers rather than reactionaries, and that in fact they fought for a kind of social justice which sought to challenge the entrenched élitism of British society by rewarding ability.[39] In their defence, it is correctly claimed that many of their theories were supported by the political Left, which was persuaded that mental testing would open up equality of opportunity. Yet why the support of several left-wing thinkers, mainly of the professional classes, for an inegalitarian procedure should be an argument in favour of its radicalism is not made clear. Rather than viewing the psychologists as fighters on behalf of social justice, it seems reasonable to suggest that the psychological dynamic of the period was far more concerned with an efficient distribution of human resources.[40]

In certain circumstances no doubt it was easy to confuse a desire for redistribution of these resources with a desire for social justice because the example given was of people in the lowest class who should by virtue of their 'intelligence' have been in a higher class.[41] However, the affinity of Spearman, Cattell, Thomson, Burt and Valentine, not to mention lesser-known figures, with the philosophy of eugenics points to other considerations, since 'at the heart of eugenics was a fear about the likely consequences of differential class fertility'.[42] All these psychologists were riddled with political anxieties. While they sought greater equality of opportunity for the middle class to challenge aristocratic privilege (itself an explicitly political undertaking), they all feared the consequences of the highly differential fertility rate between professional and labouring classes, in particular what they thought would be the reduction of average intelligence among the population.[43]

But of course social justice involves more than the relocation of persons between classes, irrespective of the mechanism of IQ. It is fundamentally about equality of access, opportunities and services. The question that was left unanswered, or rarely asked, was what happened to those who remained in the lower classes (the overwhelming majority of people). How was 'society' to treat them? While it would be a mistake to look for unilinear connections between eugenics, mental testing, psychology and education, it remains true that 'psychometrics' and the whole meritocratic ideal merely sought to substitute one form of aristocracy with another: the new meritocrats were to replace the old landed aristocrats and other unqualified élitists.[44]

Apart from the question of creating a meritocracy, what also needs to be recognised is the capture of the child's mind through the technology provided by psychology. The measurement of intelligence focused on children for ulterior motives concerned with the wider neo-hygienist strategy of public health, thereby objectifying them. The relationship between psychology, education and children in the inter-war period was one of the starkest demonstrations not only of the essentially political nature of educational psychology, but also of the condition of childhood. When all this is considered, then the scale and the nature of the new perception of children and childhood becomes obvious. The perception demanded new forms of behaviour from children as they were observed in their reactions to progressive education, to preparation for the tests and, as is shown below, to the demands of child guidance.

THE CHILD GUIDANCE MOVEMENT

Understanding produces tolerance, and tolerance gives us the power to guide.[45]

Child guidance was not without its purpose, nor did it arrive as if from heaven. It was the progeny of a strategy of preventive medicine which gradually extended beyond the body to the history, geography and technology of the mind. The late-nineteenth- and early-twentieth-century concern with mental defectiveness gave way to a more subtle anxiety about behaviour and emotions, and maladjustment and delinquency. It was often a puzzling and frustrating anxiety to contemporaries, but one to which they clung tenaciously. The 1920s and 1930s saw the home brought together (through the clinic) with the school and the juvenile court as all three strove to produce citizens with properly integrated personalities. The home, or the 'psychological family' as Nikolas Rose calls it, was never less than of central importance in terms of mature parents, and of mothers in particular, who were regarded as crucial for the successful adjustment of children to their internal and external environments.[46]

Sources and origins

The sources of the child guidance movement were threefold: the British Child Study tradition, American psychological medicine, and the 'new psychology' in Britain. Let us look first at the provenance of the movement. Although there were disputes between psychologists and psychiatrists as to who pioneered the movement and who was best-suited to direct the clinics, the psychological Child Study tradition was at least *one* of the foundations for child guidance. The difficulty in attributing responsibility for the movement is that child guidance developed along several different lines and responded to several different influences.[47] Nevertheless, it is impossible to overlook the contribution made between *circa* 1880 and 1914 by psychologists such as Galton, Sully, McDougall and Burt.

In 1884, Francis Galton had opened an 'anthropometric laboratory' to test children's 'powers'. Sully had referred to child guidance as 'the application of scientific methods to practical problems of treating, training, and supervising the development of the individual child according to his individual needs'.[48] McDougall had set up an informal centre to which teachers could send 'difficult' children for examination and report. And while Burt was at the LCC he was in effect running a psychological centre for school children. In his classic study of the psychology of juvenile delinquency published a few years later, Burt argued that punishment should not be made to fit the crime, but that 'the treatment must fit the delinquent', and an appendix to the 1927 edition called for the establishment of 'a psychological clinic for juvenile delinquents'.[49] The idea of the clinic, which was born almost as Burt was writing, was but one feature – a public one – of the more general turning to psychological examination of 'difficult' and 'delinquent' children.

Whether all this activity is dismissed as 'background influences' to child guidance proper, or whether it is seen as the foundation stone of the clinics of the 1920s onwards, is perhaps not directly relevant to an account of child welfare. But it is important to see child guidance as having 'origins' in so far as by the end of the nineteenth century the psychological study of the child was a recognised branch of scientific research, even though by the 1930s psychology had lost ground as the clinics were under the control of psychiatry in England and Wales. Child guidance developed much more slowly in Scotland where the relationship between psychology and education was institutionally closer than elsewhere in the British Isles, which probably accounted for the continuing influence of the educational psychologist and the shortage of child psychiatrists and psychiatric social workers.

The significance of 'maladjustment' and its relationship to juvenile delinquency had first been publicised in America by William Healy, founder of the Chicago Juvenile Psychopathic Institute (1909) and author of *The Individual Delinquent* (1915). The organisation of the early clinics in Britain followed the American model, though they eventually took a different form. Healy tried to establish scientific methods of approach; he encouraged the collection of detailed case-histories which were correlated with the child's conduct; and aetiological factors were formulated in preparation for rational treatment. He had always attached considerable importance to the environment of the child. However, it was not until research at the Boston Psychopathic Hospital in 1912 showed that the factors were so complex as to require investigation from psychiatrically trained social workers that these were added to the team. Healy also emphasised the importance of the school for good or ill in the mental health of the child and, therefore, looked to educational psychologists to focus on the child's intellectual ability through the use of Binet–Simon and other psychological tests. Furthermore, he soon realised that the psychologist could also be useful in a therapeutic role.[50] In this way the team approach to child guidance developed: the psychiatrist, the psychiatric social worker, and the educational psychologist.

The connection between different forms of delinquency and 'maladjustment' officially began to emerge in Britain after 1918, as evidenced in Newman's reports as CMO in which he gradually developed the view that children who were emotionally disturbed (*neuropathic* was the word used originally) at school could develop into delinquents.[51] Newman was well aware of the growing psychiatric influence emanating from the opening of the Tavistock Clinic in 1920 under the direction of Dr Hugh Carlton Miller, a 'pioneer of the new psychology'. Nikolas Rose has defined the new psychology as 'a group of English doctors and psychologists, many engaged in therapeutic work, who, whilst recognising the revolutionary discoveries of Freud, sought to dispense with certain of the central concepts of his system and combine the remainder with theories drawn from other domains'. It was, he says, 'a science of social contentment'.[52] In this science, 'character' became the product of 'instincts' rather than merely moral influence and training. The argument was that when 'instincts were correctly channelled, a child would be produced who was *adjusted* to its social environment'. This in turn meant that the normal child was produced by the normal family. Thus it followed that if the family was in conflict within itself, then it was likely to yield up the maladjusted child.[53]

This approach provided the clinic's 'practical, theoretical and therapeutic orientation'. It established a connection between the psychical, the familial and the social, which was expressed in its combination of diagnosis and therapy and investigation of domestic relations in the home.[54] The clinic's first patient was a child, though it was 1926 before a specifically children's department opened after numerous delinquents, bed-wetters and other apparently disturbed children had been referred there. In many respects this was the first child guidance clinic, except that it did not allow for the extensive role played by psychiatric social workers, which would come to be one of the characteristics of the English system.[55]

The Child Guidance Council

The emergence and development of the child guidance movement was greatly facilitated by the establishment of the Child Guidance Council (CGC) in 1927, formed 'to advance the treatment of maladjusted, difficult, and delinquent children', and later made more specific to include children with nervous conditions such as states of hysteria, anxiety, habit spasms, stammering, and difficulties in eating and sleeping. (Clearly it did not intend to confine its activities to juvenile delinquents.) The origins of the Council lay in a visit by a socially well-connected magistrate, Mrs St Loe Strachey, to America in 1925, where she saw at first hand the work of child guidance clinics and returned to propagate them in Britain. Dr R. H. Crowley, senior medical officer at the Board of Education, also visited America to study the clinic system and appears to have reported favourably.[56]

Mrs St Loe Strachey secured the collaboration of a number of individuals such as Burt, Percy Nunn and Dame Evelyn Fox of the Central Association for Mental Welfare (CAMW).[57] This organisation, together with the National Council for Mental Hygiene (NCMH), helped to establish the CGC. The CAMW was founded in 1913 to promote the Mental Deficiency Act of that year and to care for defectives who were outside public-authority responsibility. By the 1920s its brief had extended to all aspects of mental welfare. The NCMH began soon after the end of the First World War in an attempt to deal with what it considered to be preventable mental and nervous ill-health. Its aim was to educate the public in mental health problems; to promote special clinics; and to encourage the application of psychological methods in the study of prostitution and crime. Among the other organisations represented were the Institute of Hospital Almoners, the Charity Organisation Society, the Howard League, children's care committees, the probation service and magistrates.[58]

The Council set about achieving its objectives by publicising procedures and organising, on the American model, the London Child Guidance Training Centre and Clinic in Islington in 1928, under the direction of a psychiatrist, William Moodie. Newman, the CMO, perhaps on the advice of Crowley, his Senior Medical Officer, insisted that the head of the clinic be medically qualified if children were to attend in school hours. However, the first American-style clinic in England was actually the East London Child Guidance Clinic opened by the Jewish Health Organisation in 1927, with help from the LCC and the CGC, and staffed by a psychiatrist, a psychologist and a psychiatric social worker. Other independent clinics included the Children's Clinic in West London, opened by Margaret Lowenfeld in 1928, later renamed the Institute of Child Psychology, and the Institute for the Scientific Treatment of Delinquency, founded in 1931.[59]

The involvement of such a range of agencies, especially those concerned

165

with mental health and welfare, is a reminder that the child guidance movement not only had a complex agenda, but also drew on perspectives that stretched well beyond the confines of childhood. At one end of the spectrum of interest in the health and welfare of the mind was the question of insanity; at the other end, a myriad of concerns clustered around national mental hygiene. The connected issues included mental instability, criminality, fecundity, destitution, and general social and occupational inefficiency. In order to cope with these examples of public and private disturbance, it was necessary to treat them in their early stages, while simultaneously promoting familial mental health. This objective demanded a number of organisational and social service strategies.

One of these strategies involved the establishment of psychological centres where children and their families could receive psychiatric attention when appropriate, but more usually they would simply be 'guided' in their emotional responses to each other and to daily situations. This would ensure that early signs of mental sickness and emotional disturbance were recognised and treated, and that families were also brought within the frame of influence. Furthermore, these centres would themselves act as beacons of guidance for a range of voluntary and government agencies in the social and educational services. The clinic, then, was to be the hub of a comprehensive system of child welfare embracing 'the nursery, the home, the school, the playground and the courts'.[60] This explains why the CAMW and the NCMH were so instrumental in the formation of the Child Guidance Council.

Thereafter the Council published annual reports, trained psychiatrists and social workers through a fellowship system (who went on to work in hospitals, local authorities, residential institutions and other clinics), and provided a loan system (intended to 'demonstrate the value of new methods') whereby its social workers, on request, could work in a hospital, school or clinic. By the end of 1933, eighteen organisations had asked for the loan of a social worker. From 1935 the Council also kept a register of foster homes for children attending clinics. The CGC was always conscious of its propaganda and was evangelical in its role as it consciously set about entertaining visitors, answering inquiries, and arranging lectures and meetings. For instance, it provided more than one course of lectures for the Federation of Girls' Clubs, National Children's Homes, Barnardo's, the Macmillan Nursery Training College and several other teacher-training colleges. Its staff also wrote popular articles in *Woman's Outlook*, *Women's Employment*, *Hospital*, *The Guider* and *The Boy*. In addition it published a series of pamphlets circulated to professional bodies on topics including child guidance in hospital, emotional growth and development, play and leisure, the causation of difficult behaviour, physical health and behaviour, nutrition and physical development, the re-education of delinquents, opposition to whipping and young offenders and the courts.[61]

The psychiatric influence

We have seen the early influence of psychology on child study in general and observed how this gave way to the growing psychiatric influence on the promotion of child guidance clinics. The emergence and development of the psychiatric interest in children can be observed through three editions of the standard student psychiatric textbook. In its first edition, published in 1927, no mention was made of either children or childhood in the index, though children's problems were described in terms of 'emotional defect', a condition the authors held to be inborn and therefore barely susceptible to treatment. The second edition, 1930, had one reference to child guidance clinics, which noted that it was now widely accepted that the seeds of many mental disorders are 'sown in childhood'. The authors advocated a children's division in every psychiatric clinic. By the third edition, published in 1932, there was a separate chapter on the psychiatry of childhood, which could no longer be ignored since the CGC had shown it to be 'an important part of the psychiatric domain'. This reflected the influence of the CGC on psychiatry to be less physicalist or hereditarian in its explanation of child behaviour.[62]

The authors gave childhood what Rose calls 'its own specific repertoire of disorders', and it is worth listing these in detail to show the range of conditions and symptoms that allowed childhood to be emotionally excavated: (i) disorders of personality (timidity, obstinacy, irritability, sensitiveness, shyness, day-dreaming, lack of sociability, and emotional disturbances); (ii) behaviour disorders (truancy, wandering, temper tantrums, lying, stealing, begging, sex misdemeanours, food fads, and refusal of food); (iii) habit disorders (nail-biting, thumb-sucking, incontinence, constipation, vomiting and stammering); (iv) 'glycopenic' disorders (migraine, crises of collapse, insomnia, night terrors, cyclical vomiting); (v) psychoneuroses (anxiety, hysteria, phobias, obsession and compulsions); (vi) psychoses (schizophrenia and manic-depressiveness); and (vii) epilepsy and mental deficiency.[63]

By the 1930s, then, psychiatry, often in collaboration with varieties of psycho-analysis, drew upon the clinics' experience, thereby reinforcing their value and the directorial role of the psychiatrist, as it catalogued 'maladjustments' into a psychiatric expertise. But once this categorisation of child disorders was in place it became available for others besides psychiatrists to draw upon it as a source for investigation and treatment. In other words, the 'gaze' that fell upon children was immeasurably broadened and, therefore, they were subject to further observation. The treatment, on which the professionals more or less agreed, lay in the investigation of the home and the school, especially relationships within the family.

The clinics and their patients

The reports of the CGC chart the growth in the number of recognised clinics throughout the inter-war years, which were modelled on the Tavistock, grounded in the 'new psychology' and staffed by a male psychiatrist ('the presiding genius'), assisted by female psychologists and psychiatric social workers. It has been shown that the staff structure of the clinic was influenced by Healy's view of the problem of the criminal child which, he said, fell into three parts: factors within the child; those in and associated with the school; and those in the home. Hence the problems were defined as medical, educational and sociological.[64]

By 1932 there were eight recognised clinics in London, with others in Glasgow, Birmingham, Edinburgh, Liverpool, Oxford and Leicester. Three years later further clinics had been opened in Cardiff, Cheltenham, Bath, Manchester, St Albans, Cardiff and Greenock. By 1938 there were fifty-four clinics including a second Welsh clinic in Swansea, of which sixteen were wholly maintained by local authorities, ten partly so, and twenty-eight were voluntary. The provision of clinics in rural areas, as with all medical facilities, was noted as deficient. From 1935 the Board of Education approved LEA funding and empowered them also to contribute to voluntary clinics if children were referred by SMOs, thus ending the movement's purely voluntary phase. This was an important development since it marked the beginning of formal acceptance of child guidance by local education authorities, thereby bringing this area of mental health closer to education. Although there were many clinics, which for one reason or another were not officially affiliated to the CGC, by 1939 all clinics could be grouped into three main types: independent and financed by grants, fees and from other sources; those within hospitals; and those financed by LEAs.[65]

But why were children referred and by whom? Broadly speaking, children were referred when they exhibited a behaviour problem, which Moodie defined as occurring when average home and school conditions, average discipline and average physical care fail to make the child conform 'to that of the average child of similar age'.[66] Referral could be anyone in contact with the child, usually either parents, teachers, doctors or probation officers. At the East London clinic, where parental referral was on the increase, 60 per cent were from SMOs, head teachers and care committees, and the remainder were from parents, hospitals and social agencies. The majority of children attending were aged between 8 and 14, and by far the commonest reasons for referral were forms of behaviour likely to bring them into conflict with adult authority. Stealing, lying, unmanageability at home or at school, and educational backwardness were most frequently mentioned. Referral was rare for emotional disturbances such as fear, anxiety, depression and excessive shyness. However, once these children had been diagnosed the position was almost reversed as follows:

168

behavioural disorders as referred, 54 per cent – as diagnosed 41 per cent; nervous disorders as referred 4 per cent – as diagnosed 41 per cent. Next in order of frequency came habit disorders: speech defects, enuresis, and sleep and eating difficulties. As to the number of children 'guided'? In 1938 a survey of thirty clinics (out of fifty-four) returned 4,688 new cases during the year and the continued treatment of nearly 3,000 cases.[67]

Children were also referred from the juvenile courts, and the Tavistock in particular had a close relationship with the Home Office and the probation service, as it did with the LCC school inspectorate. The relationship between the home, delinquency and psychology was clearly stated in 1922: 'In nearly every case the root cause of the trouble is the fact that the child is living under such home conditions as have not led to a right upbringing.' But all was not lost since 'under right influences . . . most children respond and do well . . . The treatment of the young offender is entirely a psychological problem.'[68] And, though the clinics always looked beyond delinquents for their 'patients', juvenile delinquency was one of the original prime conditions motivating the movement. So the child found that its mental life fell under the knowing eye of psycho-social scrutiny, with a view not to 'punishing' wrongdoing, but to 'treating' it.

Principles of treatment

According to Moodie, the Director of the London Demonstration Clinic, the method of diagnosis and treatment was along the following lines. The psychiatrist first acquainted himself with background information. He next interviewed the parents, before having a short interview with the child (with young children, parents were usually present), and then saw the parents again. The examination of the 'patient' was 'quite a simple matter . . . an informal conversation'. The psychiatrist was free to decide on the nature and extent of the investigation required. If necessary, the psychologist made an assessment of the patient's intellectual capacities, while the social worker gathered essential information on the home. At the second visit to the clinic, the patient would be physically examined, and this provided the opportunity for a further conversation. The next stage required each of the staff involved to write a report before meeting to discuss the patient in a 'case conference'. However, only in cases of extreme difficulty was the three-sided approach used. Very often only the psychiatrist would treat the child, for Moodie claimed that many cases required little more than advice to parents on basic childcare or matters of diet and sleep patterns. Moodie believed that the majority of children referred to clinics were quite normal and the less mental investigation they received the better. In his view less than 5 per cent required direct mental treatment. The general intention was that 'treatment' should encompass not only the mental and physical state of the child, but also its home and

169

school environment. In cases of 'maladjustment' the two lines of treatment were modifying the environment to meet the child's capacity and increasing the capacity of the child to adapt to the existing environment.[69]

In the early days Moodie, who was also General Secretary of the CGC, stressed that the psycho-analytic method was never used. This was intended to reassure those who were hostile to psycho-analysis. The underlying principle of the work, claimed the Council, was 'to obtain information by the use of careful and scientific methods, to arrange it in a logical sequence and to present it in a non-technical language'. The general principle, soothed the report for 1933, was 'to use the simplest possible procedure which will attain the desired results'. This took the form of 'simple advice', 'special teaching', and treatment of the child's neurosis, which often involved strained relations between the child and its family.[70]

By 1936, however, the therapeutic method was being given more emphasis as less attention was paid to manipulating the environmental factors. One of the means by which psycho-analysis was introduced into English public health was through the 'new psychology', principally in works such as Emmanuel Miller's *Modern Psychotherapy* (1930) which described in a non-technical language how it could be profitably used with children. Many doctors and social workers found themselves agreeing with Miller that in the treatment of early manifestations of disturbed behaviour 'it is necessary to use some psychotherapeutic method to restore the [disordered or disturbed] child to normality'. The book also familiarised British readers with the work of Viennese psycho-analysts such as Hermione Hug-Hellmuth and Anna Freud, and their view that 'children with neuroses and normal children too, reveal their attitude to the world outside them [through] . . . play and gestures'. Alfred Adler's *Guiding the Child* (English publication 1930) was another influential text in spreading psychodynamic ideas. It was Adler who argued for the encouragement of children to become, in David Copperfield's words, 'a hero of my own life'. He encouraged self-assertion on the part of children and the careful exercise of parental power.[71]

The first proper attempt to involve parents in the 'new psychology' approach to child-rearing was to be found in H. Crichton Miller, *The New Psychology and the Parent* (1922). Miller, who was director of the Tavistock Clinic, explained basic Freudian concepts to parents telling them about the discovery of the 'Unconscious Motive', and how through a system of treatment known as psycho-analysis the unconscious motives of the patient were revealed. In this way, he said, parents could be offered a 'knowledge' of themselves. The exact extent of the Tavistock's influence on the child guidance movement is uncertain, but it seems that the clinic's method of linking the psychical, the familial and the social, by relating diagnosis and therapy to a knowledge of relationships within the family, was publicised through its own children's department, which opened in

170

1926. However, it was several years before it was fully recognised that there was a connection between the child's condition and that of the parents.[72]

The importance of knowing and treating 'the family' emerged during 1933 at the Tavistock where it was made explicit that 'children's conditions almost inevitably called for treatment of the parents' difficulties from which they "could hardly be distinguished as individual illness" '. In general terms the family was to play a major role in the treatment of children and adolescents owing in part to the prevailing interest in 'prevention and treatment' in mental welfare. The network of familial relationships was important because it provided the environment in which 'primary instincts and emotions' were organised and channelled into proper experiences and ways of thinking, which produced 'harmonious and adjusted' characters. Parents accomplished this task in part through the example of good habits, and also through the psychological relationships they developed with their children. When families failed to provide the correct environment for the growing child, through improper treatment of the instincts and emotions, often because of parental neuroses, then 'repression' occurred, conflict ensued and mental disturbance became evident. Influential medical opinion held that even major mental disturbances could be prevented if the first signs were recognised and treated, both within and outside the family. This is not to say that it was the only institutional repository of mental efficiency, but it was the main one.[73]

The jurisdiction of the clinics

The accredited importance of domestic relations to healthy mental development meant that the clinics' jurisdiction was not confined to children with 'problems', since child guidance was becoming recognised as a source of information 'about the handling of the day to day difficulties of the normal child'. Advice was given in radio talks and in popular texts such as *The Growing Child and Its Problems* (1937), edited by Dr Emmanuel Miller, director of the East London Clinic. The contents, all written by child guidance workers, provided a popular description in terms of child needs and play, educational guidance, growth, personality deviations, habits, neuroses, and adolescent girlhood. Miller stressed that children would not grow away from the emotional problems of their first five years. The Home and Schools Council, a federation of parent–teacher associations, on which the CGC was represented, also promoted the psychology of child management through its collection of essays *Advances in Understanding the Child* (1935). This process of popularisation was part of the advocacy of a system of public health in which mental welfare was regarded as an essential element, and the welfare of the mind was regarded as essentially a function of that public health.[74]

171

The CGC report for 1935 contrasted the new view of maladjustment with the old, which was that the children would 'grow out' of their difficulties when they either went to school, or left school, or when they reached puberty, or when they got married. How misguided the old view had been, proclaimed the report, and how dangerous since it ignored the child as the source of future ill-health in the community. (Such a view easily illustrated the child victim as a potential threat.) This had resulted in lost opportunities to treat the emotional disturbance before it reached adult proportions. It seems clear that the issue being presented was one that coupled preventive medical intervention with social health. As Rose has written: 'Abnormal behaviour, antisocial conduct, neuroses, eccentricities, making friendships too easily or not at all, quarrelling or being withdrawn, grieving or fearing too much or too little – all these departures from the norm could be linked together as maladjustments, *and as predictors of troubles to come.*'[75] While the clinic was to be the pivotal institutional means for dealing with maladjustment, this did not necessarily occur on its own premises, but always through its personal contacts, its recommended practices and its analyses, which were influential on surrounding social agencies: schools, the probation service, care committees, voluntary children's homes, and others, all of whom came into contact with children and their families.

Generally speaking, child guidance clinics, primarily on the basis of psychiatric knowledge, obtained their authority by claiming to be able to understand the history, geography and technology of the child patient. This knowledge allowed the clinics to become a source of reference for correct procedures in dealing with mental and emotional problems, as well as a training ground for psycho-social personnel. But of equal importance was to be their role as the focus whereby all other welfare agencies, and parents, directed their inquiries and sought approval for their actions. The clinic was to have what was described as 'the wider sphere of influence' maintained through 'interesting individuals and social agencies in the preventive side of the work, and by demonstrating to the community . . . the needs of other children less seriously maladjusted'. In this way it was hoped that the treatment of children would have a prophylactic effect on the mental health of the community. The clinic was intended to create a core of confidence and knowledge which these other agencies, including the school, could use in practice and as a reference.[76]

Child guidance, the Feversham Committee and the war

Though child guidance progressed during the inter-war years, it was a slow progress marked by shortages of staff and finance. It would also be a mistake to see that advance as the result of a single theoretical and procedural discourse. It was rather that practitioners felt their way 'among

172

the discourses of psychoanalysis, psychiatry, psychology and criminology' which only by the end of the period were coming together with any sense of unity.[77] The initial impact of the war was to halt the growth of the child guidance movement with the closing of many clinics and the shortage of staff who were drafted into the armed forces. But the experience of evacuation (and the Blitz), described as a 'cruel psychological experiment on a large scale', with the revelations of emotional and other psychological problems, in particular enuresis, revealed the need for extended child guidance facilities.

The Cambridge evacuation survey, conducted by influential figures in the child guidance movement, including John Bowlby, Melanie Klein and Lucy Fildes, found that some children 'felt not only their own insecurity but that of their parents and homes. Some who were difficult even at home in times of peace have become much more troubled. Others have shown signs of strain for the first time.' During the first ten months of the evacuation 187 cases were referred to the clinic in Cambridge. The main reasons being enuresis, 48 per cent; incontinence, 12 per cent; and stealing and petty pilfering, 16 per cent. However, the symptoms complained about by host families and teachers did not always correspond to the problems as diagnosed by the clinic, and many were said to be both exaggerated and incorrectly identified.[78]

This situation created a favourable climate for the expansion of the clinics. In fact, during the course of the war, between 15,000 and 20,000 children were 'unbilletable', so that the Government had to open special hostels for them in evacuation areas. Previously these children had exhibited their problems at home or, to a lesser extent, at school, where they had gone largely unnoticed. Evacuation, therefore, more or less compelled an increasing number of LEAs to accept the principle of child guidance. By 1944, when there were over seventy affiliated clinics in Great Britain, including seventeen in London, fifteen in Scotland and three in Wales, over half were either partly or wholly maintained by the LEA, and the remainder were attached to departments of either education or psychology in universities, or to local hospitals. Two years later there were sixty-six wholly maintained clinics, and forty-nine authorities were running a child guidance service using voluntary clinics. The 1944 Education Act made it the duty of LEAs to establish some form of child guidance service in their areas, thereby formally incorporating it into the SMS.[79]

In 1939 the semi-official Feversham Committee, established by the CGC and the National Council for Mental Hygiene, reported on the voluntary health services.[80] It was by no means simply a factual report, but rather a determined attempt on the part of the leading voluntary organisations concerned with all aspects of mental health to set priorities for mental health policy in the future through the establishment of a National Council for Mental Health. The great need, it claimed, was for sane and balanced minds, which were being undermined by modern conditions. 'The increasing speed of life . . . is tending to produce breakdown and overstrain. What would otherwise be latent maladjustment of an unimportant kind is liable to become serious mental disorder.'[81] Among other issues the report warned of the dangers from increased 'mental dullness' and greater emotional instability. It was also concerned about the treatment of juvenile delinquency, quoting Burt to the effect that about 30 per cent of delinquents were emotionally unstable, and expressed the view that argument in favour of simple punishment 'oversimplifies the whole problem'. Instead there was a need to take into account the 'needs and distinctive characteristics of the individual offender'. But magistrates paid little heed to the importance of referring delinquents to psychological clinics. Moreover the co-ordination of services was found to be unsatisfactory with the majority of areas having no psychological services in the courts. Notwithstanding such specific concerns, the Committee argued that in general mental health problems meant 'the lowering of efficiency' of the community and, therefore, the need was to do for mental health what had been done in the past for physical health.[82]

The Committee identified three aspects of a successful child health programme: prevention, guidance and treatment. The first involved child welfare in various forms, including education and sex hygiene, which was promoted by the Home and School Council and the British Social Hygiene Council. Although there was no clear distinction between guidance and treatment, it was understood that the former referred to the CGCs. However, the Committee urged a broader view of 'guidance', one that would see beyond the psychiatric clinic to incorporate 'treatment' for those children (the majority) who did not require the attention of psychiatrists, but one or more of the other social and educational agencies. At the core of the programme were to be 'children's centres' which would serve three purposes: (i) act as an information bureau; (ii) be the centre for guidance for disturbed children; and (iii) be the headquarters for voluntary agencies dealing with children and adolescents. It was also recommended that local authorities make provision for preventive curative facilities for the mental health of children. LEAs were advised to appoint psychologists to advise on educational programmes, on backward and on difficult children; and psychiatrists were to be appointed to the school medical service in order to deal with children experiencing psychiatric problems. The LEAs were advised either to establish their own CGC or to co-operate with one of the voluntary clinics through financial support.[83]

The evacuation experience was still fresh in the public mind when early in 1944 one of Feversham's recommendations was acted upon with the formation of a Provisional National Council for Mental Health, which included the Child Guidance Council, with a special child guidance committee. This organisational shift indicated that there was a movement away from what Feversham had considered to be the isolation of the CGC from other areas of mental health. Feversham argued that 'child guidance' should mean more than what goes on in the clinic – it should include the courts, probation officers, teachers, medical and social agencies, residential institutions, and other interested parties. Indeed, part of the success of the CGC was that it made it possible for other professions to deal with 'the normal child with problems'. What was required was *education* in its widest possible implication: 'the nurture of character, mind and body', which necessitated the integration of the clinics within the administrative framework of the LEAs.[84]

The emphasis in nearly all of the comments and recommendations of the Feversham Committee was on the importance of the clinics becoming part of the education system. In a revealing section of its report (which took up the theme of the preface) it focused on child guidance in national life – the former was to be seen in relation to the latter since neither should stand in isolation from the other: 'The real importance of child mental health is the contribution which it makes to the health and efficiency of the nation of working citizens.' At present, however, 'The reservoir of potential working energy and initiative of the nation is far below what it might be' and, therefore, it was desirable that the clinics should contribute to national health through preventive medicine. The background to this anxiety was the eugenic fear of national deterioration, which focused on mental degeneration as one of the causes undermining national stock.[85]

The Education Act, 1944, in addition to imposing a duty on LEAs to incorporate psychological facilities into their school medical service, also made them responsible for special education needs, which meant that they required 'a means of advising the ordinary schools, of advising parents, of conducting social surveys or test procedures as may be necessary for the allocation of children to different types of school, and for the diagnosis and treatment of individual children whether their problem be physical or mental or emotional'. The report of the Association of Education Committees, 1946, suggested to authorities that in order to comply with the Act, and no doubt with one eye on the Feversham recommendations, the child guidance clinic

> must either have added to it a psychological service as an advisory and diagnostic service of the authority or alternatively the child guidance clinic ... must give place to a child guidance service adequately staffed to provide for all those needs varying as they will do from the severe emotional problem requiring detailed psychiatric treatment through the whole range of behaviour and educational maladjustments to the relatively simple case where a whole age group have to be surveyed ... regarding the general type of secondary education appropriate to their needs.[86]

By the late 1940s, then, there was a move away from the American model of the clinic towards a greater integration of the clinic in what was a developing schools psychological service. Between 1945 and 1949 an increasing number of LEAs in England and Wales established psychological services and the number appointing educational psychologists rose from eight in 1940–4 to an additional thirty in 1945–9 and a further fifteen between 1950 and 1954.[87]

Needless to say, the issue was not simply preventive medicine in any pure sense; it was bounded by political considerations the most prominent of which was a kind of citizenship. This was clearly spelled out in the standard textbook on child guidance, first published in 1945. Apparently, the common problem of patients facing the clinics was not simply a failure of adjustment but of 'integration': the failure of diverse elements to join in harmony. What was required, therefore, was not a token readjustment, but the combination of the parts into a *willing* whole, for 'we are individuals in society'. The ultimate purpose of child guidance was to provide education and parenting in such a way as to help the child to learn the ' "value of independence" and to accept the necessity of responsibility; so only can we *get some measure of true democracy*. Psychologically speaking, this can only be achieved by bringing discipline into relation with reality instead of with power, so that external discipline can gradually make a transition *to discipline from within*.'[88] In other words, the investment in citizenship as the 'willing whole' necessitated teaching the child to invest in itself.

Child guidance, in common with other guidances, professional and otherwise, was about teaching people self-discipline and communal responsibility in pursuit of a democratic consensus. But this was not easily achieved. On the one hand, individuals could be broken through imposed discipline; on the other, the process of integration was neither natural nor without dangers. It had to be learned and it had to be taught. Consequently, parenting, education – academic, social and moral – and medicine all had their part to play in rearing and maintaining harmoniously adjusted individuals, conscious of themselves and of society. There were differences as to how best to achieve this end. One researcher found that 'different patterns of child guidance have developed in different parts of the country' just as there were 'variations in the term "child guidance" and a lack of agreement on the types of cases that should be referred'.[89] The differences occurred because this was a relatively new subject, complex and ambitious, which was seeking to chart preventive health at a national level, and always with the liberal democratic objective in mind. And, given that there were competing versions of this objective, so child guidance was open to a number of different strategies as to means and interpretations.

6

THE CHILDREN AND YOUNG PERSONS ACT, 1933

It is a striking fact that the only major piece of child welfare legislation during the inter-war period, years in which millions of young people suffered the economic and social consequences of the Depression, was an Act based on the recommendations of a committee whose concern was with juvenile offenders. In order to understand the Act, this chapter poses four questions. How did it come to be passed, and why was it thought necessary? What did it involve for the conception of juvenile delinquency? What were its main provisions? What effect did it have on those caught in its jurisdiction? In more general terms, the intention is to show the social and political strategies inherent in the motivation of reformers and politicians and in the content of the Act.

CHANGING PERSPECTIVES ON JUVENILE DELINQUENCY

The changes in the treatment of juvenile delinquency heralded by the Children Act, 1908, barely had a chance to develop before the First World War began to affect penal priorities. The war witnessed a marked rise in juvenile crime (from 37,500 children under 16 charged each year to 51,000 by 1917), which resulted in congested industrial and reformatory schools and an increase in the number of birchings from 1,702 in 1910 to 4,864 in 1916. In the immediate post-war reconstructionist period reformers called for a new approach to the problem. The mood of these reformers was influenced by what Victor Bailey calls 'the Social Conception of Delinquency' which emphasised four features: the psychology of adolescence as a distinct development stage of life, the indiscipline and character deficiencies of large sections of working-class youth, the malign influence of bad urban environments, and the lack of recreational facilities.[1]

By the mid-1920s, this conception of delinquency was giving way to a more thoroughly psychological analysis, though one that continued to draw upon the home environment and family relationships. The significance of 'mind' was clearly being imposed as an analytical and descriptive factor in the understanding of delinquency. It was a conception much influenced by Healy's work in America and by the researches of Cyril Burt, culminating in his definitive study, *The Young Delinquent* (1925).[2] Burt stressed the significance of mind and physical surroundings, explaining that delinquency was the result of 'a concurrence of subversive factors'.[3] While many reformers and practitioners looked on the environment, especially poverty, as the prime cause of delinquency, there was never much difficulty in combining this view with a belief in mental causes. So, as has been shown, child guidance happily strove to accommodate the maladjusted child to its environment. Nevertheless, it remains true that there was no 'psychiatric deluge', as in the United States; rather, the conception of delinquency which developed in England 'incorporated the insights of social and educational psychology'.[4]

Burt insisted that delinquency was really just an 'outstanding example . . . of common childish naughtiness' and that the problem as a whole was 'but one inseparable portion of the larger enterprise for child welfare'. Crime in children should not, he said, be solely the concern of the police and the law, since it touched 'every side of social work', meaning schools, care committees, youth clubs and voluntary aid societies.[5] This reinforced the belief of many boys' club workers (who were prominent among penal reformers), and others, that 'neglected' children and adolescents soon found their way into crime. It was a theme reiterated in the influential government report on juvenile offenders, which stated that 'the tendency to commit offences is only an outcome of the conditions of neglect'.[6]

This did not mean that treatment was to be the same for all delinquents. Far from it. The delinquent, according to Burt, was 'a unique human being, with a peculiar constitution, peculiar difficulties, and peculiar problems of his own'.[7] Hence he supported the view that young people brought before the courts should be subject to mental, physical and environmental investigation, for only then could the appropriate sentence be passed. The intention was that where preferable, given the importance of family relationships, children should be kept at home on probation. In those cases where the home was considered incorrigible, children were to be sent to certified schools.[8]

THE JUVENILE OFFENDERS COMMITTEE, 1927

Although the juvenile crime rate had declined by 1921 (to 30,000 cases from a peak of 51,000 in 1917), there remained an intense interest in the problem, and demands were made for some sort of government inquiry into the whole area. Furthermore, the Children's Branch of the Home Office felt that the legislation of 1908 required amendments since it was looked on as inadequate to meet current needs and, therefore, the Branch was considering a new Children's Bill.[9] When the Departmental Committee on Young Offenders was finally appointed in 1925 it was required under its terms of reference to examine the treatment of young offenders and of young people who had not committed a crime but were deemed to be in need of 'protection and training'. The Committee also gave detailed consideration to all aspects of the juvenile courts whose procedures at the time differed widely. Apart from its importance as a precursor of the 1933 Act, it is worth bearing in mind that the Committee provided the focus for the inter-war debate on the meaning of delinquency and its treatment.

After hearing evidence on the juvenile courts, the Committee unanimously concluded that as they worked under the Children Act, 1908, they were far from satisfactory and that a number of changes were necessary in order for there be a clear distinction between these courts and those in which adults appeared. The age of criminal responsibility encountered more dissension, but the final recommendation was to raise it from seven to eight years of age. There was also considerable discussion as to whether or not the legal basis of the court should be changed from criminal to chancery jurisdiction, which would have meant abandoning the laws of evidence and bringing more children before the court on the grounds of neglect. However, this was rejected in favour of the principle that young offenders should have the opportunity to counter the charges against them, and that the absence of any kind of court procedure would undermine the gravity of the offence.

None the less, the central dilemma of the juvenile court, namely justice versus welfare, was left unresolved. The crux of the problem was that while the courts focused on a criminal act, with all the judicial procedures necessary for assigning criminal responsibility, they were also concerned with the social welfare of the delinquent, whose act was seen as the product 'of distinct psychological and social conditions'. The adopted solution, implicit in the report, was to see the court as having a different function at a different time: first determine by trial the guilt or innocence of the young person, and afterwards determine a suitable treatment, bearing in mind that the welfare of the child was to be the uppermost consideration.[10] At the time, few people interrogated the notion of 'the welfare of the child'. Instead it was left to settle comfortably in the realms of adult complacency. Of course, in reality it was open to various intepretations, many of which expressed contradictions between the welfare of the child and that of 'society', or some special interest. Predictably, children were never asked for their definition of their own welfare.

In order for the second stage, the suitable treatment, to be effective it was necessary for the court to have access to the history of the offender. This required documents of observation and investigation, which were to be provided either by child guidance clinics (where they existed) or by medical examination and other forms of pre-sentence inquiry. In other words, the court had to 'know' the offender. As early as 1917 the Penal

Reform League had called for psychological studies of children which would 'diagnose the reason for so many of the acts which lead to court proceedings, and would certainly assist the magistrate in deciding the effective method of treating the child'. An investigation into juvenile crime by the Government-appointed Juvenile Organisations Committee (JOC) carried out in 1920 found that many offenders were either physically or mentally handicapped, or both, and that in the absence of examination this often went unnoticed. Consequently,'knowing' the offender was essential for the allocation of efficient – appropriate – treatment.[11] However, it was many years before inquiries on behalf of the court were anything like usual. The long delay was caused first by the time taken to convince the majority of magistrates of the need for psychological reports; and, second, by the relative absence of remand centres where the necessary examinations could be given. Thus developments in this area occurred slowly and unevenly.[12]

In the mean time, medical, legal and child-study journals carried articles debating the mental condition of delinquency and the possible role of psychology in reducing its prevalence.[13] Nor should the role of the child guidance movement be overlooked since it may well have been responding to a demand from reformers and organisations seeking a means of dealing with delinquents.[14] It should be remembered that Mrs St Loe Strachey, a well-known magistrate, was one of the prime movers in establishing the Child Guidance Council, and she was also responsible for the Howard League republishing several of Burt's articles in 1924 as *Psychology of the Young Criminal*. The trend was certainly and no doubt self-consciously reinforced by the recommendation of the Young Offenders Committee that there be established at least three residential remand centres where delinquents could be observed and examined. As Victor Bailey writes, this was an important recommendation since it underlined the principle that the courts were not to punish offenders but to ensure their readjustment to the community. Bailey is also correct in suggesting that it epitomised the view of the committee in regarding investigative medical, social and psychological reports as essential in determining the proper treatment for young people in trouble.[15]

The question is what motivated these views? We need to appreciate that the reformers were constructing an elaborate and time-consuming set of procedures for the governance of offenders and of those apparently in need of care and protection. 'Knowledge' (divided between identity and categorisation) of the individual child's life-history was seen to be essential not only for the exercise of effective external control, but also in order to bring to bear upon the young person the most appropriate influences. This is a period which saw the transformation (rather than the elimination) of punishment, albeit often very reluctantly, into welfare discipline. The assimilation of the reformatory and industrial schools into the single category 'approved' school, and the move towards psycho-medical examination should be looked on as part of the same process whereby the intention was to 'treat', i.e readjust, both offenders and non-offenders rather than to punish them. And as treatment suggests a cure – a recovery – so the emphasis was on re-establishing some perceived good in order that the individual child voluntarily entered into respectable society. This was one reason why the juvenile courts had to be made distinctly separate from institutions of criminality. 'Punishment', however, in the form of incarceration and birching, retained a place in the gallery of inducements, but it was to be used sparingly, with more thought, and more often as a last resort.

None the less, the extent of welfare discipline should not be exaggerated since on the issue of corporal punishment the Committee was divided, as was official opinion throughout the inter-war years. There was no clear-cut division between 'progressive' reformers and proponents of retribution – at least, not in the 1920s. Charles Russell, a noted reformer, favoured flogging for cruelty to animals and for *any* serious offence committed by children under 16 years old. Chief Constables were very much in favour of it, and Cyril Burt hardly less so, while Alexander Paterson, another well-known reformer, thought that the matter ought to be left to the courts to decide. William Clarke Hall, the 'progressive' magistrate, opposed this view and refrained from sentencing boys to be birched, as did the Birmingham Juvenile Court under the influence of Geraldine Cadbury. While birching continued, for example, at the Leeds and Liverpool juvenile courts, and nationally nearly 1,600 boys were so sentenced in 1919, overall the proportion of offenders birched declined from 9.7 per cent of those sentenced in 1916 to 1.8 per cent in 1923. The Committee recommended, with three dissenting voices, that, subject to safeguards, the courts should be able to order a whipping for any serious offence committed by a boy under 17. Bailey has observed that this was one of the few occasions when the Committee 'placed the punishment of the offence before the needs of the offender'.[16]

It is instructive to note that many of the 'liberal progressive' reformers, such as Clarke Hall, interpreted the needs of the children of the poor in terms of bringing even more of them before the courts, including those living in 'undesirable surroundings', since 'these children who have *not* been charged are the real danger to the community. It is they who will in the future replenish the ranks of the criminal classes.'[17] This was clearly an enterprise of some complexity, seeking as it did not only to bring additional numbers within the courts' jurisdiction, but also to mix offenders and non-offenders in a single category of 'training schools'. In some respects the bringing of children into court and the nature of the 'treatment' they received were two separate issues, but the Committee, echoing the views of its witnesses, brought them firmly together.

The original distinction between the schools went back to the mid-nineteenth century. The industrial schools had developed from the Ragged Schools and were intended for orphans and other neglected children. The reformatories were for the reformation of young offenders as an alternative to prison. The former schools took children under 14, while the latter took those under 16. In the years prior to 1914 both types of institution were heavily criticised by reformers for being repressive and unimaginative. However, the Report of the Departmental Committee on Reformatories and Industrial Schools, 1913, led to a new atmosphere in the schools – at least, officially – through the appointment of the veteran boys' club worker Charles Russell as the new Chief Inspector and the establishment of the Children's Branch at the Home Office.[18]

The terms of reference of the Young Offenders' Committee, as we have seen, required it to examine 'the treatment of young offenders and young people who, owing to bad associations or surroundings require protection and training'. This suggests that there was already an interest among officials and reformers in abolishing the distinction between the 'depraved' and the 'deprived' child, although the relationship between protection and training was left undefined. Notwithstanding, the Committee looked at young people who were 'the victims of cruelty and other offences committed by adults and whose natural guardianship [has] proved insufficient or unworthy of trust', and recommended that such guardianship be 'replaced'. In the Report 'neglected' children were put into three categories: 'Poor Law' children; those in voluntary homes; and those dealt with under the Children Act, 1908, which included children who came under the previous industrial schools legislation and those who were victims of adult offences. With respect to these categories, the 1908 Act was said to exhibit three weaknesses: (i) no provision for cases requiring urgent protection; (ii) unsatisfactory methods of treatment; and (iii) no authority whose duty it was consistently to see that all suitable cases received treatment. Hence 'a more consistent and comprehensive policy is required'.[19]

An important feature of such a policy was to be the ending of the distinction between reformatories and industrial schools which the report described as 'an unsound one'; and it echoed the sentiments of the 1913 Departmental Committee with the words:

> there is little or no difference in character and needs between the neglected and the delinquent child. It is often a mere accident whether he is brought before the court because he is wandering or beyond control or because he has committed some offence. Neglect leads to delinquency and delinquency is often the direct outcome of neglect.[20]

The schools themselves, it said, had abandoned their different names, and were now distinguished primarily by the age of boys and girls receiving treatment. The Report suggested that this practice should now be legally recognised, and by way of supporting evidence it claimed that 'the neglected child is often more difficult to train than the bad boy who in a spirit of adventure and dare devilry has committed some more or less serious offence'.[21] This, of course, would have raised questions about the implications of the word 'train' with reference to penal reform and mental health, had there been the will to do so; as it was, no one asked. What it reveals in part is that neglected children were considered to be 'difficult' because they were less easily available for treatment.

Besides considering juvenile courts, remand and observation centres, and approved schools, the committee also recommended various changes to the probation system. The basic principle of probation was that the offender should be brought under the guidance of a respectable person, which was considered particularly appropriate for first offenders. Magistrates had long been urged to make more use of probation for suitable cases (those with 'decent' and responsive parents), with penal reform groups leading the campaign. But evidence showed that the use of probation varied from town to town – in 1919 it was from 1.4 to 43.6 per cent. Moreover, 215 courts of summary jurisdiction out of a total 1,034 had not appointed even a single probation officer.[22] The Committee, however, decided to leave probation as a permissive service with the Home Office continuing to urge magistrates to make use of it.

THE SCOPE OF THE ACT

The Children and Young Persons Act, 1933, in which children were defined as up to 14 years of age, and a young person as between 14 and 17, was a consolidating measure of major significance, whose main provisions were based on the recommendations of the Young Offenders Committee, 1927. According to the preamble of the Act, it was intended 'to make further and better provision for the protection and welfare of the young and the treatment of young offenders; to amend the Children Act, 1908, and other enactments relating to the young; and for objects connected with the purposes aforesaid'. Two of the Act's most distinctive characteristics were, first, that it forged a closer link between care of delinquent and neglected children and the work of the local education authorities and, second, that it further removed the care of neglected children from the Poor Law. In terms of changes in the law the main developments concerned the constitution and procedure of the juvenile courts, the role played by LEAs, and the treatment of young people brought before the courts. The Act became famous for its concern with what it and its supporters defined as 'welfare' as well as 'punishment', and for the search for 'rehabilitation' of the juvenile through social services.

The Act was divided into six parts. The first part was concerned with the 'Prevention of Cruelty and Exposure to Moral and Physical Danger'

183

of children and young persons. It defined *wilful* cruelty and *wilful* neglect as criminal offences committed against a child who itself could be brought before the juvenile court to receive care or protection. The second part consolidated legislation restricting different forms of child employment: (i) no child under 12 shall be employed – except in certain circumstances by their parents in light agricultural or horticultural work; (ii) no child shall be employed before the close of school hours on any day on which he/ she is required to attend school; (iii) powers were given to local authority to make bye-laws with respect to employment of children and young persons up to the age 18; (iv) street-trading was prohibited to those under the age of 16.

The third part of the Act was significant in that it dealt with the complex subject of the constitution and procedures of the juvenile courts under the title of 'Protection of Children and Young Persons in Relation to Criminal and Summary Proceedings'. A number of changes were made to the previous legislation embodied in the Children Act, 1908. These may be listed as follows:

1 (i) the age limit was raised from 16 to 17; (ii) the definition of the need for care and protection was widened to include a child or young person who, either through having no parents or guardians, or those failing to exercise proper care, was (*a*) being exposed to moral danger; (*b*) falling into bad company; (*c*) beyond control; (*d*) being neglected or ill treated in a manner likely to result in unnecessary suffering or injury to health. In other words, the courts dealt with all young people, regardless of whether they were offenders or only in need of care, protection and guidance.
2 The juvenile courts 'shall have regard to the welfare of the child' and to this end the courts were to function separately from the ordinary petty sessional courts, and were to be constituted by panels of magistrates who were to be selected for their special interest in young people. The courts were to have simplified procedures in order to extract from the young person his or her own story 'unhampered' by the rules of evidence observed in criminal courts.
3 LEAs were compelled to provide magistrates with information concerning the young person's health, character, schooling and family background. These authorities were also given the primary responsibility for bringing to the courts those deemed to be in need of care or protection, as well as the duty of providing remand homes, which was transferred to them from the police.

The fourth part dealt with the treatment of offenders and others. The distinction between industrial and reformatory schools was abolished, and they were renamed 'approved' schools under the control of the Home Office. The approved school was intended for short-term training. Detention was to be for a maximum of three years if at the end of that time the young person was 15; if not, then for a further period until reaching that age. Further supervision by school managers could continue outside the school, with the power of recall until the age of 19. The Act accepted the principle of detention as expressed by the Departmental Committee on Juvenile Offenders, which denied the relevance of 'just proportions' (periods of detention commensurate with the seriousness of the offence), arguing that the guiding principle was not to be that of 'punishment' but of 'reformation', and this demanded time during which the young person would receive a training experience. Non-offenders, who were either beyond parental control or living in undesirable surroundings or with undesirable persons, could either be sent to an approved school, where they would be subject to the same period of detention as offenders, or be given probation in appropriate cases. Other sections of the fourth part limited the use of the birch to six strokes; increased the age of criminal responsibility from 7 to 8; abolished the death sentence on persons under 18; and prohibited the use of the words 'conviction' and 'sentence' in relation to juveniles dealt with summarily.

In part, attention was directed to the care given to homeless or neglected children in voluntary homes and orphanages. The homes were officially defined, and in addition to being made subject to Home Office inspection, were required to provide the Secretary of State with certain particulars. The final part of the Act dealt with administrative matters which made the Home Office responsible for inspection and made exchequer grants to local authorities, while local administration of the care of children was made the responsibility of local education authorities.

Before looking at the very substantial changes made by the Act to the juvenile court system, its intention *vis-à-vis* the prevention of cruelty to children under 16 needs to be made clear. The relevant subsection (1) was a comprehensive provision:

> If any person who has attained the age of 16 years and has the custody, charge or care of any child or young person under that age, wilfully assaults, ill-treats, neglects, abandons or exposes him or causes or procures him to be assaulted, ill-treated, neglected, abandoned or exposed, in a manner likely to cause him unnecessary suffering or injury to health (including injury to or loss of sight, or hearing, or limb or organ of the body and any mental derangement) that person shall be guilty of [an offence] . . .

Five other sections dealt with exposure to physical danger. However, it is important to realise that the Act was as much concerned with moral danger as with cruelty. Sections 2–4 dealt with causing or encouraging seduction or prostitution of girls under 16, allowing persons under 16 to be in brothels, and causing or allowing children under 16 to beg; while section 6 prohibited children from entering bars or pubs.

THE MEANING OF THE LEGISLATION

Perhaps the acceptance by the Government of the Committee's recommendations was made easier by the further increase in juvenile crime after 1928 which helped the Home Office (and *The Times Educational Supplement*) to popularise the view that institutional training ought to take place as close to childhood as possible, rather than being left to mid- or late adolescence.[23] In effect the 1933 Act brought together three separate groups of young people: (i) offenders; (ii) the neglected; and (iii) child victims of offences. Though some distinctions between them were retained, the emphasis was on their commonality. In dealing with neglected children, described as those 'in need of care and protection', the 1933 Act, in what a government official correctly described as 'the most revolutionary change in the Bill', defined the condition very generally, replacing the specific categories of the previous law. The Act also raised the maximum age at which the courts could deal with young people from 16 to 17. The creation of the 'approved' school meant that not only could offenders be sent there, but also under section 62 of the Act so could children 'in need of care and protection'. The 'offender or otherwise' could be logically lumped together since the overall concern of the court was with the 'welfare of the child' and this concern could be used to justify his or her removal 'from undesirable surroundings, and for securing that proper provision is made for [their] education and training'.[24] It has been said that the merging of the two types of school under the 1933 Act was 'simply the culmination of a process perceived as early as 1870'.[25] To say 'simply' fails to explain why the process should have culminated at this particular time.

Briefly, the reason was that notions of crime and punishment had changed; they were now more sophisticated; so, too, were those of welfare, which was no longer seen as separate from either the causes or the consequences of crime and punishment. Indeed, from the late-Victorian period onwards, welfare was becoming a means of controlling the crime rate, in part by devising new and, in the minds of reformers, hopefully more effective 'treatments', and also by unpacking the various meanings of 'crime' to reveal its numerous features and the different ways in which each was constructed. Thus 'neglect' and its consequences came to be understood more precisely (with the help of psychology) than it had been in the past, as an aspect of crime in its broadest sense.[26]

The Act has been described as 'memorable in setting a standard of welfare and rehabilitation for the delinquent and the neglected children and those in need of care which had never previously been approached . . . the welfare of the child, and not the judgement of society, was now paramount'.[27] But is this a fair evaluation, or does it merely accept the claims of the Act at face value without questioning its motivations and objectives? Although the Act dealt with delinquent and neglected children (i.e offenders and non-offenders), it was primarily a measure to deal with what was seen as the problem of juvenile delinquency, but within a much more comprehensive framework than had previously existed. Reformers had a particular understanding of what constituted delinquency and its relationship to 'neglect'. The understanding depended upon an essentially psychological perspective of young people – of the delinquent act as a symptom of mental maladjustment, and of neglect (of whatever kind) as a failure to provide the young person with the necessary education and training for proper *mental* and, therefore, social development.[28] This explains the nature of the care and protection sections and the creation of the 'approved' school system: both were to be devoted to 'education and training'.[29]

Through the mechanism of the juvenile court, before whom all deprived and depraved children would be brought, hitherto separate practices came together: 'the penal system, the educational apparatus, the organisation of social assistance and psychological, medical and psychiatric expertise' united to form 'a multidimensional social network'.[30] In order for this to work effectively, it was necessary to recognise that the social and economic conditions of the period produced a delinquency which was the product not so much of 'actual physical want' as of 'poverty, unemployment, bad housing and overcrowding'.[31] But it was not just a question of general conditions; the argument was pressed to the specific charge of the defective family, whose inadequate functioning was exacerbated, though not caused, by the consequences of the economic depression.[32] This is where the psychological approach cemented notions of depravation and deprivation, with the objective of effectively governing the family through guidance of its inner relationships and responsibilities.

The courts were to *prevent* future criminality, including 'anti-social' behaviour, by becoming part of a preventive strategy whereby young people would be 'treated' for their disposition which, though non-criminal, threatened the good order of society, since they were in the social group that produced delinquents and criminals. In this respect, the merging of the offender and the non-offender was critically important in the development of penal policy for juveniles. It is obvious that the use of the word 'protection' in the terms of reference of the Departmental Committee hardly referred to protecting children from 'cruel' treatment by parents; rather, it referred to 'protecting' children from the criminal and moral consequences of parental 'neglect'. In this context, 'training', which was linked to 'protection', was automatically assumed to be necessary, for how else could the child be 'protected'. Once it was accepted that neglect referred to exposure to conditions leading to criminality or immorality, then the term 'protection and training', as used by the Committee, is immediately comprehensible. It is also important for what it tells us about the reformers' critical perception of certain kinds of working-class family, and about the nature of young people's 'offences', whose 'delinquency' was being partially removed from the criminal sphere, much to the annoyance of 'the reactionaries'.[33]

Jean Heywood noted the extent to which 'the concept of training by alteration of the environment' had permeated the legislation.[34] The Act offered substitutes for the natural family without conceiving of the possibility of returning the child to its own 'rehabilitated' home. Hence the significance of the foster home as a refuge from 'conditions of squalor and poverty'. This strategy has been correctly attributed to contemporary poverty and mass unemployment, the absence of free medical attention for mothers, and the rising number of divorces. In such circumstances, from the perspective of reformers and legislators, it was too difficult to rehabilitate families in what was known as the 'social problem group', namely those slum families who exhibited a range of social ills including mental illness and defect, epilepsy, criminality, unemployment, inebriety and vagrancy.[35] In time, however, the Home Office came to see a value in securing the co-operation of the natural parents in 'the training and disposal of the child'.[36] The change in outlook, as we shall see, developed during the war when 'the family' began to assume a new importance.

YOUNG PEOPLE'S INSTITUTIONAL EXPERIENCES

Finally, what effect did the Act have on the treatment received by delinquent and neglected children? It will be helpful in answering this question to look back at their treatment in penal institutions prior to 1933. According to Victor Bailey, by 1908 'the crusading spirit' of the mid-Victorian founders of reformatory and industrial schools had 'evaporated', so that what remained was not much more than the 'rigid conformity' of the nineteenth-century system.[37] Whether the crusading spirit ever produced anything other than such a conformity enforced through mental and physical repression is extremely doubtful. One does not have to enter into a 'standards were different in those days' kind of debate to determine that the inmates were regularly abused. Nor did the abuse come to an end with the exposures in the government inquiry of 1913. This is not to say that all officials in the Children's Branch of the Home Office were indifferent to the sufferings of the children; it is simply to recognise the difference between official pronouncements and daily practice in the institutions.

In terms of institutional routine, and probably also of official policy, the extent to which children's bodies were the focus of attempts at reclamation on behalf of citizenship is remarkable. Under the penal regimes, their bodies were both casually and systematically beaten; they were subjected to enforced silences, so that using their tongues without permission became an offence; and with continuous labour their bodies were made to assuage their guilt. In addition to which they were compelled to discipline their bodies through drill and to subordinate their physical movements to the commands of their overseers.

The establishment of reformatory and industrial schools in the mid-nineteenth century, besides being a specific response to anxieties produced by juvenile delinquency, was part of a more comprehensive process which had been developing since the end of the eighteenth century, whereby the criminal justice code was reordered to accommodate it to new ideas and new social, political and economic interests. Briefly, imprisonment began to replace the death penalty and violent attacks on the body. In place of whipping, branding and the pillory, came the prison with solitary confinement, the silent system, a basic diet, the treadmill, and hard (and monotonous) labour. With the growing concern around juvenile delinquency, reformers argued that not only was prison for children inhuman; it was also ineffective, since the young were kept in the company of adult criminals, and expensive. Reformatories, they claimed, which would be run by voluntary societies, were much more suitable for young offenders who could be rescued from the criminal life for society. In contrast to the child in the reformatory with a criminal conviction, the Industrial Schools' Act, 1857, created residential schools for vagrant children with the intention of keeping them away from criminal temptations. By the 1880s industrial school pupils included those who had been abused, or were truants, or who in some other way were deemed to be in need of care and protection.[38]

In many important respects, there was little difference between reformatory and industrial schools. Both ran regimes founded on discipline and hard work, with brutal punishments, Spartan diets, and austere living conditions. This, it was intended, would improve children's self-discipline, respect for authority and their strength of character so that they would be fit to re-enter society. However, 'In practice so attenuated was officialdom's faith in this principle that the great aim of all concerned . . . was to ensure that discharged persons were sent well away from their old haunts and friends', which usually meant either emigration, the armed forces, the deadly fishing fleets at Grimsby and Hull, or domestic service for girls. 'There can be little doubt that the motives of some management committees were far from altruistic.' Many schools were opened in rural areas where the children were used as cheap and free labour on farms. Similarly, in starting a school in an old vessel, the director of a shipping line company was ensuring that he had a future supply of trained sailors. Very few schools received more than a cursory visit from the overworked Home Office inspectors, of whom there were seven in 1913.[39]

The Home Office generally lacked legal standing in its requests to the management committees of the schools. When, for example, it tried to curb 'excessive' corporal punishment in the 1880s, it could only *request* that schools display monthly punishment records. At a London School Board truant school in 1879, corrective discipline consisted of 'the absolute prohibition of conversation . . . and the deprivation of play, drill being substituted by way of discipline'. The only occasions when talking was allowed were during recreation, to ask for the lavatory or in the workshop and to the teacher. After a socialist member of the Board complained, an official inquiry revealed various acts of sadism towards the boys such as forcing unclean children to lie naked on the stone sink of a lavatory in a temperature below freezing, while a cold tap was turned on them; other boys who failed to wash themselves properly were drenched with buckets of cold water and kept in their wet clothes. Those who were returned for a second truancy offence were given twelve strokes of the birch and kept in total silence for three weeks. At another inquiry in 1891, concerning conditions aboard an industrial school training ship, the captain, who had ordered 4,859 recorded strokes of the birch over a three-year period, was cleared of excessive cruelty. When a new captain was appointed he punished boys found masturbating by painting their genitals with a liquid carbolic acid, which left them in a state 'so that they could neither stand, nor sit nor lie down without suffering excruciating agony'.[40]

One of the major scandals involving brutality occurred in 1910 when the ex-superintendent and the matron at the Akbar Nautical Training School wrote to a newspaper (after having their charges rejected by the Home Office), giving details of boys being gagged before being birched, sick boys being caned, and others punished by being drenched with cold water and kept standing all night. The subsequent report, conducted by C. F. G. Masterman, a leading 'New Liberal', managed to reject charges of brutality, but was forced to admit that there had been irregular punishments. However, the scandal refused to go away, and with encouragement from sections of the press a public meeting of some 7,000 persons was held in protest. Eventually, Winston Churchill, the Home Secretary, appointed the Departmental Committee on Reformatory and Industrials Schools. In its Report, the Committee was extremely critical of the schools and made a number of recommendations for reform including classification, management, inspection and methods. The war postponed many reforms and hindered the advancement of the more humane attitudes promoted by Charles Russell and his successor Arthur Norris. However, by 1920 there was a groundswell of opinion among penologists, the courts and reformers against the schools, and committals fell so drastically that forty of them were forced to close down.[41]

There seems to have been a decisive effort on the part of senior officials at the Home Office, led at first by Russell and then by Norris throughout the 1920s to liberalise the schools' regimes. The problem for the historian lies in assessing how far these liberal attitudes affected the daily routines of the children and whether their treatment was less brutal. A regime may become less brutal, and still remain wedded to the violent punishment of its inmates, with every beating meticulously recorded in an approved manner, just as it may also continue to be characterised by psychological oppression. Many of the public criticisms of the schools were not primarily concerned with the lack of sympathy shown to the children, or with beatings; rather, they focused on the quality of formal education, vocational instruction, medical care, dietary standards, staff training and their administrative efficiency.[42] Such a focus obscured the system of discipline, except where it could be shown to be 'brutal'. The fact that brutality stands at an extreme end of the spectrum of violence and authoritarianism was usually overlooked, except of course by those who experienced it.

The 1933 Act, despite introducing some improvements, did not radically alter daily life in institutions. The positive aspects of the Act were that it increased the inspection powers of the Home Office, and sought to encourage LEAs to board out a proportion of the children placed in their care by the juvenile courts, rather than send them to certified schools, which by 1938 were seen as punitive. The Home Office wrote encouraging circulars but not always with much success.[43] Broadly speaking, the schools continued to be run in much the same fashion. Julius Carlebach, a sociologist who worked for ten years after the war in homes for disturbed children, wrote in the late 1960s of approved schools that 'they do not appear to have changed very much since the turbulent days of the 1920s'.[44]

There was, however, a significant reduction in the number of public birchings before the whole school prior to 1939, although corporal punishment with the cane remained a standard punishment as did solitary confinement, restricted diet, deprivation of earnings or play, and the postponement of visits and letters, and down-grading. Oral histories indicate that the punishment for absconding continued to be birchings, for even the youngest children. One interviewee, held between the wars in a nautical training school, told how he was made to hold down his 7-year-old brother for a public birching of six strokes for trying to escape. Another man, who had been at a school in the 1940s, recalled how, after several escapes followed by canings (the cane being kept in pickle), he was taken into the governor's office:

> First, he started by by getting hold of me by the hair and giving me two black eyes. He then kicked me in the stomach and winded me . . . two officers pounced on me and held me down whilst the head beat me something terrible. When I got to my feet it was only to be knocked down by a terrific blow on the mouth. He then laid me across a chair and gave me fourteen strokes with the cane on the back and backside. After this he took his coat off and belted me all round the office.

191

This account was given to the *Mass Observation Report on Juvenile Delinquency*, and the survey stated: 'strange and improbable as such accounts may seem, this one is not unique in our files.'[45]

Alexander Maxwell, a Home Office official who became chairman of the Prison Commission, admitted during a lecture given in 1949 that not only were the children in the schools dressed in distinctive uniforms, separating them from other children, but they were

> usually confined within the school premises by locked door and gates. Within the school buildings . . . they walked in files – at some schools with their hands folded behind their backs . . . The bodily needs . . . were adequately cared for, but their lives were extremely uneventful, and the development of their minds and characters dwarfed by lack of opportunities for the exercise of responsibility and initiative, by lack of contacts with the outside world, and by a scarcity of interests and activities. Their experience was so closely pent within a narrow enclosure of school walls and school rules that they were liable to be stunted in their mental and moral growth.[46]

This lecture was given three years after the publication of the Report of the Curtis Committee on Child Care which, as is shown below, heralded a new approach to public childcare, partly in response to the shocking revelations made by the Committee. The fact is that from the closing decades of the nineteenth century up to the late 1940s not much changed in the care of institutionalized children, be they in orphanages, cottage homes or certified schools.[47] The characteristics of the period with respect to caring for the public child were those of neglect, insensitivity and violence.

The incarceration of children and young adolescents in the certified schools from the mid-Victorian years onwards is often presented as a programme of humanitarian reform, struggling against poorly trained staff, mean-minded officials and inadequate funding, and occasionally marred by the brutality of individuals. This comfortable and reassuring myth bears little resemblance to the true situation. The purpose of the system was clearly stated by the Departmental Committee on Young Offenders when it said that the duty of the court 'is not so much to punish for the offence as to readjust the offender to the community'.[48] Those who were to be readjusted were always from the working class, and usually from the poorest sections; they came from families which had most conspicuously failed to live respectable lives. With this in mind, it needs to be recognised that the reformatories and industrial schools not only protected property and person from the anti-social behaviour of the children of the poor; they also offered the possibility of reformation of character, of 'reclaiming' the offender on behalf of a stable class-structured society through the inculcation of 'obedience, discipline, honesty, cleanliness and sobriety'.[49]

It was during the process of being 'readjusted' that the children experienced their worst horrors, since failure to comply with the demands inherent in the process brought forth terrible punishments and, in cases of non-compliance, indeterminate sentences of up to three years, since in the words of one official 'six months is too short a period for any real impression to be made upon a rebellious character'.[50]

7

THE WAR YEARS

The Second World War subjected the School Medical Service (SMS) to the most severe test of all its resources, practices and assumptions. The effects of medical staff shortages, civilian bombing, blitzed schools and, most dramatically, the evacuation process all made themselves felt and exposed many of the inherent weaknesses of the Service as it had developed since the Edwardian period. Initially the main difficulties were in evacuation reception areas which were overwhelmed by the sudden influx of children who found it difficult to get treatment from doctors and dentists. The situation worsened in 1941 when SMS personnel became liable for call-up, leaving some areas with half their staff. From 1938 to 1945 the number of full-time SMOs was reduced by more than 50 per cent of the pre-war figure; part-timers by 20 per cent and full-time school nurses by 12 per cent. Moreover, an already grossly inadequate dental service lost 25 per cent of full-time dental officers and 30 per cent of its part-timers.[1]

EVACUATION

The evacuation process was one of those rare moments when prejudice, mainly shaped and articulated by sections of the rural and small-town middle class, unveils itself unashamedly. As thousands of working-class children and expectant mothers, including those with pre-school children, arrived and began to be billeted in the reception areas, so a great torrent of exaggerated and malevolent criticism descended upon them through accusations of infestation, incontinence, inadequate clothing, bad manners and a lack of gratitude. Many of the conditions described by the critics were real, but the style of the criticisms showed a complete lack of sympathy and understanding of urban working-class life. Some householders in Perth found the effect of the evacuees so shattering that they were able to obtain medical certificates confirming that their health would be injured by the continued presence of the evacuees in their home.[2] The controversy over the behaviour and attitudes of the evacuees reflected what Angus Calder has so aptly described as the English tendency to confuse manners with

194

morals.³ In this mêlée of offended sensibilities, officials gave very little thought to children's feelings on being separated from their parents and friends, and on having to come to terms with new living environments.

The first wave of evacuation in September 1939 was conducted 'in an atmosphere of haste and confusion'. During the course of a week or so, 826,959 unaccompanied children in England and Wales were evacuated, as were 523,670 mothers with pre-school children, 12,705 expectant mothers, and 173,000 in the priority classes, including 7,000 handicapped children. These evacuees, mainly from large industrial cities, went to reception areas in the South, South-West, East and West Midlands, and North Wales.⁴ The SMS in the reception areas was under great pressure as their combined school population increased from just under 2 million to 2½ million, with many thousands of the new arrivals requiring immediate medical attention. But for the assistance given by voluntary associations such as the Red Cross, the Women's Voluntary Service, and others, the situation could well have been even more serious.

The evacuees often found themselves standing in local church and school halls waiting to be picked out by their prospective hosts, who surveyed them before announcing, 'I'll take that one.' Many hosts were kindly and took in more than one child from the same family so as to avoid splitting them up. But the time spent waiting to be chosen was a humiliating experience mentioned by all those in later years who volunteered their memories. Older boys usually went quickly in rural areas, since they could help around the farms. Pretty children were also readily chosen, as were those who displayed good manners and appearance, and those who for one reason or another caught the eye of the host. 'If you were a child with glasses or with spots, they were always left till the end.' Betty Hewitson remembered being left with her friend: '. . . two plain, straight-haired little girls, wearing glasses, now rather tearful.' But then 'a large, happy-looking, middle-aged lady rushed in asking, "Is that all you have left?" ' Their teacher nodded. 'I'll take the poor bairns,' said the woman. Others were not so quickly taken in, including two sisters who were reluctantly accepted and were reminded by their hostess that she would have preferred two boys. Chance also played a part in being chosen: '. . . they wanted a little girl with MG initials because their sports car had MG on the bumper.' Laura Welford was chosen by a woman 'because I patted her dog whilst she was enquiring why we were still on the street so late at night'. Sometimes a child was taken to replace one who had died. A teacher remembered a couple choosing on this basis: '. . . she was the same age and exactly like the daughter they had lost, and they took her back to their house and even the dog went mad with happiness.'⁵ Such moments speak volumes about the use of children as investments.

The SMS in evacuation areas (as opposed to reception areas) was largely suspended at the outbreak of war, even though half the children remained in those areas, thereby leaving them with virtually no proper medical inspection or treatment. In too many instances there was no planned correlation between numbers evacuated, distribution of staff and closure of clinics. The shortages and lack of efficient organisation exacerbated the difficulties. Scabies was on the increase, and uncleanliness and persistent nits were a menace. New problems arose with the growing number of working mothers, which meant that the call for school dinners increased, as it did for nursery places. In an attempt to satisfy some of the needs war-time nurseries, nursery-classes and school canteens were opened.[6]

The main problem was that the reception areas were usually unprepared for the feeding and medical demands made by the evacuees who presented the authorities with a catalogue of physical and mental ailments, the most important of which were impetigo, pediculosis (infestation with lice), scabies and enuresis (bed-wetting). The evacuation areas had not given their children a medical inspection prior to sending them away, and as evacuation took place at the end of the school holidays it was some weeks since the children had last received even the briefest of routine medical examinations. In some areas the Service found itself having to cater for double the usual numbers, with many of the newly arrived children requiring more or less immediate attention in terms of delousing. However, the problems began to be tackled very quickly. The children were inspected by the SMOs, and after May 1940 all child evacuees were medically examined before leaving their homes and were given a record card for details of their ailments to be passed on to medical officers in the reception areas. Nurses began to make cleanliness surveys; temporary clinics were opened, as were first-aid posts, showers, cleansing stations, and hostels for children with infectious skin diseases and severe cases of infestation. In London, thirty-eight of the eighty pre-war cleansing stations were reopened, and medical and dental treatment were resumed together with provision of meals and milk.[7]

By early 1940 about 80 per cent of evacuees had returned to the cities. There were further periods of evacuation during the Blitz of late 1940 and in 1944 with the arrival of the V1 and V2 rockets. Thus throughout the war the school population in different areas changed according to the perceived dangers in urban centres. Consequently the SMS had to make a number of adjustments in difficult circumstances. However, in the subsequent waves of evacuation many of the problems associated with medical inspection, billeting, schooling and school meals were overcome.[8]

Although several of the emergencies specific to the evacuation process were soon dealt with, in some respects they merely highlighted more profound weaknesses in the SMS, especially the ineffectiveness of the routine medical inspections. It was not so much specific illnesses that were found in the children as the destitute condition of a substantial minority of them, disclosed in uncleanliness, undernourishment, inadequate footwear and clothing, and the high degree of infestation. Evacuation also revealed, by putting their destitution into context, the extent to which inter-war housing schemes had failed to eradicate the slums and related problems such as overcrowding, lack of proper toilet and washing facilities, and the presence of rats and other vermin. Through the dramatic medium of personal contact between children and their hosts, the wider influence of inter-war poverty and poor housing became self-evident, as many MOHs belatedly admitted. In effect evacuation illuminated conditions common among the poor for generations, but which had been obscured in the dark shadows cast by aggregate official statistics and ignored by the majority of politicians and administrators.[9]

One of the most seriously deficient areas of the SMS continued to be in dental care. Whatever progress may have been made between 1933 and 1938 (which was claimed by the Board of Education), the war soon put an end to it. Unsurprisingly, surveys conducted during evacuation found the service to be completely inadequate. Not the least of the problems involved payment for treatment since it was often impossible to arrange payment from parents whose children were billeted in different parts of the country, and the host families understandably did not want to pay the cost. In a cynical attempt to accommodate reduced staff to the demand for dental care, circular 1523 (August 1940) advised LEAs in reception areas that they were responsible for dental and medical treatment of evacuees, but that children whose parents had failed to take advantage of past opportunities should as a rule have their treatment limited to extractions, rather than giving them conservative treatment. No credit was allowed for the likelihood that parents might have found the cost of the fillings too high, or that the children were frightened and, therefore, unwilling to accept them. Even more staggering in both its moral discrimination and indifference to children as individuals, was the instruction that those who had persistently neglected their teeth, though they remained 'technically saveable', should not be given fillings. It was a rare official who noted that 'not one word or thought was directed to the suffering undergone by the child whilst parental permission is obtained'.[10] In other words, moral categories were to be used to allocate scarce resources. This was an unwitting testimony to the condition of 'the body' (teeth) to serve as a barometer of personal and parental responsibility.

There was some disagreement among investigators as to whether or not infestation was exaggerated. The Board of Education expressed concern and commissioned a report showing that on average the incidence of lice among urban children was about three times higher than the percentage recorded by School Medical Officers in the pre-war period. The Board found the report so 'disquieting' that only a summary was published. The effect, however, was to throw doubt on the veracity of the claim made by the SMS to have won the battle against infestation. Similar revelations with reference to impetigo and scabies also suggested that the pre-war SMS had

197

failed to eradicate these to the extent claimed in its annual reports. The inadequacy of many of the children's clothing and footwear further undermined public confidence in the official view that very few children experienced problems in this respect. As late as 1938 the London County Council was claiming that only 0.3 per cent of children had 'poor' clothing. Richard Titmuss responded to such figures by observing that 'the worship of the statistical average made the classifications meaningless'.[11]

Evacuation also in part caused and in part revealed the presence of psycho-social problems such as enuresis and other forms of emotional disturbance. In fact, evacuation was one of the means by which the full extent of the 'need' for child guidance clinics was recognised. Bed-wetting, for example, about which there was an outcry in the host areas, was a sign of deep-rooted psychological distress for a minority of children; for the majority, however, it was merely a temporary response to the stress of their situation: away from their parents, family and community, and in what was often a hostile environment, sometimes with an equally hostile host family. In such circumstances it required understanding and sympathetic treatment. Instead, it was reported as if it were 'an entirely unknown phenomenon in the past, and that evacuation produced a Niagara all over English and Scottish country beds'. The treatment, such as it was, often consisted of sending the children away to special hostels. The true nature of the psychological impact of evacuation can never be fully known. But it can be safely assumed that the trauma of separation from family, and the emotional adjustment this involved, was rarely taken seriously by those who made policy. On the other hand, many psychologists and medical personnel *did* appreciate the children's anxieties and warned of the dangers of the separation of parent (usually mother) and child. Implicit in these warnings was the risk of creating future problems in adolescents and young adults.[12]

The official reaction to most of the revelations of distress, poverty and destitution was simply to reiterate the view voiced throughout the 1930s, namely the SMS was primarily educational, and not meant either to provide comprehensive child health or to relieve the effects of poverty. The Government was always keen to stress that the subject of needy children was one of parental responsibility: 'The root cause' of the evacuees' problems 'lies in the home'. The Government preferred to focus, somewhat prophetically, on encouraging a more efficient and more psychologically mature parenthood as the solution. This was in keeping with the developing concept of the 'problem family'. Thus it has been accurately observed that 'Evacuation . . . marks the conceptual transition from the "social problem group" of the inter-war years to the "problem family" of the 1940s and 1950s'. The latter notion, as will be shown below, being less hereditarian in emphasis, was more optimistic in so far as these families appeared to be redeemable.[13]

198

Evacuation, in the words of one of its chroniclers, meant that 'An army of children, clutching tiny bags, came out of the dark and pricked a nation's conscience'.[14] It was as if, at the moment when liberal democracy faced its greatest challenge, the children of the urban poor escaped the slums to remind their rulers of their primary duties: to feed, clothe, shelter and look after the health of those over whom they exercised power. While 'conscience' was present in the development of the more universalist spirit that dominated social welfare politics in the late 1940s and early 1950s, its significance should not be exaggerated in a frenzy of nostalgia. Much more important was the influence of political and economic calculations on the part of governments and sectional interests in a revolutionised post-war world.

SCHOOL MEALS

For thousands of children, being evacuated meant having a good diet for the first time in their lives. For thousands of others who moved away from local authorities providing food services to those without any such provision, it was a disaster. Similarly, the children who were not evacuated soon found that where their schools were closed, so, too, were the feeding facilities. Authorities in the reception areas justified their mean attitude by arguing that the billeting allowance paid to the host families included the full cost of board. This was disputed by the hosts, who claimed that it was insufficient to allow for payments for school meals or milk. Consequently during the first few months of the war, when evacuation was in full swing, not only were 60 per cent of children no longer receiving school milk, but also the number of free meals being served in schools was at its lowest for fifty years.[15]

Within a year, however, the Government recognised that it could not allow such a scandalous situation to continue, and from mid-1940 it was a matter of policy that the provision of school canteens for school children should be expanded, and the Board issued a circular to this effect. But progress was slow, although there was some development in parts of the North and the Home Counties where Yorkshire, Surrey, Middlesex and Berkshire each doubled or more than doubled its figures during 1941. As late as May 1941 (when the understandable confusion of the early months of the war should have long passed) about 25 per cent of LEAs in England and Wales were failing to provide solid meals on either a free or charged basis; and paid meals were provided by only 30 per cent of authorities.

In an attempt to accelerate the pace of provision, LEAs were given Board of Education permission to provide free milk and free or reduced-price meals 'solely on evidence of financial need', thereby relaxing the previous rule which demanded both medical and financial need to be proved. As a result, the number of children taking milk on any one day rose from around 2½ million in February 1941 to nearly 3½ half million (76.3 per cent of those attending school) in February 1946. Thus ended one of the most disgraceful of the Board's feeding policies dating from the Depression.

The real reason for the expansion of milk provision was motivated by four factors other than concern with children's welfare. These were: (i) the continuation of pre-war policy to improve distribution; (ii) as part of the programme of war-time food policy in the face of the German submarine blockade; (iii) to compensate for the reduction in the meat allowance in school canteens; and (iv) the practical difficulties in wartime of implementing the pre-war means-test criteria for eligibility. Similar considerations led to an improvement in the provision of school meals, and local authorities received Treasury grants to assist them with the cost. Unfortunately, rationing further undermined the nutritional value of the meals, especially the reduction in meat content. Nor was the scheme as universal as intended since, in 1942, forty-five out of 315 LEAs still had no canteen system, and the proportion of children fed at school was only 13 per cent, having risen from 3 per cent in 1939.[16]

None the less, throughout the remaining war years the situation gradually improved. Meat, sugar, jam and milk allowances were increased, perhaps partly in response to the Beveridge Report which influenced parliamentary opinion in favour of an improved nutritional diet for everyone. By the end of the war more than one-third of children were receiving meals in schools and over 70 per cent were having milk. At this time, eighty-nine LEAs were feeding more than 40 per cent of children in their areas, with Welsh rural authorities feeding the highest proportion and South-Eastern counties being generally above average.[17]

Where the nutritional standard is concerned, it is difficult to assess the position. Many authorities ceased to weigh and measure their children, and few continued to furnish the valuable special sections on nutrition in their SMO reports. Obviously the food shortages and maldistribution of resources during the first evacuation period tended to depress standards, but perhaps other factors countered these hindrances such as improved nutritive qualities of bread and flour, supplementary rations, and the expanding school meals and milk service. For what it is worth, the official view was that the nutritional standard of elementary-school children had 'almost certainly been improved' during the war.[18]

HEALTH AND WELFARE UNDER THE EDUCATION ACT, 1944

Prior to the Act, LEAs were compelled to provide elementary-school children with treatment for defects of teeth and eyes, minor ailments, enlarged tonsils and adenoids. Many authorities, however, provided more than these basic services and generally charged parents for all treatments. The situation changed with the passing of the Education Act, 1944. In determining the structure of the SMS, the Act made it a duty of LEAs to: (i) provide school meals and milk (the LEA could remit the charge for the meal in cases of hardship); (ii) provide medical and dental inspections (only one of the latter) for all children aged 2 to 15 in state schools; and (iii) either to provide or to secure free medical and dental treatment. Medical inspection was also made compulsory with parents being given the opportunity to be present at the inspection. Not only were school children compelled to undergo examination (unlike under the 1921 Education Act, which did not compel parents to submit their children for medical examination): but so too were pre-school children aged 2 and over. The Act also extended dental care to secondary schools. However, with the establishment of the National Health Service (NHS), 200 full-time dentists left the school service for general practice, and not until 1953 was the equivalent staff of 1945 employed. Nevertheless, under the Act the range of free services on offer was extended to include: minor ailments; child guidance; orthopaedics; ear, nose and throat; audiometry; speech therapy; orthoptics; remedial exercises and chiropody; and special investigation for rheumatism, asthma and enuresis.[19]

In addition LEAs had their duties of ascertainment of handicapped pupils widened into clearly defined categories: the blind and partially sighted, the deaf and partially deaf, the diabetic, the delicate, the educationally subnormal, the epileptic, the maladjusted, the physically handicapped, and speech defects. These definitions were based on educational considerations, so that only in cases where pupils required special education did they become 'handicapped'. The powers of assessment were extended beyond medical officers (though they remained extremely influential) to include teachers, psychologists and parents, and the final decision was to rest with the LEA.[20]

Further developments occurred in the SMS under the NHS Act, 1946, which renamed the SMS as the School Health Service (SHS), but kept it separate. LEAs were enabled to make arrangements with regional hospital boards and teaching hospitals for free specialist and hospital treatment for their children, and were obliged for the first time to make provision for health visitors to give advice on the care of young children. Broadly speaking, the NHS affected the SHS in two ways: since the whole population now had free access to general practitioners, the school service was no longer so important in referral and treatment of children; and, second, the transfer of school medical treatment to the NHS meant that the school service could concentrate on preventive work.

In the 1940s concern was expressed that MOHs and GPs were too widely separated by the gulf between preventive and curative medicine. The inter-war period had witnessed the growing importance of individual preventive medicine, which convinced doctors of the connections between the two forms of medical care. One of the Board's SMOs argued that the separation was damaging to child health. Others argued, not necessarily in contradiction, that the purpose of the SMS was not the detection of disease, but the rearing of a population which would 'escape' disease. 'Its great aim is to do what is possible to promote healthy development and the growth of full physiological vigour.'[21] These ideas were influential in the post-1945 era. With the establishment of the NHS and the 'Welfare State' everything seemed possible. The first signs that this was a delusion appeared in the 1950s, but in the late 1940s disenchantment was still some way off.

CONCLUSION

It should be now obvious that during the period 1918–45 there was no clear narrative of bodies and minds, but rather that these years were marked by contradictions and tensions which only began to be harmonized towards the end of the war. Similarly, the dualism of children as victims and threats existed in a domain of reality which was also marked by contradiction and tension as policy makers and reformers strove to arrive at new understandings based on the recognition of a more complex body–mind unity. By way of drawing out several of the principal themes of the period, let us begin with an assessment of the School Medical Service between 1918 and 1939.

The single most important characteristic of the inter-war SMS was the routine medical inspection, and from the earliest days doubts had been expressed as to whether this anthropometric basis would not distract SMOs from more important, practical work. There was a danger, warned critics, that the doctor would become a 'mere collector of statistics for sociologists of the next generation'. But Newman argued that such statistics would yield an 'exact knowledge of the physical and mental condition of the school-child population'.[1] However, the statistical approach failed, mainly in its own terms, for four reasons. First, the inspections were too brief. Six minutes were allotted for each one, but in practice it seems that one or two minutes was more usual. Second, merely to catalogue defects and diseases failed to provide an understanding of the health condition of individuals. Third, there was a lack of standardisation of the data – for example, with respect to malnutrition and dental care, and in the reporting of rickets, and treatment required for tonsils or adenoids. Similarly with TB and in identifying those in need of special schooling. Finally, the statistics could not reveal the huge differences between either social classes or regions.[2]

Thus the SMS was not centrally and intellectually committed to improving children's health since in order to do so would have required an understanding of the different social contexts in which children lived, as well as a recognition of the importance of their environment *per se*. At the national level no attempt was made to understand the relationship of the child's environment to its health, except to deny the influence of poverty or bad housing and to blame parental ignorance for many of the ills suffered by the children. Instead, the Service was committed to financial retrenchment for most of the period, to securing the regular attendance of pupils at school, to ensuring that they were physically and mentally competent to benefit from the lessons, and to gathering statistics emphasising the growth of the system. It was left to a minority of local SMOs and social scientists to struggle against the complacency of the official reports.

It is true that there was some improvement in the health of children

203

who, along with other age groups, benefited from a better diet, improved housing and sanitation, and the generally higher standard of living in the 1920s and 1930s.[3] But in searching out the meaning of health and welfare reform during the inter-war period it is helpful to bear in mind the comments of John Macnicol, the historian of the movement for family allowances. He has reminded us that 'the atmosphere in which these reforms [school meals and school medical inspection] were introduced had a profound influence on how they were subsequently operated. The concept of "national health" to emerge in the early twentieth century was primarily concerned with military and industrial efficiency, though not entirely.' Consequently, he continues, 'it is hardly surprising that in the inter-war years, when this militaristic fervour had waned and a vast army of unemployed provided a pool of surplus labour, there was less immediate concern over the health of future generations'. [4] It could be said, without for a moment underestimating the importance of notions of 'efficiency', that Macnicol overlooks a more subtle and less articulated Edwardian concern with children's 'national health' as a commodity for investment in a programme of evolutionary democractic capitalism. Notwithstanding this caveat, there was certainly a more confused set of priorities during the Depression than there had been prior to 1914.

The rhetoric of reform surrounding school meals and medical inspection was that they were necessary in order to allow children to take advantage of their educational opportunities; otherwise the available educational resources were being 'wasted'. In other words, what Macnicol calls 'financial wastage' was set against the monetary and political costs of introducing these child welfare services.[5] There is some debate as to whether or not Sir Robert Morant, the influential Permanent Secretary at the Board of Education in the early 1900s, and Sir George Newman, the Chief Medical Officer, looked on the reforms as first steps in a more comprehensive national health service. There is no doubt, though, that despite the confusion over 'National Health' priorities, both the Ministry of Health and the Board of Education continued to view school feeding and medical inspection and treatment as being for educational purposes and not for the relief of poverty which, they claimed, was the responsibility of the Poor Law and the Unemployment Assistance Board.[6]

In the opinion of Charles Webster, 'the pattern of welfare in depressed areas was subject to all the bewildering permutations of permitted variation'. Given that most services, such as school meals, were subject to the 50 per cent exchequer grant, while others, such as the extension of the maternity and child welfare feeding schemes, were entirely rate-provided, local authorities could only provide services within the framework of their rate-generated financial resources. Thus those areas most in need usually had the worst services: poor authorities could not raise sufficient funds to finance the services required by their child populations.[7] Yet behind this specific explanation for the failure of local authorities adequately to provide for the health and welfare of children, there was a more general and overtly political explanation. As John Boyd Orr, Director of the Rowett Research Institute, Aberdeen, wrote at the time: '. . . the Establishment put up the strongest possible resistance to informing the public of what the true position was regarding under-nourishment among their fellow citizens.'[8] To quote Macnicol again, 'the government steadfastly denied that there was any pressing need to raise the economic status of mothers and children'. At this level there was no confusion about priorities. When the pressure group, the Children's Minimum Council, pressed the Government to introduce free school meals in 1934, an internal memorandum from the Board of Education to the Prime Minister commented:

> this demand, like that for the larger children's allowances, is largely based on the assumption that the financial assistance to be given to the unemployed under the Government's Unemployment Bill is insufficient to enable them to feed their children adequately. This is an assumption the Government cannot accept.[9]

There were several reasons for this perspective, including problems of definition of malnutrition, the emphasis on 'educational' concerns within the School Medical Service, financial retrenchment, and the conservatism of many local authorities. The fundamental reason was more brutal: '. . . the government was clearly determined not to announce a minimum needs level in cash terms, for to do so would open the way to demands that a large section of the working class . . . should have their incomes brought up to such a level. This was something to be resisted at all costs.'[10] Political choices, then, were the ultimate determining factors in the health of children during the inter-war period.

When we look at the mapping out of the emotional world of children, it is evident that there existed a very different set of priorities among psycho-medics, however varied the objectives of particular interests within the professional and political groups involved. The movement towards an understanding of the child's mind and a recognition of social significance of 'maladjustment' was often hesitant and far from universally appreciated. But, once these new knowledges began to be grasped by reformers, educationalists, politicians and the caring professions, children were among those who found themselves more comprehensively observed.[11]

The educational debates of the 1920s and 1930s coincided with the work of the Child Guidance Council and its initial commitment to treat 'maladjusted, difficult, and delinquent children'. Not only was there the beginning of an intimate relationship between education and child psychiatry, but also the vocabulary and insights of the clinics began to filter into schemes for the treatment of juvenile delinquency, in the shape of 'the welfare of the child'. Child guidance, in all its different manifestations, always paraded itself as benign; it linked itself to 'progressive' concepts of welfare. The more overtly authoritarian and disciplinary functions of the CGC, in the form of influences derived from the CAMW and the NCMH, were less conspicuous. However, the concern with national mental health, and the psychiatric delineation of childhood's 'specific repertoire of disorders' were not without their political objectives, the majority of which were moving towards the creation of the healthy and emotionally mature family. The importance of the child guidance movement was in identifying maladjustment and in providing the network of practices by which, on the one hand, it could be treated while, on the other, individuals could be tutored to avoid reaching the stage where treatment became necessary. Hence the publication of such parental guides as Dr Emmanuel Miller (ed.), *The Growing Child and Its Problems* (1936), and the Home and School Council's *Advances in Understanding the Child* (1935).

The Children and Young Persons Act, 1933, was one of the first attempts at binding the work of psychologists such as Cyril Burt, through the ideas contained in his study, *The Young Delinquent* (1925), to the developing concept of welfare, but within the framework of the mind–body unity. (In the case of juvenile delinquents this unity was graphically illustrated by the photograph reproduced as the frontispiece to the book, showing a degenerate-looking older boy with a cigarette hanging from his lips.) Burt's insistence that much delinquency was merely an exaggerated example of 'childish naughtiness' reinforced the emerging view among reformers that the young people concerned required a form of attention other than that of straightforward penal punishment, physical or otherwise. The same kind of thinking underpinned the abolition of the distinction between reformatories and industrial schools – between depravation and deprivation. In effect, Burt and those who shared his views were arguing for the new welfare whose principal insight was that it consciously recognised the complexity of the social and political tasks confronting it. In this instance these touched on mental health, procreation among the working class, and familial cohesiveness and durability. Thus, for Burt and other 'progressives', combating crime in children called upon 'every side of social work'.

In such a scenario, the distinction between concepts of 'victim' and 'threat' lost much of its relevance in the welfarist language of the time. However, this should not blind us to the continuing distinction between these conditions for the individual children concerned. To take just one example, those evacuees who were unbilletable owing to emotional disturbance of one sort or another and who were objectively victims of their circumstances were turned into witnesses against their home communities, often the urban slums, and their families. The verdict delivered by professionals was that there existed a hitherto undisclosed and threatening sub-species of the working class: the problem family. As we shall see, this

206

was the start of a new twist in the long relationship between children, families, the caring professions and the State.

Although throughout the period 1918–45 children made guest appearances as 'victims' – usually of poverty, abuse, ignorance or neglect – their regular employment in the theatre of welfare was as threats in various guises: criminal, racial, social, mental and educational, albeit that the word was rarely used openly. Sometimes the threat was seen in relation to the present; sometimes to the future; more often it was both. The solution was nearly always portrayed in the language of investment: 'The neglected toddler in everyone's way is the material which becomes the disgruntled agitator, while the happy contented child is the pillar of the State.'[12]

Part IV

CHILDREN OF THE WELFARE STATE
1945–89

INTRODUCTION

By 1945 social policy for children had a complex history. Needless to say, children themselves had remained virtually silent during the making of this history. They had been figures in that familiar landscape of adult reform programmes, shuffled (sometimes humanely) from one area to another out of the way of the architects and builders seeking to construct new structures of administration in order to accommodate the changing concepts of welfare and the growing role of the State. In some respects little changed in the presentation of children after 1945. They continued to be seen as investments of one sort or another; their victim status remained marginal to the various social-policy agendas; and their identity as 'threats' remained well focused in the minds of many reformers, politicians and professionals. But it would be a mistake to confuse similarities with historical continuity. The perception of the welfare of children was not the same after 1945 as it had been in the inter-war period, and was markedly different from what it had been in the late-Victorian and Edwardian eras.

First a number of contradictions and tensions in the body–mind understanding of children had been resolved by the end of the 1930s, or at least were well on the way to being resolved, as we have seen, through progressive education, child guidance and the critical assessments made of the efficiency of the school meals and medical services. The mental hygiene approach of child guidance, in particular, with its insistence on the family context, had added a new and far deeper dimension to the design and objectives of social policy with respect to children and the governance of the population in the future. Second, the experience of evacuation served to dramatise many of the themes which had been implicit in inter-war social debate, notably the existence of the slum child (and family) with not only its frail verminous body but also its emotionally disturbed mind which often produced physical manifestations such as enuresis. In effect it was being officially realised that children required sensitive and sympathetic treatment and understanding. Third, the politics of the period brought forth what was consciously thought of as a 'Welfare State' in which citizens had evidence of their citizenship through their right to social and health services. This deliberate democratisation of citizenship had begun to be formulated during the war-time debates on post-war reconstruction with one eye on sustaining a healthy and growing population and the other on the growth of communism throughout Europe and the Empire. At the same time, there were also important economic considerations, as in the case of family allowances which were recommended in the Beveridge Report 'almost entirely' on economic grounds.[1]

The specific welfare of children was not given much more than an afterthought in these grand schemes, except with respect to problems likely to arise after the conclusion of evacuation. It was expected that as many as 10,000 children might be unable to return to their homes (in the event the figure was 1,500). The question was how should they be dealt with? The most appropriate agency seemed to be the Poor Law, but this would be politically unacceptable given its stigma. On the other hand, to exclude evacuees from the Poor Law 'and not do the same for others, of the same classes who are now under such care' was also deemed politically undesirable. In early 1944 the Ministry of Health circulated a paper entitled 'The Break-up of the Poor Law and the Care of Children and Old People' which proposed that all homeless children should be made the responsibility of local-authority children's committees. The Home Office saw the paper as an attempt by the Ministry to assume overall control for separated children, thereby lessening its authority in such areas. By the middle of 1944 two issues were beginning to be discussed: the nature of post-war childcare services and who should be responsible for them.[2]

In February 1944 the Women's Group on Public Welfare and the National Council for Maternity and Child Welfare sponsored a conference on the care and education of young children, with the intention of influencing policies then being discussed for the post-war period. Two of those in attendance were Lady Allen and Mary Stocks, and within a month Stocks wrote to the *Manchester Guardian* to call attention to the 'legion of lost children', and to request that an inter-departmental inquiry be established to inquire into the care of deprived children. The day after her letter was published, Lady Allen wrote to the Home Secretary and to the Minister of Education about the poor standards of residential care and the absence of a properly co-ordinated administration. Several weeks later, she wrote her famous letter to *The Times*, and by the end of August an all-time record was set with the publication of sixty letters discussing the issue. Numerous influential people supported the call for some kind of inquiry, as did an editorial in the newspaper. Lady Allen continued to write to various government departments as questions were asked in Parliament. On 3 November 1944, the House of Commons passed an all-party motion calling for an inquiry into conditions in residential homes for children. After a flurry of memorandums between departments, on 7 December the Government agreed to appoint a committee, which was finally established in March 1945.[3] Less than a month later 13-year-old Denis O'Neill died at the hands of his foster parents. This became a major scandal with the press in full cry with extensive reports, pictures and interviews. It was at this point that the Home Office appointed Sir Walter Monckton to conduct an inquiry into the death of the boy, which he completed by May 1945. The report indicted the absence of co-ordination between different authorities and social workers, and showed that the problem of childcare was not confined to residential conditions but to the whole system of administration.[4]

In the meantime Lady Allen, who was discovering that no one really knew anything about residential homes, wrote a pamphlet, *Whose Children?* The astonishing number of reviews and leading articles which it received is evidence of the popularity of the topic. The picture of conditions in the homes, the overwhelming majority of which were run by religious orders, as revealed by the pamphlet gave cause for concern. In general the staff were inexperienced and insensitive; the children were grouped together for administrative convenience rather than in accordance with their emotional and physical needs; there was an absence of play material for young children, and a prohibition on children having personal belongings. In some homes, 'spotless tidiness and the polishing of linoleum is a fetish'. In others there were appalling incidences of insensitivity and brutality made all the more depressing by the openness with which staff described them. Of children under 5 years old sitting silently in rows at meal-times, a matron declared: 'We like them to be quiet.' If the children wanted a second helping, they had to put their hands on their heads. When asked why a group of 3-year-olds were so silent, the reply was: 'They do not need to talk, everything is done for them.' Meals were usually eaten in compulsory silence, with force feeding by holding the nose for those who refused to eat a particular meal, followed by being put to bed in a dark room where they were forcibly put to rest by holding blankets over their heads. Boys who wet the bed were dressed in girl's knickers or tunics and made to walk up and down in front of the other children. In one home the 'cure' for bed-wetting was confinement for three weeks. If this failed, the child would be taken to the chapel where 'lying across the feet of a plaster Virgin, was a thin cane used on the little boys'. No wonder that even school teachers felt the children from the homes to be in a state of 'acute anxiety and insecurity'.[5] Lady Allen's findings were, however, merely the prelude to the more comprehensive and far more influential report of the committee appointed in 1945 under the chairship of Myra Curtis, the principal of Newnham College, Cambridge.

8

CHILD CARE POLICY

THE CURTIS REPORT, 1946

The Curtis Committee recognised its own importance when it claimed to be 'the first enquiry in this country directed specifically to the care of children deprived of a normal home life'. The Committee's findings focused on three areas: the absence of a single centralised authority responsible for deprived children, who were left to the charge of five different authorities; the lack of properly trained staff; and the insensitive and sometimes excessive discipline of the residential regimes.[1] The children were divided into several groups, the largest being those in the care of local-authority public assistance committees, as 'poor persons in need of relief'. These were either orphans or those who had been deserted by their parents, or who had mentally or physically ill parents who were either unable or unwilling to care for them. Other categories included those who came into care from the juvenile court, either as offenders or as in need of 'care or protection'; children who were either mentally or physically handicapped and were being educated away from home; war orphans and evacuees unable to return home for one reason or another; and children supervised by local authorities because they had been put into foster care by their parents or had been offered for adoption. The total number of children and young adolescents in care was 124,900.[2]

In its 'general impressions' the Report was 'far from satisfied' with provision for those coming into local-authority care. Where long-term provision was concerned, nurseries were found to be more progressive than other forms of residential accommodation for older children and for those boarded out (though several had very low standards). Curtis and her colleagues noted that the care of both these latter groups gave rise to public anxiety, and they shared this anxiety. However, they did not believe the overall position to be as bad as particular incidents had suggested, believing that conditions had improved since the 1930s, because 'the whole attitude of society to the treatment of children has been moving towards a gentler and more sympathetic approach'. The Committee was so keen to present

214

a balanced picture that the testimony of 'a very experienced inspector' was given prominence in support of the assertion that homes and persons responsible for children 'have shared in this development'. In consequence, no adverse conclusion was formed with respect to the general administration of childcare in 'any organisation or group of institutions'. Where homes fell below a satisfactory standard, it seemed that 'the defects were not those of harshness, but rather of dirt and dreariness, drabness and over regimentation'.

Nor did the Committee find any evidence of children being 'cruelly used in the ordinary sense', adding 'but that was perhaps not a probable discovery on a casual visit'. And there the matter was left. Witnesses who drew a 'very dark' picture of their treatment were ignored. It was, however, admitted by the Report that there were 'unimaginative methods' of child-rearing, and too little effort was made to develop the children's 'full capabilities'. Members also felt that there was a danger of 'harsh or repressive tendencies or false ideas of discipline' developing among those who were in charge of groups of children, who 'may suffer without the knowledge of the central authority'. There was a need for a proper code of conduct and for inspectors to enforce it. In many homes members noted 'a lack of personal interest in and affection for the children which we found shocking'. In such homes the child 'was not recognised as an individual with his own rights and possessions, his own life to live and his own contribution to offer . . . he was without the feeling that there was anyone to whom he could turn who was vitally interested in his welfare or who cared for him as a person'. Members found the effect of this neglect pathetically obvious in the behaviour of small children towards visitors, which exhibited itself as 'an almost pathological clamouring for attention and petting'. The effect on older children was to produce 'backwardness and lack of response and . . . habits of destructiveness and want of concentration'.[3]

Despite the reluctance of the Report to endorse examples of harsh or cruel discipline and its tendency, sometimes to the point of straining credibility, to conclude that discipline was nearly always reasonable and non-violent, its own chosen examples of punishment and disciplinary systems conflict with the complacency of its conclusions. It is true that the system was characterised by indifference and neglect rather than by overt cruelty. Children in workhouses, for example, even where physical care was adequate, had little experience of 'homeliness or provision for recreation'. The child's admission to Public Assistance Homes 'was often formal, cold and hurried, just at the moment when leisured kindness, warmth and affection were his main need'. The Report admitted that judging 'methods of up-bringing' proved to be the 'most difficult part' of its observations to 'estimate and summarise'. However, this did not prevent it from accepting the official view that in the Public Assistance Homes 'corporal punishment is strictly limited by statutory order'.[4]

In homes run by voluntary (usually religious) organisations, disciplinary methods were found to be 'negative and discouraging', though only in a few homes was it the case that 'caning and deprivation of liberty and food were necessary to maintain order'. In general, there was apparently no evidence of 'unduly harsh or cruel discipline', though 'signs of repression were evident in some Homes'. Corporal punishment with a cane 'was not often used'. Two sentences later, however, it was casually stated without comment that 'In other Homes . . . in which we heard about caning this punishment was given from time to time for "anti-social behaviour", wanton destructiveness, fighting and bullying'.[5] Obviously, the Committee here is accepting definitions and accounts provided by the administrators of the homes.

One of the most implausible claims made by the Report was that the discipline of approved schools was not 'much more severe than that of children's Homes'. Having suggested that discipline in the homes was more or less reasonable, the intention behind the claim seems to have been to reassure critics of the approved schools that they were not as brutal as had been alleged, despite the testimony of former residents and liberal staff. Moreover, with reference to all types of school and home, there appears to have been an exclusive reliance on information provided by the heads of the institutions and the inspection of punishment-books. The possibility that the records were inaccurate was never raised, nor was the crucially important issue of unauthorised and casual violence.[6]

Curtis was confident that the majority of children in homes were adequately reared. Within the limits of their resources the greater number of homes were 'reasonably well run from the standpoint of physical care'. The strongest criticisms were reserved for inadequate accommodation, equipment and staffing.[7] There was a widespread shortage of the right kind of staff, with the proper qualifications and training. The position of the matron or superintendent was particularly important, as was that of house-mother: 'On the personality and skill of these workers depends primarily the happiness of the children in their care.' In the past it had not been thought necessary to provide specialist training, and 'many of the children have suffered as a consequence'. Properly trained staff were also called for at local-authority headquarters to supervise boarding-out arrangements and to visit the children. Those in charge seemed often to be working 'in a rather remote and impersonal way'. On balance, the Committee felt that 'there is probably a greater risk of acute unhappiness in a foster home, but that a happy foster home is happier than life as generally lived in a large community'.[8]

The recommendations, of which there were sixty-two, were in three main areas: (i) central responsibility for all deprived children in one government

216

department; (ii) local responsibility to be exercised by new children's committees which would take over functions of various hitherto existing committees; and (iii) the appointment of local-authority Children's Officers, well qualified academically, with chief officer status and with their own department. The Committee also gave its authority to boarding-out (fostering) as the preferred form of care for deprived children, and recommended that 'a vigorous effort' be made by local authorities to extend the system. Emigration for deprived children was recommended to be allowed only on condition that the receiving government made the same kind of arrangements for their welfare and supervision as the Report was advocating for such children in this country.[9]

THE CHILDREN ACT, 1948

In March 1947 the Government officially accepted the recommendations of the Curtis Committee, and began to act on them even before the passing of the Children Act in June 1948. The main principles of the Act included the establishment of local-authority Children's Departments; a new emphasis on boarding-out in preference to residential homes; restoration of children in care to their natural parents; greater emphasis on adoption where appropriate; and the partial responsibility by the Children's Departments for young offenders.[10]

Under section 1 of the Act local authorities were given the duty to receive into care all people under 17 years old (the maximum age under the Poor Law had been 16) whose parents or guardians were unable to care for them and whose welfare required the intervention of the local-authority. The authorities were also to continue to carry out duties laid upon them by previous child protection legislation: to supervise children fostered for reward; to register adoption societies; to provide information to magistrates on the background of children appearing in juvenile courts; and to be responsible for children sent to remand homes, approved schools, or committed by the courts to local authorities in their role as 'fit persons'.[11] The establishment of a Children's Committee was made mandatory for local authorities, as was the appointment of the Children's Officer (the majority of whom would be women). The Act also specified that the voluntary services were to be fully integrated into the national system of childcare through registration and inspection. A new provision allowed for the award of grants to voluntary homes for improvements in premises and equipment. Finally, the legislation followed Curtis in giving a high priority to fostering as the best way of providing as near a normal home life as possible. Local authorities were given a duty to board out children in their care, and where it was not possible to do this 'for the time being' to maintain them in residential homes. The average boarding-out rate rose from 35 per cent in 1949 to a peak of 52 per cent in 1963, after which the percentage declined.[12]

The Act set out to establish new principles of childcare and to break with those of the Poor Law. The theme of the Act, distinguishing it from previous legislation, was spelled out in section 12, the first part of which stated that local authorities responsible for a child in care were 'to exercise their powers with respect to him so as to further his best interests and to afford him opportunity for the proper development of his character and abilities'. This referred to what was heralded as the individuality of the child and the duty of the local authority to respect and foster this characteristic. In the second part local authorities were told that in providing for children in their care they were to 'make use of facilities and services available to children in the care of their parents'. This was an attempt to prevent the segregation of deprived children from the community while simultaneously emphasizing the importance of the family.[13]

By June 1948, before the Act became operational, sixty local authorities had already appointed Children's Committees. The immediate consequence of the new service was a rise in the numbers of *deprived* children in care (which continued until 1965) by 18 per cent between 1949 and 1953 from 55,255 to 65,309. This is partly explained by the rise in the post-war birth rate, but it was also due to the wider interpretation being given to social needs. However, discharges from care also rose steadily, commensurate with numbers received. A Home Office study found that approximately two-thirds of children coming into care during a year would leave before the end of that year. The study showed that the proportion of those taken into care on a given day who would still be there after six weeks was 50 per cent, after one year 23 per cent, after two years 19 per cent and after five years 11 per cent.[14] Nevertheless, the rise in the number of short-stay cases proved to be a new area of work which had not been fully foreseen by the legislators. In this context Children's Officers almost immediately found themselves having to deal increasingly with family problems since prior to reception into care it was necessary to investigate home circumstances. Though these procedures were comprehensive and time-consuming, it was thought worthwhile as in the long term it might help to ensure that the children of 'problem' families broke out of the cycle.[15] Thus preventive care was considered an investment in properly functioning human capital.

While the Act had not been specific about the amount of time to be given to preventive measures, the Home Office issued a circular in 1948 stressing their significance.[16] The growing emphasis on this matter was the product of two influences. First, the childcare service responded not only to the evacuation experience, but also more specifically to the work of psychologists and psycho-therapists on the consequences of the separation of parent (especially the mother) and child. The idea, closely associated

218

with John Bowlby, Director of Child Guidance at the Tavistock Clinic, and known as maternal deprivation, was popularised in his seminal study, *Maternal Care and Mental Health* (1951). This warned of the dangers of separating small children from their mothers and families, and saw separation as having short- and long-term effects on the child's normal development. More broadly, Bowlby and his supporters argued that there were connections to be made between childhood, mental health and social life. Predictably, therefore, Bowlby praised the new childcare service, saying that it 'should be first and foremost a service giving skilled help to parents, including problem parents, to enable them to provide a stable and happy family life for their children'. In the absence of natural parental care, he approved of adoption and fostering (which was increasing) in so far as they were preferable to institutional care, but the former needed to be done in the first two months of the child's life, and the latter was liable to collapse. Second, residential care was expensive and, while fostering was much cheaper, too often the placements broke down. With such considerations in mind, the Parliamentary Select Committee on Estimates (1951–2) recommended that family difficulties be 'dealt with and remedied before the actual break-up of the home occurs', thereby reducing the number of children coming into care.[17]

So it was that these two factors, economic parsimony and psychological research, gave support to those Children's Officers who believed in the maintenance of the family. This approach was further encouraged by a Home Office circular, issued in 1950, and two years later the list of objectives of the Association of Children's Officers included the aim 'to encourage and assist in the preservation of the family'.[18] The possibility that children might be placed in jeopardy by the desire to keep families together was hardly ever raised. One of the few officials to do so, D. Watkins, the Children's Officer for Cornwall, wrote 'of the danger of forgetting the possible magnitude of his (the child's) suffering when he is left where he is'.[19] But the warning was unheeded, and by the mid-1950s prevention was the dominant philosophy in the majority of children's departments.

The Children Act was only one of a number of important Acts passed at the time. In addition to the Government's commitment to the maintenance of full employment, expressed in a White Paper, there were four significant Acts regarded as underpinning the creation of the Welfare State: the Family Allowances Act (1945), the National Health Service Act (1946), the National Insurance Act (1946) and the National Assistance Act (1948). The question often asked is whether or not the Act marked a turning-point in the care of deprived children. A semi-fictionalised account of the beginnings of the Children's Service, written by one of the first Children's Officers, reveals something of the contemporary optimism:

219

There was a tremendous crusading atmosphere about the new service. Our impression at the University was that the country outside was dotted with castle-like institutions in which hundreds of children dressed in blue serge were drilled to the sound of whistles. We were going to tear down the mouldering bastions. We were going to replace or reeducate the squat and brutal custodians. I had a dream of myself letting up a blind so that sunshine flooded into a darkened room as I turned, with a frank and friendly smile, to the little upturned faces within.[20]

There was certainly an aspiration to see deprived children integrated into the ideal of the Welfare State. It has been claimed that the Act was part of the desire 'to create a better life for the community as a whole after the bitterness of economic depression in the twenties and thirties and the nightmare of the Second World War'.[21] But was it?

THE CHILDREN ACT, THE FAMILY AND THE STATE

Although the growing emphasis on preventive care has been mentioned, if we are to understand and interpret the Children Act, and much else besides in the area of child welfare in the late 1940s and throughout the 1950s, we must look more closely at the creation of the new relationship between the State and the family. This was implicit in the Home Office statement stressing the importance of family identity:

To keep the family together must be the first aim, and the separation of a child from its parents can only be justified when there is no possibility of securing adequate care of a child in his own home.[22]

There were four reasons which explain why the family should have come to be seen as so necessary for the effective care of children, whether they be deprived or living in a normal domestic situation. These same reasons also illustrate some of the influences at work on both the Curtis Committee and the shaping of the Act.

First, there was a growing concern about the reproductive rate of the population. In his report of 1942, Beveridge warned that at its present rate 'the British race cannot continue'. This was followed in 1944 by the establishment of the Royal Commission on Population and a report published by Mass Observation in 1945 which saw the birth rate as 'the coming problem for Western Civilisation'. When the Royal Commission reported in 1949, it saw the decline as threatening both 'the security and influence of Great Britain' and the 'maintenance and extension of Western values'.[23] There appeared to be a clear need for a programme of pronatalism, which would include advice on contraception, measures to avoid stillbirths and infant perinatal mortality, family allowances and income tax relief. As an adjunct to these inducements, special services for mother and child were also to be organised.[24]

Second, the history of public child care, as revealed by Lady Allen and the Curtis Report, in emphasizing the need for more *personal* care of individual children reflected the influence of Bowlby and Anna Freud, among others, on understanding of what was needed for the healthy emotional development of children. This was evident in the Curtis Report, which had commented critically on the absence of personal affection for children who exhibited 'an almost pathological clamouring for attention and petting'. However, 'where individual love and care had been given' their behaviour 'was quite different'.[25]

Third, and closely related, there were several interwoven developments beginning with the impact of the child guidance movement in emphasising the importance of childhood as a formative period and the necessity for it to have a stable environment. There was also an increasing willingness on the part of officials at the Board of Education and in social services departments to refer to psychological knowledge in the treatment of children and young adolescents, as witnessed in, for example, the growth of the school psychological service which took for granted the relationship between the child, the school and the family. Broadly speaking, interest in the psychological condition of childhood reinforced the idea of the properly functioning family, 'a therapeutic agent' as the perfect environment for the healthy development of children in the post-war democracies. Furthermore, this view was propounded by psychiatric social workers who were often heads of social work training and, therefore, in a position to encourage their students to share the same outlook.[26]

Fourth, the social experiences of the war exerted numerous influences. The effects of evacuation, with its revelations about the urban poor, coupled with the belief that many parents had failed to maintain adequate standards of childcare, all contributed to the concept of the 'problem family'. While the parents were condemned for their alleged failures, the view was also expressed that with better social services, financial provision and sympathetic assistance parents, especially mothers, could be helped towards responsible and mature behaviour. Another war-time influence was the disintegration of many families as a result of absent fathers, blitzed homes, dead relatives, demographic movement into hostile communities, illegitimacy, and the struggle to rebuild relationships on the return to normality. At the same time, the evacuation experience demonstrated what appeared to be the extraordinary tenacity and resilience of the family as mothers and children gradually returned from the reception areas to their old homes. Such families, it was thought, should be given assistance, to help them to overcome their difficulties and to continue to provide adequate childcare. Beveridge, always in favour of promoting effective individualism, had declared it a principle that children should have the necessities for life provided in such a way 'as to preserve parental responsibility as completely as possible'.[27]

For all these reasons families could no longer be left to fend for themselves, nor could their individual members who fell into difficulties. It was significant that the lesson of the death of Denis O'Neill was not that families could be murderous environments, but that they required help and encouragement. The Children Act was not only one of a number of welfare Acts at the time, which were themselves enabling legislation, but also it was part of the attack on Beveridge's five giants of want, disease, squalor, ignorance and idleness. Social security, full employment, family allowances, and health services were to help individuals to become citizens of the community. And in helping individuals these provisions were intended to assist families to withstand temporary setbacks and to fulfil their obligations to one another and to society.

DEPRIVATION AND DEPRAVATION: INGLEBY AND THE FAMILY

The euphoria that had existed in childcare circles after the 1948 Act soon fell by the wayside as anxiety increased over the rising level of juvenile delinquency. By the 1950s it was fully realised that public childcare was much more complex than had been appreciated, not only in the administrative sense involving local-authority politics (whose influence should never be underestimated in social-policy practice), but also because the nature of the 'problem families' from which the children came was now recognised to be a web of ambiguities and ambivalences requiring long-term intervention by psychodynamically trained social workers.[28] Further complications arose from the fact that there were differences of opinion within the developing childcare service as to what constituted the welfare of the child. While the concept of preventive and remedial care continued to dominate social-work thinking, it was increasingly asked what was the purpose of these preventive procedures? Moreover, it was asked who was being protected from whom? And who most needed protection?

During the course of the debate notions of prevention and protection in childcare underwent subtle reinterpretations as the focus fell on what was said to be the need of society to protect itself from juvenile delinquents who were identified as deprived children. Thus once again, as in the 1920s and 1930s, the link between *depravation* and *deprivation* was reasserted. However, war-time and early post-war studies on separation of children from their families, and the new category of 'problem families' had planted a much more informed interest among politicians, social theorists and social workers in the relationship between the two conditions.[29] The concept of prevention in local-authority Children's Departments eventually triumphed

222

but, as Jean Packman has shown, it was achieved at the cost of relating it to strategies for combating juvenile delinquency through family medition.[30] The first assertively new emphasis was demonstrated in the remit and report of the Ingleby Committee which, after pressure from the Magistrate's Association, social workers, the Council for Children's Welfare, and the Fisher Group, was appointed by the Home Office in 1956 and reported in 1960. The terms of reference of the Committee, which reveal the reappearance of an old anxiety, were to inquire into, and make recommendations on (a) the working of the law in England and Wales relating to: (i) 'juveniles brought before the courts as delinquent or as being in need of care or protection or beyond control; (ii) the constitution, jurisdiction and procedure of juvenile courts; (iii) the remand home, approved school and approved probation home systems; (iv) the prevention of cruelty to, and exposure to moral and physical danger of juveniles; and (b) (described as an after thought by a leading Fabian social-policy analyst) whether local authorities responsible for child care under the children Act, 1948 . . . should . . . be given new powers and duties to prevent or forestall the suffering of children through neglect in their own homes.' It was apparent to all concerned that the main focus would be on juvenile delinquency rather than on the prevention of cruelty and neglect of children.

The Ingleby Report, 1960

The Report paid little attention to whether or not the children's services needed new powers, for only ten of its 179 pages were devoted to the issue, and just four of 125 recommendations concerned the prevention of cruelty to children. Nor was there any recommendation that the powers advocated be imposed. Instead, the Report recommended the following: (i) a 'general duty' should be laid upon local authorities to protect children from suffering in their own homes, and they should be given the power to carry out preventive casework and to 'provide the material needs that cannot be met from other sources'; (ii) widespread arrangements were to be made for the detection of families at risk; (iii) local authorities were to be under a statutory obligation to submit their schemes for the prevention of children suffering in their own homes for ministerial approval; and (iv) there should be 'further study' by the Government and others of 'the various services concerned withthe family'.[31] The Report was met with a general feeling of disappointment among those involved in the child care services. In the words of one expert at the time, it was 'respectable and cautious, lacking all sense of urgency and offering no vision for the future structure of the social services – in fact conservative.'[32]

Ingleby was primarily concerned with the working of the juvenile court system. From the third page of the Report, the importance of children in trouble was stressed as an organising principle of investigation. It summarised the changes in different areas of social policy since the end of the war, showing how by 1956 the overall picture of 'the problems covered by our terms of reference was not altogether discouraging'. During the course of the committee hearings, however, juvenile delinquency increased so that by 1958 the rates for the 14–17 age group were 47 per cent higher than in 1954. The rate had previously risen just after the war, peaking in 1951. The explanation then focused on the upheaval of war, the absence of fathers, the loosening of parental discipline and the accompanying freedom for young people. Such explanations seemed irrelevant by the later 1950s. Thus the Committee felt it necessary 'to reconsider our approach to the whole question'. In the past the main problem had been to identify the most effective treatment of delinquents; the emphasis 'has been on cure'. In the future, however, the focus should be on 'the more difficult problem of prevention'.[33]

One of the most significant features of the Report was the link it established (or reiterated in view of the 1933 legislation) between neglect (deprivation) and delinquency (depravation). The terms of reference had assumed the existence of such a link, but Ingleby made the connection explicit, claiming that it was not sufficient to protect children from 'neglect' (which included exposure to physical, moral or mental danger or deprivation), for if they were to be prevented from becoming delinquent 'something more positive is required. Everything within reason must be done to ensure not only that children are not neglected but that they get the best upbringing possible.' Parents had a 'primary responsibility' for helping their children to become 'effective and law abiding citizens by example and training and by providing a stable and secure family background in which they can develop satisfactorily. Anything which falls short of this can be said to constitute neglect in the widest sense.' Children who were *deprived* of this upbringing were exposed to the temptations of delinquency. Moreover, in making the connection between deprivation and depravation, the emphasis was placed on a positive form of prevention, which included not simply parental education, but also 'the duty of the community to provide through its social and welfare services the advice and support which such parents and children need . . . in considering whether local authorities responsible for childcare should be given new powers and duties . . . we have had this positive aspect of the problem constantly in mind'.[34]

The Report, which in some senses portended the uncertainties and confrontations of the 1960s, promoted three themes, none of which was original: juvenile delinquency *was* a serious social problem; the deprived child often went on to become the depraved child; and courts and social services should aim not only to 'cure' the delinquent, but also to prevent the child from entering on the path to delinquency. This sequence of connections led to the family as the source of the conditions from which delinquency emerged: 'It is the situation and relationships within the family which seem to be responsible for many children being in trouble.' ('Trouble' became the catch-all category since it was defined as 'delinquency or anything else'.) The Report continued: 'It is often the parents as much as the child who need to alter their ways, and it is therefore with family problems that any preventive measures will be largely concerned.'[35]

This was really a call for an extension of the provisions of the 1948 Act which dealt with children living away from their parents, or those who were orphaned, to include children living with their parents.[36] But now the focus was more coherently on the role of families preparing their children for citizenship, and their ability to achieve this end. Consequently the new objective was for the various social services concerned with the family to be unified into a family service.[37] Ingleby was the first of a series of documents reiterating the view that forms of moral and physical neglect were the antecedents of criminal delinquency. This emphasis was especially conspicuous in the Labour Party's *Crime: A Challenge to Us All* (1964), and in two important White Papers: *The Child, the Family, and the Young Offender* (1965) and *Children in Trouble* (1968). Nowhere was much account taken of cruelty to children, except marginally in relation to the creation of delinquency.

Ingleby and the welfare model

The emphases on preventive social work, the link between delinquency and neglect, and the encouragement of a family social service were couched in the language of 'welfare' as opposed to that of the 'judicial'.[38] However, Ingleby felt that these two 'jurisdictions' posed a problem of reconcilability. After summarising the development and objectives of the juvenile court, in particular that it should have 'the welfare of the child before it', the Report acknowledged that the jurisdiction appeared to be based on principles 'that are hardly consistent'. While the court remained a criminal court, with a modified form of criminal procedure and with more or less the law of evidence, the requirement 'to have regard to the welfare of the child, and the various ways in which the court may deal with an offender, suggest a jurisdiction that is not criminal'. The problem was how to reconcile these two principles: '. . . criminal responsibility is focused on the allegation about some particular act isolated from the character and needs of the defendant, whereas welfare depends on a complex of personal, family and social considerations.'[39]

The Committee recommended maintaining the principle that allegations against juveniles had to be proved in a court of law, and raising the minimum age of criminal responsibility from 8 to 12. In its dealings with younger children, the court should move away 'from the conception of criminal jurisdiction'. All younger children who had committed an offence and all children who were in need of care or protection or who were beyond control should be brought to court as 'being in need of protection or discipline'. The powers of the court for dealing with these children were to be widened to include detention orders for remand homes or attendance centres, and payment of compensation. Parents were to be involved in the proceedings, and the court was to 'be at pains' to explain to them and to the child what it was doing and why, 'so that they will be able to accept the court's decision as reasonable and appropriate, and become willing to co-operate in carrying it out'.[40] This was an important feature of the strategy. It encouraged families to be willing contributors to their own surveillance.

Clearly the Committee were trying to create a new balance between criminal procedure, welfare procedures within the precincts of the court and the family services outside the court. The intention was to involve parents and children more intimately by drawing particular attention to 'discipline', to parental responsibility and to the inculcation of a moral duty on the part of all concerned to accept the decision of the court. In order to create this new balance, however, the courts and the social services were given powers to probe deeper into the behaviour of children. Furthermore, and revealingly, the Committee felt that all children under 12 who came before the court did so for 'the same basic reason', namely that they were in need of 'protection or discipline'.[41] The implication being that there was not much difference between the two. Thus being in need of protection for any reason was equated with being in need of discipline. In its pursuit of the welfare dimension the Committee and its witnesses were perverting the notion of welfare. Or were they?

The apparent contradiction between the welfare and the justice/punishment orientations has been the subject of much debate. But in terms of Ingleby, and the subsequent legislation, the contradiction hardly affected the objectives of the policy-makers. Since the inter-war period juvenile courts had increasingly become places where a combination of procedures, interests and social-service objectives jostled together in search of a means of incorporating the child, the parents, the family and the local community in the pursuit of individual responsibility and collective security through healthy personal relations. The significance of this approach can be understood by bearing in mind the verdict of Michel Foucault: 'the sentence that condemns or acquits is not simply a judgment of guilt, a legal decision that lays down punishment; it bears within it an assessment of normality and a technical prescription for a possible normalisation.'[42] The juvenile court, then, was concerned solely with neither punishment nor welfare but with 'normalization', that is, the return of the young person, in a thoroughly integrated form, to the community.

Similarly, in his *The Policing of Families*, Jacques Donzelot has argued that the two jurisdictions within the juvenile legal system – the judicial and the welfare – are part of the same performance. What he calls the 'old market of children' drew upon 'monastic and military techniques, linked to familial and religious, police and judicial authority'. The new 'looked to medicine, psychiatry, and pedagogy for its methods', employing, for example, 'educational screening and canvassing by social workers'.[43] As 'welfare' permeated and influenced the judicial process, so the principle of the welfare of the child – through the social services co-operating with the court – *extended* the judicial into the social life of children (and their families). There was little or no conflict between the principles, except perhaps at the level of ritual and symbol. Their forms differed, but their purposes were very similar. The two jurisdictions ensured that there was no escape for the child from the adult eye: its behaviour was surveyed and interpreted and categorised within the contexts of punishment (judicial) and treatment (welfare) which appeared as contradictory, while in reality being complementary. Both are locked doors as far as children are concerned. We shall return to this when we examine the legislation of the 1960s. For the moment it is worth observing that in retrospect Ingleby proved to be something of a watershed in the growth and legitimation of welfare practices at the national and local level throughout the 1960s.[44] Far from 'perverting' the notion of welfare, as suggested above, in building on the Children and Young Persons Act, 1933, Ingleby consolidated a politically acceptable interpretation of it.

THE CHILDREN AND YOUNG PERSONS ACTS, 1963 AND 1969

The 1963 Act

Although the 1963 Act was primarily concerned with delinquency and the juvenile court system, section 1 gave local authorities the specific powers they had been seeking in order to practise preventive social work:

> It shall be the duty of every local authority to make available such advice, guidance and assistance as may promote the welfare of children by diminishing the need to receive children into care or keep them in care . . . or to bring children before a juvenile court; and any provisions made by a local authority . . . may . . . include provision for giving assistance in kind or, in exceptional circumstances, in cash.[45]

This was the go-ahead for local-authority children's departments actively to 'promote the welfare' of children through practical assistance.[46] However, as this was to proceed within the family, in many respects, the client group ceased being children and became families, especially mothers.[47] All the same, the 1963 Act provided the children's departments with the opportunity to present themselves as the natural authorities with respect to children and juveniles, but only by aligning themselves with the Ingleby focus on the link between depravation and deprivation. Crime could be prevented, they argued, by intervening in the families of deprived children.[48]

Ingleby provided the spark to ignite the enthusiasm of preventive work in relation to delinquency, but the fuse had been set much earlier, in 1948, by J. B. Priestley, among others, in his preface to a study of neglected children. After outlining the growth of welfare provision and the array of services to deal with delinquency, he wrote:

> but while there are neglected children, who may easily grow up to hate society, we are locking stable doors after vanished horses. If we can rescue the child from his feeling of isolation and despair, we can not only give that child some security and happiness (and nothing, of course, could be better worth doing than that), but we can also begin to free the community from the strain of trying to turn into good citizens great numbers of men and women who were thoroughly warped long ago in infancy.[49]

Aside from the parenthesis which, despite the rhetoric, underlines the insignificance of the child's security and happiness as a motive, this points towards the importance attached to the creation of a stable community with emotionally healthy adults. (Emotionally healthy children were also necessary, but their future adult status was always a crucial factor in determining policy.)

Other relevant parts of the Act dealt with new definitions of 'care and protection' in line with Ingleby's recommendations for children in need of discipline; grounds for local authorities assuming parental rights were extended; the age of criminal responsibility was raised from 8 to 10; and certain changes in court procedures were introduced to clarify matters for the child. Further measures included use of approved schools and after-care; and the tightening-up of regulations governing employment of children.[50]

The Children and Young Persons Act, 1963, expressed the essence of the relationship between young people and adult society throughout the 1960s, namely that in varying presences the former posed a serious social and criminal threat to the latter. There were other intervening strands to the relationship but this was its most identifiable characteristic. Once having established the nature of the relationship, based as it was on a 'threat', the question or questions arose how to understand it and how to counter it. In part politicians, social scientists, pedagogues and social workers could easily refer to the progress of psychiatry and schooling in dealing with the problem of childhood and youth, and to the growth of the social services, notably the childcare service since 1948. This process has been identified as therapeutic, since 'therapy' of different kinds was used in categorising, preventing, curing and 'punishing' deviance whether it be social, psychological or criminal. By the 1963 Act, the therapy was being extended from children in care to include whole families with dependent children. The process began long before 1963, but the Act confirmed its legitimacy.[51]

The crisis

In 1948 the Criminal Justice Act had introduced remand centres, attendance centres and detention centres; provided financial backing for probation homes and hostels; and abolished penal corporal punishment. According to *The Times*, the guiding principle of the Act was 'that there must be no despair of humanity'. The Act, wrote *The Times* on another occasion, derived from 'a common stock of liberal thought to which men of all parties and of none have contributed'.[52] In this atmosphere, and throughout the period from the early 1950s through to the 1960s, the childcare service developed a strong sense of professional identity and was well represented in the emerging unified social-work profession and in the Home Office Children's Division. Furthermore, senior figures in the Service were involved in shaping the 1969 legislation. From the mid-1960s, however, the welfare consensus, around which children and family services had been established and grew, began visibly to dissolve. Geoffrey Pearson describes what happened: '. . . when the highly specific conditions changed, so the faith of the counsellors entered a period of convulsion. In particular the forgotten questions of power, social structure and social class posed themselves. Social work had entered its radical hour.'[53] What had brought about this radical hour, and how did it relate to the 1969 Act?

One influential factor was juvenile crime, which had been expected to decline in post-war society. However, after a lull, it began to climb again in the mid-1950s and continued to do so up to halfway through the 1960s. By 1961 the proportion of indictable offenders under 17 was 107 per cent more than in 1938, in 1963 it was 125 per cent, and in 1965 the proportion had risen to 133 per cent. By 1964 the Home Office was writing about 'the Evil of Delinquency'. The root source of this anxiety was the perception of working-class youth as posing a problem in the post-war period. These youths, it was claimed, threatened the 'British way of life'. Similarly, the new cultural icons of clothes and leisure pursuits, especially as personified by the 'Teddy Boys' in the mid-1950s and the 'teenagers' in later years, seemed to be direct challenges to discipline and respect for authority. One academic claimed that the crime wave was 'associated with certain forms of dress and other social phenomena'.[54] Delegates at the Conservative Party Conference in 1958 expressed similar fears, referring to 'this sudden increase in crime and brutality which is so foreign to our nature and our country' and to the 'make-believe gangsters strolling about the streets as if they are monarchs of all'. Conference participants had no doubt about the reasons for this deluge of violence: the 'lack of parental control, interest and support'; the 'sex, savagery, blood and thunder' in films and on television; and the 'smooth, smug and sloppy sentimentalists who contribute very largely to the wave of crime'; no wonder young people were 'no longer frightened of the police, they sneer at them'.[55] There was a certain irony in the choice of the 'Teddy Boy', with his Edwardian dress, being represented as one of the architects of social change by Conservative critics lamenting that Britain 'was not what it used to be'.

More serious critics than Conservative Party Conference-goers were also disturbed by British youth. The BMA published a pamphlet in 1961, *The Adolescent*, which argued:

> The society in which today's adolescents find themselves is one of bewildering change ... the whole face of society has changed in the last 20 years ... a decrease in moral safeguards, and the advent of the welfare state has provided a national cushion against responsibility and adversity.[56]

The standards of affluence were said to be particularly undermining of moral fibre; everywhere there seemed to be 'moral decay, uncertainty and dissatisfaction'; 'not poverty, but unaccustomed riches seems an equally dangerous inducement to wild behaviour, even crime'.[57] Another report noted that young people had 'too much pocket money and too little discipline'. In T. R. Fyvel's *The Insecure Offenders* (1961) there could be found the by now familiar juxtaposition of 'the law-abiding England of pre-1940' with 'the new juvenile crime', 'the new rebels', 'the new generation of indifferent parents', 'a new type of violence' and 'the new state of insecurity'. By 1960, he wrote, 'juvenile delinquency had for the first time in Britain become elevated to the status of a national problem'.[58] The bulk of the critical commentaries was directed at adolescents rather than at children, but the popular commentators were unconcerned with subtle distinctions between children, especially older children and adolescents. Moreover, the critical assault had no difficulty in including children in its barrage of abuse, for they, too, it was assumed, had too much pocket money, too little discipline, and were infected with the lack of respect for authority that in the eyes of the moral evangelists seemed to mark out the times.

It was in the early days of this climate that the Ingleby Committee heard evidence and produced its Report, after which came the other reports and White Papers, the combined result of which was the collision of what Packman calls 'two contradictory notions of the juvenile delinquent': 'one regarded him as a dependent victim of circumstance whose offence was a cry for help and who therefore needed care and treatment; the other saw him more as a miniature adult with free will and a keen sense of "right", "wrong" and natural "justice", which must be protected by due process of law and if necessary dealt with by control and discipline'.[59] The majority of influential voices (liberal Fabian left-of-centre conservatives) thought that family circumstances and relationships were deeply significant in explaining juvenile delinquency. The Longford Report (1964), for example, stated that 'it is a truism that a happy and secure family life is the foundation of a healthy society and the best safeguard against delinquency and anti-social behaviour'.[60]

The Children and Young Persons Act, 1969

The 1969 Act was modelled on the Labour Party White Paper *Children in Trouble* and, while representing a compromise between a number of competing recommendations, was very much in the mould of incorporating 'welfare' into 'classical justice'. The paper reflected the progressive thinking of the Home Office Children's Inspectorate: '... professional casework for deprived families, delinquency and neglect being a mere symptom of deprivation, an awareness of the contribution of social deprivation and a commitment to de-institutionalisation.'[61] Briefly, the aim of the Act was to substitute non-criminal care procedures in place of criminal procedures for the 10–14 age group, and to encourage a more liberal use of non-criminal care proceedings for the 14–17 age group. The main clauses involving children (those aged 14 and below) were: (i) raising the age of criminal responsibility from 10 to 14; and (ii) voluntary agreements between parents and social workers to decide 'treatment' without a court appearance, in appropriate cases. Other clauses included (i) using care proceedings for older adolescents; (ii) mandatory consultation by police with social services prior to prosecution of 14–17 year olds; and (iii) Approved School and Fit Persons orders to be replaced with care orders. In general social workers were given power to vary the disposition orders made by courts; and, within the limits of particular orders, social workers rather than magistrates determined the most appropriate form of treatment.[62] In the words of Nikolas Rose, the Act was intended to represent 'the high point of therapeutic familialism as a strategy for government through the family'.[63]

The juvenile court was retained with its dual justice and welfare functions. The intentions were to reduce the number of young persons appearing before the court; and to minimise the differences in the treatment of offenders and non-offenders, both in the court and in the provision of their care facilities. The reduction in the number of juveniles appearing in court was to be achieved by strengthening the intervention process undertaken by children's departments under section 1 of the 1963 Act. This in turn was to be accomplished by a new 'family service', established through the remit of the Local Authority Social Services Act, 1970. As Jean Packman observes, the 1969 Act assumed the restructuring of the personal social services in much the same way as the Beveridge Report in the 1940s had assumed full-employment policies and a National Health Service.[64]

The Act attempted to keep down the number of *offending* children aged between 10 and 14 from appearing in court by substituting care proceedings for criminal prosecution. In addition to the offence, however, it had to be shown that the child was 'in need of care or control which he is unlikely to receive unless the court makes an order under this section'. Thus the court could only intervene if it could be shown that the offender's home situation was unsatisfactory. If it could be improved on a voluntary basis, then there were no grounds for care proceedings and the offender need not be brought before the juvenile court. Both offenders and non-offenders would be dealt with by the social workers from the new social services departments. The Act aimed to make the court 'a place of last resort' by bringing a number of interventions to bear upon the child: wherever possible offenders would either be cautioned by the police, attended to by social workers or teachers, or be admitted into care under the Children Act, 1948. The court was to be kept for the 'chronic delinquent' who had failed to respond to these measures, and whose home environment was considered to be beyond voluntary assistance.[65]

In the treatment of offenders measures were to be similar to those used for non-offenders; punitive sanctions were lessened, and new methods were introduced. Approved schools and probation hostels became 'community homes'; adolescents aged 15 and 16 were no longer eligible for borstal training; attendance and detention centres were to be phased out to be replaced by forms of 'intermediate treatment'. There was to be an emphasis on adventure training of the 'Outward Bound' variety, community service, club activities, and for young offenders the old 'probation order' was to be replaced by a 'supervision order', applicable to both offenders and non-offenders. All children under 14 and those between 14 and 17 not already on probation were to be supervised by social workers (who were seen as crucial to the success of the welfare model of juvenile justice). The intention was further to remove young offenders (except for a hard core) from all aspects of the penal system.[66]

Jacques Donzelot has written of the juvenile court that it 'administers children' over whom hangs the threat of punishment. The rituals of intervention and preventive action aim 'at encircling the offending boy instead of stigmatizing him in an ostentatious way'. The system allows the guilty child ' "his chance" by sentencing him only to measures of control. In another sense, by obliterating the separation between the assistancial and the penal, *it widens the orbit of the judicial to include all measures of correction*'. The juvenile court, he says, does not so much pronounce judgement on individual crimes; 'it examines individuals'. It is not a minor jurisdiction, but rather 'the mainstay of a tutelary complex'. It occupies 'a pivotal position . . . between an agency that sanctions offenses . . . and a

232

composite group of agencies that distribute norms'.[67] He is writing here about social workers and their institutions acting as guardians of sets of values and as the inculcators of approved forms of personal and collective behaviour.

This is very close to being an accurate description of the ethos and procedures gradually being introduced throughout the 1950s and 1960s in the juvenile legal system. The expanding role of the social worker in childcare and in the newly developing family social services was integral to the juvenile court becoming the 'junction point of the various social-work practices'; moreover, it became 'the privileged arena for registering the interrelationships between the practices – penal, educational, assistential and psychiatric – which come to bear on the child and on the family'.[68] In effect, children – offenders and non-offenders – who came within the orbit of social services (including the court) found themselves under constant observation accompanied by constant judgement; they were continually having to prove themselves citizens. However, they were not alone in being observed and judged, for they were seen from the perspective of their relationship with their parents (in particular their mother), which meant that the social services' intervention more often than not focused on the failings of the family, as in the unhygienic and unhealthy nurturing of children, failure to send the child to school, inadequate moral environment, sickness of parents, desertion of children, and so on.

The 1969 Act, however, was not implemented in its entirety, for in 1970 the Labour government lost the election to the Conservatives who were developing a different policy on crime, one that made 'welfare' completely subservient to 'justice'.[69] The characteristics of the *classical* justice model are: proportionality of punishment and crime; determinate sentences; no judicial or administrative discretion; equality in sentencing; and protection of rights through due process. Those parts of the Act which were implemented included new provisions about care proceedings; the replacement of approved school orders and fit person orders with care orders; and new provisions on supervision and intermediate treatment. On the other hand, it was announced that

> The age for prosecution will not be changed; children from ten upwards will remain liable to criminal proceedings. The courts will retain their present powers to order borstal training, to commit to junior detention centres and to order attendance at junior attendance centres. Probation orders will be replaced by supervision orders for those under 17; but courts will retain complete discretion to select probation officers as supervisors for children of 10 upwards in both care proceedings and criminal proceedings.

The Government declared that it did not intend to raise the minimum prosecution age above 12 (nor did it intend to limit prosecution of 14–17-

233

year-olds). Furthermore, existing forms of treatment were to be retained until it considered adequate alternative measures were fully available.[70]

The Act quickly became controversial, drawing criticism from virtually all the professional groups: magistrates, lawyers, police, approved school and remand home staff, and social workers. It was originally intended to be a compromise piece of legislation, with the goal of a less punitive approach to offenders. The Conservative government's interference with its implementation disturbed the balance. As one observer commented: '. . . the lesson is clear: tamper with a complex structure and all sorts of strains and defects are created'.[71] Moreover, the fact that prosecution of children under 14 continued, with social-work reports on the family presented to the courts, meant that social workers became part of the sentencing system. In this respect, court procedures devalued the family's responsibility.[72] Despite the frustration of some of the reformers' aims, the number of children (under 14) appearing in court did decline as the police, in an unanticipated move, increased their cautioning procedure. In Devon, for example, in the early 1970s, over 70 per cent of juvenile offenders were cautioned each year. This tended to shift the balance in out-of-court action away from social workers in favour of the police.[73]

At the centre of the 'struggle between the old and new philosophies of treatment', stood the care order. This was seen by many magistrates as undermining the judiciary (themselves) in favour of the executive (social workers). The former alleged that the latter ignored their intentions in making care orders by removing any punitive aspects of the order and returning the child to its own home rather than to, say, a community home. But this difficulty was exacerbated by the failure to provide a number of alternative forms of residential accommodation to borstal and remand centres. Indeed, where appropriate, custodial measures were used more frequently, ensuring that they were far from being the 'last resort' as envisaged by the reformers of the 1960s.[74]

The 1969 Act accepted the reformers' argument that a link existed between delinquency and family stability, and that 'intervention' by social workers offered the best hope of reducing delinquency rates (and also of helping the family to create its own stable environment). However, even before the end of the 1960s this view was being challenged, and by the mid-1970s there was a counter-argument to the effect that in some urban areas more than half of all persistent offenders came from apparently 'normal' families and, therefore, the search for the causes of delinquency should move to the schools and the community.[75] Social workers were put in the position of having to expand their horizons for means of dealing with their young charges. Writing in 1981, Packman concluded: 'The 1969 Act challenges social workers to develop a very wide range of approaches to delinquency and past practice and current problems meant that, so far, the challenge has been only fitfully taken up.'[76]

234

Such a conclusion seems barely to recognise the implications of the change that occurred in the notion of juvenile justice during the 1960s and 1970s, which has been described as 'the retreat from welfare'.[77] But it would be wrong to see the retreat in terms of a simple division of opinion between penal and political reactionaries on one side and liberal social democrats on the other. Nikolas Rose argues that it was part of 'a much more widespread shift in the techniques for governing the family and its troublesome offspring'. In many respects this was the result of the break-up of the alliance of political, medical and social-work progressives, which since the 1950s had thought in terms of the family as the 'therapeutic agent' at work in rehabilitative interventionism. The realisation that the Welfare State had not solved the basic problem of poverty was a major political moment and, coupled with the political upheavals of the 1960s, the rise of feminism, anti-psychiatry, 'radical' social work, and the undermining of Bowlby's theories, played a principal role in the loss of direction by the liberal left as the New Right began to gain intellectual and political credibility.[78] These developments account for the growing popularity of the justice model throughout the period. In such an environment,

> A society that cannot offer rewards to secure the consent of its members must find some new controls. The justice model provided an acceptable rationale for the necessary shift to coercive controls, and its major function has not been as a pragmatic set of procedural reforms to correct abuses, but as an ideological underpinning of the movement to get tough on crime.[79]

THE 'FAMILY SERVICE' IN THE COMMUNITY, 1970–5

Around the same time as the problem of juvenile delinquency was being debated, so, too, was the nature of social work itself, which in turn was part of a wide-ranging discussion centring on, among other issues, the 'rediscovery' of poverty in the 1960s. As preventive work developed throughout the 1950s and 1960s, social workers found themselves more intimately involved in the lives of families and their needs, many of which could only be met by personnel from other departments such as day care for small children and home help services. The 1963 Act, in allowing Children's Officers to give material and financial aid to families, further extended their interest in and involvement with a whole range of family experiences, well beyond the narrow confines of childcare, and from within the childcare service there were increasing calls for greater co-ordination between different departments. Where juvenile delinquency was concerned it appeared to make good sense to forestall delinquency by every possible means thereby reducing the likelihood of creating adult criminals and the costs of borstals and prisons. Influential Children's Officers, such as Barbara Kahan of Oxfordshire, argued long and hard for the acceptance of a correlation between crime and deprivation. It seemed, therefore, that there were shrewd economic, social (and political) reasons for a more comprehensive approach to preventive welfare work.[80]

But the move towards a 'family service' did not develop naturally out of experience; it was predicated on a developing Fabian theory of social-democratic welfare vis-à-vis working-class families, which was articulated in evidence to the Ingleby Committee.[81] While Ingleby acknowledged that some reorganisation of services involving the family might be necessary in the future, it made no specific recommendations to this effect. The idea, however, reappeared in 1964 in the Labour Party's Crime – a Challenge to Us All, which as part of the efforts to combat rising delinquency called for 'the establishment of a new Family Service'. This was followed in 1965 by the White Paper The Child, the Family and the Young Offender, which stated that the government believed in the concept of such a service.

A few months later the Seebohm Committee was appointed to review the 'personal social services' and to suggest changes desirable to secure 'an effective family service'.[82] At the time of its appointment the focus of attention was on children and juvenile delinquency within the family setting, though since the mid-1950s there had been calls for a more generically oriented social-work practice.[83] Child Care Officers were cautious in their approach to the proposals, arguing for gradualism. However, the childcare lobby failed to persuade the Committee, and other representations such as that made by Professor Richard Titmuss, who argued that preventive thinking was 'too family and child-centred', proved more influential.[84] Seebohm reported in 1968 with a general recommendation for the establishment of a new local-authority Social Services Department which, though 'family oriented', was to be 'community based'. The family, then, remained partly in focus, but the child was virtually subsumed.

In addition to children's departments, the organisation was to comprise welfare services for the elderly, homeless and handicapped, education welfare and child guidance, mental health social provision, home helps, day nurseries, and the social-welfare work provided by health and housing departments. Moreover, the responsibilities of the new structure were to extend beyond those of existing departments. The objective was to reach out 'far beyond the discovery and rescue of social casualties; it will enable the greatest possible number of individuals to act reciprocally, giving and receiving service for the well-being of the whole community'.[85] In practice this meant the disbandment of a specific childcare service (and in many respects of a family service, too). However, neither the professional associations involved nor influential figures in childcare circles raised any objections.[86] These recommendations were incorporated in the Local Authority Social Services Act, 1970, which came into effect in April 1971.

The change in emphasis away from social casework for children in favour of 'service provision' for all deprived groups in the community (including families) was not accidental. The new service was described by a group of influential Fabian theorists as the 'fifth social service', whose objective was to personify the 'rehabilitative ideal' through a personalised, liberal, humanistic approach to welfare.[87] Its purpose reflected the continuing movement, evident on reflection since the Curtis Report called for the identification of a central authority and the professional training of child-care officers, towards what has been called 'a sharpening of surveillance, and its displacement over as wide a field as possible'.[88] This had been recommended by the Ingleby Committee when it urged special arrangements for the detection of 'families at risk':

> Many different sorts of agency and worker will function in this role. Neighbours, teachers, medical practitioners, ministers of religion, health visitors, district nurses, education welfare officers, probation officers, childcare officers, housing officers, officers of the National Assistance Board and other social workers may all spot incipient signs of trouble.[89]

The gradual move towards a 'family service', then, was the result of a continual reappraisal of the ability of the Welfare State to solve social and economic problems and those involving personal relationships. It is no secret that as the character of social democracy changed between 1945 and the 1960s, so, too, did the objectives of the social services. At first the task seemed to be confined to 'residual' groups, who for one reason or another were unable to take advantage of welfare provision. But this was soon seen to be wildly optimistic, especially in the face of the rediscovery of poverty and its accompanying problems.[90]

FOSTERING, ADOPTION AND THE CHILDREN ACT, 1975

Since 1889, Poor Law Boards of Guardians had been able to 'adopt' children, who were often then fostered out, through the assumption of parental rights until the children were aged 18. (In 1908, 12,417 were 'adopted' in this way.) But the majority of 'adoptions' and 'fosterings' occurred informally. Prior to the Adoption of Children Act, 1926, parents could give their children permanently to relatives, friends or even strangers, without relinquishing either their parental rights or obligations. The children had no legal status in respect of their foster parents, and their natural parents could remove them whenever they wished. The practice was a clear demonstration of the chattel-like regard in which children were held by society at the time.

The difficulty concerning adoption reflected the problems faced by illegitimate children, in particular the legal, economic and social disqualifications surrounding them. These in fact were often responsible for the

237

child being left to the care of the Poor Law guardians. The extent of illegitimacy throughout the First World War encouraged the growth of adoption societies and the establishment of the National Council for the Unmarried Mother and Her Child. (By 1918, 6.26 per cent of all live births in England and Wales were illegitimate.) It was felt that illegitimacy added to the problems involving children who, for one reason or another, were without parents either temporarily or permanently. The matter proved to be controversial, and between 1920 and 1926 no fewer than six parliamentary Bills were introduced and two committees of inquiry were appointed.[91]

When the Adoption of Children Act was finally passed in 1926 it dealt with the legality of the adoption procedure between natural and foster parents resulting in the irrevocable change of legal status of the child and of the natural and adopting parents. (In the same year a Legitimacy Act was passed, allowing with certain excluding provisions for illegitimate children to be legitimated by the marriage of their parents.) Adoption became increasingly popular with a corresponding growth in adoption societies and in the numbers of individuals who arranged private adoptions. The main groups of children adopted were (i) the majority who went to non-relatives; (ii) those being transferred from parents to relatives; and (iii) adoption of illegitimates by the natural mother or father, usually with the spouse, in order to give the child 'respectability'. Approximately 80 per cent of adopted children were illegitimate, with the remainder coming from broken homes or single-parent homes (where a parent had died), or having been abandoned.[92]

There were various attempts to regulate adoption societies and others involved in adoption between 1926 and the 1940s, but it was the Children Act, 1948, which sought to provide a coherent and centralised structure for all homeless children. In addition to long-standing duties imposed on them by earlier child protection legislation, such as registering adoption societies, local authorities were given a duty to receive into care on a voluntary basis children whose parents were either unfit or unable to care for them.[93] The local authority was also responsible for supervising *all* children placed for adoption. The Act stipulated that prior to an adoption hearing the court was to appoint a guardian *ad litem* to act on its behalf as an independent agent in order to investigate all aspects of the proposed adoption and everyone involved. Some form of independent guardianship was clearly necessary since throughout the 1950s and 1960s approximately 37 per cent of children in care were with foster parents, and in the 1950s between 13,000 and 15,000 children were adopted. Besides these children there were several thousand others who had been placed in foster care by their parents or guardians and were not subject to the same supervision as were those placed by a local authority.[94]

After the Curtis Report, 1946, developments in adoption law and practice are hard to follow. The law was often under review and was amended in

238

1949. A committee of inquiry sat from 1953 to 1954, and further amendments followed in the Children Act and the Adoption Act, both passed in 1958.[95] The Children Act was in two parts. The first part dealt with child-life protection and the second with adoption. Part 2 was repealed with the passing of the Adoption Act which consolidated all previous adoption legislation. Of particular importance was the clause giving local authorities the power to 'make and participate in arrangements for the adoption of children', regardless of whether those children were in care. However, it appeared from the research of Robert Holman that as far as *private* fostering was concerned there was much less local-authority supervision than for foster children in care. He concluded that 'In Britain it is easier to get a child than an extension to one's garage'.[96]

Local-authority attitudes towards supervision and regulation of private fostering and adoption remained ambivalent throughout the 1950s and 1960s, although most of the amendments to adoption law in the 1950s favoured the adopters. Nevertheless, there was a press campaign in the 1960s for greater consideration to be given to the claims of foster parents over natural parents, and as a result there developed a new but discriminating emphasis on fostering as the best substitute for the loss of natural parents, and as a means to the eventual rehabilitation of children with those parents after they (the parents) have been subject to social casework.[97]

The Houghton Report, 1972

Generally speaking, the adoption laws were regarded as unsatisfactory. They had last been looked at in 1954 (followed by the 1958 Adoption Act), and it was felt that the welfare of the child was not paramount in either the 1948 or the 1958 Act. There were also problems about the timing of the mother's consent to adoption and the legal position of the putative father, and the position of the guardian *ad litem* required re-examination. Moreover, foster parents feared adopting their children because it was possible for the natural parents to reclaim the child at any stage. Furthermore, voluntary agencies were under strain from mounting pressures.[98]

Consequently in 1969 a Department Committee on the Adoption of Children (the Houghton Committee) was appointed to 'consider law, policy and procedures on the adoption of children and what changes are desirable'. The Houghton Report, published in 1972, made ninety-two recommendations, which formed the basis of the Children Act, 1975. Not all of its recommendations secured unanimous approval, though it was generally agreed that the welfare of children (rather than of parents) should be 'the first and paramount consideration' and that the principle should be reinforced throughout the whole process of adoption. It has been suggested that this marks the final break in regarding children as chattels of their parents. It certainly ended the presumption that parents were always the best people to represent their children's interests.[99]

Although initially the Government had shown little interest in Houghton, a series of child abuse cases pushed it into taking some form of action. In January 1973, Maria Colwell, after being fostered, had been returned to her family where she was killed by her step-father. Critics argued that excessive emphasis had been given to the blood-tie between Maria and her natural mother and to the policy of rehabilitating the natural family. The rights of the natural parents, it was claimed, had been put above those of the foster parents and of the child.[100] Further pressure came from the Association of British Adoption Agencies (ABAA), a campaigning group known as the Adoption and Guardianship Reform Organisation (AGRO), and from professional anxiety concerning children held in long-term care and those who were privately fostered. There was also a certain amount of parliamentary interest shown in adoption and related issues, especially in the Bills sponsored by Dr David Owen who, after Labour won the 1975 general election, became a Minister of State at the DHSS. A government Bill, first introduced in the Lords in January 1975, received the Royal Assent in November of the same year, becoming the Children Act. The main provisions were improving the law on adoption; legalising custodianship so as to give improved security for children who, for one reason or another, could be neither fostered nor adopted; and extending the powers of local authorities in dealings with children in care and those who were privately fostered.[101]

In broad terms the Act introduced a limited extension of the rights of children through the 'welfare test' and their separate representation; it reduced the rights of natural parents (much criticised as working against the interests of working-class families); it gave potentially greater security to foster parents (in line with the view that fostering is a valuable form of childcare); and it offered the possibility of integrating adoption provisions into the childcare service. More specifically, it was made a duty for local authorities to provide comprehensive adoption facilities, and all adoption societies were to be officially approved by the Minister of State. The courts and adoption agencies, in addition to applying a 'welfare test' in deciding a child's future, were to give due consideration to the wishes and feelings of the child, wherever possible. Furthermore, the new 'custodianship order' allowed for long-term fostering and for application (by a relative or foster parent) for the legal custody of a child where adoption was thought inappropriate for one reason or another. The Act also amended the law (as it stood under the Children Act, 1948, and the Children and Young Persons Act, 1969) concerning children in care, claiming that the intention was to give these children better protection. Overall it reversed the trend of the 1950s and 1960s which looked to the eventual return of children in care to their natural or 'birth' families.[102]

However, the Act was only very gradually, and never completely, implemented. In 1980 it was observed that the Act

> has yet to get off the ground as at present there is no comprehensive Adoption Service, no central approval of voluntary societies, no freeing for adoption option, no payment of allowances to adopters, no separate representation of children's interests in adoption and care proceedings, no custodianship orders, no measures to improve private fostering.

The result was that not only did many children 'grow up without the experience of family life and without security because plans cannot be made for their future', but also an increasing number of voluntary adoption societies 'are closing through lack of finance, a decline in the number of referrals, or an inability to adapt to the changing needs in adoption'.[103]

The Act can be seen in part as the result of the public reaction to child abuse in 1973–4, and as representing 'an attempt to institute wider changes in childcare policy and practice'. There was a new focus on security and permanence for the child within a family (adoptive or natural) environment. The emphasis, says Parton, 'is on the child as a unit distinct from his family'.[104] But this should not be confused with a 'children's rights' approach on the part of the legislators. It is true that sections 3 and 59 of the Act refer to the wishes and feelings of the child being ascertained where practicable. Similarly, sections 64–6 admitted the possibility of conflict between parent and child and, therefore, allowed for separate representation of these two parties in certain circumstances. To this extent it may be reasonable to speak of a 'children's rights perspective'.[105] Perhaps, however, a more realistic interpretation of the Act is to view it as a signpost marking the end of the rehabilitative ideal; it signalled a loss of faith in the natural family, usually that of the poor. Children were to be distinct units only in so far as they served this end.

9

THE REDISCOVERY OF
CHILD ABUSE

The history of child abuse since the 1960s perfectly illustrates how little credence should be given to official declarations of concern about physically and sexually abused children as *subjects*. Instead, such declarations have tended to focus on children merely as *objects* in the struggles and ambitions of professions, and as *figures* in expressions of ideological and cultural value systems. In discussing cruelty to children it is important to recognise that over the last century public and professional anxiety for the 'problem' has come in two waves: between the 1880s and early 1900s and since the 1960s (moving from physical to sexual abuse). We need to inquire into why this hiatus occurred. What happened to 'cruelty' between those dates? And why does the 'problem' resurface first as 'the battered baby syndrome', followed by 'child abuse' which in the 1980s was redefined as 'child sexual abuse'? What's in a name? It will be necessary to look back and forth across the years in order to answer these questions, and constantly to bear in mind that we are dealing with a shifting set of definitions and interests used to describe and identify a particular condition for groups of children which may or may not have altered much over the last century. In other words, 'abusing' parents are ever present and, therefore, it is the definition of cruelty and abuse and public interest in the 'problem' which is subject to 'rediscovery'. In the arguments and debates over meanings and solutions we should never forget the 'abused' children themselves.[1] If much of history comprises vast silences of oppressed people, then the silence of these children engulfs us in its enormity.

This chapter, which relies heavily upon the writings of Nigel Parton, begins by looking at the discovery of the 'battered baby' in the 1950s and 1960s, before going on to examine the Maria Colwell Inquiry (1974) which marked the beginning of popular interest in 'child abuse'. It concludes with an attempt to begin to explain the hiatus (often commented upon but never discussed) between late-nineteenth- and early-twentieth-century interest in the problem and its 'rediscovery' in the 1960s.

THE DISCOVERY OF THE 'BATTERED BABY'

It is generally agreed that the discovery of the 'battered baby' began in the United States in the 1940s with the work of Dr John Caffey, a distinguished paediatric radiologist. Caffey drew attention to a group of infants whose principal disease consisted of a collection of blood immediately underneath the skull (subdural haematoma) but who, upon X-ray, were found to have either fresh, healing or healed multiple fractures in their arms and legs (long bones). However, he could not find any case in which there was a history of injury to which the skeletal lesions could be attributed; nor was there evidence of any disease which would predispose to fractures. Caffey was led to conclude that the two conditions, subdural haematoma and long-bone fractures, were related and that their origin was traumatic. Other doctors began to voice their support for Caffey's findings and many identified parents as the source of the trauma. This connection was made explicit in 1955 when Doctors Woolley and Evans published a paper on the significance of skeletal lesions, linking them directly to parental behaviour. The lesions, they concluded, were produced by 'undesirable vectors of force', and went on to refer to the causes of the injuries as 'parental indifference', 'alcoholism', 'irresponsibility' and 'immaturity manifested by uncontrollable aggressions'.[2]

Around the same time the Children's Division of the American Humane Association began a national survey of maltreated children and distributed the results to a variety of interested parties including child welfare departments and the Federal Children's Bureau, hitherto not a particularly well respected agency. The Bureau became convinced that child abuse was a national problem and saw in the issue an opportunity to raise its own profile and credibility. Thus the Bureau supported research into child abuse, in particular that of Dr Henry Kempe who made his findings public under the title of the 'Battered Child Syndrome' at the American Academy of Paediatrics in November 1961. In the published paper, Kempe and his colleagues described the syndrome to the readers of the prestigious journal of the American Medical Association:

> The battered child syndrome, a clinical condition in young children who have received serious physical abuse, is a frequent cause of permanent injury or death. The syndrome should be considered in any child exhibiting evidence of fracture of any bone, subdural hematoma, failure to thrive, soft tissue swellings or skin bruising, in any child who dies suddenly, or where the degree and type of injury is at variance with the history given regarding the occurrence of the trauma. Psychiatric factors are probably of prime importance in the pathogenesis of the disorder, but knowledge of these factors is limited. Physicians have a duty and responsibility to the child to require a full evaluation of the problem and to guarantee that no

expected repetition of traumas will be permitted to occur . . . Unfortunately, it is frequently not recognised or, if diagnosed, is inadequately handled by the physician because of hesitation to bring the case to the attention of the proper authorities.

The abuse was said to be caused 'generally from a parent or foster parent'. Kempe also denied that the problem was simply one of the consequences of poverty, arguing that abusing parents were 'immature, impulsive, self-centred, hypersensitive and quick to react with poorly controlled aggression'.[3]

The 'problem' was soon popularised in the United States, and by 1967 every state had some form of legislation compelling professionals who suspected child abuse or neglect to report their suspicions to the police or to a child-care agency. Such a rapid emergence of the social and medical significance of the 'battered child syndrome' has been attributed in part to the 'entrepreneurial efforts' of Kempe and his colleagues and other 'organizational and professional interests' in American medicine, in particular the alliance formed between paediatric radiology, paediatrics and psychodynamic psychiatry. More generally it seems that American medicine was in search of a new frontier to cross and in particular that paediatric radiology was a low-ranking speciality seeking to enhance its status. However, the critical fact to emerge from Kempe's entrepreneurship was that child abuse was labelled a 'syndrome' ('a group of concurrent symptoms of a disease': *OED*) which identified the problem as an individual illness and, second, as primarily a medical province thereby relegating its social and legal aspects.[4] So was born the 'disease model' of child abuse.

The discovery in Britain occurred more gradually, even though cruelty to children was recognised and Caffey had spoken in London in 1956 and published his classic paper on traumatic lesions in growing bones in the *British Journal of Radiology*.[5] It is perhaps significant, however, that the 'problem' was referred to in terms of 'cruelty' rather than those of 'battering'. The change in nomenclature began to appear in 1963 with the publication of an article in the *British Medical Journal*, by two orthopaedic surgeons, which was subtitled 'Battered Baby Syndrome: '. . . a syndrome which we think commoner than is usually believed, and which would appear often to be misdiagnosed'.[6] This article claimed that, for every child treated as abused in hospital, there were another hundred treated by unsuspecting doctors, and that the syndrome 'may be a more frequent cause of death than . . . leukaemia, cystic fibrosis and muscular dystrophy'. In the same issue, a leader article thanked the authors for drawing attention to the problem, reminding readers that the work of the NSPCC confirmed that it was by no means uncommon and concluded that 'clearly this tragic matter deserves more attention than it has received'. The importance of medical involvement, it argued, was that clinical and radiological investigations could produce proof necessary for court convictions. This assisted the NSPCC and the police since previously lack of evidence had contributed to the low percentage (2 per cent) of NSPCC cases going to court.[7]

Though initially the problem was categorised very much within a medical framework, this soon broadened into a medico-legal context with the relevant vocabulary. As one author proclaimed, the doctor 'is the first line of defence in the fight to combat the problem', while another wrote of the syndrome as a 'widespread crime that can only too easily escape detection'. Further medical involvement came in 1966 with an official pronouncement from the British Paediatric Association which stressed the role of hospital casualty doctors. However, unlike previous medical writings, the BPA spoke of the need to consult local-authority Children's Officers, thereby reducing the focus on what it called the 'purely punitive attitude', which it regarded as ill-advised. Thus the BPA was calling for a link between medical authorities and the social agencies of the State.[8] However, the point to bear in mind is that the definitions continued to be provided through medical expertise, especially that of forensic pathologists and paediatricians.

Between 1968 and 1972 the issue of the battered baby took on a new dimension with the establishment of the NSPCC Battered Child Research Unit, which was set up after the Society's director, the Reverend Arthur Morton, had visited Dr Kempe and others in the United States.[9] Since the early days of its foundation, there had been a fundamental shift of emphasis in the work of the Society, so that by the early 1960s it was no longer certain of its role. The Reverend Morton claimed that by the 1950s the main call upon the Society was for cases of neglect rather than of 'cruelty'. In 1964, there were said to be only 9,632 cases of assault out of a total 120,000 children assisted by the Society. Furthermore, since prior to 1900, when 21 per cent of cases were prosecuted, the Society had ceased to be a prosecuting agency, so that by 1968 the figure was 0.5 per cent.[10] But in its search to become a professional childcare agency the Society found itself competing with the expanding local-authority Children's Departments, created by the 1948 Act, which had been given the power to investigate cruelty and neglect (by the 1952 Amendment to the 1948 Act) and which employed over 3,700 Childcare Officers by 1970. And, potentially more damaging to its future, the NSPCC found itself facing a financial crisis in 1964–5 when its expenditure exceeded its income by more than a quarter of a million pounds. This, then, was the context in which the Society established its 'battered child' research unit.[11]

Within four years members of the unit had published seventeen articles and had conceptualised child-battering as a 'medico-social problem' with an emphasis on early identification and non-punitive treatment. The aim of all treatment was 'primary prevention', so that the Society social worker was not to be concerned with the law, but with forming a 'consistent, trusting, professional relationship'. The unit perceived the problem as a symptom of family breakdown, and identified abusing parents as themselves having been children in inadequate families, which produced mothers with an inability to mother. The solution, it claimed, lay in a 'psychosocial diagnosis' in order to provide a 'transfusion of mothering . . . in the hope that they will identify with us and eventually interject a less punitive self image'. The success of the unit was reflected in media and journal coverage of the problem which to a large extent echoed its views and looked to it as the principal research agency. However, as Parton shows, during the period child guidance workers, solicitors and the police were becoming aware of child abuse, although *Social Work Today* did not carry an article on the topic until 1974.[12]

In the early 1970s the first sign of state intervention in the matter was evident with the publication by the DHSS of two circulars for MOHs and Children's Officers, which were intended to promote local activity. Both documents reflected the views of the NSPCC, especially the interprofessional team approach. The influence of the Society was strengthened by the appointment of the senior researcher at the Society's Unit to the Social Work Service at the DHSS where it seems that one of her primary tasks was to promote awareness within the Department. By 1972 many areas had established review and case committees to deal with child abuse in their localities. Once again the medical influence was strongly present in the committee membership with the convenor usually being a consultant paediatrician.[13] Nevertheless, with the exception of sections of the medical profession and the NSPCC, up to the early 1970s the 'battered baby syndrome' was not treated as especially significant either by the media or by professional groups. This was to change with the death of Maria Colwell and the subsequent public inquiry.

MARIA COLWELL: CHILD ABUSE COMES OF AGE

The inquiry into the death of Maria Colwell, published in September 1974, 'proved crucial in establishing the issue as a major social problem and in introducing fundamental changes in policy and practice'.[14] Maria Colwell was one of nine children borne by her mother and had spent more than five years in foster care with her aunt before being returned to her mother and step-father when she was aged 6 years and 8 months. Maria herself opposed the return, and on earlier visits had showed signs of trauma, so much so that in June 1971 she was diagnosed as depressed. However, the child's feelings were ignored by the Social Services Department, which had a long-term plan to reintegrate Maria with her natural mother's family. In the last nine months of her life, thirty complaints were made by various people about her treatment by her mother and step-father. The complaints concerned weight-loss, neglect, physical injuries, scapegoating and excessive physical demands. The family received visits from a variety of social workers. On 6–7 January 1973, approximately two weeks before her 7th birthday, Maria was killed – 'battered' – by her step-father. It has been said that 'Reaction to the case and the events that followed signified a dramatic event such that it took on the proportions of a moral panic', defined by the sociologist Stanley Cohen as 'A condition, episode, person or group of persons emerges to become defined as a threat to societal values and interests'.[15] We shall see that the prevailing explanation for this 'moral panic' was couched in terms of the national condition in the late 1960s and early 1970s, in particular the reactions to the so-called 'permissiveness' of the 1960s, and the perceived threat of violence in society, both of which were seen as undermining the family in its role as the basic social institution.

First, let us look at events leading up to the public inquiry following the child's death. Initially the tragedy and the trial of her step-father received little publicity except in East Sussex where the local press campaigned for central government to hold a public inquiry. However, once the inquiry was under way the media played an important part in publicising its hearings and in setting the agenda for public interest. A crucial role was also played by the 'Tunbridge Wells Study Group on Child Abuse', a self-appointed group of professionals anxious to highlight the problem and to encourage inter-professional co-operation in dealing with it. The Group organised a conference in May 1973 which was attended by Sir Keith Joseph, Minister of State for Social Services and a strong advocate of the 'cycle of deprivation' theory which claimed that deprived and inadequate parents pass on to their children their own weaknesses and inadequacies, and these are then reproduced in the next generation.[16]

Maria had died in January. The conference was held between 15 and 18 May. The public inquiry was announced on 24 May. It seems that the Tunbridge Wells Group had good connections with the DHSS and with other state agencies, and was instrumental in the setting-up of the inquiry. The chairperson of the Group later commented: 'While the timing of Maria Colwell and Tunbridge Wells was coincidental the combination was explosive.'[17] Sir Keith made a speech on the day the inquiry opened which revealed the influence of the NSPCC unit, the Tunbridge Wells Group, and the work of Kempe and his colleagues in the United States. He called for more aid for 'battered babies' and urged magistrates and social workers to be more confident in dealing with the problem.

The role of social workers was to become extremely important in the ensuing debate on child abuse and on child care in general, as was the work of the Social Services Departments created after the Seebohm Report of 1968. The basic theme was that child care had deteriorated.[18] How had this happened? The good intentions of the 'fifth social service' were soon frustrated by the challenge from the emerging New Right (and the radical left) which was fundamentally critical of the Welfare State in virtually all its forms, especially in terms of its costs and the alleged permissiveness and liberalism of social work in its attitudes towards the poor, the inept and the deviant. The Maria Colwell inquiry provided a stage on which these critiques, graphically illuminated by the media, could be performed. The drama was to have a didactic purpose: to inform the public about the inefficiency, and confused and misplaced liberalism, of democratic welfarism.[19]

Prior to the inquiry, as we have seen, there had been some agitation in the press on behalf of foster parents and the law on adoptions. In the late 1960s there was a spate of cases involving parents who were demanding the return of their children from foster homes where they had been for years. The death of Maria Colwell appeared to be proof of the dangers of removing a child against its will from a loving foster home. The Houghton Report, 1972, as has been shown, called for improved rights for foster parents, but the Government had no plans to legislate on the matter. Once the inquiry got under way, the press began to report and comment on the issues raised on a daily basis by the different witnesses. The *Sunday Times* and *The Times* were both prominent in campaigning for a new emphasis on the child as opposed to the natural parents. At the conclusion of the inquiry, Barbara Castle, the Secretary of State, was quoted as saying that she hoped social workers would place less emphasis on the 'blood-tie' (natural parents) in the future. The new mood was expressed by a correspondent to the *British Medical Journal* who stated that social-work intervention should be 'authoritative, intrusive and insistent'.[20]

In many respects the Maria Colwell case illustrated a number of controversial issues of childcare: the child's relationship with its foster parents; the weak or nonexistent bond with the natural mother; the problems surrounding the step-father figure; the failure of welfare agencies to respond adequately to signs of abuse; and the failure to take notice of the child's wishes. Furthermore, while the inquiry report condemned the failure of the *system*, it also implicated child care *policy*.[21] Unsurprisingly, then, in its wake there was a proliferation of new procedures detailed in a number of DHSS circulars issued between 1974 and 1976 which 'established the framework of the administrative system for detecting, investigating and processing child abuse cases'. The main features were: Area Review Committees whose members were senior staff of various welfare agencies; case conferences for individual cases with 'front-line' practitioners; abuse registers for those at risk, and child abuse manuals.[22] The focus was 'exclusively on how to recognise child abuse and manage cases, with particular emphasis on ensuring good interprofessional communication'.[23]

The reaction to the death of Maria Colwell and subsequent cases of abuse provided the impetus for a House of Commons Select Committee on Violence in the Home. The Committee began by considering 'violence in marriage' in 1975, but on being reconstituted in 1976 its brief had been broadened to include violence in the family. In its Report, *Violence to Children*, (1977), it opined that 'violence against children is only part of the much larger problem of child abuse and neglect and how children should be brought up', and it acknowledged that children had to contend with physiological violence and passive forms of neglect. Evidence seemed to suggest that perhaps as many as 40,000 children suffered from moderate abuse. The causes were said to be 'diverse', but emphasis was given to the 'cycle of violence', stress, isolation, 'bonding' and unwanted pregnancies. The Committee's recommendations were obviously designed to benefit families in general rather than to deal with particular abusive cases.

The main concern of the Committee was with preventive methods for a problem which it tended to see in terms of the 'social pathology' of the family, rather than of individualism. Consequently, it stressed that the community should be more conscious of its duty towards families with young children, and that the Government should give local authorities assistance with initiatives to prevent child abuse through the rate-support grant and with grants to agencies such as the NSPCC. Its specific recommendations were that (i) there should be adequate care facilities for children under 5, especially child-minders, play-groups and nurseries; and education should be provided for parenthood together with self-help groups for anxious parents; (ii) social workers and the police should be given more training and the police should be involved in managing abuse cases; (iii) social services departments should be made more welcoming and offer an 'open door' for worried parents; and (iv) the health services should be made more aware of the importance of 'early bonding' between mother and infant and be more sensitive to the birth experience; and all children under 5 should be medically examined as a means of contacting the 'unreachables'.

In its response to the Report, the Government produced a number of consultative documents and circulars on health and well-being, especially of children, with titles such as *Prevention and Health: Everybody's Business. A Reassessment of Public and Personal Health* (1976), *Priorities for Health and Personal Social Services* (1976) and *The Way Forward* (1977). However, all the proposals were frustrated by limited resources.

THE HIATUS OF CONCERN FOR ABUSED CHILDREN BETWEEN 1908 AND THE 1960s

Before looking at the context of the so-called 'moral panic' surrounding the killing of Maria Colwell, it will be helpful to examine the absence of concern about cruelty to children during the period *circa* 1908 to the 1960s. The socio-legal researchers Dingwall, Eekelaar and Murray have argued that in the nineteenth century children were regarded as 'threats' to society, primarily in the form of juvenile delinquency, though it was also recognised that such children might be delinquent owing to 'the improper conduct of parents, the want of education and the want of suitable employment'.[24] It is well known that Mary Carpenter, the mid-Victorian reformer, maintained that there was little practical difference between offenders and neglected non-offenders. However, she retained a classificatory distinction between the two groups, with the latter being sent to industrial schools. These schools, as the Departmental Committee on Juvenile Offenders, 1927, remarked, dealt with their pupils 'by providing education and industrial training for the class of children from whom delinquents were mainly drawn'. Undoubtedly the children were in the schools as much because they were deemed to be 'a *risk* to society as being *at risk* themselves'.[25] And we are already familiar with the view of the Departmental Committee that there was 'little or no difference in character and needs between the neglected and the delinquent child . . . Neglect leads to delinquency and delinquency is often the outcome of neglect.'[26] Thus the Children and Young Persons Act, 1933, reflecting its influence, abolished the distinction between reformatory and industrial schools, renaming them approved schools. Clearly, then, the protection of children from neglect and from cruelty was overladen with other concerns.

We have also seen that under the 1933 Act children whose parents had been convicted for their wilful ill-treatment, neglect or abandonment were included along with those who were considered to be 'in need of care and protection' and, therefore, could be committed to an approved school. Despite being obviously in need of protection *from* adults, the children were being dealt with under the same statutory provisions as those who were deemed to be a threat to society. This situation had arisen because the Departmental Committee felt obliged to look at non-offenders who for whatever reason required protection *and* training. This made it appear that the two courses of action – 'protection' and 'training' – were necessarily related. It was recognised that many children were 'the victims of cruelty or other offences committed by adults', but this was very much an afterthought.

The Committee began by dividing 'neglected' children into three groups: Poor Law children; children in voluntary homes; and children who came under the provisions of the 1908 Children Act (the second part of which dealt with prevention of cruelty). In place of tripartite categorisation, it recommended the broader definition of 'being in need of care and protection' which was enacted in the 1933 Act. On the one hand, this enhanced the protection of children since local authorities were now compelled to inquire into all such cases and the courts were empowered to put the children into local-authority care. On the other hand, 'these children had now become irredeemably intertwined with a group of children with

250

entirely different problems, who were regarded by society as being virtually inseparable from delinquent'.[27]

Nor was there much more recognition of cruelly treated children by the Ingleby Committee when it was appointed in 1956. The last-mentioned of its four duties was to inquire into and make recommendations on the working of the law in relation to 'the prevention of cruelty to, and exposure to moral and physical danger of juveniles'. The subordinate position of children as victims in the placing of the terms of reference, and the subsidiary manner in which the Committee treated the subject, has already been mentioned.[28] The attitude of the Committee can be seen in its remark relating to child neglect that the 'difficulty has not arisen for several years over the reasonable requirements for nutrition, housing, clothing and schooling'.[29] Thus neglect (and by implication cruelty) were dismissed as insignificant issues. The Ingleby emphasis was continued in the 1960s White Papers *The Child, the Family and the Young Offender* (1965) and *Children in Trouble* (1968), and in the Children and Young Persons Act, 1969. The Act sought to define delinquents as suffering from a kind of moral neglect and to substitute civil care proceedings for those of a criminal nature. The outcome confirmed what had been the case since the 1933 Act, namely that abused and neglected children were dealt with under legislation designed primarily to meet the threat from juvenile delinquency.[30]

The exception to the trend since 1933 was the Children Act, 1948, with its new approach to child-care policy, and the Children and Young Persons (Amendment) Act, 1952, which brought in a 'no-fault' approach to child protection, thereby focusing on the condition of the child, rather than on those responsible for creating its condition. It was also made a duty for Children's Departments to look into allegations of child mistreatment brought to their attention. By 1956 over 90 per cent of local authorities had established co-ordinating machinery for dealing with neglect and ill-treatment, though inter-occupational rivalries prevented about 50 per cent from making the Children's Officer the central figure in the system. The primacy of the Children's Departments in this area was only achieved, as we have seen, by relating deprived families to the Ingleby conception of the prevention of delinquency.[31]

However, the Ingleby Committee showed how quickly the mood and emphasis of the 1948 Act had evaporated as far as child abuse was concerned, despite there being ample evidence of child cruelty and neglect to children to anyone who cared to look for it.[32] In Manchester alone during 1951 the NSPCC investigated 1,500 cases affecting 3,700 children, sixty per cent of which were for neglect and 10 per cent for brutality.[33] One of the principal reasons why Children's Departments failed to focus on *cruelty* to children in the late 1940s and throughout the 1950s was the near-obsession among social services personnel with the 'problem family', which

251

identified a general form of neglect rather than physical cruelty. The perception was clearly expressed in a study made by the influential Women's Group on Public Welfare and published in 1948 as *The Neglected Child and His Family*. The emphasis throughout the study was on child neglect within problem families. Reference to cruelty was limited to a three-page description of the law relating to offences against children. A distinction was made between cruelty and neglect with the former being dismissively attributed to 'subconscious motives'. Less than five years later, this was reiterated by Penelope Hall in her standard text when she described cruelty as 'only a small part of the whole problem', and reminded readers of the recent government circular which, in her words, recognised that

> Child neglect is frequently found in problem families and is both a symptom and a result of the general collapse of morale which characterises this particular social group, and in these cases it cannot be treated as an isolated phenomenon. Instead an effort must be made to rehabilitate the family as a whole.

Such families were said to be suffering the effects of 'Poverty, ignorance, bad housing, mental sub-normality or abnormality, too many children for the mother's capacity to manage, the broken home, ill health, marital disharmony, [and] excessive child-bearing'.[34] These same factors could just as easily have been used to explain cruelty had it been counted as a serious matter. However, as the social problem was constructed in terms of the problem family, which was seen primarily as the neglectful family, so 'cruelty', either physical or mental, was never given its proper consideration.

The more fundamental answer must be found in the politics of age relations, in particular those between parents and their children and those implicit in the attitude of the State towards young people. The fact was that, in the absence of what certain groups of adults considered to be *necessary* political, economic or cultural reasons, there was little or no interest in protecting children from physical abuse (this would change with the medical interest in the 1960s), and even the interest in neglected children was usually expressed within the context of either combating the sources of delinquency or in support of family regulation. This does not mean that the majority of parents were indifferent to the welfare of their children or that the courts were uninterested in cases of 'cruelty'. But it does mean that, in terms of child-protection legislation and the enforcement and interpretation of that legislation by the State through social policy, the *primary* concerns were with the efficient functioning of the family and the maintenance of respectability through socialisation.

The protection of children against 'abuse' or 'cruelty' depends in part on how these terms are socially constructed and in part on their position at any one time in the list of a society's political priorities. The social construction of abuse is of some significance since 'abuse and neglect come to exist as socially recognizable phenomena, and hence as a cause of action, only as a result of processes of identification, confirmation and disposition within health, welfare and legal agencies'.[35] The process of definition, which is discussed below, is itself, in general terms, the principal explanation of the hiatus in concern for cruelly treated children.

THE REDISCOVERY OF CHILD ABUSE

This brings us to the 'discovery' of child abuse in the 1950s and 1960s. By the end of the 1960s it was clear that many areas of social policy were causing concern to different political, religious, philanthropic and professional interests. The anxiety exploded as a 'moral panic' which focused on the death of Maria Colwell in 1973. However, as Parton writes in a nice understatement: 'It would be wrong . . . to see the panic . . . as simply arising from the more specific concerns about injury to children.' By the late 1960s the post-war political consensus (to the extent that there was one of any significance) on welfare, crime and the economy had collapsed. There were many factors involved in the collapse, two of the most influential being the rediscovery of poverty in the 1960s and the associated social problems, notably inner-city deprivation, poor housing and racial conflicts, and the emergence of counter-cultures, new movements, especially feminism, and youth's perceived revolt against authority. A third factor was what appeared to be the growth of criminal, social and political violence, including trade-union militancy. Many of these developments were understood in terms of 'the violent society' – a portrayal effectively exploited by the New Right, which made much capital out of the alleged decline of the traditional family and its values. Thus the stage was set for the upsurge of what has been called 'moral fundamentalism', as it appealed to the middle class and to sections of the working class.

The significance of the Maria Colwell inquiry was that she seemed to personify the 'innocent' victim, to represent that which was being destroyed by alien forces. The child's death pointed the finger at the range of groups allegedly threatening 'the British way of life' – social workers, feminists, Marxists, radical students and teachers, divorcees – and at the equally threatening trends: criminality, pro-abortion, anti-authoritarianism, pop culture, drugs, and lack of self-reliance, each of which was seen as the product of 'permissiveness' in all its forms, especially the sexual, the social and the cultural. The reformist legislation of the 1960s on censorship, homosexuality and divorce appeared to confirm that there had indeed been an erosion of traditional morality.

It is also worth remembering that by the time of the inquiry in 1974 these social anxieties were regularly aired so that the ground was prepared for the ensuing 'moral panic'. A major role was played by the media,

253

which familiarised the general public with experiences and events about which it would otherwise have had little or no knowledge; it provided an interpretation for people as to what was wrong with society and in so doing helped to create 'child abuse' as a social problem. This is not to say that all sections of the media promoted conservative and traditional values, but in general the press tended to express serious concern about the principles and practices of welfare. In effect child abuse, and the social workers who were said to allow it to happen, became the scapegoat for a multitude of fears and uncertainties.[36]

There is much more that could be said about the nature of the British 'crisis' in the late 1960s and 1970s, but our main concern is with suggesting a framework which can help to explain the discovery of child abuse and the particular attention generated by the death of Maria Colwell. We should not be surprised that a single death can have such dramatic repercussions. This is exactly what happened with the Denis O'Neill case after the war, which came be linked to the Curtis Report and the beginning of a new approach to child welfare. Sometimes a single criminal act, such as the killing of a child, can act as a catalyst in so far as it serves either to lance a boil of frustration and anger, as with the Colwell affair, or to open up a boulevard of concern characterised by prominent elements of humanitarianism and political liberalism, as with Lady Allen's campaign in the 1940s, the Curtis Report and the subsequent establishment of Children's Departments.

Concepts of child abuse

When child abuse was 'discovered' it was as an individualistic *disease* rather than as a sociological and political malaise. The Reverend Arthur Morton, Director of the NSPCC, described it in 1972 as 'a contagious disease which must be notified'. The concept of disease tends to mask responsibility; it is something one catches or is exposed to; it is random in its choice of subject. The concept operates at two levels: one concerns the individuality of the abuser – the diseased person; the other concerns the identification and treatment of the problem as conforming to the conventional evolution of 'a serious disease model'. It was suggested, for example, that an appropriate analogy was with progress in combating cystic fibrosis – from a time in the 1950s at which doctors had difficulty in treating the disease to that where, as they gained experience, research progressed making it better understood, so that treatment began to be available which would help the children. 'Early diagnostic methods were developed and the problem began to be recognised at a point when much of the irreversible pathology could be prevented.'[37] This assumes that a particular virus or bacteria is responsible for the disease, whose causal links can be demonstrated, and whose 'habits, strengths and weaknesses' can be assessed in order to fight the disease.[38] Parton and others correctly maintain that this provides an inadequate explanation of child abuse which can best be understood as social phenomena. It is a political issue, rather than one of individual or family pathology.[39]

From the perspective of age relations and the attitude of adult society towards children it is the first level – the diseased individuality of the abuser (and Parton's critique) – which interests us here. The concept of child abuse as a medical-type 'disease' afflicting individual parents ignores the social context of violence towards children. It says nothing about the general approval of violence in the form of corporal punishment in schools (finally abolished in the state sector in 1986), care institutions and the domestic home. It is significant that one of the reasons advanced to explain why casualty doctors and paediatricians failed to inquire further about signs of what came to be called the 'battered baby syndrome' was that they were psychologically unwilling to believe that parents could 'abuse' their own children.[40] Perhaps, then, it is not surprising that abused children had to wait for the advocacy of an organised interest (in this case paediatric radiologists pursuing their own professional objectives) before their plight was made known. However, even after abuse was 'discovered' in America and every state had passed legislation to deal with it, surveys showed that public sympathy was with parents rather than with children.[41] This suggests the depths of adult antipathy towards children.

The work of David Gil has most forcefully drawn attention to the *societal* nature of child abuse, and it is he who in 1970 offered the comprehensive definition:

> any act of commission or omission by individuals, institutions, or society as a whole, and any conditions resulting from such acts or inaction, which deprive children of equal rights and liberties, and/or interfere with their optional development, constitute, by definition, abusive or neglectful acts or conditions.[42]

This led him to argue that physical abuse of children *resulting in serious injury* is not a major social problem, 'at least in comparison with several more widespread and more serious social problems that undermine the developmental opportunities of many children . . . such as poverty, racial discrimination, malnutrition and inadequate provisions for medical care and education'.[43] Such a definition obviously has little to do with the disease model of abuse.

In addition to that provided by Gil, there are three other main positions. The first argues against the 'myth of classlessness', maintaining instead that child abuse is more predominant among the poor than in any other sector of society. The second looks to the 'ecological perspective' to explain abuse, seeing it as the product of ecological dysfunction, such as social isolation, bad neighbourhoods and generally inadequate environments. The third position is the 'socio-cultural approach' which states that 90 per cent of violence in American families derives from the nature of the family as a social institution and from society itself, rather than being an aberration found among certain individuals. This argument, associated with the work of Straus, Gelles and Steinmatz, stresses the cultural acceptance of 'normal' violence towards children in American families, and they quote from their national survey of family violence to illustrate the high percentages of children who had been slapped, kicked, caned, punched, bitten, and so on. For Straus *et al.* child abuse is not a rarity, but is a persistent condition for many children.[44]

Before commenting we should be clear about the process of defining child abuse. The clearest explanation of this process is given by Gelles, who maintains that in

> all the cases that make up the data on incidence, all the explanatory analyses and all the prevention and treatment models are influenced by the *social process* by which individuals and groups are labeled and designated deviants. In other words there is no objective behavior we can automatically recognise as child abuse ... when I speak of the social construction of abuse, I mean the process by which: (*a*) a definition of abuse is constructed; (*b*) certain judges or 'gatekeepers' are selected for applying the definition; and (*c*) the definition is applied by designating the label 'abuse' and 'abuser' to particular individuals and families.[45]

Thus abuse and neglect 'are the products of complex processes of identification, confirmation and disposal rather than inherent in a child's presenting condition and, at least in some sense, self-evident'. Nor can they be discussed 'intelligibly without an understanding of the way in which such processes operate, an understanding which must necessarily be moral rather than technical'.[46]

So what are we to make of the discovery of child abuse? Looking at the period 1945–1970s, it can be seen that in the early years the focus of child-care policy was on reforming institutions and preventing neglect through support for the family. Child cruelty was known to exist – at least, for those who read the annual reports of the NSPCC, and several social scientific works published in the 1950s. Yet not until after the medical 'discovery' of the 'battered baby' in the mid-1960s was there any significant interest shown in 'child abuse' with the establishment of the NSPCC research unit in 1967, followed by the Tunbridge Wells Group (1973), which in turn was followed by the 'moral panic' surrounding the aftermath of the Colwell inquiry in 1973–4. It would be perverse to conclude that the 'discovery' of abuse had much to do with an uncluttered concern for the welfare of children. Nevertheless, many of the people involved were deeply concerned for the welfare and happiness of children, which they saw as their *only* objective. But there were others, professionally, politically and religiously motivated, who, while also having a genuine interest in child health and development, were governed by less altruistic considerations. For these participants, child abuse was just *another* issue in the larger world of ideological certainties, moral revivals, scientific ambitions and professional skills.

The disease model of abuse suited such people since it individualised the problem and offered a solution based on treatment. Of equal significance for the perception of child abuse, it individualised not only the *abuser*, but also the *abused*. This served to divert any questioning of the social status of children *per se*. Similarly, the disease model portrayed abuse as being found *within* society but not as being *of* society – the problem was said to arise from the behaviour of deviant parents or guardians, rather than from 'normal' attitudes towards children. However, it is the work of Gil and Straus *et al.* which points us in the most fruitful direction for understanding both the nature of the discovery of child abuse and its sources. The emphasis in Gil on 'the structural obstructions to human development' is of critical importance since it reminds us that 'the activities of schools, institutions, unemployment, social security systems, racial discrimination, class differentials' do indeed 'have far more deleterious effects upon the life chances and development of children than the traditional concerns of child abuse literature, policy and practice'.

At the same time, there is a danger that in following Gil alone we would be led into a position which locates the problem simply in the inequalities of resources in society, with all the familiar attendant disastrous consequences, But we also need to keep in mind the basic premiss of Straus and his colleagues, which is that violence in families occurs in 'normal' circumstances, and that the family is an institutional means of teaching violence to its members. It is so because within the majority of families physical punishment of children is regarded (certainly by parents) as culturally acceptable and to be expected. Physical abuse is probably less widespread in middle-class families but mainly because their relative affluence allows parents to 'buy' their way out of the stresses and strains that lead to 'abuse'. The lesser prevalence of middle-class abuse does not, however, mean that attitudes towards children and perceptions of parental rights to inflict violence are fundamentally different from those in the working class. Instead it suggests that those explanations of abuse which seek to show the importance of social structure, and look to remedies in the form of 'a comprehensive anti-poverty strategy', are incomplete when they do not give due consideration to the generally low and oppressed status of children throughout society.[47] It is this latter understanding which reminds us that social welfare problems are essentially about the suffering of certain groups of people, and in this case it focuses our attention on the abused children themselves.

10

HOSPITAL WELFARE, HEALTH AND POVERTY

THE WELFARE OF CHILDREN IN HOSPITAL

The welfare of children in hospital is an interesting and revealing topic to examine in relation to social policy and child welfare since it raises in an undisguised form professional attitudes towards children's emotional contentment, which perhaps can be described more simply as their happiness. It was in the 1920s that paediatric work began to develop in hospitals, and under the influence of the child guidance clinics a new consciousness of the importance of children's emotional security soon emerged, although it was not until the 1940s that the issue of their welfare in hospital first assumed any kind of prominence. The Curtis Report (1946) on the care of deprived children highlighted the importance of a secure and loving environment, and no doubt this impressed itself upon progressive medical personnel. Moreover, the establishment of the National Health Service in 1948, in making hospital treatment available to an ever increasing number of children, underlined the need for a more sensitive policy with regard to their residential needs.

On the census night of 1951 in England and Wales there were 36,856 children between the ages of 4 weeks and 14 years in hospital, and a sample analysis undertaken by the Ministry of Health in 1955 suggested that approximately 685,000 children under 15 were admitted to non-mental hospitals during the year, compared with a total of 3.5 million persons of all ages.[1] It was clear that hospital welfare involved large numbers of children and young adolescents. Between 1949 and 1956, the year in which the Platt Committee on the Welfare of Children in Hospital was appointed, the Central Health Services Council at the Ministry of Health issued three memoranda to hospital managements asking them to allow daily visits for children in their care. The Council also published a report in 1953 dealing with the reception and welfare of all hospital patients which included recommendations concerning visiting hours for children and the proper advice to be given to parents on how to prepare their children for admission. Once again, as a result of the psychological gaze, the child was being perceived in terms of mind and body, rather than simply as a physical being.

The principal sources for the concern about hospitalised children were the Central Council for Health Education and especially the Tavistock Institute for Human Relations. There was a direct link between the Institute, its psychological perspective and that of the child guidance movement, and the Platt Committee, for one of its principal witnesses was James Robertson, a member of the Institute. Since 1948 the Tavistock's Child Development Research Unit had been doing research into the effects of loss of maternal care in the early years upon children's personality development. Robertson, a leading advocate of their welfare in hospital, had worked with Anna Freud on the psycho-analytic treatment of young children, collaborated with Bowlby at the Unit, and made films chronicling maternal deprivation.[2] Robertson believed that separation from the principal carer (nearly always the mother) was the major factor in the child's experience of hospitalisation, in addition to the 'obviously alarming events, such as anaesthetics and operations'. In psychological terms, the two main dangers of hospitalisation were the traumatic, which referred to the shock of losing the mother and led to feelings of insecurity and hostility, and the deprivational, which could result in the 'impoverishment of personality'.[3]

These views would certainly have been known to the Central Health Services Council when it appointed Sir Harry Platt, President of the Royal College of Surgeons, to chair its committee with terms of reference to 'make a special study of the arrangements made in hospitals for the welfare of ill children – as distinct from their medical and nursing treatment – and to make suggestions which could be passed on to hospital authorities'. Platt reported in 1959 with a list of fairly radical recommendations. The general recommendation signalled the importance being attached in some medical circles (there was by no means unanimity on the matter) to children's emotional contentment and to their fundamental reliance upon the home for personal stability:

> Great attention need be paid to the emotional and mental needs of the child in hospital, against the background of changes in attitudes towards children, in the hospital's place in the community, and in medical and surgical practice. The authority and responsibility of parents, the individuality of the child, and the importance of mitigating the effects of the break with home should all be more fully recognised.

The specific recommendations, of which there were fifty-five, included wherever possible finding alternatives to in-patient treatment; care and consideration being given to hospital organisation, design and staffing; the importance of sensitive preparation for admission; the reception process; and a number of recommendations under the heading of 'the child as in-patient', including the admission of mothers, visiting hours, education, recreation, personal possessions, discipline, food, toilet needs, and religious instruction. Unpleasant medical treatment was to be kept to a minimum; parents were to be warned about behaviour problems that may arise after discharge and advised how to deal with them; and more training was to be given to staff in 'the emotional needs' of children. Special attention was drawn to children in long-stay and infectious-diseases hospitals, and to those who were blind and deaf.[4]

The Report was at pains to stress that medical and nursing staffs in hospitals were generally sympathetic towards children, and that they faced problems in dealing with children in buildings that were more than fifty years old and, therefore, without the amenities or services that had come to be regarded as essential for their welfare. Nevertheless, the Committee was also 'unanimous in our opinion that the emotional needs of a child in hospital require constant consideration'. Furthermore, echoing the influence of the child guidance movement, the work of Bowlby and the research findings of the Tavistock Institute, it continued, 'changes of environment and separation from familiar people are upsetting, and frequently lead to emotional disturbances which vary in degree and may sometimes last well into adult life'. The connection between medicine, emotional stability and environment was reinforced by direct reference to the Curtis Report which, in looking at the deprived childhad 'emphasised the part played by unfamiliarity and separation'. The child in hospital, 'particularly when separated completely from his parents, encounters conditions similar to those of the deprived child, with the added risk of painful and frightening experiences'. Hospital staff were also reminded 'of the great advances in child care which have been made during the past 20 years or so'. Their attitudes to parents 'should take into account the general rise in the standard of living and the influence of health education on the mind of the public ... it must be remembered that the school education of many mothers has included at least elementary physiology, nutrition and hygiene'. In other words, the mothers at least could be trusted, so that hospitals should respect 'the authority of parents and respect their methods of handling their children'.[5]

What, then, happened to the Platt recommendations? The Conservative government accepted them as soon as the Report was published in early 1959. They were approved by a Ministry of Health circular which in particular called for an end to the placing of children in adult wards and restricted visiting-times. Further circulars were also issued arguing for the implementation of other recommendations. The *Visiting of Children in Hospital* (1966) and the *Accommodation of Children in Hospital in Children's Departments* (1969) emphasised the need for the relaxation of visiting-times, providing accommodation for mothers to stay overnight, and repeated the desirability of ending the practice of putting children into adult wards. A comprehensive paper, *Hospital Facilities for Children*, detailing the essential requirements for a proper hospital service for children, was published in 1971. A circular in 1972 reiterated the importance of unrestricted visiting and of close contact between parents and staff, and in addition to further circulars there was a White Paper in 1971 on *Better Services for the Mentally Handicapped* and in 1974 on *Long-Stay Children in Hospital*.[6]

It was evident that these circulars were having a limited effect on hospital administrators and medical staff. When Robertson came to publish the second edition of *Young Children in Hospital* in 1970, he noted that the Platt Report, though Ministry of Health policy, was not enforced. Instead, the Ministry left its implementation in the hands of the medical professions. Consequently, there was no uniform progress throughout the country. In an attempt to monitor the situation, the National Association for the Welfare of Children in Hospital (NAWCH) was formed in 1961, and within ten years it had fifty local groups and four thousand members. By 1969 the Association described the situation as 'extremely disappointing'. While the Department of Health claimed that unrestricted visiting was allowed in 85 per cent of children's hospitals, NAWCH disputed this figure, pointing specifically to its survey of hospitals in the South-West Metropolitan area which showed only 57 per cent with unrestricted visiting. Another survey in 1970 revealed that, of 800 hospitals admitting children, approximately 20 per cent had 'some accommodation for mothers', 8 per cent offered accommodation routinely, and 12 per cent would provide a bed for the mother in certain circumstances. By 1975 there was a 'gradual improvement' in unrestricted visiting since the early 1960s. Almost 20 per cent of all children's wards now had twenty-four-hour visiting with 33 per cent allowing daytime visits at any time. Visiting on the day of an operation, however, was rarely allowed.[7]

Nearly twenty years after Platt, the report of the Court Committee on the Child Health Services proclaimed: 'It is our belief that children have special needs which they cannot articulate for themselves and that society has therefore a duty to ensure that these are identified and cogently represented.'[8] This sentiment expressed the tone of much of the Committee's thinking about child health. The report identified the continued practice of nursing children and adolescents in adult wards where they would witness many distressing and frightening scenes. It called for a child- and family-centred health service which could meet the needs of all children and, in arguing for the advocacy of children's interests, was critical of the lack of will in the health services to act on behalf of children. Court recognised that some of the difficulties were caused by financial restrictions, but commented that 'this is by no means always so'.

By the end of the 1970s most hospitals were producing leaflets advising parents on how to prepare their children for admission, and NAWCH produced its own literature to help parents and children. There had been laudable progress made in the extension of play schemes, just as by this time the importance of play itself was generally accepted. Visiting-hours were much more flexible than in the 1960s, and accommodation for parents was available in six out of every ten wards. Progress in this area was probably helped by the fact that the average stay in hospital had fallen from two weeks in 1964 to under four days by 1980. During the period the reasons for going into hospital changed, especially the growth of 'social' admissions, with perhaps as many as 20 per cent of children admitted for other than medical or clinical reasons.[9]

Studies in 1970 and 1974, however, showed that it was the failure of hospital staff to understand children which was primarily responsible for the gradualist approach in implementing the Platt recommendations. One researcher referred to the 'fundamental lack of knowledge among nursing staff of the emotional needs of children and of the basic assumptions on which the recommendations were made'. Even when unrestricted visiting was officially allowed, the obvious disapproval of the nurses deterred the faint-hearted parent.[10] It is difficult to assess the extent to which this attitude was the result of inadequate training, as opposed to a deeper inability to conceptualise children's needs in a professional environment where those needs conflicted with administrative convenience. In general, as late as 1976, despite the progress made in some hospitals, it remained true that 'a great deal of evidence we have received underlined that it is in the sphere of social understanding of their needs that children are least well cared for'.[11]

A national survey of fifty-eight hospitals and 300 parents carried out in 1980 by the Consumers' Association to assess how far Platt's recommendations had been adopted found a substantial change in staff attitudes, especially those in paediatric departments, towards the emotional welfare of hospitalised children.[12] Non-paediatric staff, however, were much less sensitive in their dealings with the children. Nor was much attempt made to develop relationships between children and their own nurse since individual children tended to be looked after by a number of nurses. Few hospitals recognised any need to nurse children within the same age group, except in the case of babies. Furthermore, there had been little improvement in arrangements for alternatives to in-patient treatment, and it was rare to find a hospital with special provision for seeing children in a permanent out-patients' department. When temporary arrangements were made, they often excluded a paediatric nurse.

In terms of preparation for admission and reception, the hospitals were found to be laggardly in their procedures for the sympathetic treatment of children: leaflets explaining procedures were only occasionally produced specially for them; on admission to the ward they were rarely welcomed by the ward sister; and few hospitals had special casualty departments for them. In fact 15 per cent of children were admitted to adult wards.

Unsurprisingly, opportunities for outdoor play were rare. More surprisingly, many hospitals were without special playrooms and only a minority had any organised recreational schemes. On the other hand, children were no longer put straight to bed on admission during the day; they could bring their own clothes and toys, and were given individual lockers for personal possessions, and if readmitted most children went back to the same ward.

In the contentious area of parental accommodation and visiting-times, though hospitals claimed to allow parents to stay with their sick children, in practice the facilities were limited and inadequate, and it was left to parents to take the initiative. Visiting-times varied enormously both between hospitals and between wards within the same hospital. Real twenty-four-hour visiting was rarely to be found, with most hospitals discouraging evening visiting, and parents were hardly ever told of the necessity for the child's emotional health of early and frequent visiting. Parental contact immediately before and after an operation was usually forbidden, while general visits from other members of the family were not encouraged.

'FIT FOR THE FUTURE': THE CHILD HEATH SERVICES

The liberal interest in the welfare of hospitalised children was developing at a time of fundamental change in the running of the child health services. The reorganisation of the National Health Service (NHS) in 1973 transferred responsibility for all local-authority health services to Area Health Authorities, who were under the jurisdiction of the NHS. This meant that the NHS was responsible for preventive services, including school health. One result of the reorganisation was that several of the professional groups involved in health care, including Medical Officers of Health who worked in child health clinics, and who were renamed Clinical Medical Officers, not only had no clearly defined career structure but were also uncertain whether their work was to be within either the hospital or the community health services. It was thought that an inquiry would help to solve these and other organisational problems. Such an inquiry would also consider the place of the child health services as a whole in the light of the new policy of integrating the hospital, general practitioner and community services. Second, since 1972 health care had been viewed in relation to specific 'client' groups, of which children were one group. Child health, however, had never been studied from the client perspective and, therefore, an inquiry seemed to present a good opportunity to carry out such a review. Third, the contemporary interest in the 'cycle of deprivation' theory, which was much favoured by Sir Keith Joseph, Minister of State for Social Services, encouraged the view that an inquiry would provide material for an analysis of the incidence of disease in relation to social class.[13]

At the end of 1973, Professor Donald Court was appointed to chair a Committee of Inquiry into the Child Health Services, the first of its kind in Britain, with terms of reference to 'review the provision made for the health services for children up to and through school life; to study the use made of these services by children and their parents, and to make recommendations'. The Committee prefaced its report with a quotation from Katherine Mansfield: 'By health I mean the power to live a full, adult, breathing life in close contact with what I love – I want to be all that I am capable of becoming.' This at least signalled an aspiration towards some sort of ideal with respect to children's welfare.

The inquiry and the subsequent report provided one of the clearest demonstrations of the perception of the child through body *and* mind in post-war Britain. From the outset the child was viewed in its social, economic, racial and cultural environment. The Report opened with a survey of children and families, and among its twenty-one chapters it went on to look at the changing picture of health and disease, the origins and growth of services, their present strengths and weaknesses, future objectives, an integrated child health service, particular needs, and remedies for special groups. The Report was notable for including the chapter 'A Voice for Children', and for its introductory declaration that the training of anyone in professional contact with children should further 'their understanding of a child's emotional, educational, social, psychological and physical needs; that is, their understanding of the essence of being a child'.[14] What we see here is not only the claim that children have an essence which can be comprehended, but also the component features of this essence, and the linking-together of the environmental, physical and mental features into a harmonious whole. The notion of 'need', however, was not investigated. It was assumed to be unproblematic.[15]

There is little doubt that the Committee was appointed primarily for administrative reasons. While for some time there had been disquiet concerning children's health, no one disputed that there had also been 'an impressive improvement in the health of children this century'. Many of the improvements were due to better living conditions, better nutrition, smaller families, immunisation, improved treatments and standards of medical and nursing care, and health education. The main factor in saving children's lives was the decline in deaths from infectious diseases. Increased survival was matched by increased growth. Between 1900 and the 1970s children 'in average economic circumstances' gained height at ages 5–7 by 1–2 centimetres each decade, and at ages 10–14 by 2–3 centimetres each decade.

Nevertheless, there were several nagging anxieties. During the last twenty years, the infant mortality rate had fallen behind those of Sweden, France, the Netherlands, Switzerland, Japan and Finland. In England and Wales eleven out of every 1,000 births was stillborn; eleven out of every 1,000 babies died within their first four weeks, and a further sixteen died within their first year. One in seven children had a moderate or severe handicap causing educational problems. In inner-city areas the proportion was almost double and many children, it was claimed, would carry their handicap with them into adult life. Moreover, while physical health had improved steadily, mental health was seen to have lagged behind. Between 5 and 10 per cent of children were thought to have disorders of sufficient severity as to handicap them in everyday life. One of the most worrying of medical concerns was the degree of dental dilapidation: less than one third of children reached the age of 5 with their teeth free from decay, and by the age of 7, half were affected by gum disease. It was estimated that approximately 6 million schoolchildren had active caries, and about 10 per cent of 9–15-year-olds had decaying teeth. Accidents in the home and on the roads were another source of concern, being the main cause of death among those aged 1–15 (for those under 5 years old the home was more dangerous than the roads).[16]

Of course the national statistics for death, illness and disabilities concealed regional, local and social-class differences. Children in families headed by either unskilled or semi-skilled workers were twice as likely to die before the end of their first month and their first year of life as children born into class I and II. But disadvantage was not due to class alone. Those born to young mothers who did not use the ante-natal services and who smoked heavily during pregnancy were also likely to be disadvantaged. These infants were more likely to be premature and to have a low birthweight. Children in inner cities were more likely than others to be ill, and those in London were twice as likely to be psychologically disturbed as their rural contemporaries. Furthermore, the health services in the North and the Midlands were more likely to be less numerous and of poorer quality than elsewhere. Variation in regional provision of service was still much the same as it had been in 1948. Conditions were even worse for handicapped children. The Court Committee was most dejected by the services for, and the treatment of, physically and mentally handicapped children. The Report explicitly stated that the standard of diagnosis, assessment, treatment and care did not reach the normal level achieved for the treatment of acute illness: 'Some of the most depressing evidence we have received concerned handicapped children both at home and in hospital.'[17]

Child health problems no longer referred to acute episodic illness, but to malformations, chronic illness, physical and mental handicap, psychiatric disorder, and ill health arising out of social and family distress. Given this changed and changing picture of health and disease, health services for children claimed the Report, continuing its critical tone, had not developed sufficiently in response to their needs and those of their families, and the

265

In practice the majority of the fundamental recommendations were ignored. The suggestions for the new posts of Child Health Visitor, a General Practitioner Paediatrician and a Consultant Community Paediatrician were all rejected. It was claimed that the professions concerned were not sufficiently forthcoming in their support. Nor were the dental services reformed. By 1980, approximately 17,000 15-year olds had false teeth and three out of ten people over 16 had no teeth. However, the idea of a district handicap team was accepted in principle, though in practice the comprehensiveness and quality of the teams were left variable. The Government also established a Joint Committee for Children, along the lines recommended by Court, charged with advising it on the health and personal social services where they concerned children and their families. The generally disappointing government response was attributed to a lack of resources and to the powerful opposition from sections of the medical profession. In effect it was left to local health authorities and the various professional bodies to integrate the child health services in the manner they thought most appropriate, with or without regard to Court's proposals.[20]

THE BLACK REPORT AND THE HEALTH DIVIDE

The Court Report had repeatedly drawn attention to what it described as 'the correlation between social class and the prevalence of ill-health and disability in children . . . There is now extensive evidence that an adverse family and social environment can retard physical, emotional and intellectual growth, lead to more frequent and more serious illness and adversely affect educational achievement and personal behaviour'.[21] As part of its contribution to the debate on 'cycle of deprivation' theory, the DHSS funded several studies for research into the whole problem of what it called the 'conspicuous persistence of deprivation and maladjustment'. The first of these was a review of research which examined factors such as income, housing, educational attainment, intelligence, occupational status, delinquency and psychiatric disorder; the second was a micro-study of four families in Sheffield; and the third was a review of research on health and sickness as factors in the cycle.[22]

Thus the issues given voice by Court continued to attain prominence with these studies, as well as through the House of Commons Report of the Social Services Committee on Perinatal and Neonatal Morality (1980). The most devastating and controversial critique, however, came in the DHSS Report on Inequalities in Health chaired by Sir Douglas Black (1980), described by the *British Medical Journal* as 'the most important medical report since the war'.[23] Unsurprisingly the incoming Conservative government rejected the recommendations. The Secretary of State for Social Services was dismissive:

267

I must make it clear that additional expenditure on the scale which could result from the report's recommendations – the amount could be upwards of £2 billion a year – is quite unrealistic in present or any foreseeable economic circumstances, quite apart from any judgement that may be formed of the effectiveness of such expenditure in dealing with the problems identified. I cannot, therefore, endorse the Group's recommendations.[24]

The Report was updated in 1988 to include *The Health Divide* (a study commissioned by the Health Education Council, thereby bringing more recent research to bear on the debate). This also met with government interference on its publication with a press conference being cancelled an hour before it was due to begin. In the event it was widely covered in the media and discussed in the House of Commons, where the Government attempted to deflect criticisms of its health policy by pointing to improvements in the overall health condition of the population, with rising life expectancy and a falling infant mortality rate.[25]

Sir Douglas Black (formerly Chief Scientist at the Department of Health) and his Research Working Group examined the links between social class and ill-health, and concluded that class differences in morbidity and mortality were a constant feature throughout people's lives, though 'in general they are more marked at the start of life and in early adulthood'.[26] Black, however, went much further in providing a detailed account of the relationship between social class, standard of living, ill-health and mortality, and by declaring that '*the abolition of child poverty should be adapted as a national goal for the 1980s*'.[27] This was a crucial consideration throughout the Report, linked as it was to the recommendation for 'radically improving the material conditions of life of poorer groups, especially children . . . by increasing or introducing certain cash benefits, like child benefit, maternity grant and infant care allowance . . .'.[28] At the same time, it was wary of arguing that class inequalities *caused* ill-health, but nevertheless it felt that material deprivation was a 'key concept' in 'explaining the pattern of inequalities'.[29] Indeed, while both Black and *The Health Divide* agreed that in absolute terms the British people (including children) were healthier in the 1970s than they had been in the 1940s, it remained a fact that serious social inequalities in health persisted; and that socio-economic factors influenced these differentials to the extent that they had widened.[30]

Several examples of the class-related causes of child illness and death will illustrate the specifics of child ill-health during the 1970s and 1980s. The principal causes of death among the 1–14 age group were, in descending order, accidents, respiratory disease, neoplasms, congenital abnormalities and infections. According to Black, '*almost all* the differences in mortality between occupational classes I and V are due to accidents, respiratory disease (bronchitis and pneumonia) and to a much lesser extent congenital abnormality'. The explanation for this pattern appears to have been that the class gradient in bronchitis was largely caused by parental smoking, family size, a parental history of lung disease, and environmental pollution. Where accidents were concerned, the risk of death to child pedestrians was multiplied from five to seven times in moving from class I to class IV, and in cases of accidental death caused by falls, fires and drowning there was an even greater gap between the classes. The explanation here referred to material resources, domestic environment, and the supervision of children's time out of school: 'Households in occupational classes IV and V simply lack the means to provide their children with as high a level of protection as that which is found in the average middle-class home.'[31]

It was also emphasised that 'material deprivation affects physical development in young children and that ill-health contracted in childhood can dog an individual for life'. For instance, nutritional deprivation could affect physical growth, the brain and the nervous system. Improper physical development made children susceptible to illness. Moreover, as the Court Report suggested, inadequately treated childhood illness could 'cast long shadows forward'. *The Health Divide*, in looking at the *indirect* influence of income on health, drew attention to the fact that low-income families ate less fruit, vegetables and high-fibre foods, and more fat and sugar, than high-income families. A lack of money was found to be a major factor in restricting food choice and in limiting the amount consumed, thereby pushing people towards the purchase of cheap foods, which tend to be high in fat and sugar content. Poor families were particularly susceptible since for them food was the flexible item, unlike rent and rates.[32]

However, it was not only a question of poor nutritional standards. Studies of factors influencing the health and development of children showed the importance of low-income mothers coping with stress through a supply of sweets to keep children quiet and obedient, the abandonment of breast-feeding to provide time for other family duties, mixing babies' milk with cereal as a means of coping with crying and sleep difficulties, and cigarette-smoking to relieve tension (thus polluting the domestic environment). Such behaviour, while 'irresponsible' in professional terms, involved *rational* decisions on the part of the mother as she struggled to achieve family peace, contentment and survival on a limited income.[33]

The Black Report made a number of recommendations specific to the needs of children. Among the more important were more funds for accident-prevention programmes; a shift of NHS resources towards child health and community care; other improvements in the health and welfare of pre-school and school children, including a school health service linked up to general practice in order to intensify surveillance and follow-up procedures; general availability of screening procedures for neural-tube defects and Down's Syndrome; an increase in the level of child benefits;

and the introduction of an infant care allowance. Alas, the general response to these recommendations was that they were ignored.

Several years later, *The Health Divide* found that 'the child health services, provision of day care for under-fives, and the schools health services, which were seen as ways of giving children a better start in life, are all giving cause for concern'. The sense of pessimism was shared by the National Children's Bureau, in its view that since the mid-1970s 'Progress in the organization and delivery of treatment and more especially preventive services to children has been, at best, patchy. In some respects there has been a decline in those areas in which the Court Committee had hoped to see improvement.' Changes in the organisation of services away from particular client groups, like children, had discouraged the development of integrated services for them, and possibly caused administrators to lose sight of them as a priority. The Bureau put forward two main reasons to explain the decline in children's services. First, economic constraints; second, inter-professional disagreements made worse by the absence of leadership from government. Moreover, underlying so many of the difficulties, there was no attempt to adopt policies deliberately aimed at reducing child poverty; instead rising unemployment affected families with young children in particular (so that the number of children living in poverty had increased since 1980), as did the shortage of housing for the poor and state of disrepair of existing houses.[34]

The extent of ill health (and poverty) among children throughout the 1970s was well known from the DHSS studies, one of which concluded that 'there is overwhelming evidence that adverse social factors are associated with health disadvantage in children, and probably with disadvantage in the children's future'. Furthermore, 'a great deal of effort has gone into the task of proving again and again, that these socially-associated differences in the health status of children do exist; almost as if this were something that society did not wish to believe'.[35] Several years later, in a publication to mark the Diamond Jubilee of the British Paediatric Association, Professors Court and Alberman noted that the Black Report had called for the abolition of child poverty as a national goal for the 1980s, and that to date 'there is no evidence that this is a political priority'. After reminding their readers of the importance of child health for adult health, the professors observed: '*Not* to put children as a political priority is shortsighted in every way, and the consequence serious and long-standing.'[36]

The various studies and reports of the period illustrated how little attention was given either to the Bodies or the Minds of children from poor families, many thousands of whom were consequently suffering emotional and physical distress and stunted development. This neglect occurred at the same time as child abuse scandals were gathering headlines throughout the media. It is tempting to suggest that the vast majority of child victims were ignored by influential interests, so that those suffering deliberate

270

physical injury and sexual abuse could be mythologised. The purpose being, as was suggested in the previous chapter, to counter social and political threats emanating from those welfare policies which were deemed to be the products of consensual social-democratic beliefs and the 'permissiveness' of the 1960s.

11

'CHILDREN ARE PEOPLE, TOO': CHILD CARE POLICY IN THE 1980s

CHILD CARE POLICY IN THE 1980s

The legacy of the 1970s

The child care services initiated in the wake of the Curtis Report (1946) continued to develop in the 1960s when, as has been shown, they sought to prevent the breakdown of families and to bring juvenile delinquents within the care system, and again in 1971 when as part of the Seebohm proposals they were merged with other local-authority services. For the most part these years were marked not only by expansion, but also by a sense of optimism, a belief that it *was* possible to change people's lives, to enhance their experiences, in effect to patch up the consequences of economic and social deprivation.[1] However, by the mid-1970s, if not before, a feeling of disquiet had arisen within social work circles over certain child care issues, such as adoption and fostering. Other criticisms concerned the damaging effects of 'drift' in care, so that a campaign was launched as the 'Permanence Movement', which sought early decision-making. This gave rise to another opposition lobby, the Family Rights Group, which campaigned in defence of parents against what it saw as premature decisions.[2]

The appearance of this organisation reflected the emergence from the late 1960s of what has been termed 'Individual Rights and legalism', namely, the Children's Rights Movement, Childright and Child Line; the civil liberties critique which focused on local-authority intervention in people's lives in cases of mental illness and juvenile delinquency; the related group of 'due process' lawyers in organisations such as the National Association for One Parent Families, Justice for Children, the Children's Legal Centre, the above-mentioned Family Rights Group and, from the mid-1980s, Parents Against Injustice. Furthermore, with respect to young offenders, there was growing criticism, from a legalistic perspective, of the 'welfare' orientation towards delinquency (focusing on their families and their relationships) which was held to be inherently unjust. These and other conflicts were exacerbated by the shortage of resources, with cutbacks in services, as family poverty increased and the problems of inner cities multiplied. When all is considered, it is hardly surprising that social work became more conflict-ridden from the late 1970s onwards than it had been in the years between 1948 and 1975.[3]

The 1980s

It would be hard to disagree with Parton's observation that there was 'a growing set of constituencies developing during the 1980s' (albeit without a shared focus of criticism) 'which emphasized the need for a greater reliance on individual rights firmly located in a reformed statutory framework where there was a greater emphasis on legalism'.[4] The 1980s were the decade in which long-smouldering tensions concerning the relationship between child care, family responsibility and the jurisdiction of the State finally erupted. The problem has usually been perceived as one of *balance* between too much and too little intervention. The child abuse cases of the 1980s exemplified the dilemmas of the State and its professionals: the public inquiries surrounding the deaths of Beckford, Carlile, Henry and Mason suggested that there was too little intervention and that it occurred too late, while the Cleveland affair – focusing on sexual abuse – pointed to the reverse. The concern for all interested parties was how to strike a *new* balance between the competing claims of parents, children, social workers and local-authority social services departments.[5]

The feelings of unease and dissatisfaction were aired in studies by the National Children's Bureau, the DHSS, and the Parliamentary Social Services Committee, which called for 'a thorough-going review of the body of statute law, regulations and judicial decisions'.[6] The DHSS *Review of Child Care Law* (1985) emphasised the concept of 'partnership' between parents and local authorities. This was followed by a government White Paper, *The Law on Child Care and Family Services* (1987), and by two papers from the Law Commission on *Guardianship and Custody* (1988), and *Wards of Court* (1987). Among other criticisms, these appeared to confirm the impression of hasty and badly planned decision-making when children were taken into care.[7] A particular point of tension was the increased use of the 'place of safety' order – between a quarter and a third – which suggested that large numbers of children within care had entered in a traumatic manner. This served to intensify the polarisation between different political perspectives.[8] Much of the criticism was aimed at social workers who were seen as authoritarian and adversarial, though the researchers were sympathetic to the profession as a whole.

Increasingly, the call was made for the philosophy of *partnership* which, so its advocates claimed, had been present in the early days of post-war

273

child care practice, to be reintroduced in national policy.[9] However, almost simultaneously with the publication of these studies came the reports of major child abuse scandals (Beckford, 1985; Henry, 1987; and Carlisle, 1987), which criticised social workers, not for being too adversarial, but for being too trusting of parents, too willing to believe in the ability of the family to survive as a whole unit. Nevertheless, the feeling remained that 'decision making was little more than crisis management' and that social work had become 'confrontational, antagonistic and defensive'.[10]

On the one hand, the DHSS studies pointed to the 'mismatch between the very different elements in the work of services for families and children, and the unhelpfulness of the legalistic and adversarial approach to most of this work.' On the other hand, the child abuse reports provided the 'major catalyst' of public disquiet about issues over and above the behaviour of social workers – issues concerning more fundamental questions about the family, feminism, law and order, and ethnic integration.[11] Thus, when the Cleveland affair broke, it proved to be a cartharsis for a number of political anxieties which often had no clear party-political identity and, for the first time, found expression through a sexual abuse scandal. Once again children were about to become bit-part players in a drama where their welfare was of lesser significance than other and more overtly political priorities.

The Cleveland story began early in June 1987 when a local paper started to publish accounts of 200 children being taken into care since May by the local-authority social workers on the basis of a diagnosis of sexual abuse made by two paediatricians, Dr Marietta Higgs and Dr Geoffrey Wyatt. The parents protested and soon found articulate supporters in local clergy, the national press and the local MPs, Stuart Bell and Tim Devlin. The caring professions, in particular social workers and certain paediatricians, were accused of acting in an authoritarian manner – Tim Devlin and the *Daily Mail* actually compared the social workers to the German SS – and matters were made worse through disagreements within the professions concerned, especially in relation to the reliability of anal dilatation as evidence of buggery.[12] Less than a month later a parliamentary question was asked of the Minister of State for Health, who promised an inquiry. Mrs Justice Butler-Sloss was appointed to head the inquiry, which began to hear evidence on 11 August 1987 and concluded its business on 29 January 1988.[13]

But the real significance of the threat posed by Cleveland was that, through the minority of middle-class parents among those suspected of child sexual abuse, in part it challenged 'the integrity of the *bourgeois* family, not merely the private conduct of the loose and demoralised black or white working-class unit of living'.[14] Hence the jacket cover of Stuart Bell's book on the affair proclaimed that at the heart of events in Cleveland 'lay the fundamental question: who has ultimate power over children – the family or the State?'. Clearly the political representatives of 'the family'

274

saw the issue in terms of power. The bourgeois family *per se* was presented as being under threat from the range and scale of social-work and medical intervention in family life. The significant moment occurred when the middle class decided to fight back against the social workers and their medical allies, and gathered around them the support of those interests which for sometime had feared for the sanctity of the family as it came under a variety of assaults from doctrines of permissiveness, feminists, gays and lesbians, and a variety of socialists and radicals. The new emphasis on the family was apparent in the Cleveland Report's criticism of the professionals involved for having 'a strong focus on the needs of the child *in isolation from the family*'. The professionals had failed to appreciate 'the unique features of each family as a family'. So it was that social workers could be accused of 'missing out a vital dimension of proper assessment – a family diagnosis'.[15]

The shift towards 'the family' and parents' rights can be seen in the DHSS response to Cleveland. After the Beckford inquiry, the Department circulated a draft guide, *Child Abuse – Working Together* (1986), for inter-agency co-operation, which saw child protection in terms of protecting children *from* parents and guardians *per se*. However, the Cleveland crisis began prior to publication of the final draft, and in order to consider the findings of the Inquiry publication was postponed until the same day as the Report was published in 1988. In the intervening period, and no doubt under the influence of Cleveland, the emphasis changed. In the final version the phrase 'working together' was emphasised to mean that professionals and agencies should work together *with* parents (and in some respects also with children). This denoted a subtle shift of direction in child protection policy from that exposed in the draft guide. Where the draft spoke of protecting children *from* parents, the final version looked to their protection through more circumscribed relations between professionals and families which in effect meant protecting the 'rights' of parents. Furthermore, where the draft held that 'a child's statement that he or she is being abused should be accepted as true until proved otherwise', by 1988 this had become 'a child's statement about an allegation of abuse . . . should always be taken seriously'.[16] The new phrasing was such as to cast doubt upon the child's integrity.

Confirmation of the lessening of the child's importance between the draft and the published version could also to be seen by comparing the declaration of the former, that 'the child's welfare must be the overriding concern of professional staff', with the latter, which advised that while social services should give 'the first and highest priority to protecting the child', 'they also have responsibilities in relation to the child's parents and other family members or carers'.[17] In important respects the change of emphasis meant that the issue was no longer one of recognising and combating child abuse; instead the focus was moved to that of the search for a new set of 'balances' between the 'rights' of children, parents and the State. Despite the rhetoric of the Cleveland Report in describing the child as 'a person – and not an object of concern', in reality it was seen primarily through the prism of 'the family', which could not but limit the scope of its individual personhood.

This was a revealing development, given that it was children who were being sexually abused, rather than 'the family' or parents. And even more so when it is recognized that the Inquiry did not attempt to assess the extent of sexual abuse or to discover how many of the Cleveland children taken into care had in fact been sexually abused. Instead it preferred to limit itself to examining how the problem should be *managed*. Indeed, management of child abuse became the dominant theme of the manner in which the 'problem' was officially perceived. No wonder a commentator wrote that 'One could be forgiven for reading the DHSS circulars and reports on child abuse as arguing that "lack of coordination" is the *cause* of child abuse'.[18] A perception of this kind had little time for a more searching or more unsettling analysis – such as inquiring into patriarchy and the inherent powerless of children when confronted by adults. In a very important sense, 'mismanagement' of cases of child abuse turned the *victims* into figures who threatened to undermine the comforting imagery of family and home.

THE CHILDREN ACT, 1989

The majority of commentators seem to agree that throughout the decade – indeed, from about the mid-1970s – all roads in child care led to the Children Act, 1989.[19] However, the Act was not a response to events in Cleveland but rather the culmination of a review of child care law which began with the Short Report in 1984. The Act was described by the Lord Chancellor when introducing the Bill as 'the most comprehensive and far reaching reform of childcare law in living memory'.[20] In the words of Michael Freeman, the leading legal advocate of Children's Rights, it 'rewrites the language of childcare law and practice ... it represents a change in attitude towards children and their families'.[21] Or, as Parton writes, it attempts to construct 'a new consensus', often referred to as 'a new set of balances'.[22] The Act is about 'parental responsibility', 'support for children and families' and 'partnership (in many respects the key concept). In the following summary, the intention is not simply to describe the main provisions of the Act, but to incorporate it into a historical interpretation of child-welfare policy and, with reference to the last decade or so, to assess its significance for children, for parent–child relations, and for the welfare of children in the broadest sense of the term.

The Act, which reiterates the Inquiry's proclamation that 'the child is a person and not an object of concern', is commonly described as compre-

276

hensive and coherent, bringing together public and private law involving children – in areas covering childcare, child protection, wardship and divorce (although child-support law and adoption remain more or less without alteration).[23] Old concepts such as custody, care and control and access were abolished, as were 'voluntary care', custodianship or the assumption of parental rights, and the 'place of safety' order. Children who persistently truanted were no longer to be committed to care; criminal care orders were abolished; and the powers of the court to supervise arrangements for children in divorce matters were reduced. New 'orders' were also introduced, among which were those relating to family assistance (s.16), education supervision (s.36), emergency protection (s.44), child assessment (s.43) and private orders (s.8). The distinction between private law involving children (e.g disputes between parents) and public law (matters relating to their public welfare) was dissolved. New categories of children were included, in particular those with disabilities, long-stay hospital patients, the mentally handicapped, and pupils in independent boarding schools.[24]

A key part of the Act concerns the powers and duties of local authorities in providing family support or, as it is sometimes known, 'primary prevention'. Under the new legislation a distinction was drawn between *all* children in need and those defined by the Act as *children in need*. Section 17 gave local authorities a number of duties, to be implemented through the provision of services, to look after the welfare of children. These duties were imposed for the 'principal' purpose of providing for children who are 'in need'.[25] The definition of 'in need' was laid down by statute for the first time, and is fairly broad. This, says Freeman, clearly indicates the emphasis on 'preventive support and services for families'. It refers to achieving or maintaining 'a reasonable standard of health or development'; being in a position where health or development 'is likely to be significantly impaired'; or being disabled. Local authorities were also given a number of *powers* which would allow them to provide various facilities for *all* children in their area, such as day care for children under 5.[26] However, the emphasis on children 'in need' constitutes what has been called 'the new ideology of residualism' which will 'provide a challenge for good practices in childcare'. This means that under pressure from resource deficiencies there will be the temptation to apply the concept of 'need' to a restricted group of children, probably those 'at risk'.[27] Local authorities are also permitted to provide cash assistance in 'exceptional circumstances' to families. The origins of this provision go back to the 1950s and to the Children and Young Persons Act, 1963, which linked it to keeping children out of juvenile courts. The new provision does not have this overtone since it is to be seen as part of the support services.[28]

In order to appreciate the distinctive nature of the Act it is essential to understand the triad of 'Principles, Parents and Partnership'.[29] There are four principles. The first declares that whenever the court has to determine issues relating to the upbringing of the child, or the administration of a child's property, or the income arising from it, 'the child's welfare shall be the court's paramount consideration'. The second principle urges rapid procedures and decision-making since delay is viewed as prejudicial to the child's welfare. The novelty here is that for the first time Parliament, rather than the courts, has expressed this view. Third, there is a checklist to which courts considering certain categories of order must have regard. Again, the significant aspect is that Parliament has decreed a checklist in order to assist the courts to operate the welfare principle. The fourth principle, which arguably may be 'the key to an understanding of the whole Act', is that of 'minimal intervention' – a reluctance to make an 'order' unless it is clearly 'better' for the child. It has been said, with some accuracy, that these principles mean that the Act is fundamentally concerned with a change in *attitude*.[30]

In addition new concepts were introduced. Of particular importance was the insertion of the term 'parental responsibility' in place of the traditional emphasis on parental rights and duties (s.2). But it should not be thought that this is an expression of the children's rights philosophy. In fact the whole matter was virtually ignored by the Act, probably because it would have proved controversial and delayed the introduction of other important reforms.[31] Instead, the new concept emphasised the notion of 'responsibility' as being in relation to 'rights'. In other words, parents had the latter only in so far as they exercised the former. The effect of this distinction was to promote the parent as the authority figure. Thus the legislation reinforces parental authority so long as parents behave 'responsibly'. Moreover, in an affirmation of the Conservative doctrine of 'privatisation', the emphasis on parental responsibility makes parents, rather than the state, responsible for their children. Nor can they divest themselves of their obligation (though others can exercise it for them in certain circumstances); only where legal adoption occurs do the natural parents get released. This explains why 'voluntary care' was replaced by 'accommodation', meaning in effect that the local authority would care for children only on *behalf* of their parents, until such time as they could resume their proper role.[32]

The third concept, partnership, although not actually mentioned in the Act, derives from the *Review of Child Care Law* (DHSS, 1985). The *Review* argued that the emphasis should be on maintaining family links in order 'to care for the child in partnership with rather than in opposition to his parents, and to work towards his return to them'.[33] This theme has since been officially reiterated several times, most recently in an official guide, *Principles and Practice* (DHSS): 'The development of a working partnership with parents is usually the most effective route to providing supplementary or substitute care for their children.' However, the concept of 'accommodation' (mentioned above) showed that the Government's notion of partnership was based on what Parton calls 'consumerist criteria', which sees parents as consumers who in time of need turn to the local authorities, who in turn are seen as suppliers, for a 'service' – as in the commercial market-place. So parental responsibility cannot be surrendered; instead the parent can only ask for or be given assistance in the form of the local-authority 'service' to 'look after' the child for a limited period. Freeman comments: 'The emphasis on partnership, like that on parental responsibility, is in part an exercise in social engineering.'[34] Or, put another way, it is the reinforcement of market values.

The Act was also notable for confirming the importance of 'legalism' in childcare, as defined by the 'superimposition of legal duties and rights upon the therapeutic and preventative responsibilities [of local-authority social workers], essentially for the protection of clients'.[35] It has already been shown that a feature of the focus of developments from the late 1960s onwards was a set of criticisms (often contradictory) of social workers, and of welfare practices in general, as being authoritarian and almost beyond the law. Moreover, the criticisms came from both the Left and the Right.[36] No doubt with this critique in mind, the Act was distinctive in making social workers more accountable to the law, especially where the transfer of parental responsibility to the local authority is concerned. This shift is of interest in understanding more than just the formal legal arrangements involved in childcare since, as Parton shows, in drawing upon Durkheim's concept of the *visible symbol*, 'the degree of legalism [*visible symbol*] in the regulation of certain social practices can provide an index of important changes in the relationship between the state and civil society and ... the state and the family'. The emergence of legalism is seen as 'evidence of the collapse of the political consensus upon which the institutional fabric of the welfare state was so dependent' during the period *circa* the 1950s to the early 1970s. It is also evidence of 'the development of an influential liberal individualist critique of the professionalised paternalism and bureaucratic decision-making', which was alleged to have been the hallmark of social-work activity during the period 1945–1980s.[37]

Alongside the importance of legalism in the Act, must also be placed the concept of 'dangerousness', which developed from the 1970s onwards and is relevant to several areas of penal and mental-health policies. Dangerousness assumes the existence of a small number of highly dangerous individuals who are liable to cause serious harm to others through physical, sexual or psychological violence. Where child abuse is concerned, the central objective of social workers is to concentrate on the 'assessment of past, present, and future dangerousness, which can result in the long-term or permanent removal of children from a family'.[38] Since the emphasis is on identifying the extreme in human behaviour, and not on working towards the possibility of prevention or rehabilitation, the policy can be characterised as conservative rather than liberal in terms of remedying family problems. This approach is also politically significant since it focuses on limited resources, whereas rehabilitation disperses resources throughout a number of social channels.[39]

The theoretical significance of 'dangerousness' is that it provides a clear demarcation-line between legitimate and illegitimate interference in the family by social workers. In this respect it can be seen as part of the structure of 'balance' in the Act. On the one hand, those with an interest in child protection could look to the criterion of dangerousness to protect children; while, on the other hand, those who were interested in family rights could look to the concept to ensure that families are not subjected to unnecessary interference. This view of 'child protection' is perhaps 'fundamental' to the Act, which clearly distinguishes between the *voluntary* services for 'children in need' and the care system which involves itself only when the child 'is *suffering, or is likely to suffer significant harm.*'[40]

The development of dangerousness and legalism highlighted the construction of *child protection* during the 1980s as *the* concern of the child care profession, often to the neglect of other child care services. The focus on *child protection* was also another means of targeting resources at a time, since the end of the 1970s, when the number of children in conditions of social and economic distress has grown to millions.[41] It may well turn out that 'child protection' will allow social services departments to ignore many of those children in need of preventive assistance, in favour of those suffering or likely to suffer 'significant harm' (the term emphasises the severity of the 'harm' thought necessary to justify local-authority intervention in parental child-rearing). And, even then, budgetary considerations may force priorities to be made within the area of child abuse itself. Hence the concept of 'dangerousness' (in conjunction with 'significant harm') allows for priorities to be rigidly identified. This can hardly be seen as coincidental given that during the passage of the 1989 Bill the Government reiterated its opposition to more generous provision in housing and social security policies and made clear that by and large no extra resources would be made available for dealing with 'child protection'.[42]

The Act did not begin to come into force until October 1991 and, therefore, it will be some time before the reality of day-to-day practice exerts its influence on the structural principles. There is, however, little doubt that the Act forms an integral part of Conservative Party social policy for the 1990s which does not, as is sometimes mistakenly alleged, promote the abdication of post-war social collectivism, so much as rather 'a reformulation of what those responsibilities really mean. Service boundaries, resource allocation and assessment and the means to "police" and review each are key determinants of the new welfare.'[43]

AN ASSESSMENT OF THE ACT

It is generally agreed that the Children Act represents a consensus among interested parties, except of course for children, who were not consulted. It seems clear that its sense of direction stemmed from government priorities. While all major viewpoints are present, none is more so than that of *laissez-faire* since one of the basic objectives of the Act is to keep compulsory intervention to a minimum. At the same time, representing the interventionist perspective, local authorities have also been strengthened in their powers of intervention, principally through the clause which allows social workers to begin care proceedings on the basis that the child is 'likely' to suffer 'significant harm' (s.31.2). Similarly, under the terms of an 'assessment order', a child may be removed from its family for investigative purposes. The pro-birth-family principle is also clearly evident in an official guide to the Act which proclaims that the legislation 'rests on the belief that children are generally best looked after within the family with both parents playing a full part and without resort to legal proceedings'.[44] The children's rights position is just about present in so far as children may initiate court actions; there is also to be a greater recognition of their wishes and feelings; and greater use made of guardians *ad litem* to represent them. However, the position of the child is weakened in relation to divorce since the power of the court to inspect child care arrangements has been reduced. Assessing the relative strengths of these different perspectives is difficult. It has been argued that paternalism and the defence of birth parents' rights are the dominant strands in the Act, while others see it as being characterised by non-interventionism.[45]

In Freeman's view, the 'presence of such different ideologies suggests the conflicts of the 1980s have not truly been resolved, that divisions were papered over and that, not far below the surface, conflict remains'.[46] The issue of consensus, balance and conflict is, of course, basically one of ideology. Thus, as Freeman says, legislation is always political – indeed, it is a political process – and, therefore, the consequences also must be political. The official Guide to the Act claims that it strikes a 'new balance between the autonomy of the family and the protection of children'. Similarly, it has been argued that the Act 'treads a tightrope' and tries 'to safeguard the weak . . . [and] the state's duty to support families in their task of bringing up children and its duty to protect children from significant harm are *both* enhanced'.[47] And yet, to quote Freeman again, Acts 'do not strike balances'; instead they 'establish frameworks within which [political] decisions are taken by lawyers, social workers, local-authority officials, and the courts'. Consensus can be constructed by projecting 'images' which appeal to those of a different 'value position', but, as Freeman argues, this may turn out to be 'fragile and precarious'.[48]

The image around which the consensus arose was that of the family in so far as it drew upon social theories of both Right and Left. The former sees the family as the arena of the 'domestic ideal', inherited from the nineteenth century with its emphasis on privacy, hierarchy, order, obedience and patriarchy. Such a family – whose adults were self-conscious citizens – required little or no interference from the State, except in exceptional circumstances.[49] For the Left the idea of the family is usually lodged within the working class, which is seen as being harassed by bureaucrats and social workers, with parents being made the scapegoats for an inequitable social and economic system. The Act appealed to the Left because it offered the likelihood of reducing coercive interventions by state officials and, equally if not more significantly, it also offered the possibility of support for the families of 'children in need' through day care, financial assistance, and family centres.[50]

As might be expected, there were significant differences in the way in which the MPs viewed the debate on the Act when it was a Bill passing through Parliament. For the Conservative Dame Jill Knight, child abuse arose from the collapse of old values under the impact of permissive divorce laws and the general inability of many interests to recognise 'the crucial importance to society of stable family life'. The right-wing Labour MP Stuart Bell (one of the leading supporters of parents during the Cleveland affair) stated that 'Family life has come under a fundamental and serious attack over the years . . . we have seen a steady erosion of the family base'. It was left to certain Labour MPs to argue for the relationship between child abuse and economic and social deprivation. Max Madden pointed to the irony that while the Bill was being debated child benefit had been frozen and over 2 million children were estimated to be living around the poverty line: 'the bill will be no more than words on paper unless we ensure that Britain's children and families receive a fair share of the wealth that they have been creating over the years.'[51]

But the polarisation has not been simply one of Left versus Right, or that arising out of the different perspectives represented in the Act.[52] The fundamental source of the problem is to be found in the heritage of a liberal capitalist democracy as it has evolved since the end of the nineteenth century. At the heart of this heritage is the whole question of what Jacques Donzelot has called 'the social', by which he means the conceptual (and historical) space between the 'public' and the 'private' domain as it comes to settle on the family, and in particular on child-rearing, in pursuit of its universal aim of creating 'a general solidarity and the production of a lifestyle'.[53] On the other hand, 'the social' might more easily be seen – at least, as a form of shorthand – as the issue of citizenship, that is, relations over the last 150 years or so in liberal society between individuals and the State.[54] Given that in liberal theory the family stands as a primary moral source and as the bulwark against the abuse of state power, how should the State relate to its citizens in terms of duties, responsibilities, rights and 'needs'. Liberal philosophers from Mill to Hayek have acknowledged that children do not enter the parent–child relationship of their own free will and, therefore, the relationship is based on an unequal contract. With specific reference to the family, including childcare, the crucial question remains 'how can we devise a *legal* basis for the power to intervene into the family which does not convert *all* families into clients of the State?'[55] The family must behave as if it were an autonomous entity, and it must be seen as such by the State and its welfare agencies, and yet the State must also be free to intervene when the family fails in its child-rearing functions.[56]

The State finds this freedom in the Act which allows for the supervision of the privatised family. The 'partnership' referred to above is one which allows for unobtrusive state supervision – at least, that is the intention. It is a subtle partnership; to a large extent it is dependent upon goodwill from both parties. Indeed, in many respects it is a liberal compromise.[57] Nevertheless, the partnership is not entirely free to find its own equilibrium since, as the family is an instrument of social regulation, it must conform to certain social disciplines.

With this in mind, we should see the debate about welfare intervention not only in terms of 'rights' or 'the best interests of the child', but also in those of 'state forms' – the organic variety of interests forever struggling for superiority at any one time, and 'households' – not just the nuclear family but the plurality of family forms in modern Britain. Only when this context is recognised does it make sense to use concepts such as 'rights' and 'interests'. In a passage which expresses one of the principal themes of this history, Nick Frost writes that in a divided society 'we cannot understand child protection work as being simply about the protection of children'. Child-protection practice, he continues, 'in an environment of inequality and marginalization becomes a process of judging and disciplining households defined as outside the mainstream'.[58] This observation is substantially correct, though child protection was and is about much more than either exercising discipline over a kind of underclass or, following the thesis of Nikolas Rose, a feature of the self-government of our souls.[59] Child-protection practice is integral to definitions of childhood and to the social lives of individual children.

The problem of family regulation in the liberal state only occasionally attends to children's rights *within* the family. The decision of Parliament to shift the emphasis in child care legislation towards 'the family', however much this may be disguised in the language of partnership (one that excludes children), cannot but endanger children's rights since as has been shown it removes the child from the centre of child protection policy and relocates it within what is very often no more than a spurious domesticity. The family autonomy theorists, of both Left and Right, throughout the 1980s reformulated children's rights 'in terms of adult freedoms'.[60] These theorists thought in terms of a child's right to 'family integrity', the 'privacy of family life', the 'principle of respect for family autonomy' and respect for 'parental autonomy in child-rearing'.[61] Such a concept of children's rights reduces them to 'a parental right to freedom from state supervision on the basis of an assertion that children have a right to develop and maintain unconstrained psychological ties with their parents'.[62] As Dingwall and Eekelaar have observed, 'this is not a theory of children's rights at all so much as a political theory about the proper relationship between families and the state', since a true theory 'would need to express claims that enhanced their [children's] interests as a matter of principle rather than coincidence'. There can 'be no escape from the fact that the recognition of children's interests necessarily entails the abridgement of family autonomy. The trade-off between these objectives is a political decision.'[63] Since the focus of the 1989 Act rarely falls in this direction, it has little interest in furthering children's rights.

CONCLUSION

There have been four main developments in post-war social policy, only one of which was clearly concerned with children as investments, though all used notions of victims and threats, albeit in different combinations, to fashion policies convenient for dominant economic and political interests. The period began on a wave of optimism which was largely the product of war-time reconstructionist thinking along the lines of planning for democratic families, 'problem' families, and the creation of universal welfare schemes. Despite all the revisionist historical writing which has correctly called into question the extent of the post-war consensus and the reality of so-called social solidarity, it remains true that for thousands, if not millions, of Liberal and Labour voters in their working lives the new social services and the desire to build a more egalitarian democracy than had existed in the inter-war period represented years of hope, of a belief in the possibility of change. Children were given roles in this scenario – not large or significant roles in and for themselves, but none the less positive roles. The other influence on the new perception of child care emerged from the evacuation experience, especially as it affected middle-class social attitudes in alerting the philanthropic and professional caring sections of the class to the extent and nature of life in the slums. However, it was not simply the trauma of evacuation that attached a new importance to childcare. Professional (and perhaps even governmental) attitudes were influenced by the knowledge gathered from the 1920s through the child guidance movement, and from the war-time psychological studies of Susan Isaacs, John Bowlby and Anna Freud.

Although much of the rhetoric of the late 1940s and early 1950s implied an image of the child as a victim (of evacuation, the Blitz, the slums, and separation), the overall emphasis was on its membership of a family, an institution regarded as the basis of a revitalised liberal capitalist democracy. This emphasis was projected in collaboration with the desire to counter fears about a declining birth rate (and consequently the possible decline of 'the security and influence of Great Britain': Beveridge) through the encouragement of pronatalism.[1] While both these projects viewed children as investments, there was a subtle difference between the two. In the case of the family, the importance of the child was as a properly functioning member of a properly functioning group – in other words, the child was important for itself in the present; its healthy emotional and physical development was evidence of the harmonious domestic environment, and of the likely continuance of such harmony in the next generation of parents. Of course, the possibility of children as threats was always likely, since failure to thrive in the family, for whatever reason, made them a threatening presence along a spectrum from 'naughtiness through criminality to frank insanity'.[2] The child as a figure in pronatalist ambitions was more directly

285

restricted to the future and so could hardly be viewed as any kind of threat. The importance of these children was primarily numerical rather than personal: they were points on a birth-rate graph. Overall it was the child as investment that mattered; the child as victim or threat was very much a secondary consideration.

The second development was a particularly focused concern which emanated from a medical expertise before becoming an integral feature of a complex socio-moral analysis of post-war and post-1960s society. The 'battered baby', the 'abused child' and finally the 'sexually abused child' took their place in a gallery of social constructions which paradoxically reveal the monumental indifference of adults to this form of child persecution throughout the greater part of the last century. It has been shown that prior to the emergence of the 'battered baby' in the 1960s very little official concern had been expressed about the plight of abused or neglected children since the late-Victorian and Edwardian periods. The evolving portraits of cruelly used children – from 'battered' to 'sexually abused' – could well represent a series of mirrors in which there was (and is) reflected an amalgam of professional (medical, legal, social, academic) and political interests of both the Right and the Left (the latter influenced by feminism), which saw in the child's abused condition an opportunity to campaign for their own ends, often with little regard for the children concerned. We are probably too close to the issues, emotionally and temporally, to offer an enlightening analysis. There is little doubt, however, that in time the peculiar interest in 'child abuse' during the period 1960s–1980s will come to be seen as a profoundly significant moment in British culture.

One reason why the interest will appear so curious is that it coincided with the third development, namely the extensive research by university and government departments and pressure groups into child health and welfare. The health inquiries of Professors Platt, Court and Black, together with that of the Health Education Council, *The Health Divide*, when added to DHSS studies, the sociological accounts of health and poverty by Professors Abel-Smith and Townsend, and their colleagues, and the research publications of the CPAG, all pointed towards a situation of such inequity as to be 'inexcusable in a democratic society which prides itself on being humane'.[3] From the rediscovery of poverty in the 1960s it was clear that the children of the poor, and even those who were marginally above the poverty line, were in grave danger of suffering from deteriorating standards of health and social life. Time after time throughout the 1960s, 1970s and 1980s, the condition of these children was reiterated in publication after publication.[4] But increasingly children's welfare was made subject to the same economic criteria as was applied to other groups. In the more stringent economic climate beginning with the sterling crisis of 1966 and devaluation in 1967, their needs were more or less ignored.

It would be untrue to say that either the media or the Government was completely unmoved by child ill-health and poverty, for there were expressions of concern. However, it would be equally untrue to say that the media treated child poverty in the same dramatic fashion as it did the child abuse scandals of the period. No politician responsible for social security payments to poor families was harrassed by journalists as were social workers and doctors involved in child abuse cases. There were few in-depth analyses of the effects of poverty and bad housing on child health and welfare, as there were of local-authority social service departments, and as the Institute of Economic Affairs performed on what it called 'the failure of the Welfare State'.[5] Of course there was widespread abuse of children, including their murder and manslaughter (usually by fathers or step-fathers). But what needs to be questioned is why these relatively few deaths caused such public anguish, while the quiet mental, physical and emotional retardation of so many hundreds of thousands of children raised hardly a murmur outside professional and academic circles.

Unfortunately, it is usually the case that the most influential ideological perspective is that which coincides with what is economically feasible in the minds of representative élites. The fact is that notions of child health and welfare are inseparable from economic values and priorities. Child abuse protection services, though relatively expensive, are of marginal financial significance in comparison with the cost of comprehensive anti-poverty programmes.

The fourth development was the creation of the Children Act, 1989, about which volumes have been and are being written by lawyers and social scientists. The importance of the Act for our purposes is that it illustrates how far present childcare concerns are from those of the 1940s and the Children Act, 1948. It might appear at first sight that the two Acts have much in common. Both seem to be concerned with procedures and administration; both are concerned with the family and with the relationship between it, the local authority and the State; and both seek to protect children. However, the 1989 Act is much more circumscribed than its post-war predecessor. True, it is generous in its attempt to be comprehensive and universal. But the earlier Act set out to create a system of child welfare in keeping with the broader understanding of a 'Welfare State'. Nothing of the sort can be said about the 1989 Act, which slithered on to the statute-book as a tired consensus arrived at between a dispirited, fragmented and largely defunct Left and a morally arrogant Right, confident of its own ability to continue successfully to articulate social (and, therefore, political) agendas. In essence the Act is about the privatised family; the 1948 Act, whatever its interest in 'problem' parents, was concerned with the family in a democracy. Neither, however, offered much to children as people.

One other area remains to be considered here: the dualism of Body/Mind. The public debate on child care in the 1970s and 1980s was domi-

287

nated by the child as 'body' – by its physicality; very little attention was paid to its 'mind'. This does not mean that children were perceived almost entirely through their bodies, but since the influence of the 1948 Act began to wane the emotional condition of the child figured less prominently in its public image. It is almost as if the child guidance movement, having identified the Mind dimension, subsided into the anonymity of local-authority social service departments. Once the importance of emotional development in children was recognised, as it was in the Children Act, 1948, child guidance seems to have lost much of its influence. It looks as if it became subsumed within the child welfare legislation of the 1960s and 1970s and is difficult to find in the Children Act, 1989. By and large the political, social and economic contexts of the years since the late 1940s have directed attention towards the body as the issues involving child health and welfare have been those relating to poverty, housing, delinquency, and physical and sexual abuse. This has been particularly true of the 1980s where the image of the abused child recalls the studied photographs used by Barnardo and the NSPCC in their pioneering days. Such a bodily image is not without its significance, for it simplifies the child for us. Make the body better, it suggests, and there are no more problems. Rescue me, cries out the body, from abuse – physical or sexual – and I shall be whole again. What you see is what you know. Invest your love and care in me and I will be good.

JUSTIFICATIONS AND
EXPLANATIONS

This has been a long textbook. I have two defences. First, so much has happened in the area of social policy for children over the last 120 years, and so little is known about these developments among a general audience (aside from specialists), that in order to provide a proper historical perspective it has been necessary to offer a broad and comprehensive sweep. In bringing together so many different policies I have tried to show the ways in which children were gradually incorporated into a kind of social citizenship (which has not always benefited them), and also to describe the continuities and discontinuities in the motives and objectives of reformers and other policy-makers. The implicit argument of this book is that future historical surveys of social policy should not ignore the connections between children and welfare. It should now be clear that the relationship has been sometimes indicative of, and very often central to, debates about the role of the State, the family, education, citizenship and social stability, not to mention more grandiose themes concerning national culture and morality. The hope is that by considering the variety of developments across a wide range of policies we may begin to appreciate the complex roles demanded of children by these inquiries.

My second defence refers to the period covered by the book. The original intention was to confine it to the twentieth century. However, I soon concluded that it was necessary to begin with a description of how this thing called 'childhood' and those associated with it, generally known as 'children', came into such prominence vis-à-vis the State and its philanthropic agencies. Thus it became necessary to explain the 'emergence' of childhood. I do not mean to suggest that childhood literally emerged into public consciousness for the first time in the nineteenth century, but it certainly did begin to occupy a new position in what Donzelot refers to as the 'social' space of the 'tutelary' or wardship complex. That is to say it began to figure in the plans of reformers, educationalists, economists, politicians and those with a professional interest in public health and urban planning, many of whom were also moved by the evangelical spirit. The arguments about factory children, the conception of juvenile delinquency, and compulsory elementary education each provided opportunities for the itemisation of childhood, usually with one eye on those cultural and religious understandings associated with Rousseau, Wordsworth and evangelical political economy. These debates formed the background for the development of the psycho-medically dominated Child Study movement which mushroomed in the 1890s and early 1900s. The movement was crucial in portraying childhood as something more than the subject-matter of education, and part of the subject-matter of law and religion. Child Study made children the province of science. This served to provide a more subtle understanding of childhood as a stage of life and of children as human beings. In my view, we need to know about the emergence of this childhood in the nineteenth century if we are to make full sense of the developing social policies connecting children to the State, the family and the social services in the twentieth century.

Furthermore, to begin the narrative of social policy in, say, 1900, would have been akin to joining a conversation already well under way, for without an awareness of the impact of compulsory schooling on the social and economic perception of children, and the sanitation issues relating to child health, together with the campaigns for school meals for necessitous children in families of the poor and the unemployed, and the continuing fear of urban degeneration, it would be impossible to make sense of legislation for school feeding and medical inspection and treatment. We would also have remained ignorant of how sexual norms for young people were established by the age-of-consent legislation. Perhaps of even more importance, would be our ignorance of the Infant Life Protection campaign, the NSPCC, and the successive legislative curtailments of parental autonomy. Without this knowledge it is difficult to understand the structuring of the governance of working-class families from the late 1940s onwards. (The First World War and the subsequent mass unemployment prevented a fully articulated policy from developing prior to the 1940s.)

My hope is that by beginning the book with a discursive introduction to the emergence of childhood, and including so many different subject-areas throughout the chapters, I have compelled readers to be aware of the centrality of children in the history of English social policy. The material has been organised through the dualisms of Bodies/Minds and Victims/Threats, and the notion of Investments. It seems to me that bodies and minds are integral to all concepts of childhood. Bodies in particular are widely used because they appear to offer an easily comprehensible discourse on meaning and purpose. This is especially so given the vulnerability of the child's body and the apparently self-evident changes in appearance as it develops. 'Looking' at children has for centuries been a way of knowing them. And, though the form of this 'knowing' began to change fairly radically during the nineteenth century, the body continued to be used in debates on inter-war malnutrition, post-war surveys of health and poverty, and exposés of abuse. Of course, the intrusion of Mind, beginning with the Child Study movement and reaching a kind of apotheosis in the child guidance clinics in the 1920s and 1930s before surfacing anew in the Children Act, 1948, served profoundly to alter both the understanding of children and the possibilities of what might be done to them.

The other dualism, Victims/Threats, is more difficult to interpret. The position adopted in these pages has been to emphasise the role of children as threats, even when they were ostensibly defined as victims. It seems to me that whichever policy we choose – their physical or mental well-being, their material comforts, or their education – the spectre of them as a threat nearly always overshadows their 'needs'. It is as if when they confront us we think first about the consequences for us and 'our' society should we ignore them. In the history of social policy it is very hard to find any occasion when the child has been seen purely and simply as a victim. Even when the general condition of victimism is recognised, children are usually the last to be included in that condition. The outstanding example here, recently brought to light by Jane Morgan and Lucia Zedner in *Child Victims* (1992) is children as victims of crime, hitherto an almost entirely neglected area of study and welfare practice. If at times I have exaggerated the extent to which children have been seen as threats, it is to counter the generally complacent tone of so many historical texts which portray them more or less as adjuncts to adult humanitarianism.

Finally, to children as investments. It is hardly original or controversial to say that much of what is done for the welfare of children is motivated by the need to protect future interests of an economic, social and political order, which do not necessarily include their own. However, I have used the term here to reinforce the nature of the social policies described in these chapters. Too often the investment aspect is overlooked in favour of political critiques which focus on 'capitalism'. No doubt it is impossible to escape from the influences of this as system, but it would be well also to consider investment from the age perspective. In other words, certain groups of adults formulate specific social policies for a specific age group, children. The formulation of these policies is not simply heavily influenced by social class, which is always present, but also by age. For example, through the idea of 'adjustment' (and helped by psycho-analysis) it became possible to think of children beyond their individual psychologies in terms of the human relations of the family. To paraphrase Nikolas Rose in his *Governing the Soul* (1990), children could be used to 'adjust the bonds of love' in pursuit of what he calls the 'responsible autonomous family'. Thus an analysis of the investment should not be restricted to class terms, any more than such analyses are now devoid of gender perspectives. We have only to look to the prevention of cruelty to children, school feeding, child guidance clinics, and services for children in care to see the importance of age in prioritising investments in social welfare.

NOTES AND REFERENCES

Introduction: Bodies and Minds, Victims and Threats, and Investments

1 Roy Porter, 'History of the Body', in Peter Burke (ed.) *New Reflections on Historical Writing*, Cambridge: Polity Press, 1991: 206–32; Carolyn Steedman, *Childhood, Culture and Class in Britain: Margaret McMillan, 1860–1931*, London: Virago Press, 1990: 189–202, and her 'Bodies, Figures and physiology: Margaret McMillan and the Late Nineteenth Century Remaking of Working-Class Childhood', in Roger Cooter (ed.), *In the Name of the Child: Health and Welfare, 1880–1940*, London: Routledge, 1992: 19–44; D. Armstrong, *The Political Anatomy of the Body*, Cambridge: Cambridge University Press, 1983; John Eekelaar, Robert Dingwall and Topsy Murray, 'Victims or Threats? Children in Care Proceedings', *Journal of Social Welfare Law*, March 1982: 68–82; Jane Morgan, and Lucia Zedner *Child Victims: Crime, Impact, and Criminal Justice*, Oxford: Clarendon Press, 1992.

2 B. S. Turner, *The Body and Society*, Oxford: Basil Blackwell, 1984: 2.

3 ibid.: 180.

4 Porter, op. cit.: 208.

5 ibid.: 213 and 215.

6 ibid.: 217.

7 Armstrong, op. cit.: passim.

8 ibid.: 2.

9 ibid.: 4.

10 ibid.: 13. He has in mind the view of the child's body as expressed in works such as J. F. Goodhart, *The Diseases of Children*, London, 1885; R. Hutchison, *Lectures on Diseases of Children*, London, 1904; and the formation in 1900 of the Society for the Study of Diseases in Children.

11 For a contemporary discussion of their bodily nature, see Sir John Gorst, *The Children of the Nation*, London: Methuen, 1906. Arising from compulsory mass schooling there developed an interest in identifying 'feeble-minded' children which introduced a limited focus on Mind, but this was dwarfed by the far more comprehensive and universal concern with the general welfare of children's bodies. On the 'visibility' of the feeble-minded, see Nikolas Rose, *The Psychological Complex: Psychology, Politics and Society in England, 1869–1939*, London: Routledge & Kegan Paul, 1985: 97–8, 101–3. For health of body, see 57, 59, 78, 103, 150.

12 Steedman, *Childhood, Culture and Class*: 189–214.

13 Bruce Haley, *The Healthy Body and Victorian Culture*, Cambridge, Mass.: Harvard University Press, 1978: 4.

14 ibid.: 12, 21, 23–45.

15 ibid.: 141–60, 253–62; J. A. Mangan, *Athleticism in the Victorian and Edwardian Public School*, Cambridge: Cambridge University Press, 1981.

16 For child psychology, see Denise Riley, *War in the Nursery*, London: Virago Press, 1983: 42–59. On the medical profession seeing patients as a 'mind–body unity' in the late nineteenth century, see L. L. Whyte, *The Unconscious before Freud*, London: J. Friedman, 1979: 161; and Steedman, *Childhood, Culture and Class*, 204. See also Hugh Cunningham, *The Children of the Poor: Representations of Childhood since the Seventeenth Century*, Oxford: Basil Blackwell, 1991: 197.

17 Armstrong, op. cit.: 19–21, 24–5; For Eder, see Steedman, *Childhood, Culture and Class*: 209. D. Forsyth, *Children and Health and Disease*, London: University of London Press, 1904, quoted in Armstrong, op. cit.: 27.

18 Hector Cameron, *The Nervous Child*, London: Oxford University Press, 1919: v.

19 Cathy Urwin and Elaine Sharland, 'From Bodies to Minds in Childcare Literature: Advice to Parents in Inter-War Britain', in Roger Cooter (ed.), op. cit.: 175.

20 Armstrong, op. cit.: 55.

21 Jean Packman, *The Child's Generation*, London: Blackwell & Robertson, 1981; Jean Heywood, *Children in Care: The Development of the Service for the Deprived Child*, London: Routledge & Kegan Paul, 1978.

22 Armstrong, op. cit.: 55–63.

23 It will become clear that in one sense this dualism is less concerned with 'two independent underlying principles' (*OED*), and more concerned with the respective conditions being perceived as interdependent.

24 Ian Bradley, *The Call to Seriousness*, London: Jonathan Cape, 1976: 50.

25 Quotations from Cunningham, op. cit.: 9–17, 104–7, 86–7, and 97–132 for stimulating discussion on 'Savages'. For Barnardo's views on 'The Dangerous Classes', see June Rose, *For the Sake of the Children*, London: Futura, 1989: 85–6. See also Robert Pattison, *The Child Figure in English Literature*, Athens, Ga: University of Georgia Press, 1978: 71–2.

26 See, for example, Deborah Gorham, 'The "Maiden Tribute of Babylon" Re-Examined: Child Prostitution and the Idea of Childhood in Late-Victorian England', *Victorian Studies*, 21, 3, 1978: 353–79; George K. Behlmer, *Child Abuse and Moral Reform in England, 1870–1908*, Stanford, Calif.: Stanford University Press, 1982; Deborah Dwork, *War Is Good for Babies and Other Young Children: A History of the Infant and Child Welfare Movement in England, 1898–1918*, London: Tavistock, 1987; Bentley B. Gilbert, *The Evolution of National Insurance in Great Britain: The Origins of the Welfare State*, London: Michael Joseph, 1966: 102–58; June Rose, op. cit.: passim; Gorst, op. cit.: 1.

27 Geoffrey Pearson, *Hooligan: A History of Respectable Fears*, London: Macmillan, 1983; Margaret May, 'Innocence and Experience: The Evolution of the Concept of Juvenile Delinquency in the Mid-Nineteenth Century', *Victorian Studies*, 18, 1, 1973: 7–29; Eekelaar, *et al.*, op. cit.: *Departmental Committee on the Treatment of Young Offenders, Report*, XII, 1927: 71–2.

28 For a clear description of official policy, see Victor Bailey, *Delinquency and Citizenship: Reclaiming the Young Offender, 1914–1948*, Oxford: Clarendon Press, 1987: 91–114.

29 Nick Frost and Mike Stein, *The Politics of Child Welfare*, London: Harvester Wheatsheaf, 1989: 32–6.
30 ibid.: 37–9.
31 ibid.: quotations from 47. See also 48.
32 Nikolas Rose, *Governing the Soul*, London: Routledge, 1990: 121.
33 Gilbert, op. cit.: 152, 107 and, for quotation from speech by Lord Rosebery, 72. For relevance to infant mortality, see Dwork, op. cit.: 3–21; and, for children as communal investments *vis-à-vis* school meals, see Michael Freeden, *The New Liberalism: An Ideology of Social Reform*, Oxford: Clarendon Press, 1978: 227.
34 Emmanuel Miller (ed.), *The Growing Child and Its Problems*, London: Kegan Paul, Trench & Trubner, 1937: xii.
35 Quotations cited in Jeffrey Weeks, *Sex, Politics and Society: The Regulation of Sexuality since 1800*, London: Longman, 1981: 232.

PART I THE EMERGENCE OF THE CHILD, *c.*1800–1894

Introduction

1 Michael Anderson, *Approaches to the History of the Western Family, 1500–1914*, London: Macmillan, 1980: 61.
2 Alan Prout and Alison James, 'A New Paradigm for the Sociology of Childhood? Provenance, Promise and Problems', in Prout and James (eds), *Constructing and Reconstructing Childhood: Contemporary Issues in the Sociological Study of Childhood*, London: Falmer Press, 1990: 26.
3 Anderson, op. cit.: 60.

1 Identities and definitions

1 J. H. Plumb, 'The New World of Children in Eighteenth-Century England'. *Past and Present*, 67, 1975: 64–95.
2 ibid.: 65; R. A. Houlbrooke, *The English Family, 1450–1700*, London: Longman, 1984: 32, 155–6.
3 Plumb, op. cit.: 70; K. Thomas, *Man and the Natural World: Changing Attitudes in England, 1500–1800*, Harmondsworth: Penguin, 1983: 172–91, 301; Roy Porter, *English Society in the Eighteenth Century*, Harmondsworth: Penguin, 1982: 284–8; P. Coveney, *The Image of Childhood*, 2nd edn, Harmondsworth: Peregrine, 1967: 29; Robert Pattison, *The Child Figure in English Literature*, Athens, Ga: University of Georgia Press, 1978: 51; James Walvin, *A Child's World: A Social History of English Childhood, 1800–1914*, Harmondsworth: Penguin, 1982: 46; John Lawson and Harold Silver, *A Social History of Education in England*, London: Methuen, 1973: 233.
4 Boutet de Monvel (ed.), J.-J. Rousseau, *Émile*, London: Dent, 1963: vii.
5 Pattison, op. cit.: 52; Coveney, op. cit.: 4–9; J. Somerville, *The Rise and Fall of Childhood*, London: Sage, 1982: 127–31. For the term 'Nature', see Ludmilla Jordanova, 'Children in History: Concepts of Nature and Society', in Geoffrey Scarre (ed.), *Children, Parents and Politics*, Cambridge: Cambridge University Press, 1989: 4–19, and her *Languages of Nature*, London: Free Association Books, 1986: 36–47, 86.
6 Coveney, op. cit.: xii, 30–43; Pattison, op. cit.: 50, 56–64.
7 ibid.: 69; Coveney, op. cit.: 16, 18, 27, 48–9.

295

8 ibid.: xiii, 1, 4.
9 A. D. Gilbert, *Religion and Society in Industrial England*, London: Longman, 1976; D. Rosman, *Evangelicals and Culture*, London: Croom Helm, 1984: 21; see also chs 1 and 2: Leonore Davidoff and Catherine Hall, *Family Fortunes: Men and Women of the English Middle Class, 1780–1850*, London; Hutchinson, 1987: 81–99; Hugh Cunningham, *The Children of the Poor: Representations of Childhood since the Seventeenth Century*, Oxford: Basil Blackwell, 1991: 48.
10 Quoted in Walvin, op. cit.: 45.
11 Quoted in Priscilla Robertson, 'Home as a Nest: Middle Class Childhood in Nineteenth-Century Europe', in Lloyd de Mause (ed.), *The History of Childhood*, London: Souvenir Press, 1976: 421. But see also Rosman, op. cit.: 97–118.
12 Davidoff and Hall, op. cit.: 321–56.
13 Cunningham, op. cit.: ch. 4.
14 Rosman, op. cit.: 47–53; C. Hall, 'The Early Formation of Victorian Domestic Ideology', in S. Burman (ed.), *Fit Work for Women*, London: Croom Helm, 1979: 15–32.
15 Cunningham, op. cit.: 65, 69.
16 C. Driver, *Tory Radical: The Life of Richard Oastler*, New York: Oxford University Press, 1946: 244.
17 Quotations from ibid.: 47, 243–4. See also Cunningham, op. cit.: 69–71.
18 Margaret May, 'Innocence and Experience: The Evolution of the Concept of Juvenile Delinquency in the Mid-Nineteenth Century', *Victorian Studies*, 18, 1, 1973: 7–29; see also Ivy Pinchbeck and Margaret Hewitt, *Children in English Society*, Vol. 2, London: Routledge & Kegan Paul, 1973: 530, 476–7, 483–4; Geoffrey Pearson, *Hooligan. A History of Respectable Fears*, London: Macmillan, 1983.
19 Quoted in May, op. cit.: 7.
20 M. Hill, 'Prize Essay on Juvenile Delinquency', in M. Hill and C. F. Cornwallis, *Two Prize Essays on Juvenile Delinquency*, London: Smith, Elder, 1853: 9.
21 H. Worsley, *Juvenile Depravity*, London: Gilpin, 1849: 81–93.
22 M. Carpenter, *Juvenile Delinquents: Their Condition and Treatment*, London: Cash, 1853: 298–9; Hill, op. cit.: 9; May, op. cit.: 19; Worsley, op. cit.: 79–81, 95; Pearson, op. cit.: ch. 7.
23 May, op. cit.: 22, 27–8; Pearson, op. cit.: 165.
24 Quoted in J. Manton, *Mary Carpenter and the Children of the Streets*, London: Heinemann, 1976: 109.
25 Carpenter, op. cit.: 292–3, 297–9.
26 May, op. cit.: 15–17, 19, 21–2.
27 Pearson, op. cit.: 159, 161–7, 171–9.
28 Clark Nardinelli, *Child Labor and the Industrial Revolution*, Bloomington Ind.: Indiana University Press, 1990: 119; Cunningham, op. cit.: 166. See also Lionel Rose, *The Erosion of Childhood. Child Oppression in Britain, 1860–1918*, London: Routledge, 1991: Chs 1–3.
29 Nardinelli, op. cit.: 119; Pamela Horn, *The Victorian and Edwardian Schoolchild*, Gloucester: Alan Sutton, 1989: 105–6; J. S. Hurt, *Elementary Schooling and the Working Classes, 1860–1918*, London: Routledge & Kegan Paul, 1979: 183–213.
30 R. L. Schnell, 'Childhood as Ideology: A Reinterpretation of the Common School', *British Journal of Education Studies*, 27, 1, 1979: 10.

31 Viviana Zelizer, *Pricing the Priceless Child: The Changing Social Value of Children*, New York: Basic Books, 1985.

32 Quoted in Pearson, op. cit.: 179–82; R. Johnson, 'Educational Policy and Social Control in Early Victorian England', *Past and Present*, 49, 1970: 96–8, 104; Robert Colls, ' "Oh Happy English Children!" ': Coal, Class and Education in the North-East', *Past and Present*, 73, 1976: 97.

33 Hurt, op. cit.: chs 7 and 8.

34 H. Bosanquet, *Rich and Poor*, London: Macmillan, 1908: 50.

35 Wayne Dennis, 'Historical Beginnings of Child Psychology', *Psychological Bulletin*, 46, 1949: 224–45; Denise Riley, *War in the Nursery*, London: Virago Press, 1983: 43–9; Cunningham, op. cit.: 196–7; James Sully, 'Babies and Science', *Cornhill Magazine*, 43, 1881: 539–54; G. S. Hall, 'The Content of Children's Minds', *Princeton Review*, 11, 1883: 249–72.

36 Gillian Sutherland, *Ability, Merit and Measurement: Mental Testing and English Education, 1880–1940*, Oxford, Clarendon Press, 1984: 6–13.

37 ibid.: 6.

38 ibid.: 6–13; Hurt, op. cit.: chs 5–6; Bentley B. Gilbert, *The Evolution of National Insurance in Great Britain: The Origins of the Welfare State*, London: Michael Joseph, 1966: ch. 1.

39 F. B. Smith, *The People's Health, 1830–1910*, London: Croom Helm, 1979: 183.

40 Sutherland, op. cit.: 7–13; A. Wooldridge, 'Child Study and Educational Psychology in England, c.1880–1950', Oxford University DPhil thesis, 1985: 21–2.

41 ibid.: ch. 1; L. S. Hearnshaw, *A Short History of British Psychology, 1840–1940*, London: Methuen, 1964: 254–74.

42 Wooldridge, op. cit.: abstract.

43 Gertrude Keir, 'The History of Child Guidance', *British Journal of Educational Psychology*, 22, 1952: 10.

44 Wooldridge, op. cit.: 44.

45 ibid.: 52–3, 59.

46 ibid.

47 Coveney, op. cit.: xiii, 242–8.

48 Cunningham, op. cit.: 129–31. For the threat from older children and adolescents, see Harry Hendrick, *Images of Youth, Age, Class and the Male Youth Problem, 1880–1920*, Oxford: Clarendon Press, 1990: chs 4 and 5.

PART II FROM RESCUE AND REFORM TO 'CHILDREN OF THE NATION', *c.*1872–1918

Introduction

1 T. N Kelynack, *Childhood*, London: Charles H. Kelly, 1910: 3.

2 The Morally Reforming State: Rescue, Reclamation and Protection, 1872–1908

1 *Select Committee on Protection of Infant Life, Report*, VII, 1871: 607. (Hereafter *SC on Infant Life*.)

2 Ludmilla Jordanova, 'Children in History: Concepts of Nature and Society',

in Geoffrey Scarre (ed.), *Children, Parents and Politics*, Cambridge: Cambridge University Press, 1989: 8–9.

3 Lionel Rose, *Massacre of the Innocents: Infanticide in Great Britain 1800–1939*, London: Routledge & Kegan Paul, 1986: 31–2, 36; L. G Houseden, *The Prevention of Cruelty to Children*, London: Jonathan Cape, 1955: 126–7; Ivy Pinchbeck and Margaret Hewitt, *Children in English Society*, Vol. 2, London: Routledge & Kegan Paul, 1973: 596–7.

4 ibid.: 591–4; Rose, op. cit.: 35; Jean Heywood, *Children in Care: The Development of the Service for the Deprived Child*, London: Routledge & Kegan Paul, 1965: 94, 97.

5 Quoted in George Behlmer, *Child Abuse and Moral Reform in England, 1870–1908*, Stanford, Calif.: Stanford University Press, 1982: 17–18. See also Rose, op. cit.: 37.

6 ibid.: 41–2; Behlmer, op. cit.: 20–1.

7 Rose, op. cit.: 41, 43–5; Behlmer, op. cit.: 22–43; James Greenwood, *The Seven Curses of London*, Oxford: Basil Blackwell, 1869 (1981 edn): 21–38.

8 Behlmer, op. cit.: 26–36; Pinchbeck and Hewitt, op. cit.: 597, 617–18; Rose, op. cit.: 108–9; Houseden, op. cit.: 126–46.

9 Behlmer, op. cit.: 38; Rose, op. cit.: 110.

10 Behlmer, op. cit.: 38; Rose, op. cit.: 110–11; Pinchbeck and Hewitt, op. cit.: 619–20; Heywood, op. cit.: 98.

11 Behlmer, op. cit.: 40–1; Pinchbeck and Hewitt, op. cit.: 598 and 604. For Charley's arguments, see *Hansard*, 3rd series, cccxxv, col. 1494.

12 Rose, op. cit.: 122–35.

13 Behlmer, op. cit.: 151–2.

14 *SC on Infant Life*, Vol. 13, 1890; Vol. 10, 1896; Behlmer, op. cit.: 153–6; Rose, op. cit.: 161; Heywood, op. cit.: 99–100.

15 Rose, op. cit.: 161.

16 Behlmer, op. cit.: 156–7, 221; Rose, op. cit.: 162.

17 *SC on Infant Life*, Vol. 9, 1908; Rose, op. cit.: 168. The Infanticide Act, 1922, finally created a capital offence distinct from murder.

18 Behlmer, op. cit.: 2–3, 16.

19 Quoted in ibid.: 51.

20 ibid.: 52.

21 ibid.: 42

22 *The Lancet*, 20 November 1880: 823, also quoted in Behlmer, op. cit.: 45; J. S. Hurt, *Elementary Schooling and the Working Classes, 1860–1918*, London: Routledge & Kegan Paul, 1979: 106–8; Gillian Sutherland, *Ability, Merit and Measurement: Mental Testing and English Education, 1880–1940*, Oxford: Clarendon Press, 1984: 10–11, 30–1, 37.

23 C. Sherrington, 'The NSPCC in Transition, 1884–1983: A Study in Organizational Survival', University of London PhD thesis, 1985: 60.

24 A. S. Wohl (ed.), Andrew Mearns, *The Bitter Cry of Outcast London*, Leicester: Leicester University Press, 1970: Samuel Smith, 'Social Reform', *The Nineteenth Century*, 13, 1883: 896–912. See also Sherrington, op. cit.: 55, 61–2; Houseden, op. cit.: 48–68; B. Waugh, *The Gaol Cradle: Who Rocks It?*, London: Daldy, Isbister, 1876: 101; Harry Ferguson, 'Rethinking Child Protection Practices: A Case for History', in Violence Against Children Study Group, *Taking Child Abuse Seriously*, London: Unwin Hyman, 1990: 127–8.

25 Behlmer, op. cit.: 52–3; Pinchbeck and Hewitt, op. cit.: 621–3.

26 Liverpool Society for the Prevention of Cruelty to Children, *Tortured*

Children: A Third Year's Experience in Their Defence, Liverpool: LSPCC, 1887: 16.

27 *The Child's Guardian*, January 1887: 14.

28 Quoted in Behlmer, op. cit.: 55. See also Ferguson, 'Rethinking Child Protection', 131.

29 Smith, op. cit.: 902.

30 Ferguson, 'Rethinking Child Protection': 131.

31 Houseden, op. cit.: 19–22; Anne Allen and Arthur Morton, *This Is Your Child*, London: Routledge & Kegan Paul, 1961: 15–26.

32 Letter from Bordett-Coutts to *The Times*, October 1888, quoted in John Stewart, 'Children and Social Policy in Great Britain, 1871–1909', University of London, MPhil thesis, 1988: 80.

33 Behlmer, op. cit.: 78–9, 100–2; *The Child's Guardian*, January 1889: 129. Teachers feared the Act because, between 1870 and 1889, 172 of them had been brought before the courts for assault and thirty-two had been convicted. *Hansard*, 5, 3 July, 1889: 1381–4.

34 Behlmer, op. cit.: 98–108; Pinchbeck and Hewitt, op. cit.: 623–7.

35 *Prevention of Cruelty and Protection of Children Act*, 52 & 53 Vict., c.44.

36 Behlmer, op. cit.: 119–57.

37 ibid.: 159.

38 ibid.: 208; Allen and Morton, op. cit.: 33; Heywood, op. cit.: 108–9.

39 ibid.: 108–9.

40 Behlmer, op. cit.: 55.

41 National Society for the Prevention of Cruelty to Children, *Five Years with Cruelty to Children: Review and a Statement*, 1889: 19–20.

42 Liverpool Society for the Prevention of Cruelty to Children, *Report for 1884*.

43 National figures given in National Society for the Prevention of Cruelty to Children, Oxford Branch, *Reports 1890–1901*, 22. For a similar emphasis in the North-East between 1889–1914, see Harry Ferguson, 'Cleveland in History: The Abused Child and Child Protection, 1880–1914', in Roger Cooter (ed.), *In the Name of the Child: Health and Welfare, 1880–1940*, London: Routledge, 1992: 162.

44 Behlmer, op. cit.: 181.

45 ibid.: 71 and 181. NSPCC, Oxford Branch, *Reports, 1899–1900*. EC Report: 11.

46 For a comparison with the United States see Linda Gordon, *Heroes of Their Own Lives*, London: Virago Press, 1989: 68–75. For case-study of parental neglect, see Ferguson, 'Rethinking Child Protection', 122–5.

47 Behlmer, op. cit.: 196–7.

48 London Society for the Prevention of Cruelty to Children, *Third Annual Report, 1887–88*: 8.

49 Sherrington, op. cit.: 85.

50 *Report of the NSPCC, 1888–89*: 19 and 21.

51 Behlmer, op. cit.: 176–7, 183–15. The Society was always a little confused over what caused cruelty and neglect. At various times it emphasised drink, poverty and individual personality.

52 LSPCC, *Report for 1884*: 16.

53 Ferguson, 'Rethinking Child Protection': 130.

54 D. Garland, *Punishment and Welfare*, Aldershot: Gower, 1985: 30.

55 LSPCC, *Report for 1884*: 15. It is important not to see the Society in isolation from other instruments of social discipline and reformation. See Sherrington, op. cit.: 186.

56 *Report of the NSPCC, 1888–89*: 25. On 'rights', see also report of fourth annual meeting of the Society in *The Children's Guardian*, 1 June 1888: 45.

57 On this process, see Nikolas Rose, *Governing the Soul: The Shaping of the Private Self*, London: Routledge, 1990.

58 Robert Parr, *Wilful Waste: The Nation's Responsibility for Its Children*, London: NSPCC, 1910: 7.

59 For excellent overviews, see Frank Mort, *Dangerous Sexualities: Medico-Moral Politics in England since 1830*, London: Routledge & Kegan Paul, 1987: 2 and 3; Jeffrey Weeks, *Sex, Politics and Society: The Regulation of Sexuality since 1800*, London: Longman, 1981: ch. 5.

60 Quotations from ibid.: 87; see also Mort, op. cit.: 105.

61 Weeks, op. cit.: 81.

62 ibid.: 85–6, 89–91; Mort, op. cit.: 68–76, 86, 88; Edward Bristow, *Vice and Vigilance: Purity Movements in Britain since 1700*, Dublin: Gill & Macmillan, 1977: 75–93.

63 Behlmer, op. cit.: 73–4; D. Gorham, ' "The Maiden Tribute of Babylon" ' Re-examined: Child Prostitution and the Idea of Childhood in Late-Victorian England', *Victorian Studies*, 21, 3, 1978: 353–4, 358–60; Weeks, op. cit.: 87; Mort, op. cit.: 103, 126–8; *Select Committee on the Law Relating to the Protection of Young Girls from Artifices to Induce Them to Lead a Corrupt Life, Report*, IX (HL), 1881. Snagge's report forms an appendix to this report. Michael Pearson, *The Age of Consent*, Newton Abbot: David & Charles, 1972: 20, 21, 26, 28–31.

64 Gorham, op. cit.: 361; Weeks, op. cit.: 87, Bristow, op. cit.: 106–14; Mort, op. cit.: 103–4.

65 ibid.: 105 and 126; Gorham, op. cit.: 363; Weeks, op. cit.: 88.

66 Gorham, op. cit.: 355 and 365. On female adolescence, see Carol Dyhouse, *Girls Growing Up in Late Victorian and Edwardian England*, London: Routledge & Kegan Paul, 1981: ch. 4.

67 Gorham, op. cit.: 362.

68 ibid.: 363–5. See also Mort, op. cit.: 103–50; and Weeks, op. cit.: 81–95.

69 Gorham, op. cit.: 366–8.

70 Harry Hendrick, *Images of Youth, Age, Class and the Male Youth Problem, 1880–1920*, Oxford: Clarendon Press, 1990: ch. 4; John Springhall, *Coming of Age: Adolescence in Britain, 1860–1960*, Dublin: Gill & Macmillan, 1986: 133–7.

71 Gorham, op. cit.: 369–70. On psychologists and girls, see Dyhouse, op. cit.: ch. 4.

72 Gorham, op. cit.: 370–1.

73 ibid.: 372–4.

74 Wohl (ed.), Mearns, op. cit.: 61; William Booth, the Salvationist, quoted in A. S. Wohl, 'Sex and the Single Room: Incest among the Victorian Working Classes', in Wohl (ed.), *The Victorian Family*, London: Croom Helm, 1978: 210; *Royal Commission on the Housing of the Working Classes*, Vol. 2, XXX, 1884–5: Qs 1954, 1519, 2228, 3690, 4989, 5461; *Select Committee on the Law Relating to the Protection of Young Girls . . . Second Report*, XIII, 1882.

75 Wohl, 'Sex and the Single Room': 197–216. See also B. Webb, *My Apprenticeship*, 2nd edn, London: Longmans, Green, n.d: 275 n.

76 Wohl, 'Sex and the Single Room': 201.

77 Quoted in ibid.: 203.

78 Mort, op. cit.: 135; V. Bailey and Sheila Blackburn, 'The Punishment of Incest Act 1908: A Case Study of Criminal Law Creation', *Criminal Law Review*,

November 1979: 709. For the role of the State in the regulation of sexual behaviour, see Weeks, op. cit.: 82–3.

79 Bailey and Blackburn, op. cit.: 711–12.

80 Quotation from Home Office internal document cited in ibid.: 713.

81 ibid.: 717–18. See also Mort, op. cit.: 103–50.

82 Board of Education, *Annual Report of the Chief Medical Officer of Health* (hereafter *CMO Report*), 1914: 16.

83 Quoted in Harry Hendrick, 'Child Labour, Medical Capital, and the School Medical Service, *c.*1890–1918', in Cooter (ed.), op. cit.: 49.

84 Jane Lewis, 'Anxieties about the Family and the Relationships between Parents, Children and the State in Twentieth-Century England', in Martin Richards and Paul Light (eds), *Children of Social Worlds*, Cambridge: Polity Press, 1986: 35 and 37. See also Anna Davin, 'Child Labour, the Working-Class Family, and the Domestic Ideology in 19th Century Britain', *Development and Change*, 13, 1982: 633–52.

85 Marjorie Cruickshank, *Children and Industry*, Manchester: Manchester University Press, 1982: 94, 96–8; Hugh Cunningham, *The Children of the Poor: Representations of Childhood since the Seventeenth Century*, Oxford: Basil Blackwell, 1991: 174–6.

86 For descriptions of child labour see ibid.: 174–82; Pamela Horn, *The Victorian and Edwardian Schoolchild*, Gloucester: Alan Sutton, 1989: 102–34; Lionel Rose, *The Erosion of Childhood: Child Oppression in Britain, 1860–1918*, London: Routledge, 1991: chs 1–8.

87 See Hendrick, 'Child Labour', in Cooter (ed.), op. cit.: 51.

88 Quoted in Cunningham, op. cit.: 174; and Harry Hendrick, 'Child Labour, Medical Capital, and the School Medical Service, *c.*1890–1918', in Roger Cooter (ed.), op. cit.: 50.

89 E. Hogg, 'School Children as Wage-Earners', *The Nineteenth Century*, 42, 187: 235–44.

90 Hendrick, 'Child Labour': 50.

91 *Inter-departmental Committee on the Employment of School Children, Report*, XXV, 1902 (hereafter *Report, 1902*): 17; Frederic Keeling, *Child Labour in the United Kingdom*, London: P. S. King, 1914: xxvii–xxxii; P.P. *Select Committee on Homework*, Minutes of Evidence, VI, 1907: Qs 446, 449–51, 1286, 1866–7, 2351, 3183; *Education: Elementary Schools (Children Working for Wages*, Pt 2, 1899, LXXV, (hereafter *Return, 1899*): 25; *Departmental Committee on Conditions of School Attendance and Child Labour, Report*, LXVIII, 1893–4, 22–3.

92 Hendrick, 'Child Labour': 50–1.

93 *Report, 1902*: 13, 18; Hogg, 'School Children': 239–42; Keeling, op. cit.: xxviii; *Return, 1899*: 25; Hurt, op. cit.: 206–12.

94 Quoted in Cunningham, op. cit.: 181.

95 Pamela Horn, 'The Employment of Elementary School Children in Agriculture, 1914–1918', *History of Education*, 12, 3, 1983: 203–15.

96 Grace Paton, *The Child and the Nation*, London: Student Christian Movement, 1915: 79; Arthur Greenwood, *The Health and Physique of School Children*, London: P. S. King, 1913: 48; A. Paterson, *Across the Bridges*, London: Edward Arnold, 1911: 104–6; Sir John Gorst, *The Children of the Nation*, London: Methuen, 1906: 91.

97 Greenwood, op. cit.: 30, 33, 57–8. See also *School Hygiene*, 6, 1, 1910: 362; *Inter-departmental Committee on Physical Deterioration, Report and Evidence*, XXXII, 1904, Vol. 2, Minutes of Evidence, Qs 1924 and 2453.

98 *Inter-departmental Committee on Partial Exemption from School Attendance, Report*, XVII, 1909: 6.
99 Peter Sandiford, 'The Half-Time System in the Textile Trades', in M. E. Sadler (ed.), *Continuation Schools in England and Elsewhere*, Manchester: Manchester University Press, 1907: 330; Henry Dunckley, 'The Half-Timers', *Contemporary Review*, 306, 1891: 801; Cruickshank, op. cit.: 98–100.
100 D. M. Taylor, 'The School Child Worker', in T. N. Kelynack (ed.), *School Life*, London: P. S. King, 1911: 53–4. See also *CMO Report for 1911*, 249.
101 ibid.: 249–57.
102 Quoted in Margaret Alden, *Child Life and Labour*, London: Headley Bros, 1908: 116. See also Clive Riverie, 'Heart Strain in Boys', *School Hygiene*, 3, 1, 1910: 155; Eric Pritchard, 'The Physiology of the Child'. *Child-Study*, 11, 1, 1909: 6–14.
103 Alice Ravenhill, 'Some Results of an Investigation into Hours of Sleep among Children in the Elementary Schools of England', *Child-Study*, 1, 4, 1909: 116–22; Clive Riverie, 'On Sleep', *School Hygiene*, 2, 3, 1912: 108–18.
104 *The Lancet*, 11 March 1899: 707; 13 May 1899: 1309; 16 March 1901: 806; 28 September 1907: 307–8; *British Medical Journal*, leader, 25 July 1903.
105 *Report, 1902*: 261–85.
106 Heywood, op. cit.: 67–93; Pinchbeck and Hewitt, op. cit.: 496–545; Vic George, *Foster Care: Theory and Practice*, London: Routledge & Kegan Paul, 1970: 6–41; Sidney and Beatrice Webb, *English Poor Law Policy*, 2 vols, London: Cass Reprint, 1963.
107 Quoted in George, op. cit.: 6. See also Heywood, op. cit.: 67–71.
108 *The Education and Maintenance of Pauper Children in the Metropolis, Report*, Vol. 1, XLIII, 1896 (hereafter Mundella Report): 104, 129; Nigel Middleton, *When Family Failed*, London: Victor Gollancz, 1971: 92–7. See also A. M. Ross, 'Care and Education of Pauper Children', University of London PhD thesis, 1955: 108–9; 11 and 162–74.
109 Quoted in Heywood, op. cit.: 82.
110 Quoted in ibid.: 85–6. See also Middleton, op. cit.: 102–8.
111 Heywood, op. cit.: 89–90. George, op. cit.: 25–41.
112 Middleton, op. cit.: 83. A slightly different set of figures is given in Heywood, op. cit.: 90.
113 ibid.
114 Reference to Mundella Report in ibid.: On parental relief, see R. Holman, *Putting Families First*, London: Macmillan, 1988: 5.
115 Senior's report quoted in Ross, op. cit.: 103; also 110–11. Mundella Report, quoted in Middleton, op. cit.: 89.
116 Quoted in ibid.: 88–9.
117 ibid.: 114–15, 176.
118 Quoted in ibid.: 91.
119 Gillian Wagner, *Barnardo*, London: Eyre & Spottiswoode, 1979: 38–51; Heywood, op. cit.: 49–66; Kathleen Heasman, *Evangelicals in Action*, London: Geoffrey Bles, 1962: 88–106; June Rose, *For the Sake of the Children*, London: Futura, 1989; John Stroud, *Thirteen Penny Stamps: The Story of the Church of England Children's Society from 1881–1970*, London: Longmans, 1860, 1971; W. Waugh, *These My Little Ones*, London: Daldy, Isbister, 1876, 1911.
120 Holman, op. cit.: 5.
121 Quoted in Heywood, op. cit.: 53.
122 Quoted in Holman, op. cit.: 9, 11–12. By the end of the century the Societies, the NSPCC and the Poor Law had secured rights to keep children against the

wishes of their parents. See Wagner, *Barnardo*; 214–36; Heywood, op. cit.: 63–5; Holman, op. cit.: 10.

123 ibid.: 8–14, original emphasis. See also Lewis in Martin and Richards (eds), op. cit.: 37–9; Heywood, op. cit.: 92.

124 Ferguson, 'Cleveland in History', in Cooter (ed.), op. cit.: 163. See also Behlmer, op. cit.: 163.

125 Pinchbeck and Hewitt, op. cit.: 546–81; Philip Bean and Joy Melville, *Lost Children of the Empire*, London: Unwin Hyman, 1989: 28–37; Joy Parr, *Labouring Children*, London: Croom Helm, 1980: 27–9, 39; Gillian Wagner, *Children of the Empire*, London: Weidenfeld & Nicolson, 1982: 1–8; June Rose, op. cit.: 82–112.

126 Quoted in Parr, op. cit.: 31; see also 62–81; Wagner, *Children of the Empire*: 137.

127 Quoted in Pinchbeck and Hewitt, op. cit.: 572; see also 546–81; Heywood, op. cit.: 61–2; Heasman, op. cit.: 102–6.

128 Parr, op. cit.: 33; June Rose, op. cit.: 85–6.

129 Wagner, *Children of the Empire*: xiv–xv, 100–2, 112–13; Wagner, *Barnardo*: 38–51; Bean and Melville, op. cit.: 43; Parr, op. cit.: 27–44, 142–3.

3 The Social Services State: Providing for the Children of the Nation, 1889–1918

1 Gillian Sutherland, *Ability, Merit and Measurement: Mental Testing and English Education, 1880–1940*, Oxford, Clarendon Press, 1984: 38.

2 David G. Pritchard, *Education and the Handicapped, 1760–1960*, London: Routledge & Kegan Paul, 1963: chs 2–5.

3 Charity Organisation Society, *Report of a Special Committee on the Education and Care of Idiots, Imbeciles and Harmless Lunatics*, London: Longmans, Green, 1877.

4 Pritchard, op. cit.: ch. 6.

5 *Royal Commission on the Blind, Deaf, Dumb ... Report and Minutes of Evidence*, (hereafter Egerton Commission) XIX–XX, 1889: liii–liv; Pritchard, op. cit.: ch. 7.

6 ibid.: 97.

7 Egerton Commission, Vol. I: xii.

8 ibid.: 38.

9 ibid.: xiii and xxxix.

10 ibid.: xc–xci.

11 ibid.: 95 and 100.

12 *Departmental Committee on Defective and Epileptic Children, Report* (hereafter *Report of DCDEC*), XXVI, 1898: Vol. 2; Pritchard, op. cit.: 153–7; Board of Education, *Annual Report of the Chief Medical Officer of Health* (hereafter *CMO Report*), 1910: 118.

13 By 1913 the Board was inspecting 397 special schools and institutions in England and Wales with a total of 26,759 pupils. *CMO Report for 1914*, 1914–16: 12–13.

14 Alfred F. Tredgold, *Mental Deficiency*, London: Baillière, Tindall & Cox, 1908: 123; Sutherland, op. cit.: 6–7.

15 Pritchard, op. cit.: 116–17.

16 Egerton Commission, Vol. 3; Francis Warner, *Report on the Scientific Study of the Mental and Physical Conditions of Childhood, with Particular Reference to Children of Defective Constitution and with Recommendations as to*

Education and Training, London: Royal Sanitary Institute, 1895; Charity Organisation Society. *The Feeble-Minded Child and Adult*, London, 1893,

17 Pritchard, op. cit.: 120–2, 126, 131; Sutherland, op. cit.: 19; J. S. Hurt, *Outside the Mainstream: A History of Special Education*, London: Batsford, 1988: 127.

18 Sutherland, op. cit.: 21; Pritchard, op. cit.: 136; *Report of DCDEC*: 3.

19 *CMO Report for 1909*, 1910: 152.

20 Sutherland, op. cit.: 24; Pritchard, op. cit.: 150.

21 Nikolas Rose, *The Psychological Complex. Psychology, Politics and Society in England, 1869–1939*, London: Routledge & Kegan Paul, 1985: 96–7.

22 Kathleen Jones, *A History of the Mental Health Services*, London: Routledge & Kegan Paul, 1972: 48; Ellen Pinsent, 'On the Permanent Care of the Feeble-Minded', *The Lancet*, 21 February 1903: 513–15; Sutherland, op. cit.: 31–2; Pritchard, op. cit.: 180–4. See C. Paget Lapage, *Feeblemindedness in Children of School Age*, Manchester: Manchester University Press, 1920: app. 1 for an account of such a school.

23 *Royal Commission on the Care and Control of the Feeble Minded, Report*, (hereafter the Radnor Report), XXIX, 1908: 105; Pritchard, op. cit.: 183–5.

24 ibid.: 116 and 354–7.

25 *CMO Report for 1912*, 1914: 115–16, 239.

26 Hurt, op. cit.: 148.

27 Pritchard, op. cit.: 178–80; Jones, op. cit.: 49–52; Hurt, op. cit.: 140; Rose, op. cit.: 113.

28 Sutherland, op. cit.: 25–56; Jones, op. cit.: 185–210; R. A. Lowe, 'Eugenicists, Doctors and the Quest for National Efficiency: An Educational Crusade, 1900–1939', *History of Education*, 7, 1979: 293–306; Greta Jones, *Social Hygiene in Twentieth Century Britain*, London: Croom Helm, 1986: chs 1 and 2; Rose, op. cit.: 92–103.

29 Sutherland, op. cit.: 33–41; Hurt, op. cit.: 137–8; Radnor Report: 185 (369); Lapage, op. cit.: vii.

30 Anna Davin, 'Imperialism and the Cult of Motherhood', *History Workshop Journal*, Spring 1978: 9–65; Deborah Dwork, *War Is Good for Babies and Other Young Children: A History of the Infant and Child Welfare Movement in England, 1898–1918*, London: Tavistock, 1987: 3–21; Jane Lewis, *The Politics of Motherhood: Child and Maternal Welfare in England, 1900–1939*, London: Croom Helm, 1980.

31 G. F. McCleary, *The Maternity and Child Welfare Movement*, London: P. S. King, 1935: 4–5; Sir John Gorst, *The Children of the Nation*, London: Methuen, 1906: 15–16; George Newman, *Infant Mortality: A Social Problem*, London: Methuen, 1906: 1–19; Janet Layne-Claypon, *The Child Welfare Movement*, London: G. Bell, 1920: 1–7; Charles Webster (ed.), *Biology, Medicine and Society, 1840–1940*, Cambridge: Cambridge University Press, 1981: introduction, 1–8.

32 G. F. McCleary, *The Early History of the Infant Welfare Movement*, London: H. K. Lewis, 1933: 35; Dwork, op. cit.: 93–166; Lewis, op. cit.: 61–113.

33 ibid.: 62; McCleary, *Early History*: 22; Layne-Claypon, op. cit.: 179–86; Carnegie United Kingdom Trust, *Report on the Physical Welfare of Mothers and Children*, Liverpool: C. Tinling, 1917: 4–5.

34 Quoted in McCleary, *Early History*, 26. See also Newman, op. cit.: 139–76; Layne-Claypon, op. cit.: 182–4; F. B. Smith, *The People's Health, 1830–1910*, London: Croom Helm, 1979: 85–104.

35 Lewis, op. cit.: 61, 65–82; McCleary, *Maternity and Child Welfare*, 6–8.

36 Quoted in McCleary, *Early History*, 31–4; see also his *Maternity and Child Welfare*, 49–53.
37 Layne-Claypon, op. cit.: 3; G. F. McCleary, *Infantile Mortality and Infant Milk Depots*, London: P. S. King, 1905: 71, and his *Early History*: 69–73, 80.
38 Dwork, op. cit.: 99, 103, 104–24; Lane-Claypon, op. cit.: 56–64; McCleary, *Early History*: 81, 83.
39 Lewis, op. cit.: 105.
40 McCleary, *Early History*: 85–6.
41 Quoted in Dwork, op. cit.: 160. See also 114 and 134.
42 Quoted in ibid.: 131. See also Caleb Saleeby, 'The Human Mother', *Report of the Proceedings of the Second National Conference on Infant Mortality*, London: P. S. King, 1908; Smith, op. cit.: 115–17; Lewis, op. cit.: 89–113; Dwork, op.cit.: 124–5, 135–9; McCleary, *Early History*: 89–94.
43 Quoted in ibid.: 92–3.
44 Carnegie Trust, op. cit.: 34.
45 McCleary, *Early History*: 93, 135–6; Layne-Claypon, op. cit.: 8–26; Dwork, op. cit.: 137–8, 143.
46 Quoted in Lewis, op. cit.: 97. See also 13–14, 19, 96–100, 103; Layne-Claypon, op. cit.: 38–80; Dwork, op. cit.: 144–56.
47 Quoted in Lewis, op. cit.: 95 and Dwork, op. cit.: 133 and 164.
48 Quoted in ibid.: 154.
49 Lewis, op. cit.: 64–7.
50 McCleary, *Early History*: 138; Lewis, op. cit.: 16; Bentley B. Gilbert, *The Evolution of National Insurance in Great Britain: The Origins of the Welfare State*, London: Michael Joseph, 1966: 349.
51 McCleary, *Early History*: 134. By 1910 the Local Government Board had published three reports in four years on the subject.
52 ibid.: 139–44; and his *Maternity and Child Welfare*: 12–14, 17–19.
53 ibid.: 17, 56–9; Lewis, op. cit.: 33; J. M. Winter, *The Great War and the British People*, London: Macmillan, 1986: 194–5; Lewis, op. cit.: 96.
54 McCleary, *Maternity and Child Welfare*: 20–2; Layne-Claypon, op. cit.: 52–5; Lewis, op. cit.: 151. See also Caroline Rowan, 'Child Welfare and the Working-Class Family', in Mary Langan and Bill Schwarz (eds), *Crises in the British State, 1880–1930*, London: Hutchinson, 1985: 226–39.
55 Carnegie Trust, op. cit.: passim.
56 Quoted in Winter, op. cit.: 199. See also 198, 200–4; Dwork, op. cit.: 214.
57 McCleary, *Early History*: 146–9; Winter, op. cit.: 143.
58 Lewis, op. cit.: 13–14, 202; Winter, op. cit.: 143–53; Smith, op. cit.: 113–14, 123–8; Dwork, op. cit.: 209–12, 215, 220; Arthur Newsholme, *The Last Thirty Years in Public Health*, London: George Allen & Unwin, 1936: 188–94; George Newman, *The Building of a Nation's Health*, London: Macmillan, 1939: 234–48, 281–321.
59 M. E. Bulkley, *The Feeding of School Children*, London: G. Bell, 1914: R. H. Tawney in the introduction, xi.
60 ibid.: 206.
61 ibid.: ch. 1; *Inter-departmental Committee on Medical Inspection and Feeding of Children Attending Public Elementary Schools*, Report (hereafter *Medical Inspection and Feeding of Children*), XLVII, 1906: 54–6; John Stewart, 'Children and Social Policy in Great Britain, 1871–1909', University of London, MPhil thesis, 1988: 171–83.
62 B. Webb, *My Apprenticeship*, London: Longmans, Green, 2nd edn, n.d.: 213, n. 1; John Welshman, 'The School Medical Service in England and Wales,

1907–1939', Oxford University, DPhil thesis, 1988: 132; S. D. Fuller, 'Penny Dinners', *Contemporary Review*, 48, 1885: 428, 432.

63 Bulkley, op. cit.: 6 and 10; quotation from *The Lancet* cited in Stewart, op. cit.: 172–3; *Report of Dr Crichton-Browne on Over-Pressure*, LXI, 1884; Gorst, op. cit.: 1; Gorst in *Hansard*, vol. 125, 194; vol. 141, 143; vol, 133, 782–4.

64 Stewart, op. cit.: 80–116; Keith Layburn, 'The Issue of School Feeding in Bradford, 1904–1907', *Journal of Educational Administration and History*, 14, 2, 1982: 30–9.

65 *CMO Report for 1910*, 1911: 246; *British Medical Journal*, 12 December 1903: 1557; Stewart, op. cit.: 152–3.

66 Bulkley, op. cit.: 27; Dwork, op. cit.: 169–70.

67 *Royal Commission on Physical Training (Scotland), Report*, XXX, 1903: 30, 31, 37.

68 *Inter-departmental Committee on Physical Deterioration, Report and Evidence*, XXXII, 1904: 66, 69.

69 Gorst, op. cit.: 76 and 80; *Medical Inspection and Feeding of Children*: 68, 70, 84.

70 *British Medical Journal*, 4 April 1903: 791. See also 22 August 1903: 424; 12 December 1903: 1541–2; 1 October 1904: 850; 22 August 1903: 424–5.

71 John Burns, President of the Local Government Board, quoted in Bulkley, op. cit.: 44. See also Gorst, op. cit.: 86; *Medical Inspection and Feeding of Children*: 83. Order reprinted in app. iv.

72 Gilbert, op. cit.: 109; *Hansard*, vol. 145: 531, 554.

73 It seems that the Board of Education was unprepared for the Bill, and in an almost casual manner supported it. Gilbert, op. cit.: 110–11.

74 On the passing of the Act, see ibid.: 102–17.

75 Bulkley, op. cit.: 54–5.

76 *CMO Report for 1913*, 1914–16: 244–5.

77 *CMO Report for 1912*, 1914: 274; Bulkley, op. cit.: 59 and 61; Henry Iselin, 'The Story of a Children's Care Committee', *Economic Journal*, 22, 1912: 43.

78 *CMO Report for 1911*, 1912–13: 322–4; J. Lambert, 'The Feeding of the School Child', in T. N. Kelynack (ed.), *Medical Examination of Schools and Scholars*, London: P. S. King, 1910: 231–48; Bulkley, op. cit.: 81.

79 Quotations in ibid.: 83; see also Margaret Alden, *Child Life and Labour*, London: Headley Bros, 1908: 108; *CMO Report for 1911*, 1912–13: 278; *Report on the Working of the Education (Provision of Meals) Act, 1906, for the Year 1910*, 1911: 8–9.

80 *CMO Report for 1910*, 1911: 1. See also *CMO Report for 1912*, 1914: 271.

81 *Hansard*, vol. 51: 1381; Arthur Greenwood. *Health and Physique of School Children*, London: P. S. King, 1913: 48.

82 Bulkley, op. cit.: 184–98; *CMO Report for 1911*, 1912–13: 282–3.

83 *CMO Report for 1910*, 1911: 1.

84 *CMO Report for 1912*, 1914: 27; Welshman, op. cit.: 139.

85 ibid.: 140 and 142.

86 Ralph Crowley, *The Hygiene of School Life*, London: Methuen, 1910: 2.

87 Gilbert, op. cit.: ch. 3 and p. 117.

88 J. David Hirst, 'The Growth of Treatment through the School Medical Service, 1908–1918', *Medical History*, 33, 3, 1989: 323.

89 ibid.: Hirst argues that George Newman, the Chief Medical Officer (CMO) at the Board of Education, pressed this point internally. See also N. P. Daglish,

'Robert Morant's Hidden Agenda? The Origins of the Medical Treatment of Children', *History of Education*, 19, 2, 1990: 144–5.

90 Crowley, op. cit.: 3–5; A. H. Hogarth, *Medical Inspection of Schools*, London: Hodder & Stoughton, 1909: 20–44; J. David Hirst, 'The Origins and Development of the School Medical Service, 1870–1919', University of Wales (Bangor) PhD thesis, 1983: 5–40; Bernard J. Harris, 'Medical Inspection and the Nutrition of Schoolchildren in Britain, 1900–1950', University of London PhD thesis, 1988: ch. 2; *Report of Dr Crichton-Browne*: passim.

91 Hirst, 'Origins and Development': 43, 50, 56, 145; quotations in Dwork, op. cit.: 187.

92 Rose, *Psychological Complex*: 132; Leslie W. MacKenzie, *The Health of the School Child*, London: Methuen, 1906: 4–12, 51.

93 Crowley, op. cit.: 6; Harris, op. cit.: 6; *CMO Report for 1908*: 5–6; Welshman, op. cit.: 26; Newman, op. cit.: 21–5.

94 Gilbert, op. cit.: 123; Dwork, op. cit.: 186.

95 Gilbert, op. cit.: 120.

96 ibid.: 123–6.

97 *CMO Report for 1908*: 5–10.

98 *Board of Education Circulars 576 and 596*; Crowley, op. cit.: 9–11, 72.

99 ibid.: 73; *Board of Education Circular 596*; *CMO Report for 1908*: 15–18.

100 Crowley, op. cit.: 73–5; *CMO Report for 1908*, 31–2; Hirst, 'Origins and Development': 291–2.

101 Crowley, op. cit.: 78–9, 82–4.

102 *CMO Report for 1910*: 256.

103 Crowley, op. cit.: 163–7; L. D. Cruickshank, *School Clinics at Home and Abroad*, London: National League for Physical Education and Improvement, 1913: 38–9; Welshman, op. cit.: 72, 77–8, 80; *CMO Reports* (1908): 33–4; (1909): 96–7; (1910): 109–10; *Medical Inspection and Feeding of Children*: 10 and 27.

104 Hirst, 'Origins and Development': 367–71. Welshman, op. cit.: 80, argues that treatment was primarily a way of improving school attendance.

105 Hirst, 'Growth of Treatment': 327–8, 332, 334–5; Cruickshank, op. cit.: 43–51; *CMO Report for 1909*, 101.

106 Hirst, 'Growth of Treatment': 328, 335–6, 391–4; W. H. Dawson, *School Doctors in Germany*, London: Board of Education, 1906; MacKenzie, op. cit.: passim; Brian Simon, *Education and the Labour Movement, 1870–1920*, London: Lawrence & Wishart, 1965: 285–97.

107 *CMO Report for 1909*: 27, 120–1; Hirst, 'Origins and Development': 372; Crowley, op. cit.: 168–79; Cruickshank, op. cit.: 76.

108 *Board of Education Circular 596*; *CMO Reports* (1908): 85–97 and 101; (1909): 104–5; (1910), 147–8, 155; Hirst, 'Origins and Development': 377–91.

109 Cruickshank, op. cit.: 58–9, 62, 122, 130–4; Hirst, 'Origins and Development': 401.

110 ibid.: 411–12.

111 ibid.: 411–16; 424–30.

112 *CMO Reports* (1915): 27; (1916): 2; (1917): 2; (1918): 1–3, 99; Hirst, 'Origins and Development': 429, 433, 438–9, 442; Welshman, op. cit.: 39–41.

113 *CMO Report for 1919*: 41–3, 45 and 47; Hirst, 'Origins and Development': 448–9.

114 *CMO Reports for 1917–18*, xi, 99, vi.

115 Jean Heywood, *Children in Care: The Development of the Service for the Deprived Child*, London: Routledge & Kegan Paul, 1965: 108.

116 Harry Ferguson, 'Rethinking Child Protection Practices: A Case for History', in Violence Against Children Study Group, *Taking Child Abuse Seriously*, London: Unwin Hyman, 1990: 130.
117 For parliamentary references to overlaying and burning, see John Stewart, 'Children and Social Policy in Great Britain, 1871–1909', University of London, MPhil thesis, 1988: 354–9.
118 ibid.: 360–2.
119 The distinction had been disappearing since the Reformatory Schools Amendment Act, 1889, abolished the period of preliminary imprisonment which had always accompanied the reformatory sentence.
120 Robert Dingwall, J. M. Eekelaar and T. Murray, 'Childhood as a Social Problem: A Survey of the History of Legal Regulation', *Journal of Law and Society*, 11, 2, 1984: 223.
121 Quoted in Heywood, op. cit.: 109.
122 Probation had first been allowed by the Probation of First Offenders Act, 1887, but magistrates were reluctant to invoke it. However, the Youthful Offenders Act, 1901, and the Probation Act, 1907, effectively established this form of non-custodial supervision.
123 H. K. Bevan, *Child Law*, London: Butterworth, 1989: 622.
124 J. R. Gillis, 'The Evolution of Juvenile Delinquency in England, 1890–1914', *Past and Present*, 67, 1975: 124.
125 The number of children sent to prison declined from 1,151 in 1904–5 to 143 in 1909–10. For young people held 'on remand', see I. M. Baker, 'Remand Homes', in *Legislation in Regard to Children: Report of the Proceedings at a Special Conference, May, 1906*, London: P. S. King, 1906.
126 Bevan, op. cit.: 622.
127 John Clarke, 'Managing the Delinquent: The Children's Branch of the Home Office, 1913–30', in Mangan and Schwarz (eds), op. cit.: 251. On reformation programmes for youth, see Harry Hendrick, *Images of Youth: Age, Class and the Male Youth Problem, 1880–1920*, Oxford: Clarendon Press, 1990: pts 2 and 3.
128 Quotations in Stewart, op. cit.: 367–8. See also Rose, op. cit.: 169–91.
129 Quoted in Stewart, op. cit.: 375.
130 Quoted in ibid.: 342.

Conclusion

1 Newman quoted in Nikolas Rose, *The Psychological Complex: Psychology, Politics and Society in England, 1869–1939*, London: Routledge & Kegan Paul, 1985: 131, see also 84–5 and 150 for 'Neo-hygienism'; George Newman, *The Building of a Nation's Health*, London: Macmillan, 1939: 28–33; David Armstrong, *The Political Anatomy of the Body*, Cambridge: Cambridge University Press, 1983: 13.
2 George Newman, *The Health of the State*, London: Headley Bros, 1907: 135–6 (my emphasis).
3 Rose, op. cit.: 150–1. For health as a civic virtue, see E. de Bruin, 'The Correlation of Hygiene and Civics', *School Hygiene*, 1, 1913: 26–34. See also Armstrong, op. cit.: 13–18.
4 See, for example, Ernest Jones, 'Psycho-analysis and Education', *School Hygiene*, 2, 1911: 94–9; and 3, 1911: 130–9; and Oskar Frister, 'Psycho-analysis and Child Study', *School Hygiene*, 7, 1911: 366–74; and 8, 1911: 432–42.

PART III MINDS AND BODIES: CONTRADICTION, TENSION AND INTEGRATION 1918–45

4 Health and welfare between the wars

1 *Annual Report of the Chief Medical Officer at the Ministry of Health (hereafter MH Report), 1932*: 223; *1933*: 9; *1934*: 15. These reports are also cited in Charles Webster, 'Healthy or Hungry Thirties?', *History Workshop Journal*, 13, 1982: 110–29.

2 ibid.: Charles Webster, 'Health, Welfare and Unemployment during the Depression', *Past and Present*, 109, 1985: 204–30; Charles Webster, 'The Health of the School Child during the Depression', in Nicholas Parry and David McNair (eds), *The Fitness of the Nation – Physical and Health Education in the Nineteenth and Twentieth Centuries*, Leicester: History of Education Society, 1983: 70–85; John Macnicol, *The Movement for Family Allowances*, London: Heinemann, 1980: 43–74; John Hurt, 'Feeding the Hungry School-child in the First Half of the Twentieth Century', in D. J. Oddy and Derek S. Miller (eds), *Diet and Health in Modern Britain*, London: Croom Helm, 1985: 179–206; Margaret Mitchell, 'The Effects of Unemployment on the Social Condition of Women and Children in the 1930s', *History Workshop Journal*, 19, 1985: 105–27.

3 Quoted in John Welshman, 'The School Medical Service in England and Wales, 1907–1939', Oxford University DPhil thesis, 1988: 152; see also 87 and 89.

4 *The Health of the School Child (hereafter HSC), 1921*: 11; *1928*: 8. From 1921 onwards the Annual Reports of the Chief Medical Officer at the Board of Education were titled *The Health of the School Child*.

5 Welshman, op. cit.: 97; *HSC for*, (1927): 14 and 16; (1929): 7; (1932): 16; and (1933): 141; Hurt, op. cit.: 180–1, and 185–6; Webster, 'Health, Welfare and Unemployment': 214.

6 *Annual Report of the Chief Medical Officer at the Board of Education for 1920*: 148; internal memo cited in Welshman, op. cit.: 145.

7 ibid.: 146; Webster, 'Health, Welfare and Unemployment': 215; Hurt, op. cit.: 181–4; S. and V. Leff, *The School Health Service*, London: H. K. Lewis, 1959: 70–1, 77–8.

8 ibid.: 72–3.

9 *HSC for* (1926): 139; (1929): 10.

10 Quoted in Welshman, op. cit.: 147.

11 Leff, op. cit.: 83–5; J. Boyd Orr, *Food, Health and Income*, London: Macmillan, 1936.

12 Welshman, op. cit.: 152–7.

13 Macnicol, op. cit.: 46–8.

14 Bernard J. Harris, 'Medical Inspection and the Nutrition of Schoolchildren in Britain, 1900–1950', University of London, PhD thesis, 1988: 137–8.

15 Macnicol, op. cit.: 49; Hurt, op. cit.: 191–3; John Stevenson, *British Society, 1914–45*, Harmondsworth: Penguin, 1984: 214–16; Webster, 'Health of the Schoolchild': 79.

16 Webster, 'Healthy or Hungry Thirties?': 112–14; *HSC for 1932*: 126.

17 Orr, op. cit.: C. E. McNally, *Public Ill Health*, London, Victor Gollancz, 1935: 72–117; R. Huws Jones, 'Physical Indices and Clinical Assessments of the Nutrition of Schoolchildren', *Journal of the Royal Statistical Society*, 100, 1938: 1–52; G. C. M. M'Gonigle and J. Kirby, *Poverty and Public Health*, London: Victor Gollancz, 1936; Allen Hutt, *The Condition of the Working*

Class in Britain, London: Martin Lawrence, 1933: 86; Webster, 'Health of the Schoolchild', 78; *HSC for 1934*; Stevenson, op. cit.: 283.

18 Jane Lewis, *The Politics of Motherhood: Child and Maternal Welfare in England, 1900–1939*, London: Croom Helm, 1980: 175–90; Webster, 'Health and Welfare': 214.

19 *Board of Education Circular 1443*, 16 February 1935.

20 Welshman, op. cit.: 168–71; Webster, 'Health and Welfare': 216; Macnicol, op. cit.: 62–5; Hurt, op. cit.: 180; Political and Economic Planning, *Report on the British Health Services*, London: PEP, 1937: 321–37.

21 Webster, 'Healthy or Hungry Thirties?': 113; Hutt, op. cit.: passim: Hurt, op. cit.: 195; Harris, op. cit.: 118; M'Gonigle and Kirby, op. cit.: 54–8.

22 Harris, op. cit.: 119. See also *HSC for 1933*: 17–19.

23 R. M. Titmuss, *Poverty and Population. A Factual Study of Social Waste*, London, Macmillan, 1938: 97–100.

24 *HSC for 1934*, 27.

25 Welshman, op. cit.: 163.

26 ibid.: 165–6; Leff, op. cit.: 87; *Board of Education Circular 1443*, 16 February, 1935.

27 Welshman, op. cit.: 366–72; Webster, 'Healthy or Hungry Thirties?', 112; Macnicol, op. cit.: 52–61; Harris, op. cit.: 151.

28 Quoted in Hurt, op. cit.: 187.

29 *Board of Education Circular 1437*, 5 September 1934; *HSC for* (1933): 28; (1935): 33–5; Welshman, op. cit.: 158–61; Macnicol, op. cit.: 65–6; Hurt, op. cit.: 186–91; Welshman, op. cit.: 186–7; *Ministry of Health Circular 1840*, 2 August 1939.

30 *The Health of the School Child, 1939–45*, London: HMSO, 1947: 23.

31 Leff, op. cit.: 87–8; Webster, 'Health of the Schoolchild': 77; F. Le Gros Clark, *The School Child and the School Canteen*, Hereford: Herts. County Council, 1942.

32 Hurt, op. cit.: 185; Leff, op. cit.: 68–70; Webster, 'Health of the Schoolchild': 76; John Lawson and Harold Silver, *A Social History of Education in England*, London: Methuen, 1973: 388.

33 *HSC for* (1925): 65; (1926): 22; (1927): 14 and 16; (1929): 7.

34 Leff, op. cit.: 67–8; Welshman, op. cit.: 90–4.

35 There was some growth during the period. By 1936 all 315 LEAs provided clinic treatment for minor ailments, dental care and ophthalmic services; slightly fewer made provision for patients with nose and throat complaints; and fewer still had either X-ray facilities for treating ringworm or offered orthopaedic treatment. The staff of the SMS numbered 1,458 SMOs (of whom only 275 were full-time), 907 dentists (of whom 404 were full-time), and 6,014 nurses (of whom 1,619 were full-time). PEP, op. cit.: 121; see also Webster, 'Health of the Schoolchild': 70–5.

36 Welshman, op. cit.: 89.

37 ibid.: 99–105, 120–30; PEP, op. cit.: 119, 123.

38 Hutt, op. cit.: 88; PEP, op. cit.

39 Webster, 'Health, Welfare and Unemployment': 219; quotation from *HSC for 1924* quoted in *The Health of the School Child: Fifty Years of the School Health Service*, London: HMSO, 1956–7: 50; McNally, op. cit.: 112; Jennie Riddell, 'A Study of the History and Development of the School Medical Service in Liverpool from 1908 to 1939', University of Liverpool MA thesis, 1946: 217–18.

40 Leff, op. cit.: 75; *HSC for 1926 and 1928*; PEP, op. cit.: 115; McNally, op. cit.: 91 and 94; M'Gonigle and Kirby, op. cit.: 42–3.

41 Royal College of Obsteticians and Gynaecologists, *Maternity in Great Britain*, London: Oxford University Press, 1948: 201; Webster, 'Health, Welfare and Unemployment': 220, 225; Webster, 'Healthy or Hungry Thirties?': 222–5; G. F. McCleary, *The Maternity and Child Welfare Movement*, London: P. S. King, 1935: 44–6, 58–9.

42 Webster, 'Health, Welfare and Unemployment': 222–3.

43 Quoted in Macnicol, op. cit.: 46.

44 Webster, 'Healthy or Hungry Thirties?': 116; R. M. Titmuss, *Birth, Poverty and Wealth: A Study of Infant Mortality*, London: Macmillan, 1943: 52, table xv; Hutt, op. cit.: 83–6; McNally, op. cit.: 113; Jay Winter, 'Unemployment, Nutrition and Infant Mortality in Britain, 1920–50', in Jay Winter (ed.), *The Working Class in Modern British History*, Cambridge: Cambridge University Press, 1983: 245.

45 Webster, 'Healthy or Hungry Thirties?': 123–4; Stevenson, op. cit.: 204; Lewis, op. cit.: 178–80; Titmuss, *Birth, Poverty and Wealth*: 57–9. For a contrary view, see J. M. Winter, 'Infant Mortality, Maternal Mortality and Public Health in Britain in the 1930s', in *Journal of European Economic History*, 8, 1979: 440 and 462, and his 'Unemployment . . . 1920–50'.

46 Roy Lowe, 'The Early Twentieth Century Open-Air Movement: Origins and Implications', in Nicholas Parry and David McNair (eds), *The Fitness of the Nation – Physical and Health Education in the 19th and 20th Centuries*, Leicester: History of Education Society, 1983; D. Turner, 'The Open-Air School Movement in Sheffield', *History of Education*, 1, 1972: 58–78; Linda Bryder, ' "Wonderlands of Buttercup, Clover and Daisies": Tuberculosis and the Open-Air School Movement in Britain, 1907–39', in Roger Cooter (ed.), *In the Name of the Child: Health and Welfare, 1880–1940*, London: Routledge, 1992: 72–95.

47 Welshman, op. cit.: 263–4, 287–90, 293–4, 310–11; J. Hurt, *Outside the Mainstream: A History of Special Education*, London: Batsford, 1988: 160, 165–6; David G. Pritchard, *Education and the Handicapped, 1760–1960*, London: Routledge & Kegan Paul, 1963: 202–6.

48 Alfred F. Tredgold, *Mental Deficiency*, London: Baillière, Tindall & Cox, 1908: 351; C. Paget Lapage, *Feeblemindedness in Children of School Age*, Manchester: Manchester University Press, 1920: 84–5; Welshman, op. cit.: 280–5.

49 Pritchard, op. cit.: 188;

50 *Royal Commission on Lunacy and Mental Disorder, Report*, London: HMSO, 1929: 14–15; Pritchard, op. cit.: 190–2.

51 Quoted in Welshman, op. cit.: 309–10.

52 Quoted in Bryder, op. cit.: 81.

53 ibid.

5 Psychologising the Child

1 Gillian Sutherland, *Ability, Merit and Measurement: Mental Testing and English Education, 1880–1940*, Oxford: Clarendon Press, 1984: 95, 128–9; L. S. Hearnshaw, *A Short History of British Psychology, 1840–1940*, London: Methuen, 1964: chs xiv–v.

2 Charles Fox, *Educational Psychology: Its Problems and Methods*, London:

Kegan Paul, Trench, Trubner, 1925: ch. 1; James Drever, *An Introduction to the Psychology of Education*, London: Edward Arnold, 1925: ch. V.

3 Quoted in Hearnshaw, op. cit.: 254, and A. Wooldridge, 'Child Study and Educational Psychology in England, c.1850–1950', University of Oxford DPhil thesis, 1985: 65, respectively.

4 R. J. W. Selleck, *English Primary Education and the Progressives*, London: Routledge & Kegan Paul, 1972; Hearnshaw, op. cit.: 257–60; John Lawson and Harold Silver, *A Social History of Education in England*, London, Methuen, 1973: 397–401; Board of Education Consultative Committee, *The Primary School*, London, HMSO, 1931, xxii.

5 Selleck, op. cit.: 102–8; Cyril Burt, 'The Permanent Contribution to Psychology of McDougall', *British Journal of Educational Psychology*, 25, 1955: 10–22; Wooldridge, op. cit.: 173 and 222; Feversham Committee, *Report on the Voluntary Mental Health Services*, London: Feversham Committee, 1939: 147–8, 175; *The Primary School*, 47–52, 268–79.

6 For a clear account, see Wooldridge, op. cit.: 81–102.

7 Selleck, op. cit.: 101–13; Sutherland, op. cit.: 95–6; Hearnshaw, op. cit.: 256–7.

8 Burt and Nunn worked on the drafting of the *The Primary School*. See Wooldridge, op. cit.: 200–54; Selleck, op. cit.: 126.

9 Wooldridge, op. cit.: 201, 253–4; Selleck, op. cit.: 110–11.

10 Gillian Sutherland, 'Measuring Intelligence: English Local Education Authorities and Mental Testing, 1919–1939', in Charles Webster (ed.), *Biology, Medicine and Society, 1840–1940*, Cambridge: Cambridge University Press, 1981: 315; Sutherland, *Ability, Merit and Measurement*: 97–111.

11 Quoted in Nikolas Rose, *The Psychological Complex: Psychology, Politics and Society in England, 1869–1939*, London: Routledge & Kegan Paul, 1985: 117.

12 ibid.: 124–31. See also Sutherland, *Ability, Merit and Measurement*: 53–5.

13 *Annual Report of the Chief Medical Officer at the Board of Education* (hereafter *CMO Report*), 1911, XVII: ch. x; *CMO Report for 1911*, XXI: app. E and 196; Rose, op. cit.: 123–4; Sutherland, *Ability, Merit and Measurement*: 55–6.

14 Wooldridge, op. cit.: 215–16; *Royal Commission on Lunacy and Mental Disorder, Report*, London: HMSO, 1929, Vol. I, ch. 6, para. 15; J. F. Foulton, 'Factors Influencing the Growth and Pttern of Child Guidance Services and School Psychological Services in Britain from 1900 to the Present', University of Belfast MA thesis, 1964: 41.

15 Sutherland, *Ability, Merit and Measurement*: 97–127; Rose, op. cit.: 128–9.

16 Sutherland, *Ability, Merit and Measurement*: 110–44; Rose, op. cit.: 124–30; Bernard Norton, Charles Spearman and the General Factor in Intelligence', *Journal of the History of the Behavioural Sciences*, 15, 1979: 142–54.

17 Quoted in Rose, op. cit.: 140. See also Brian Simon, *The Politics of Educational Reform, 1920–1940*, London: Lawrence & Wishart, 1974: 237.

18 Wooldridge, op. cit.: 221–2; *The Primary School*: 35.

19 Quoted in L. S. Hearnshaw, *Cyril Burt: Psychologist*, London, Hodder & Stoughton, 1979: 111–16.

20 R. M. Titmuss, *Birth, Poverty and Wealth: A Study of Infant Mortality* London: 1943: 62–6.

21 Sutherland, *Ability, Merit and Measurement*: 145–63; Stephen Jay Gould, *The Mismeasure of Man*, New York/London: W. W. Norton, 1981: 293.

22 *Departmental Committee on Scholarships, Free Places and Maintenance Allowances, Report* (hereafter Hilton Young Report), XV, 1920; Sutherland, *Ability,*

Merit and Measurement: 164–9; Michael Sanderson, *Education Opportunity and Social Change in England*, London: Faber & Faber, 1987: 26.

23 Sutherland, *Ability, Merit and Measurement*: 174 and 176; Selleck, op. cit.: 135–7; Board of Education Consultative Committee, *The Education of the Adolescent* (hereafter the Hadow Report), 1929: para. 89.

24 Sanderson, op. cit.: 27–8.

25 Simon, op. cit.: 239. The origin of the threefold streaming system lay partly in a report written by Cyril Burt for the London County Council in 1925 in which he called for a 'treble track system'. The Board of Education gave its authority to Burt by printing his report in its *Handbook for Teachers*, 1927. On the choice of 11+ as the age for the test, see Hilton Young Report, paras 57 and 62–4. See also Gould, op. cit.: 294–5 and Sutherland, op. cit.: 170–1.

26 Simon, op. cit.: 240.

27 Cyril Burt, *Mental and Scholastic Tests*, London: LCC, 1921: 1.

28 Simon, op. cit.: 215.

29 ibid.: 239–40.

30 ibid.: 240. On the influence of social class and secondary education, see Sanderson, op. cit.: 34, and Sutherland, op. cit.: 283–90.

31 Board of Education Consultative Committee, *Secondary Education with Special Reference to Grammar Schools and Technical High Schools*, (hereafter the Spens report), 1938: 123–4 and 357. Original emphasis.

32 ibid.: 126 and 358; Simon, op. cit.: 250.

33 Olive Banks, *Parity and Prestige in English Secondary Education*, London: Routledge & Kegan Paul, 1955: 129; also quoted in Sutherland, op. cit.: 189, and 188 for quotation; Simon, op. cit.: 245, 248–9.

34 Sutherland, op. cit.: 189–90, 283, and her essay in Webster (ed.), op. cit.: 335.

35 Sutherland, op. cit.: 155, 160, and 288 for quotation.

36 Simon, op. cit.: 226.

37 Quoted in Gould, op. cit.: 295–6. On 11+ see 293–6.

38 Hadow Report, 2–3; Selleck, op. cit.: 141; Bernard Norton, 'Psychologists and Class', in Webster (ed.).

39 Wooldridge, op. cit.: 256–310.

40 G. R. Searle, 'Psychologists and Class', in Webster (ed.) op. cit.

41 C. Burt, 'Intelligence and Social Mobility', *British Journal of Statistical Psychology*, 14, 1961: 12.

42 Searle in Webster (ed.), op. cit.: 217.

43 For discussion of class politics and psychology (especially Burt's influence), see Norton in Webster (ed.), op. cit.: 289–314.

44 Searle in Webster (ed.), op. cit.

45 Emmanuel Miller (ed.), *The Growing Child and Its Problems*, London, Kegan Paul, Trench & Trubner, 1937: xii.

46 Rose, op. cit.: 176–96.

47 Deborah Thom, 'Wishes, Anxieties, Play and Gestures: Child Guidance in Inter-War England', in Roger Cooter (ed.), *In the Name of the Child: Health and Welfare, 1880–1940*, London: Routledge, 1992: 200–19; Gertrude Keir, 'A History of Child Guidance', *British Journal of Educational Psychology*, 22, 1952: 5–29; Rose, op. cit.: Olive Sampson, *Child Guidance: Its History, Provenance and Future*, British Psychological Society, Occasional Papers No. 3, 1980; Cyril Burt, 'Symposium on Psychologists and Psychiatrists in the Child Guidance Service', *British Journal of Educational Psychology*, 23, 1, 1953: 8–29; Hearnshaw, op. cit.: 268–75.

48 Quoted in Keir, op. cit.: 7.

49 Cyril Burt, *The Young Delinquent*, London, University of London Press, 1925, 1948 edn: 607 and 611.

50 R. G. Gordon, *A Survey of Child Psychiatry*, London: Oxford University Press, 1939: 257–9.

51 *CMO Report for* (1921): 109; (1928): 31; (1930): 26.

52 Rose, op. cit.: 198, 182; and his *Governing the Soul: The Shaping of the Private Self*, London: Routledge, 1990: 155.

53 Rose, *Governing the Soul*: 155. See also Cathy Urwin and Elaine Sharland, 'From Bodies to Minds in Childcare Literature: Advice to Parents in Inter-War Britain', in Roger Cooter (ed.), *In the Name of the Child: Health and Welfare, 1880–1940*, London: Routledge, 1992: 183–8.

54 Rose, *Psychological Complex*; 198.

55 Henry V. Dicks, *Fifty Years of the Tavistock Clinic*, London: Routledge & Kegan Paul, 1970; Thom, op. cit.: passim; Hugh Crichton Miller, *The New Psychology and the Teacher*, London, Jarrolds, 1921.

56 *The Child Guidance Council*, London, Child Guidance Council, 1928; *The Establishment of a Child Guidance Clinic*, London, Child Guidance Council, 1938; Board of Education, *The Health of the School Child, 1939–45*, London: HMSO, 1947: 63.

57 Rose, *Psychological Complex*: 200.

58 ibid.: Feversham Committee, *Report on the Voluntary Mental Health Services* (hereafter Feversham Report), London: Feversham Committee, 1939: 2–3; *The Child Guidance Council*, London: Child Guidance Council, 1928: 3–4.

59 ibid.: Keir, op. cit.: 24; Thom, op. cit.: passim; N. H. Burke and Emmanuel Miller, 'Child Mental Hygiene', *British Journal of Medical Psychology*, 9, 3, 1929: 222; G. Renton, 'The East London Child Guidance Clinic', *Journal of Child Psychology and Psychiatry*, 19, 1978: 309–12; Cathy Urwin and John Hood-Williams (eds), *Child Psychotherapy, War and the Normal Child: Selected Papers of Margaret Lowenfeld*, London: Free Association Books, 1989.

60 National Council for Mental Hygiene quoted in Rose, *Psychological Complex*: 199–200.

61 Child Guidance Council Reports, 1933–43 (hereafter CGC Reports); Child Guidance Council, series of pamphlets in the 1930s: *The Promotion of Healthy Educational Growth and Development; Play and Leisure; Some Causes of Difficult Behaviour in Children; Physical Health in Relation to Behaviour; Relation of Nutrition to Physical Development and Bodily Mechanics; The Case against Whipping; Young Offenders in Courts*.

62 David K. Henderson and Robert Gillespie, *A Textbook of Psychiatry*, London: Oxford University Press, 1927; 2nd edn, 1930: 10; 3rd edn, 1932: vii, 458–536. See also Urwin and Sharland in Cooter (ed.), op. cit.: 190.

63 Henderson and Gillespie, op. cit.: 1932 edn: 504.

64 Rose, *Psychological Complex* 202; Sampson, op. cit.: 10–11; William Moodie, *Child Guidance by Teamwork*, London: Child Guidance Council, 1931: 2–4; William Moodie, 'Child Guidance and the Schools', reprinted from *Educational Research* supplement of the *Head Teachers' Review*, St Albans, 1931: 3.

65 Ministry of Education, *Report of the Committee on Maladjusted Children*, London: HMSO, 1955: 12; Sampson, op cit.: 8, 17.

66 Moodie, *Child Guidance by Teamwork*: 1.

67 Gordon, op. cit.: 266–7. Mental defectives were not accepted as patients. CGC Report, 1938: 16; Renton, 'East London': 311.

68 Dicks, op. cit.: 45; Rose, *Psychological Complex*: 199; M. Hamblin Smith,

Medical Officer of Birmingham Prison, quoted in W. Clarke Hall, *Children's Courts*, London: George Allen & Unwin, 1928: 110–11.

69 Moodie, *Child Guidance and the Schools*: 5–8; and his *Child Guidance by Team Work*: 4–6; Burke and Emmanuel, op. cit.: 222–9.

70 CGC Report, 1933: 4.

71 Emmanuel Miller, 'Early Treatment and Prevention', in his *Modern Psychotherapy*, London: Jonathan Cape, 1930: 110, quoted in Thom, op. cit.: 211–12. See also Rose, *Psychological Complex*: 81–2.

72 Hugh Crichton Miller, *The New Psychology and the Parent*, London: Jarrolds, 1922: 24, 112; Dicks, op. cit.: 57; Rose, *Psychological Complex*: 198.

73 Dicks, op. cit.: 57; CGC Report, 1935: 3; Rose, *Psychological Complex*: 159, 186–7.

74 CGC Report, 1936: 7–8; Dicks, op. cit.: 57–8; Miller (ed.), *The Growing Child and Its Problems*: viii.

75 Rose, *Psychological Complex*: 165 (my emphasis); CGC Report, 1935: 3.

76 Douglas R. MacCalman, 'The Present Status and Functions of the Child Guidance Movement in Great Britain, and Its Possible Future Developments', *Journal of Mental Science*, 85, 1939: 510; Gordon, op. cit.: 262: Rose, *Governing the Soul*: 154.

77 Thom, op. cit.: 216.

78 Richard Titmuss, *Problems of Social Policy*, London: HMSO/Longmans, 1950: 102–22; Susan Isaacs (ed.), *The Cambridge Evacuation Survey*, London: Methuen, 1941: 109–22; William Boyd (ed.), *Evacuation in Scotland: A Record of Events and Experiments*, Bickley, Kent: University of London Press, 1944: 65–6; Women's Group on Public Welfare, *Our Towns: A Close-Up*, London: Oxford University Press, 1943: 81–91; *Underwood Report*, 1955: para. 47; Dorothy Burlingham and Anna Freud, *Young Children in War Time*, London: Allen & Unwin, 1942.

79 Keir, op. cit.: 26; *The Health of the School Child, 1939–45*: 65–6, 75; Rose, *Governing the Soul*: 161.

80 Feversham Report.

81 ibid.: x.

82 ibid.: 135–7, 139, 141–5.

83 ibid.: 147–52, 155–7, 223.

84 ibid.: 151–2; *The Health of the School Child, 1939–45*: 66–7; Greta Jones, *Social Hygiene in Twentieth Century Britain*, London: Croom Helm, 1986: 137.

85 Feversham Report: 164; Greta Jones, 'Eugenics and Social Policy between the Wars', *Historical Journal*, 25, 1982: 717–28. For a different view, see Michael Freeden, 'Eugenics and Progressive Thought: A Study in Ideological Affinity', *Historical Journal*, 22, 1979: 645–71, and his 'Eugenics and Ideology', *Historical Journal*, 26, 1983: 959–62.

86 Quoted in Foulton, op. cit.: 142–3.

87 *The Health of the School Child, 1939–45*: 67–8; Keir, op. cit.: 36–7; C. P. Blacker, *Neurosis and the Mental Health Services*, Oxford: Oxford University Press, 1946: 53; Foulton, op. cit.: 144.

88 Winifred Burbury, E. M. Balinet and B. J. Yapp, *An Introduction to Child Guidance*, London: Macmillan, 1950: 6–8, 37, 18 (my emphasis). See also Urwin and Sharland in Cooter (ed.), op. cit.: 191–2.

89 Foulton, op. cit.: 164. Thom, op. cit.: 216.

6 The Children and Young Persons Act, 1933

1 Victor Bailey, *Delinquency and Citizenship: Reclaiming the Young Offender, 1914–1948* , Oxford: Clarendon Press, 1987: 8–12. For the 'invention' of adolescence and the reformers' social critique, see Harry Hendrick, *Images of Youth, Age, Class and the Male Youth Problem, 1880–1920*, Oxford: Clarendon Press, 1990: chs 4 and 5.

2 See also Cyril Burt, 'The Causal Factors of Juvenile Crime', *British Journal of Medical Psychology*, 3, 1923: 1–33.

3 Cyril Burt, *The Young Delinquent*, London: University of London Press, 1927 edn: 600.

4 Bailey, op. cit.: 16.

5 Burt, *Young Delinquent*: 610.

6 *Departmental Committee on the Treatment of Young Offenders* (hereafter Young Offenders Committee), *Report*, XII, 1927: 964.

7 Burt, *Young Delinquent*: 610.

8 Bailey, op. cit.: 17.

9 ibid.: 18–21.

10 ibid.: 30. In the years between the publication of the Report and the passing of the Act, there was much discussion between the Children's Branch of the Home Office and the various reform groups. The Howard League wanted to see schoolchildren brought under 'the ultimate guardianship of the state', known as the 'chancery' principle, but the Home Office decided against this and supported the position of the Departmental Committee. ibid.: 74–6.

11 ibid.: 31. It appears that Birmingham was one of the few towns where juveniles were sent for examination for mental deficiency. The Young Offenders Committee recommended that such referrals be universal, and from then on magistrates were encouraged to send juveniles for medical examination.

12 ibid.: 34.

13 For example, A. M. Hutchison, 'Symptoms in Children: Bad Habits, Sexual Precocity, Thieving', *The Lancet*, 1926; Margaret Fry, 'A Belgian Psychological Laboratory', *Howard Journal*, 1, 1924: 121–7; Edgar Hamilton-Pearson, 'The Problem of the Delinquent Child', *Child*, 11, 1921: 357–61.

14 Bailey, op. cit.: 34.

15 ibid.: 35.

16 ibid.: 57–61; W. Clarke Hall, *Children's Courts*, London: George Allen & Unwin, 1928: 75–82; Burt, *Young Delinquent*: 121–3; Young Offenders Committee, 1025–7, 1087. The three members who opposed all corporal punishment were Mrs Cadbury, Rys Davies and Wemyss Grant-Wilson.

17 Hall, op. cit.: 188. For the 'liberal progressives', see Bailey, op. cit.: passim.

18 *Departmental Committee on Reformatories and Industrial Schools, Report* (hereafter Reformatories and Industrial Schools Committee), XXXIX, 1913. For a historical sketch of the schools, see Young Offenders Committee: 965–70.

19 ibid.: 964, 1067, 1077.

20 ibid.: 1029.

21 ibid.: 1030.

22 Bailey, op. cit.: 39–41.

23 ibid.: 97–8.

24 ibid.: 110.

25 John Eekelaar, Robert Dingwall and Topsy Murray, 'Victims or Threats? Children in Care Proceedings', *Journal of Social Welfare Law*, March 1982: 73.

26 D. Garland, *Punishment and Welfare*, Aldershot: Gower, 1985. The work of Cyril Burt was important in this context.

27 Jean Heywood, *Children in Care*, London: Routledge & Kegan Paul, 1965: 130.

28 Burt, *Young Delinquent*: 420–537; Nikolas Rose, *The Psychological Complex: Psychology, Politics and Society in England, 1869–1939*, London: Routledge and Kegan Paul, 1985: 194–5.

29 Burt, *Young Delinquent*: 515–26.

30 Rose, *Governing the Soul: The Shaping of the Private Self*, London: Routledge, 1990: 154.

31 Parliamentary Under-Secretary of State at the Home Office, 1938, quoted in Bailey, op. cit.: 125–6.

32 ibid.: 126, 147–70.

33 ibid.: 118–21.

34 Heywood, op. cit.: 130.

35 Greta Jones, *Social Hygiene in Twentieth Century Britain*, London: Croom Helm, 1986: 89–90. See also Joan Conquest, *The Naked Truth: Shocking Revelations about the Slums*, London: T. Werner Laurie, 1933.

36 Heywood, op. cit.: 132.

37 Bailey, op. cit.: 48.

38 John Hurt, 'Reformatory and Industrial Schools before 1933', *History of Education*, 13, 1, 1984: 45–58. On the development of the certified schools, see Julius Carlebach, *Caring for Children in Trouble*, London: Routledge & Kegan Paul, 1970: 66–94.

39 Quotations in Hurt, op. cit.: 49–51. See also J. A Slack, 'The Provision of Reformatory Schools, the Landed Class, and the Myth of the Superiority of Rural Life in Mid-Victorian England', *History of Education*, 8, 1, 1979: 33–44.

40 Quotations in Hurt, op. cit.: 52–3.

41 Carlebach, op. cit.: 83–91; Bailey, op. cit.: 48–9; Reformatories and Industrial Schools Committee, 1913. The schools had been criticised since the 1890s by penal reformers who were anxious to see new methods introduced, such as probation. See John Clarke, 'Managing the Delinquent: The Children's Branch of the Home Office, 1913–30', in Mary Mangan and Bill Schwarz (eds), *Crises in the British State, 1880–1930*, London: Hutchinson, 1985: 242. For the use of irregular punishments in other institutions, see I. G. Briggs, *Reformatory Reform*, London: Longmans, Green, 1924.

42 Stephen Humphries, *Hooligans or Rebels? An Oral History of Working-Class Childhood and Youth, 1889–1939*, Oxford: Basil Blackwell, 1981: 215. Education was crucial in the transformation of the delinquent into the citizen. See Clarke in Mangan and Schwarz (eds), op. cit.: 243–4.

43 Nigel Middleton, *When Family Failed*, London: Victor Gollancz, 1971: 228–9, 231, 286.

44 Carlebach, op. cit.: 95.

45 Quoted in Humphries, op. cit.: 224–6, 267 n. 36.

46 Quoted in Bailey, op. cit.: 16.

47 Middleton, op. cit.: 16.

48 Quoted in Bailey, op. cit.: 35.

49 Humphries, op. cit.: 212, 214.

50 Quoted in R. G. Hood, *Borstal Re-Assessed*, London, 1965: 15. See also Bailey, op. cit.: 98–103.

7 The war years

1 S. and V. Leff, *The School Health Service*, London: H. K. Lewis, 1959: 96; Jennie Riddell, 'A Study of the History and Development of the School Medical Service in Liverpool from 1908 to 1939', University of Liverpool MA thesis, 1946: 197.

2 John Macnicol, 'The Evacuation of Schoolchildren', in Harold L. Smith (ed.), *War and Social Change: British Society in the Second World War*, Manchester: Manchester University Press, 1986: 15.

3 Angus Calder, *The People's War*. London, Panther, 1971: 49.

4 ibid.: 38; Macnicol, op. cit.: 6; Richard Titmuss, *Problems of Social Policy*, London: HMSO/Longmans, 1950: 103.

5 Ben Wicks, *No Time to Wave Goodbye*, London: Bloomsbury, 1988: 62–7; see also B. S. Johnson (ed.), *The Evacuees*, London: Victor Gollancz, 1968, and Ruth Inglis, *The Children's War. Evacuation, 1939–45*, London: Fontana: 49–68.

6 Board of Education, *The Health of the School Child, 1939–45* (hereafter *HSC*), London: HMSO, 1947: 31–44; Riddell, op. cit.: 91–2.

7 *HSC*: 31; Leff, op. cit.: 94.

8 Macnicol, op. cit.: 17; Riddell, op. cit.: 194–6; Leff, op. cit.: 94.

9 Titmuss, op. cit.: 114, 124, 130–2; Women's Group on Public Welfare, *Our Towns: A Close-Up*, London: Oxford University Press, 1943: 54–63, 66–100; Barnett House Study Group, *London Children in Wartime Oxford: a Survey of Social and Educational Results of Evacuation*, London: Oxford University Press, 1947; John Welshman, 'The School Medical Service in England and Wales, 1907–1939', Oxford University DPhil thesis, 1988: 117–23, 314–15, 318, 324, 329–30, 332, 339, 373.

10 Richard Padley and Margaret Cole (eds), *Evacuation Survey: A Report to the Fabian Society*, London: Routledge, 1940): 102–4; Titmuss, op. cit.: 148; Welshman, op. cit.: 106–9; *HSC*: 44–6; Peter Henderson, *The School Health Service, 1908–1974*, London: HMSO, 1975: 35–6.

11 Macnicol, op. cit.: 18; Welshman, op. cit.: 314–15, 331–5, 345–8; Titmuss, op. cit.: 115–20, 165–6; Cole and Padley, op. cit.: 95; *Our Towns*, 66–81, 127.

12 Titmuss, op. cit.: 120–2; *Our Towns*, 81–91; Leff, op. cit.: 92–4; Susan Isaacs (ed.), *The Cambridge Evacuation Survey*, London: Methuen, 1941: 47; Dorothy Burlingham and Anna Freud, *Young Children in War Time*, London: Allen & Unwin, 1942; J. Bowlby, 'Forty-Four Juvenile Thieves: Their Characters and Home Lives', *International Journal of Psychoanalysis*, 25, 1944: 19–53, 107–28.

13 Macnicol, op. cit.: 21, 24–6; Titmuss, op. cit.: 130–165; Tom Stephens (ed.), *Problem Families*, Liverpool: Pacifist Service Units, 1947; Women's Group on Public Welfare, *The Neglected Child and His Family*, London: Oxford University Press, 1948.

14 Wicks, op. cit.: xi.

15 Cole and Padley, op. cit.: 180; Isaacs (ed.), op. cit.: 79 and 177; John Hurt, 'Feeding the Hungry Schoolchild in the First Half of the Twentieth Century', in D. J. Oddy and Derek S. Miller (eds), *Diet and Health in Modern Britain*, London: Croom Helm, 1985: 197–8; Leff, op. cit.: 96; *HSC*: 23.

16 Macnicol, op. cit.: 24; Hurt, op. cit.: 198–9; Frederick Le Gros Clark, *The Social History of the School Meals Service*, London: National Council for Social Service, 1948: 16–19; *HSC*: 24–30; *Board of Education Circular 1567*, 21 October 1941; Titmuss, op. cit.: 509–11.

17 Clark, op. cit.: 21–3; Leff, op. cit.: 96.

18 *HSC*: 11–22.
19 Henderson, op. cit.: 36; *HSC*: 29, 91–6.
20 ibid.: 98–9.
21 MOH for Swindon quoted in Bernard J. Harris, 'Medical Inspection and the Nutrition of Schoolchildren in Britain, 1900–1950', University of London PhD thesis, 1988: 87–9.

Conclusion

1 George Newman, *The Building of a Nation's Health*, London: Macmillan, 1939: 194 and 208.
2 Charles Webster, 'The Health of the School Child during the Depression', in Nicholas Parry and David McNair (ed.), *The Fitness of the Nation – Physical and Health Education in the Nineteenth and Twentieth Centuries*, Leicester: History of Education Society, 1983: 79.
3 John Stevenson, *British Society, 1914–45*, Harmondsworth: Penguin, 1984: 205–14.
4 John Macnicol, *The Movement for Family Allowances*, London: Heinemann, 1980: 44.
5 ibid.: 45.
6 ibid.: Bentley B. Gilbert, *The Evolution of National Insurance in Great Britain: The Origins of the Welfare State*, London: Michael Joseph, 1966: 123–6.
7 Charles Webster, 'Health, Welfare and Unemployment during the Depression', *Past and Present*, 109, 1985: 228; John Hurt, 'Feeding the Hungry Schoolchild in the First Half of the Twentieth Century', in D. J. Oddy and Derek S. Miller (eds), *Diet and Health in Modern Britain*, London: Croom Helm, 1985: 185.
8 Quoted in John Welshman, 'The School Medical Service in England and Wales, 1907–1939', Oxford University DPhil thesis, 1988: 173.
9 Quoted in Jane Lewis, *The Politics of Motherhood: Child and Maternal Welfare in England, 1900–1939*, London: Croom Helm, 1980: 178.
10 Macnicol, op. cit.: 67. See also Margaret Mitchell, 'The Effects of Unemployment on the Social Condition of Women and Children in the 1930s', *History Workshop Journal*, 19, 1985: 114, quoting an internal Ministry of Health memo written in 1934.
11 Nikolas Rose, *Governing the Soul: The Shaping of the Private Self*: London: Routledge, 1990: 121–31.
12 Cathy Urwin and Elaine Sharland, 'From Bodies to Minds in Childcare Literature: Advice to Parents in Inter-War Britain', in Roger Cooter (ed.), *In the Name of the Child: Health and Welfare, 1880–1940*, London: Routledge, 1992: 191.

PART IV CHILDREN OF THE WELFARE STATE, 1945–89

Introduction

1 John Macnicol, 'Family Allowances and Less Eligibility', in Pat Thane (ed.), *The Origins of British Social Policy*, London: Croom Helm, 1978: 173–202; Hilary Land, 'The Introduction of Family Allowances', in P. Hall *et al.* (eds), *Change, Choice and Conflict in Social Policy*, London: Heinemann, 1975: 158–230.

2 Ministry of Health internal document quoted in R. A. Parker, 'The Gestation of Reform: The Children Act 1948', in P. Bean and S. McPherson (eds), *Approaches to Welfare*, London: Routledge & Kegan Paul, 1983: 197–8.
3 ibid.: 198–202.
4 ibid.: 204–5.
5 Marjorie Allen (Lady Allen of Hurtwood), *Whose Children?*, London: Simpkin Marshall, 1945: 5–9; and her *Memoirs of an Uneducated Lady*, London: Thames & Hudson, 1975: 171–92.

8 Child care policy

1 *Report of the Care of Children Committee* (hereafter the Curtis Report), London: HMSO, 1946: 25–6, 139–40.
2 Peter Boss, *Exploration in Child Care*, London: Routledge & Kegan Paul, 1971: 4–5; Curtis Report: 8–10, 27.
3 These paragraphs drawn from Curtis Report: paras 415–22.
4 ibid.: paras 153, 186, 207, 214.
5 ibid.: paras 260–2.
6 ibid.: paras 303–6, 322. Nigel Middleton, *When Family Failed*, London: Victor Gollancz, 1971: 197; Steve Humphries *et al.*, *A Century of Childhood*, London: Sidgwick & Jackson, 1988: 91; Lucy Sinclair, *The Bridgburn Days*, London: Victor Gollancz, 1956; Frank Norman, *Banana Boy*, London: Secker & Warburg, 1969.
7 Curtis Report: paras 418–19.
8 ibid.: 134–5, 418–22.
9 ibid.: 177–82; Boss, op. cit.: 15–16.
10 Lorraine Fox Harding, *Perspectives in Child Care Policy*, London: Longman, 1991: 136; Boss, op. cit.: 20–1; Jean Heywood, *Children in Care: The Development of the Service for the Deprived Child*, London: Routledge & Kegan Paul, 1965: 147–8.
11 ibid.: 137.
12 Harding, op. cit.: 137.
13 For the working of the Act, see Boss, op. cit.: 34–62, and Heywood, op. cit.: 160–75.
14 Boss, op. cit.: 38–9.
15 ibid.: 42.
16 It was legally clarified only in 1963. Parker, 'Gestation of Reform': 212; Robert Holman, *Putting Families First*, London: Macmillan, 1988: 35–41; Boss, op. cit.: 43.
17 John Bowlby, *Child Care and the Growth of Love*, Harmondsworth: Penguin, 1953: 175. Parliamentary Select Committee quoted in Heywood, op. cit.: 165–6.
18 *Home Office Circular 15/20*, 1 February 1950; ACO quoted in Holman, op. cit.: 39. See also Heywood, op. cit.: 170–1.
19 Quoted in Holman, op. cit.: 39–40. See also Jean Packman, *The Child's Generation*, Oxford: Basil Blackwell, 1975: 62.
20 John Stroud, *The Shorn Lamb*, London: Longmans, 1960: 8.
21 ibid.: 24.
22 *Home Office Circular 160/1948*, quoted in Packman, op. cit., 1981 edn: 73.
23 Quoted in Jeffrey Weeks, *Sex, Politics and Society: The Regulation of Sexuality since 1800*, London: Longman, 1981: 232.
24 Denise Riley, *War in the Nursery*, London: Virago Press, 1983: 150–97; Niko-

las Rose, *Governing the Soul: The Shaping of the Private Self*, London: Routledge, 1990: 157.

25 Curtis Report, para. 418.

26 P. Henderson, *The School Health Service, 1908–1974*, London: HMSO, 1975; Board of Education, *The Health of the School Child, 1939–1945*, London: HMSO, 1947; Valerie MacLeod, *Whose Child? The Family in Child Care Legislation and Social Work Practice*, London: Study Commission on the Family, Occasional Papers No. 11, 1982: 29.

27 Women's Group on Public Welfare, *Our Towns: A Close-Up*, London: Oxford University Press: 1943; James Marchant (ed.), *Rebuilding Family Life in the Post-War World*, London: Odhams Press, n.d: 136; Richard Titmuss, *Problems of Social Policy*, London: HMSO/Longmans 1950. Beveridge quoted in Holman, op. cit.: 36–7. Illegitimacy rose from 4.19 per cent of all live births in 1939 to 9.35 per cent in 1945.

28 Rose, op. cit.: 167–9; MacLeod, op. cit.: 29–32; Packman, op. cit.: 32; Eileen Younghusband, *Social Work in Britain, 1950–1975*, London: George Allen & Unwin, 1978: 36–43; R. Dingwall, J. M. Eekelaar and T. Murray, 'Childhood as a Social Problem: A Survey of the History of Legal Regulation', *Journal of Law and Society*, 11, 2, 1984: 226–7.

29 For references to problem families, see ch. 7, n. 13. See also Rose, op. cit.: 170, and see his references: 281–2.

30 Packman, op. cit.: 63–8.

31 *Report of the Committee on Children and Young Persons* (hereafter the Ingleby Report), London: HMSO, 1960: 154.

32 Professor D. V. Donnison, quoted in Packman, op. cit.: 64.

33 Ingleby Report: 4–5.

34 ibid.: 5–6.

35 ibid.: 7.

36 Packman, op. cit.: 65.

37 Ingleby Report, para 47.

38 Allison Morris and Mary Isaac, *Juvenile Justice?*, London: Heinemann, 1978: 17–20.

39 Ingleby Report, para 60.

40 ibid.: 154–5. See also P. Priestly, *et al.*, *Justice for Juveniles*, London: Routledge & Kegan Paul, 1977: 8–9.

41 Ingleby Report: para 84.

42 Michel Foucault, *Discipline and Punish*, London: Allen Lane, 1979: 20–1, also quoted in Rose, op cit.: 154.

43 Jacques Donzelot, *The Policing of Families*, London: Hutchinson, 1979: 105.

44 N. Frost and M. Stein, 'Educating Social Workers: A Political Analysis', in Roger Fieldhouse (ed.), *The Political Education of Servants of the State*, Manchester: Manchester University Press, 1988: 167–74.

45 Packman, op. cit.: 67.

46 Many local authorities had been doing this on dubious legal grounds for many years.

47 Packman, op. cit.: 67–8, and 1981 edn: 53–4; MacLeod, op. cit.: 28 and 39.

48 Packman, op. cit.: 64–7, 103–30. See also Boss, op. cit.: 74–9.

49 Women's Group on Public Welfare, *The Neglected Child and His Family*, London: Oxford University Press, 1948: xi.

50 Heywood, op. cit.: 192–3; Younghusband, op. cit.: 43–5.

51 Boss, op. cit.: 78–9.

52 Quoted in Victor Bailey, *Delinquency and Citizenship: Reclaiming the Young Offender, 1914–1948*, Oxford: Clarendon Press, 1987: 302–3.
53 Geoffrey Pearson, *The Deviant Imagination*, London: Macmillan, 1975: 132. See also A. E. Bottoms, 'On the Decriminalization of English Juvenile Courts', in R. G. Hood (ed.), *Crime, Criminology and Public Policy*, London: Heinemann, 1974; John Clarke, 'Social Democratic Delinquents and Fabian Families', in National Deviancy Conference (ed.), *Permissiveness and Control: The Fate of the Sixties Legislation*, London: Macmillan, 1980: 73–94. Nor should it be forgotten that ethnic diversification was assuming problem proportions – if only in terms of the disproportionate number of Afro-Caribbean children in care.
54 Quoted in John Davis, *Youth and the Condition of Britain*, London, Athlone Press, 1990: 90.
55 Quoted in Geoffrey Pearson, *Hooligan: A History of Respectable Fears*, London: Macmillan, 1983: 12–13; see also ibid.: 142–74.
56 Quoted in ibid.: 15.
57 ibid.: 16.
58 Quoted in ibid.: 16–17.
59 Quoted in Packman, op. cit.: 113.
60 ibid.: 114; see also 113, and Bailey, op. cit.: 306–7.
61 Nick Frost and Mike Stein, *The Politics of Child Welfare*, London: Harvester Wheatsheaf, 1989: 81.
62 ibid.; Boss, op. cit.: 91–4; Morris and Isaac, op. cit.: 25; Younghusband, op. cit.: 48–9.
63 Rose, op. cit.: 175.
64 Packman, op. cit.: 118.
65 ibid.: 119–20.
66 ibid.: 121.
67 Donzelot, op. cit.: 108–12. For a helpful discussion of the 'tutelary complex', see Nigel Parton, *Governing the Family*, London: Macmillan, 1991: 11–16.
68 Jill Hodges and Athar Hussain, 'Review Article: Jacques Donzelot, La police des familles', *Ideology and Consciousness*, 5, 1979: 105.
69 Frost and Stein, *Politics of Child Welfare*: 82–9.
70 Quoted in Packman, op. cit.: 121–2.
71 Quoted in ibid.: 122.
72 MacLeod, op. cit.: 44.
73 Packman, op. cit.: 123–4.
74 ibid., 1981 edn: 124–6, 128.
75 Michael Power, *et al.*, 'Delinquency and the Family', *British Journal of Social Work*, 4, 1, 1974: 13–38.
76 Packman, op. cit., 1981 edn: 129.
77 Frost and Stein, *Politics of Child Welfare*, 82.
78 Rose, *Governing the Soul*: 175–6; MacLeod, op. cit.: 29.
79 B. Hudson, *Justice through Punishment*, London: Macmillan, 1987: 165.
80 Packman, op. cit., 1975 edn: 155–6; Heywood: 196, 203; Younghusband, op. cit.: 43–5.
81 See evidence of Donnison and Stewart to Ingleby Committee; D. Donnison, P. Jay and M. Stewart, *The Ingleby Report: Three Critical Essays*, London: Fabian Society, 1962. See also Nigel Parton, *The Politics of Child Abuse*, London: Macmillan, 1985: 84; Younghusband, op. cit.: 227–38.
82 *Report of the Committee on Local Authority and Allied Personal Social Services* (hereafter Seebohm Report), London: HMSO, 1968: 11 and, for section on

'Social Services for Children', 52–89. For details of the Report, see Boss, op. cit.: 85–90; Kathleen Jones, *The Making of Social Policy in Britain, 1830–1990*, London: Athlone Press, 1991: 172–5; Packman, op. cit.: 1981 edn: 156–71; Younghusband, op. cit.: 239–49; J. Cooper, *The Creation of the British Personal Social Services*, London: Heinemann, 1983.

83 Younghusband, op. cit.: 218–26.

84 Packman, op. cit., 1975 edn: 158–61,

85 Para 2 quoted in Packman, op. cit., 1981 edn: 162–3.

86 Boss, op. cit.: 87; MacLeod, op. cit.: 48–9.

87 Peter Townsend (ed.), *The Fifth Social Service: A Critical Analysis of the Seebohm Proposals*, London: Fabian Society, 1970; Parton, op. cit.: 83. Integrated social-work departments were also established in Scotland under the Social Work (Scotland) Act, 1968. See Kathleen Murray and Malcolm Hill, 'The Recent History of Scottish Child Welfare', *Children and Society*, Autumn and Summer 1991.

88 Mike Collison, 'Questions of Juvenile Justice', in P. Carlen and M. Collinson (eds), *Radical Issues in Criminology*, Oxford: Martin Robertson, 1980: 160.

89 Ingleby Report: para. 40; J. Clarke, Mary Langan and Phil Lee, 'Social Work: The Conditions of Crisis', in Carlen and Collinson (eds), 179–81.

90 Kathleen Jones, op. cit.: 168–71; Brian Abel-Smith, *The Poor and the Poorest*, Occasional Papers in Social Administration, London: Bell, 1966; Keith Banting, *Poverty, Politics and Policy: Britain in the 1960s*, London: Macmillan, 1979.

91 Lettice Fisher, *Twenty One Years and After: The Story of the NCUMC*, London: National Council for the Unmarried Mother and her Child, 1937; Margaret Kornitzer, *Adoption in the Modern World*, London: Putnam, 1952; *Departmental Committee on the Adoption of Children, Report*, VIII, 1953–4.

92 Packman, op. cit., 1981 edn: 86–7.

93 For earlier legislation, see Heywood, op. cit.: 152 n. 1.

94 Packman, op. cit., 1975 edn: 75–7, 87–8, 90–1; Heywood, op. cit.: 151–2; Frost and Stein, *Politics of Child Welfare*, 108.

95 Heywood, op. cit.: 183–4; Packman, op. cit., 1975 edn: 77–9.

96 Robert Holman, *Trading in Children: A Study of Private Fostering*, London: Routledge & Kegan Paul, 1973; Packman, op. cit., 1975 edn: 78–9, 91.

97 Packman, op. cit., 1975 edn: 89; Heywood, op. cit., 1978 edn: 185–6; Parton, op. cit.: 89–90.

98 Rick Rogers, *From Crowther to Warnock: How Fourteen Reports Tried to Change Children's Lives*, London: Heinemann, 1980: 141.

99 ibid.: 141–2; Heywood, op. cit.: 204–5; Packman, op. cit., 1975 edn: 97–8. The Act gave no support to birth parents.

100 Parton, op. cit.: 115; Harding, op. cit.: 92–3.

101 Rogers, op. cit.: 144–5; J. Rowe and Lydia Lambert, *Children Who Wait*, London: Association of British Adoption Agencies, 1973; Harding, op. cit.: 68, 76–7.

102 Frost and Stein, *Politics of Child Welfare*: 39; Packman, op. cit., 1981 edn: 100–1; Harding, op. cit.: 93–4, 141; R. Holman, *Inequality in Child Care*, London: Child Poverty Action Group, 1980: 29.

103 Rogers, op. cit.: 152–3.

104 Parton, op. cit.: 116–17; Frost and Stein, *Politics of Child Welfare*, 39. For a critique of the blood-tie, see J. G. Howells, *Remember Maria*, London: Butterworth, 1974; J. Goldstein, A. Freud and A. Solnit, *Beyond the Best*

Interests of the Child, New York: Free Press, 1973. For details of the Act, see Rogers, op. cit.: 145–51; Harding, op. cit.: 93–4.
105 ibid.: 94.

9 The rediscovery of child abuse

1 Nigel Parton, 'Taking Child Abuse Seriously', in Violence Against Children Study Group, *Taking Child Abuse Seriously*, London: Unwin Hyman, 1990: 10–13.
2 Nigel Parton, *The Politics of Child Abuse*, London: Macmillan, 1985: 49; S. J. Pfohl, 'The Discovery of Child Abuse', *Social Problems*, 24, 3, 1977: 315.
3 C. H. Kempe, F. N. Silverman, B. F. Steele, W. Droegemueller and H. K. Silver, 'The Battered Child Syndrome', *Journal of the American Medical Association*, 18, 1, 1962: 17–18.
4 Pfohl, op. cit.: 310–23; Parton, *Politics of Child Abuse*: 52–4.
5 ibid.: 211 n. 23; J. Caffey, 'Some Traumatic Lesions in Growing Bones other than Fractures and Dislocations: Clinical and Radiological Features', *British Journal of Radiology*, 30, 1967: 225–38. See also *Cruel and Neglectful Parents*, London: British Medical Association/Magistrates Association, 1966.
6 D. L. Griffiths and F. J. Moynihan, 'Multiple Epiphyseal Injuries in Babies ("Battered Baby Syndrome")', *British Medical Journal*, 21 December, 1963: 1558–61.
7 *British Medical Journal*, leader, 21 December, 1963: 1544–5.
8 Quoted in Parton, *Politics of Child Abuse*: 56–7.
9 op. cit.: 58–63.
10 A. Allen and A. Morton, *This Is Your Child: The Story of the National Society for the Prevention of Cruelty to Children*, London: Routledge & Kegan Paul, 1961; Parton, *Politics of Child Abuse*: 59.
11 ibid.: 58–63.
12 Quoted in ibid.: 61–2, 65–6.
13 ibid.: 215 n. 69; 66–7, and 259 n. 72.
14 ibid.: 69.
15 ibid.: 70; S. Cohen, *Folk Devils and Moral Panics: The Creation of Mods and Rockers*, London: Paladin, 1973: 9; Department of Health and Social Security, *Non-Accidental Injury to Children*, LASSL (74) 13, 1974; c. 1.
16 A. W. Franklin (ed.), *Concerning Child Abuse*, London: Churchill-Living-stone, 1975. For Sir Keith Joseph's views, see his speech reprinted in E. Butterworth and R. Holman (eds), *Social Welfare in Modern Britain*, London: Fontana, 1975.
17 Quoted in Parton, *Politics of Child Abuse*: 77.
18 Leader, 'Caring for Children', *New Society*, 24, 55, 1973: 742.
19 Parton, *Politics of Child Abuse*: 84.
20 ibid.: 89–97.
21 Lorraine Fox Harding, *Perspectives in Child Care Policy*, London: Longman, 1991: 92–3.
22 ibid.: 93; Parton, *Politics of Child Abuse*: 102–9.
23 B. Corby, *Working with Child Abuse: Social Work Practice and the Child Abuse System*, Milton Keynes: Open University Press, 1987.
24 Unofficial Committee Report, 1816, quoted in John Eekelaar, Robert Dingwall and Topsy Murray, 'Victims or Threats? Children in Care Proceedings', *Journal of Social Welfare Law*, March 1982: 71.
25 ibid.: 72.

26 *Departmental Committee on the Treatment of Young Offenders, Report*, XII, 1927: 71.
27 Eekelaar, *et al.*, op. cit.: 75.
28 See p. 223.
29 *Report of the Committee on Children and Young Persons (Ingleby Report)*, London, HMSO, 1960: ch. 2, para. 65.
30 R. Dingwall, J. M. Eekelaar and T. Murray, 'Childhood as a Social Problem: A Survey of the History of Legal Regulation', *Journal of Law and Society*, 2, 2, 1984: 224.
31 Packman, op. cit.: 63–8, 113–14. See also ibid.: 226–7.
32 Women's Group on Public Welfare, *The Neglected Child and His Family*, London: Oxford University Press, 1948; Eustace Chesser, *Cruelty to Children*, London: Victor Gollancz, 1951; Arthur T. Collis and Vera Poole, *These Our Children*, London: Victor Gollancz, 1950; D. V. Donnison, *The Neglected Child and the Social Services*, Manchester: Manchester University Press, 1954; L. G. Houseden, *The Prevention of Cruelty to Children*, London: Jonathan Cape, 1955; T. C. N. Gibbens and A. Walker, *Cruel Parents – Case Studies of Prisoners Convicted of Violence towards Children*, London: Institute for the Study and Treatment of Delinquency, 1956.
33 Donnison, op. cit.: 78.
34 *The Neglected Child and His Family*: 71; for problem families, see 20 and 89–90; M. Penelope Hall, *The Social Services of Modern England*, London: Routledge & Kegan Paul, 1952 (1955 edn): 191–2; see also 49, 96, ch. 9, 157, 291, 312. For samples of contemporary literature, see ch. 7 n. 13.
35 Robert Dingwall, John Eekelaar and Topsy Murray, *The Protection of Children: State Intervention and Family Life*, Oxford: Basil Blackwell, 1983: 3. In this they are following R. J. Gelles, 'The Social Construction of Child Abuse', in his *Family Violence*, Beverly Hills, Calif.: Sage, 1979.
36 Nick Frost and Mike Stein, *The Politics of Child Welfare*, London: Harvester Wheatsheaf, 1989: 37; Arthur Marwick, *British Society since 1945*, Harmondsworth, Penguin, 1982: pts 2 and 3; Parton, *Politics of Child Abuse*: 77–82; N. Parton, 'Child Abuse, Social Anxiety and Welfare', *British Journal of Social Work*, 11, 4, 1981: 404–6; R. Wallis, 'Moral Indignation and the Media: An Analysis of the NV&LA', *Sociology*, 10, 1976: 271–95.
37 Quoted in Parton, *Politics of Child Abuse*: 132.
38 ibid.: 132.
39 ibid.: ch. 7. See also Frost and Stein, op. cit.: ch. 4.
40 Pfohl, op. cit.: 316.
41 ibid.: 314; D. Gil and J. H. Noble, 'Public Knowledge, Attitudes and Opinions about Physical Abuse', *Child Welfare*, 49, July 1969: 395–401; D. Gil, *Violence against Children*, Cambridge, Mass.: Harvard University Press, 1970: 63–7, 141.
42 ibid.: 16.
43 ibid.: 137.
44 These positions are well summarised in Parton, *Politics of Child Abuse*: ch. 7.
45 R. J. Gelles, 'The Social Construction of Child Abuse', *American Journal of Orthopsychiatry*, 45, 1979: 363–71 .
46 Dingwall, *et al.*, *Protection of Children*: 3, 31.
47 Parton, *Politics of Child Abuse*: 188.

10 Hospital welfare, health and poverty

1 Central Health Services Council, *The Welfare of Children in Hospital* (hereafter the Platt Report), London: HMSO, 1959: 1.

2 James Robertson, *Young Children in Hospital*, London, Tavistock, 1958, 2nd edn. 1970.

3 ibid.: xiii and 19–20.

4 Platt Report: 37–41.

5 ibid.: 2–3.

6 Rick Rogers, *From Crowther to Warnock: How Fourteen Reports Tried to Change Children's Lives*, London: Heinemann, 1980: 31–2.

7 Robertson, op. cit., 2nd edn: 100–6; Rogers, op. cit.: 35–6.

8 Department of Health and Social Security, *Fit for the Future: The Report of the Committee in Child Health Services* (hereafter the Court Report), Vol. I, London: HMSO, 1977: 279, para 16.19.

9 Rogers, op. cit.: 38–9; 41.

10 M. Stacey, *et al.*, *Hospitals, Children and Their Families: A Pilot Study*, London: Routledge & Kegan Paul, 1970; P. J. Hawthorn, *Nurse I Want My Mummy*, Royal College of Nursing, 1974; Dr Desmond MacCarthy, *Nursing Mirror*, 2 November 1978.

11 Court Report: 190, para. 12.39.

12 Consumers' Association, *Children in Hospital*, 1980.

13 Judy Allsop, *Health Policy and the National Health Service*, London: Longman, 1984: 157.

14 Court Report: 4.

15 See Martin Woodhead, 'Psychology and the Cultural Construction of Children's Needs', in Allison James and Alan Prout (eds), *Constructing and Reconstructing Childhood: Contemporary Issues in the Sociological Study of Childhood*, London: The Falmer Press, 1990: 60–77.

16 Court Report: 4–6, 39, 42, 45–6. See also R. H. Jackson and A. W. Wilkinson, 'Why Don't We Prevent Childhood Accidents?', *British Medical Journal*, 2, 1976: 1258; M. Rutter, J. Tizard and K. Whitmore, *Educational Health and Behaviour*, London: Longman, 1970.

17 Court Report: 6. See also the Department of Education and Science, *Special Educational Needs* (hereafter the Warnock Report), London: HMSO, 1978: 279–89.

18 Court Report: 18, 20 and ch. 2. Conclusion quoted in Allsop, op. cit.: 157.

19 Court Report: 7 and pt III.

20 Rogers, op. cit.: 229–30, 233–4; Caroline Moorhead, 'What happened to the Court Report?', *The Times*, 4 April 1978.

21 Quoted in Allsop, op. cit.: 158.

22 M. Rutter and N. Madge, *Cycles of Disadvantage: A Review of Research*, London: Heinemann, 1976; F. Coffield, P. Robinson and J. Sarsby, *A Cycle of Deprivation? A Case Study of Four Families*, London: Heinemann, 1980; Mildred Blaxter, *The Health of Children: A Review of Research on the Place of Health in Cycles of Disadvantage*, London, Heinemann, 1981.

23 Department of Health and Social Security, 'Inequalities in Health: Report of a Research Working Group Chaired by Sir Douglas Black' (hereafter the Black Report), London: 1980, reprinted in *Inequalities in Health: The Black Report, The Health Divide*, Harmondsworth: Penguin, 1990. All references are to this edition.

24 Quoted by Peter Townsend and Nick Davidson (eds), introduction to *Inequalities in Health*: 3–4.

25 ibid.: 6–11. Margaret Whitehead, *The Health Divide*.
26 Quoted in Allsop, op. cit.: 158.
27 Black Report: 169. Original emphasis.
28 Introduction, *Inequalities in Health*: 2–3.
29 ibid.: 6.
30 ibid.: 13.
31 Black Report: 118–21.
32 Court quoted in ibid: 121–2; *The Health Divide*, 299–300. For a brief discussion of health in the cycle of disadvantage, see Blaxter, op. cit.: 1–9 and passim.
33 *The Health Divide*: 301–2.
34 ibid.: 316–18, 350, 355–6.
35 Blaxter, op. cit.: 219.
36 Donald Court and Eva Alberman, 'Worlds Apart', in John O. Forfar (ed.), *Child Health in a Changing Society*, Oxford: Oxford University Press, 1988: 28.

11 'Children are people too': Child care policy in the 1980s

1 P. Hall, *Reforming the Welfare*, London, Heinemann, 1976; J. Cooper, *The Creation of the British Personal Social Services, 1962–1974*, London: Heinemann, 1983.
2 J. Rowe and L. Lambert, *Children Who Wait*, London: Association of British Adoption Agencies, 1973; J. Goldstein, A. Freud and A. Solnit, *Beyond the Best Interests of the Child*, New York: Free Press, 1973.
3 Nigel Parton, *Governing the Family: Child Care, Child Protection and the State*, London: Macmillan, 1991: 19–51; Kathleen Jones, *The Making of Social Policy in Britain, 1830–1990*, London: Athlone Press, 1991: chs 13–14.
4 For the differing viewpoints in this, see J. Packman and B. Jordan, 'The Children Act: Looking Forward, Looking Back', *British Journal of Social Work*, 21, 1991: 316–18; Nigel Parton, 'The Contemporary Politics of Child Protection', *Journal of Social Welfare and Family Law*, 1992: 101–3; Nigel Parton, 'Child Abuse, Social Anxiety and Welfare', *British Journal of Social Work*, 11, 4, 1981: 392; Nigel Parton, 'Children in Care: Recent Changes and Debates', *Critical Social Policy*, 13, 1985: 107–17; Parton, *Governing the Family*: 25; R. Dingwall, J. Eekelaar and Topsy Murray, *The Protection of Children: State Intervention and Family Life*, Oxford: Basil Blackwell, 1983: 208–10; Robert Dingwall and John Eekelaar, 'Rethinking Child Protection', in Michael Freeman (ed.), *State, Law, and the Family. Critical Perspectives*, London: Tavistock/Sweet & Maxwell, 1984: 93–103; J. Packman, J. Randal and N. Jacques, *Who Needs Care? Social Work Decisions about Children*, Oxford: Basil Blackwell, 1986: 3–4.
5 Parton, 'Contemporary Politics of Child Protection': 100–1; Robert Harris, 'A Matter of Balance: Power and Resistance in Child Protection Policy', *Journal of Social Welfare Law*, 1990: 332–40.
6 R. Parker (ed.), *Caring for Separated Children: Plans, Procedures and Priorities: A Report by the Working Party Established by the National Children's Bureau*, London, Macmillan, 1980; Social Services Committee (HC 360), *Children in Care* (the Short Report), London: HMSO, 1984. For DHSS and ESRC studies, see Parton, *Governing the Family*: 26. On the conflict of interests between local authorities, parents and children, see Madeleine Colvin, 'Children, Care and the Local State', in Freeman (ed.), op. cit.: 115–23.

7 Parton, *Governing the Family*: 23–42.
8 Packman, *et al.*, op. cit.; S. Millham, R. Bullock, K. Hosie and M. Haak, *Lost in Care: The Problems of Maintaining Links between Children in Care and their Families*, Aldershot: Gower, 1986; Dingwall, *et al.*, op. cit.: passim; Department of Health and Social Security, *Social Work Decisions in Child Care: Recent Research Findings and Their Implications*, London: HMSO, 1985.
9 M. Fisher, P. Marsh, and D. Phillips with E. Sainsbury, *In and Out of Care: The Experience of Children, Parents and Social Workers*, London: Batsford/BAAF, 1986: 124–5.
10 Michael D. A. Freeman, *Children, Their Families and the Law*, London: Macmillan, 1992: 3; Packman and Jordan, op. cit.: 320.
11 ibid.; Parton, 'Contemporary Politics of Child Protection': 101; and his *Governing the Family*: 52–78.
12 Harris, 'A Matter of Balance': 338; Parton, *Governing the Family*: 81.
13 For different interpretations of Cleveland, see Parton, *Governing the Family*: 79–115; S. Bell, *When Salem Came to the Boro: The True Story of the Cleveland Child Abuse Crisis*, London: Pan, 1988; B. Campbell, *Unofficial Secrets: Child Sexual Abuse – the Cleveland Case*, London: Virago, 1988; *Report of Inquiry into Child Abuse in Cleveland* (hereafter Cleveland Report), London: HMSO, 1988.
14 Harris, op. cit.: 338.
15 Cleveland Report: para. 4.57; Packman and Jordan, op. cit.: 322.
16 Para 6.4 quoted in Parton, *Governing the Family*: 121–2.
17 Para 6.7 quoted in ibid.: 132.
18 ibid.: 83, 118–21; quotation in Nick Frost, 'Official Intervention and Child Protection: The Relationship between State and Family in Contemporary Britain', in Violence Against Children Study Group, *Taking Child Abuse Seriously*, London: Unwin Hyman, 1990: 39.
19 Parton, 'Contemporary Politics of Child Protection'; Freeman, op. cit.: 1; Packman and Jordan, op. cit.
20 Quoted in Parton, *Governing the Family*: 147. For details of the Act see Freeman, op. cit.; J. Eekelaar and R. Dingwall, *The Reform of Child Care Law: A Practical Guide to the Children Act 1989*, London: Routledge, 1989; A. Bainham, *Children – the New Law*, Bristol: Family Law, 1990; Nick Allen, *Making Sense of the Children Act*, London: Longman, 1992 edn.
21 Freeman, op. cit.: 1.
22 For a discussion of how the new consensus was reconstructed, see Parton, *Governing the Family*: 147–92.
23 For the new framework for public and private law, see Eekelaar and Dingwall, op. cit.: 19–48. For a list of public and private law concerning child care legislation since 1969, see Allen, op. cit.: 2–3.
24 Freeman, op. cit.: 6–8; Packman and Jordan, op. cit.: 315; Eekelaar and Dingwall, op. cit.: 2.
25 Quoted in ibid.: 70.
26 ibid.: 70–1; Freeman, op. cit.: 50–1.
27 Quoted in ibid.: 51.
28 ibid.: 55–6.
29 ibid.: 10–28. See also Parton, *Governing the Family*: 152–60.
30 Packman and Jordan, op. cit.: 323.
31 Eekelaar and Dingwall, op. cit.: 23–6.
32 ibid.: 19–23; Parton, *Governing the Family*: 155 and 173.

33 Quoted in Freeman, op. cit.: 22.
34 Department of Health, *Principles and Practice in Regulations and Guidance*, London: HMSO, 1990: 8; Freeman, op. cit.: 25; Parton, *Governing the Family*: 172–4. See also Packman and Jordan, op. cit.: 323, and Eekelaar and Dingwall, op. cit.: 22–3.
35 Parton, *Governing the Family*: 194.
36 For a brief summary of these positions, see Dingwall and Eekelaar in Freeman (ed.), op. cit.: 104–5, and Parton, *Governing the Family*: 196–8.
37 ibid.: 194–5.
38 Barrie Clark, Wendy Parkin and Martin Richards, 'Dangerousness: A Complex Practice Issue', in Violence Against Children Study Group, op. cit.: 144; Christine and Nigel Parton, 'Child Protection: The Law and Dangerousness', in Olive Stevenson (ed.), *Child Abuse: Public Policy and Professional Practice*, London: Harvester Wheatsheaf, 1989: 54–73.
39 On dangerousness and the failure of the rehabilitative ideal, see A. E. Bottoms, 'Reflections on the Renaissance of Dangerousness', *Howard Journal of Penology and Crime Prevention*, 16, 2, 1977: 70–96; S. Cohen, *Visions of Social Control: Crime, Punishment and Classification*, Cambridge: Polity Press, 1985; F. A. Allen, *The Decline of the Rehabilitative Ideal: Penal Policy and Social Purpose*, London: Yale University Press, 1981.
40 Parton, *Governing the Family*: 198. On the difficulties in identifying 'dangerousness' and 'high risk', see Robert Dingwall, 'Some Problems about Predicting Child Abuse and Neglect', in Stevenson (ed.), op. cit.: 28–53.
41 In 1983 approximately one-third of all children in Britain were living in families in or on the margin of poverty. Margaret Whitehead, *The Health Divide* in *Inequalities in Health: The Black Report, The Health Divide*, Harmondsworth: Penguin, 1990: 334. On government social policy in the 1980s see Anne Digby, *British Welfare Policy: Workhouse to Workfare*, London: Faber & Faber, 1989: 100–25, and Jones, op. cit.: 188–208.
42 Parton, *Governing the Family*: 203–6, 209–10, and 156 for 'significant harm'. See also Freeman, op. cit.: 102–3.
43 M. McCarthy, 'The Personal Social Services', in M. McCarthy (ed.), *The New Politics of Welfare: An Agenda for the 1990s*, London: Macmillan, 1990: 46, also quoted in Parton, *Governing the Family*: 211.
44 Quoted in Freeman, op. cit.: 4 and 6. See also Lorraine Fox Harding, *Perspectives in Child Care Policy*, London: Longman, 1991: 228–9.
45 Freeman, op. cit.: 4. For the claim that there is 'a good deal' in the Act which 'leans to a children's rights viewpoint', see Lorraine Fox Harding, 'The Children Act 1989 in Context: Four Perspectives in Child Care Law and Policy', *Journal of Social Welfare and Family Law*, 1991: 179–93 and 285–302.
46 Freeman, op. cit.: 4.
47 Packman and Jordan, op. cit.: 324.
48 Freeman, op. cit.: 5.
49 N. Frost in Violence Against Children Study Group, op. cit.: 31–5. See also an important text for the New Right's thinking about the family: F. Mount, *The Subversive Family*, London: Jonathan Cape, 1983.
50 Freeman, op. cit.: 5–6.
51 Quotations in Parton, *Governing the Family*: 162–6, and, for a discussion of the Short Report, 27–39. The relationship between poverty and deprivation and childcare also figured prominently in the Short Report, and in Packman et al., op. cit.

52 Harding, 'The Children Act 1989 in Context': passim.
53 Jacques Donzelot, *The Policing of Families: Welfare versus the State*, London, Hutchinson, 1979: xxvi–xxvii. I focus on 'the social' not simply in relation to 'discourses' of knowledge, such as law, medicine and psychiatry, but also in relation to the problem of living in a democratic community, where one of the most infectious of liberal goals is making real the notion of citizenship.
54 On citizenship, see Julia Parker, *Social Policy and Citizenship*, London: Macmillan, 1975; Michael Freeden, *The New Liberalism: An Ideology of Social Reform*, Oxford: Clarendon Press, 1978: passim; Andrew Vincent and Raymond Plant, *Philosophy, Politics and Citizenship*, Oxford: Basil Blackwell, 1984; Harry Hendrick, *Images of Youth, Age, Class and the Male Youth Problem, 1880–1920*, Oxford: Clarendon Press, 1990: 234–49.
55 Parton, 'Contemporary Politics of Child Protection': 100. See also Dingwall, *et al.*, *Protection of Children*: 211–21; Frost in Violence Against Children Study Group, op. cit.: 25–40; Donzelot, op. cit.: 53–4.
56 Packman and Jordan, op. cit.: 315. For an interesting essay on the 'autonomous family', see Nikolas Rose, *Governing the Soul: The Shaping of the Private Self*, London: Routledge, 1990: 200–9.
57 Eekelaar and Dingwall, op. cit.: 21; Dingwall, *et al.*: 218.
58 Frost in Violence Against Children Study Group, op. cit.: 26, 39. I would probably place more emphasis on the continuing relevance of the use of 'rights' and 'interests' as evaluative concepts than would Frost.
59 Rose, op. cit.: especially pt 3.
60 Dingwall and Eekelaar in Freeman (ed.) op. cit.: 104.
61 Quotations from J. Goldstein, A. Freud and A. Solnit, *Before the Best Interests of the Child*, London: Burnett Books/André Deutsch, 1980: 9; and A. Morris, H. Giller and E. Szwed, *Justice for Children*, London: Macmillan, 1980: 127 cited in Dingwall and Eekelaar in Freeman (ed.) op. cit.: 104.
62 ibid.: 104.
63 ibid.: 104–6.

Conclusion

1 Denise Riley, *War in the Nursery*, London: Virago Press, 1983: ch. 6.
2 Nikolas Rose, *Governing the Soul: The Shaping of the Private Self*, London: Routledge, 1990: 156.
3 *Inequalities in Health: The Black Report, The Health Divide*, Harmondsworth, Penguin, 1990: preface to *Health Divide*.
4 A list of references is given in ibid.
5 Kathleen Jones, *The Making of Social Policy in Britain, 1830–1990*, London: Athlone Press, 1991: 169–70.

SELECT BIBLIOGRAPHY

PARLIAMENTARY PAPERS AND OFFICIAL PUBLICATIONS

Annual Reports of the Chief Medical Officer at the Board of Education.
Hansard.
Select Committee on Protection of Infant Life, Report, VII, 1871.
Select Committee on the Law Relating to the Protection of Young Girls From Artifices to Induce Them to Lead a Corrupt Life, First Report, IX (HL) 1881; *Second Report,* XIII, 1882.
Report of Dr Crichton-Browne on Over-Pressure, LXI, 1884.
Royal Commission on the Housing of the Working Classes, Vol. 2; XXX, 1884–5.
Education: Elementary Schools (Children Working for Wages), Pt 2, 1899, LXXV.
Select Committee on the Infant Life Protection Bill, Report, XIII, 1890.
Departmental Committee on Conditions of School Attendance and Child Labour, Report, LXVIII, 1893–4.
Select Committee . . . on the Infant Life Protection Bill and Safety of Nurse Children Bill, Report, X (HL), 1896.
The Education and Maintenance of Pauper Children in the Metropolis, Report, Vol. 1, XLIII, 1896.
Departmental Committee on Defective and Epileptic Children, Report, XXVI, 1898.
Royal Commission on the Blind, Deaf, Dumb . . . Report and Minutes of Evidence, XIX–XX, 1899.
Inter-departmental Committee on the Employment of School Children, Report, XXV, 1902.
Royal Commission on Physical Training (Scotland), Report, XXX, 1903.
Inter-departmental Committee on Physical Deterioration, Report and Evidence, XXXII, 1904.
Inter-departmental Committee on Medical Inspection and Feeding of Children attending Public Elementary Schools, Report, XLVII, 1906.
Royal Commission on the Care and Control of the Feeble Minded, Report, XXIX, 1908.
Select Committee on Infant Life Protection, Report, IX, 1908.
Inter-departmental Committee on Partial Exemption from School Attendance, Report, XVII, 1909.
Departmental Committee on the Employment of Children Act, 1903, Report, XXVIII, 1910.
Departmental Committee on Reformatories and Industrial Schools, Report, XXXIX, 1913.

Departmental Committee on Scholarships, Free Places and Maintenance Allowances, Report, XV, 1920.

Departmental Committee on the Treatment of Young Offenders, Report, XII, 1927.

Board of Education, *Handbook for Teachers*, 1927.

Board of Education Consultative Committee, Report, *The Education of the Adolescent* (Hadow), 1929.

Royal Commission on Lunacy and Mental Disorder, Report, London: HMSO, 1929.

Board of Education Consultative Committee, Report, *The Primary School*, 1931.

Board of Education Consultative Committee, Report, *Secondary Education with Special Reference to Grammar Schools and Technical High Schools* (Spens), 1938.

Ministry of Health and Ministry of Education, *The Care of Children Committee, Report* (Curtis), London: HMSO, 1946.

Departmental Committee on the Adoption of Children, Report, VIII, 1953–4.

Ministry of Education, *Report of the Committee on Maladjusted Children*, London: HMSO, 1955.

Central Health Services Council, *The Welfare of Children in Hospital* (Platt), London: HMSO, 1959.

Report of the Committee on Children and Young Persons (Ingleby), London: HMSO, 1960.

Department of Health and Social Security, *Fit for the Future: The Report of the Committee on Child Health Services* (Court), Vol. 1, London: HMSO, 1977.

Report of the Committee on Local Authority and Allied Personal Social Services (Seebohm), London: HMSO, 1968.

Department of Education and Science, *Special Educational Needs* (Warnock), London: HMSO, 1978.

Report of Inquiry into Child Abuse in Cleveland, London: HMSO, 1988.

Department of Health and Social Security, 'Inequalities in Health: Report of a Research Working Group Chaired by Sir Douglas Black', in Townsend, Peter, and Davidson, Nick (eds), *Inequalities in Health: The Black Report, The Health Divide*, Harmondsworth: Penguin, 1990. (This includes report commissioned by Health Education Council from Margaret Whitehead, *The Health Divide*.)

NON-GOVERNMENTAL REPORTS, PROCEEDINGS, ETC.

Carnegie United Kingdom Trust, *Report on the Physical Welfare of Mothers and Children*, Liverpool: C. Tinling, 1917.

Charity Organisation Society, *Report of a Special Committee on the Education and Care of Idiots, Imbeciles and Harmless Lunatics*, London: Longmans, Green, 1877.

Charity Organisation Society, *The Feeble-minded Child and Adult*, London, 1893.

The Child Guidance Council, London, Child Guidance Council, 1928.

The Establishment of a Child Guidance Clinic, London: Child Guidance Council, 1938.

Child Guidance Council, reports, 1933–43.

Child Guidance Council, pamphlets, 1930s.

Feversham Committee, *Report on the Voluntary Mental Health Services*, London: Feversham Committee, 1939.

Legislation in Regard to Children: Report and Proceedings at a Special Conference, May, 1906, London: P. S. King, 1906.

Liverpool Society for the Prevention of Cruelty to Children, *Report for 1884*.

Liverpool Society for the Prevention of Cruelty to Children, *Tortured Children: A Third Year's Experience in Their Defence*, Liverpool: LSPCC, 1887.

London Society for the Prevention of Cruelty to Children, *Third Annual Report, 1887–88*.

National Deviancy Conference (ed.), *Permissiveness and Control. The Fate of the Sixties Legislation*, London: Macmillan, 1980.

National Society for the Prevention of Cruelty to Children, *Report of the NSPCC, 1888–89*.

National Society for the Prevention of Cruelty to Children, *Five Years with Cruelty to Children: Review and a Statement*, 1889.

National Society for the Prevention of Cruelty to Children, Oxford Branch, *Report, 1899–1900. EC Report*.

Political and Economic Planning, *Report on the British Health Services*, London: PEP, 1937.

Report of the Proceedings of the Second National Conference on Infant Mortality, London: P. S. King, 1908.

Royal College of Obstetricians and Gynaecologists, *Maternity in Great Britain*, London: Oxford University Press, 1948.

BOOKS AND PAMPHLETS

Abel-Smith, Brian, *The Poor and the Poorest*, Occasional Papers in Social Administration, London: Bell, 1966.

Alden, Margaret, *Child Life and Labour*, London: Headley Bros, 1908.

Allen, Anne, and Morton, Arthur, *This Is Your Child: The Story of the National Society for the Prevention of Cruelty to Children*, London: Routledge & Kegan Paul, 1961.

Allen, F. A., *The Decline of the Rehabilitative Ideal: Penal Policy and Social Purpose*, London: Yale University Press, 1981.

Allen, Marjorie (Lady Allen of Hurtwood), *Whose Children?*, London: Simpkin Marshall, 1945.

Allen, Marjorie (Lady Allen of Hurtwood), *Memoirs of an Uneducated Lady*, London: Thames & Hudson, 1975.

Allen, Nick, *Making Sense of the Children Act*, London: Longman, 1992 edn.

Allsop, Judy, *Health Policy and the National Health Service*, London: Longman, 1984.

Anderson, Michael, *Approaches to the History of the Western Family, 1500–1914*, London: Macmillan, 1980.

Armstrong, David, *The Political Anatomy of the Body*, Cambridge: Cambridge University Press, 1983.

Bailey, Victor, *Delinquency and Citizenship: Reclaiming the Young Offender. 1914–1948*, Oxford: Clarendon Press, 1987.

Bainham, A., *Children – the New Law*, Bristol: Family Law, 1990.

Banks, Olive, *Parity and Prestige in English Secondary Education*, London: Routledge & Kegan Paul, 1955.

Banting, Keith, *Poverty, Politics and Policy: Britain in the 1960s*, London: Macmillan, 1979.

Barnett House Study Group, *London Children in Wartime Oxford: A Survey of Social and Educational Results of Evacuation*, London: Oxford University Press, 1947.

Bean, Philip, and Melville, Joy, *Lost Children of the Empire*, London: Unwin Hyman, 1989.

SELECT BIBLIOGRAPHY

Behlmer. George K., *Child Abuse and Moral Reform in England, 1870–1908*, Stanford, Calif.: Stanford University Press, 1982.

Bell, Stuart, *When Salem Came to the Boro: The True Story of the Cleveland Child Abuse Crisis*, London: Pan, 1988.

Bevan, H. K., *Child Law*, London: Butterworth, 1989.

Blacker, C. P., *Neurosis and the Mental Health Services*, Oxford: Oxford University Press, 1946.

Blaxter, Mildred, *The Health of Children: A Review of Research on the Place of Health in Cycles of Disadvantage*, London: Heinemann, 1981.

Bosanquet, H., *Rich and Poor*, London: Macmillan, 1908.

Boss, Peter, *Exploration in Child Care*, London: Routledge & Kegan Paul, 1971.

Bowlby, John, *Child Care and the Growth of Love*, Harmondsworth: Penguin, 1953.

Boyd, William (ed.), *Evacuation in Scotland: A Record of Events and Experiments*, Bickley, Kent: University of London Press, 1944.

Bradley, Ian, *The Call to Seriousness*, London: Jonathan Cape, 1976.

Briggs, I. G., *Reformatory Reform*, London: Longmans, Green, 1924.

Bristow, Edward, *Vice and Vigilance: Purity Movements in Britain since 1700*, Dublin: Gill & Macmillan, 1977.

Bulkley, M. E., *The Feeding of School Children*, London: G. Bell, 1914.

Burbury, Winifred. Balinet, E. M., and Yapp, B. J., *An Introduction to Child Guidance*, London: Macmillan, 1950.

Burlingham, Dorothy and Freud, Anna, *Young Children in War Time*, London: Allen & Unwin, 1942.

Burt, Cyril, *Mental and Scholastic Tests*, London: London County Council, 1921.

Burt, Cyril, *The Young Delinquent*, London: University of London Press, 1925.

Butterworth, E., and Holman, R. (eds), *Social Welfare in Modern Britain*, London: Fontana, 1975.

Calder, Angus, *The People's War*, London: Panther, 1971.

Cameron, Hector, *The Nervous Child*, London: Oxford University Press, 1919.

Campbell, B., *Unofficial Secrets: Child Sexual Abuse – the Cleveland Case*, London: Virago, 1988.

Carlebach, Julius, *Caring for Children in Trouble*, London: Routledge & Kegan Paul, 1970.

Carpenter, M., *Juvenile Delinquents: Their Condition and Treatment*, London: Cash, 1853.

Chesser, Eustace, *Cruelty to Children*, London: Victor Gollancz, 1951.

Clark, F. Le Gros, *The School Child and the School Canteen*, Hereford, 1942.

Coffield, F., Robinson, P., and Sarsby, J., *A Cycle of Deprivation? A Case Study of Four Families*, London: Heinemann, 1980.

Cohen, S., *Folk Devils and Moral Panics: The Creation of Mods and Rockers*, London: Paladin, 1973.

Cohen, S., *Visions of Social Control: Crime, Punishment and Classification*, Cambridge: Polity Press, 1985.

Collis, Arthur T., and Poole, Vera, *These Our Children*, London: Victor Gollancz, 1950.

Conquest, Joan, *The Naked Truth: Shocking Revelations about the Slums*, London: T. Werner Laurie, 1933.

Cooper, J., *The Creation of the British Personal Social Services, 1962–1974*, London: Heinemann, 1983.

Corby, B., *Working with Child Abuse: Social Work Practice and the Child Abuse System*, Milton Keynes: Open University Press, 1987.

Coveney, Peter, *The Image of Childhood*, 2nd edn, Harmondsworth: Peregrine, 1967.

Crowley, Ralph, *The Hygiene of School Life*, London: Methuen, 1910.

Cruickshank, L. D., *School Clinics at Home and Abroad*, London: National League for Physical Education and Improvement, 1913.

Cruickshank, Marjorie, *Children and Industry*, Manchester: Manchester University Press, 1982.

Cunningham, Hugh, *The Children of the Poor: Representations of Childhood since the Seventeenth Century*, Oxford: Basil Blackwell, 1991.

Davidoff, Leonore, and Hall, Catherine, *Family Fortunes. Men and Women of the English Middle Class, 1780–1850*, London: Hutchinson, 1987.

Davis, John, *Youth and the Condition of Britain*, London: Athlone Press, 1990.

Dawson, W. H., *School Doctors in Germany*, London: Board of Education, 1906.

Dicks, Henry V., *Fifty Years of the Tavistock Clinic*, London: Routledge & Kegan Paul, 1970.

Digby, Anne, *British Welfare Policy. Workhouse to Workfare*, London: Faber, 1989.

Dingwall, Robert, Eekelaar, John, and Murray, Topsy, *The Protection of Children: State Intervention and Family Life*, Oxford: Basil Blackwell, 1983.

Donnison, D. V., *The Neglected Child and the Social Services*, Manchester: Manchester University Press, 1954.

Donnison, D., Jay, P., and Stewart, M., *The Ingleby Report: Three Critical Essays*, London: the Fabian Society, 1962.

Donzelot, Jacques, *The Policing of Families: Welfare versus the State*, London: Hutchinson, 1979.

Drever. James, *An Introduction to the Psychology of Education*, London: Edward Arnold, 1925.

Driver, C., *Tory Radical: The Life of Richard Oastler*, New York: Oxford University Press, 1946.

Dwork, Deborah, *War Is Good for Babies and Other Young Children: A History of the Infant and Child Welfare Movement in England, 1898–1918*, London: Tavistock, 1987.

Dyhouse, Carol, *Girls Growing Up in Late Victorian and Edwardian England*, London: Routledge & Kegan Paul, 1981.

Eekelaar, J., and Dingwall, R., *The Reform of Child Care Law: A Practical Guide to the Children Act, 1989*, London: Routledge, 1989.

Fisher, Lettice, *Twenty One Years and After: The Story of the NCUMC*, London: National Council for the Unmarried Mother and her Child, 1937.

Fisher, M., Marsh, P., Phillips, D., and Sainsbury, E., *In and Out of Care: The Experience of Children, Parents and Social Workers*, London: Batsford/BAAF, 1986.

Foucault, Michel, *Discipline and Punish*, London: Allen Lane, 1979.

Fox, Charles, *Educational Psychology: Its Problems and Methods*, London: Kegan Paul, Trench, Trubner, 1925.

Franklin, A. W. (ed.), *Concerning Child Abuse*, London: Churchill-Livingstone, 1975.

Freeden, Michael, *The New Liberalism. An Ideology of Social Reform*, Oxford: Clarendon Press, 1978.

Freeman, Michael D. A., *Children, Their Families and the Law*, London: Macmillan, 1992.

Frost, Nick, and Stein, Mike, *The Politics of Child Welfare*, London: Harvester Wheatsheaf, 1989.

335

Garland, D., *Punishment and Welfare*, Aldershot: Gower, 1985.

George, Vic, *Foster Care: Theory and Practice*, London: Routledge & Kegan Paul, 1970.

Gil, D., *Violence against Children*, Cambridge, Mass.: Harvard University Press, 1970.

Gilbert, Bentley B., *The Evolution of National Insurance in Great Britain: The Origins of the Welfare State*, London: Michael Joseph, 1966.

Goldstein, J., Freud, A., and Solnit, A., *Beyond the Best Interests of the Child*, New York, Free Press, 1973.

Goldstein, J., Freud, A., and Solnit, A., *Before the Best Interests of the Child*, London: Burnett Books/André Deutsch, 1980.

Gordon, Linda, *Heroes of Their Own Lives*, London: Virago Press, 1989.

Gordon, R. G., *A Survey of Child Psychiatry*, London: Oxford University Press, 1939.

Gorst, Sir John, *The Children of the Nation*, London: Methuen, 1906.

Gould, Stephen Jay, *The Mismeasure of Man*, New York: W. W. Norton, 1981.

Greenwood, Arthur, *The Health and Physique of School Children*, London: P. S. King, 1913.

Greenwood, James, *The Seven Curses of London*, Oxford: Basil Blackwell, 1869 (1981 edn).

Haley, Bruce, *The Healthy Body and Victorian Culture*, Cambridge, Mass.: Harvard University Press, 1978.

Hall, M. Penelope, *The Social Services of Modern England*, London: Routledge & Kegan Paul, 1952.

Hall, P., *Reforming the Welfare*, London: Heinemann, 1976.

Hall, W. Clarke, *Children's Courts*, London: George Allen & Unwin, 1928.

Harding, Lorraine Fox, *Perspectives in Child Care Policy*, London: Longman, 1991.

Hearnshaw, L. S., *A Short History of British Psychology, 1840–1940*, London: Methuen, 1964.

Hearnshaw, L. S., *Cyril Burt, Psychologist*, London: Hodder & Stoughton, 1979.

Heasman, Kathleen, *Evangelicals in Action*, London: Geoffrey Bles, 1962.

Henderson, David, K., and Gillespie, Robert, *A Textbook of Psychiatry*, London: Oxford University Press, 1927, 1930 and 1932.

Henderson, Peter, *The School Health Service, 1908–1974*, London: HMSO, 1975.

Hendrick, Harry, *Images of Youth. Age, Class and the Male Youth Problem, 1880–1920*, Oxford: Clarendon Press, 1990.

Heywood, Jean, *Children in Care: The Development of the Service for the Deprived Child*, London: Routledge & Kegan Paul, 1959, 1965, 1978.

Hogarth, A. H., *Medical Inspection of Schools*, London: Hodder & Stoughton, 1909.

Holman, Robert, *Trading in Children. A Study of Private Fostering*, London: Routledge & Kegan Paul, 1973.

Holman, Robert, *Inequality in Child Care*, London: Child Poverty Action Group, 1980.

Holman, Robert, *Putting Families First*, London: Macmillan, 1988.

Holmes, G. V., *The Likes of Us*, London: Muller, 1948.

Horn, Pamela, *The Victorian and Edwardian Schoolchild*, Gloucester: Alan Sutton, 1989.

Houlbrooke, R. A., *The English Family, 1450–1700*, London: Longman, 1984.

Houseden, L. G., *The Prevention of Cruelty to Children*, London: Jonathan Cape, 1955.

Howells, J. G., *Remember Maria*, London: Butterworth, 1974.

Hudson, B., *Justice through Punishment*, London: Macmillan, 1987.

Humphries, Stephen, *Hooligans or Rebels? An Oral History of Working-Class Childhood and Youth, 1889–1939*, Oxford: Basil Blackwell, 1981.

Humphries, Steve, Mack, Joanna, and Perks, Robert, *A Century of Childhood*, London: Sidgwick & Jackson, 1988.

Hurt, J. S., *Elementary Schooling and the Working Classes, 1860–1918*, London: Routledge & Kegan Paul, 1979.

Hurt, J. S., *Outside the Mainstream. A History of Special Education*, London: Batsford, 1988.

Hutt, Allen, *The Condition of the Working Class in Britain*, London: Martin Lawrence, 1933.

Inglis, Ruth, *The Children's War. Evacuation, 1939–45*, London: Fontana, 1989.

Isaacs, Susan (ed.), *The Cambridge Evacuation Survey*, London: Methuen, 1941.

Johnson, B. S. (ed.), *The Evacuees*, London: Victor Gollancz, 1968.

Jones, Greta, *Social Hygiene in Twentieth Century Britain*, London: Croom Helm, 1986.

Jones, Kathleen, *A History of the Mental Health Services*, London: Routledge & Kegan Paul, 1972.

Jones, Kathleen, *The Making of Social Policy in Britain, 1830–1990*, London: Athlone Press, 1991.

Jordanova, Ludmilla, *Languages of Nature*, London: Free Association Books, 1986.

Kelynack, T. N., *Childhood*, London: Charles H. Kelly, 1910.

Kelynack, T. N., *Medical Examination of Schools and Scholars*, London: P. S. King, 1910.

Kornitzer, Margaret, *Adoption in the Modern World*, London: Putnam, 1952.

Lapage, C. Paget, *Feeblemindedness in Children of School Age*, Manchester: Manchester University Press, 1920.

Lawson, John, and Silver, Harold, *A Social History of Education in England*, London: Methuen, 1973.

Layne-Claypon, Janet, *The Child Welfare Movement*, London: G. Bell, 1920.

Leff, S. and V., *The School Health Service*, London: H. K. Lewis, 1959.

Lewis, Jane, *The Politics of Motherhood. Child and Maternal Welfare in England, 1900–1939*, London: Croom Helm, 1980.

Mackenzie, Leslie W., *The Health of the School Child*, London: Methuen, 1906.

McCleary, G. F., *Infant Mortality and Infant Milk Depots*, London: P. S. King, 1905.

McCleary, G. F., *The Early History of the Infant Welfare Movement*, London: H. K. Lewis, 1933.

McCleary, G. F., *The Maternity and Child Welfare Movement*, London: P. S. King, 1935.

M'Gonigle, G. C. M., and Kirby, J., *Poverty and Public Health*, London: Victor Gollancz, 1936.

MacLeod, Valerie, *Whose Child? The Family in Child Care Legislation and Social Work Practice*, London: Study Commission on the Family, Occasional Papers No. 11, 1982.

McNally, C. E., *Public Ill Health*, London: Victor Gollancz, 1935.

Macnicol, John, *The Movement for Family Allowances*, London: Heinemann, 1980.

Mangan, J. A., *Athleticism in the Victorian and Edwardian Public School*, Cambridge: Cambridge University Press, 1981.

Manton, J., *Mary Carpenter and the Children of the Streets*, London: Heinemann, 1976.

337

Marchant, James (ed.), *Rebuilding Family Life in the Post-War World*, London: Odhams Press, n.d.

Marwick, Arthur, *British Society since 1945*, Harmondsworth: Penguin, 1982.

Middleton, Nigel, *When Family Failed*, London: Victor Gollancz, 1971.

Miller, Emmanuel (ed.), *The Growing Child and Its Problems*, London: Kegan Paul, Trench & Trubner, 1937.

Miller, Hugh Crichton, *The New Psychology and the Teacher*, London: Jarrolds, 1921.

Miller, Hugh Crichton, *The New Psychology and the Parent*, London: Jarrolds, 1922.

Monvel, Boutet de (ed.), J.-J. Rousseau, *Émile*, London: Dent, 1963.

Moodie, William, *Child Guidance by Teamwork*, London: Child Guidance Council, 1931

Morgan, Jane, and Zedner, Lucia, *Child Victims, Crime, Impact and Criminal Justice*, Oxford: Clarendon Press, 1992.

Morris, A., Giller, H., and Szwed, E., *Justice for Children*, London: Macmillan, 1980.

Morris, Allison, and Isaac, Mary, *Juvenile Justice?*, London: Heinemann, 1978.

Mort, Frank, *Dangerous Sexualities: Medico-Moral Politics in England since 1830*, London: Routledge & Kegan Paul, 1987.

Mount, F., *The Subversive Family*, London: Jonathan Cape, 1983.

Nardinelli, Clark, *Child Labor and the Industrial Revolution*, Bloomington, Ind.: Indiana University Press, 1990.

Newman, George, *Infant Mortality: A Social Problem*, London: Methuen, 1906.

Newman, George, *The Building of a Nation's Health*, London: Macmillan, 1939.

Newsholme, Arthur, *The Last Thirty Years in Public Health*, London: George Allen & Unwin, 1936.

Norman, Frank, *Banana Boy*, London: Secker & Warburg, 1969.

Orr, J. Boyd, *Food, Health and Income*, London: Macmillan, 1936.

Packman, Jean, *The Child's Generation*, Cambridge: Basil Blackwell, 1975 and 1981.

Packman, J., Randal, J., and Jacques, N., *Who Needs Care? Social Work Decisions about Children*, Oxford: Basil Blackwell, 1986.

Padley, Richard, and Cole, Margaret (eds), *Evacuation Survey: A Report to the Fabian Society*, London: Routledge, 1940.

Parker, Julia, *Social Policy and Citizenship*, London: Macmillan, 1975.

Parker, R. (ed.), *Caring for Separated Children: Plans, Procedures and Priorities. A Report by the Working Party established by the National Children's Bureau*, London: Macmillan, 1980.

Parr, Joy, *Labouring Children*, London: Croom Helm, 1980.

Parr, Robert, *Wilful Waste: The Nation's Responsibility for Its Children*, London: National Society for the Protection of Cruelty to Children, 1910.

Parton, Nigel, *The Politics of Child Abuse*, London: Macmillan, 1985.

Parton, Nigel, *Governing the Family: Child Care, Child Protection and the State*, London: Macmillan, 1991.

Paterson, A., *Across the Bridges*, London: Edward Arnold, 1911.

Paton, Grace, *The Child and the Nation*, London: Christian Student Movement, 1915.

Pattison, Robert, *The Child Figure in English Literature*, Athens, Ga: University of Georgia Press, 1978.

Pearson, Geoffrey, *The Deviant Imagination*, London: Macmillan, 1975.

Pearson, Geoffrey, *Hooligan: A History of Respectable Fears*, London: Macmillan, 1983.

Pearson, Michael, *The Age of Consent*, Newton Abbot: David & Charles. 1972.

Pinchbeck, Ivy, and Hewitt, Margaret, *Children in English Society*, 2 vols, London: Routledge & Kegan Paul, 1969 and 1973.

Porter, Roy, *English Society in the Eighteenth Century*, Harmondsworth: Penguin, 1982.

Priestly, P., *et al.*, *Justice for Juveniles*, London: Routledge & Kegan Paul, 1977.

Pritchard, David, *Education and the Handicapped, 1760–1960*, London: Routledge & Kegan Paul, 1963.

Riley, Denise, *War in the Nursery*, London: Virago Press, 1983.

Robertson, James, *Young Children in Hospital*, London: Tavistock, 1958; 2nd edn, 1970.

Rogers, Rick, *From Crowther to Warnock: How Fourteen Reports Tried to Change Children's Lives*, London: Heinemann, 1980.

Rose, June, *For the Sake of the Children*, London: Futura, 1989.

Rose, Lionel, *Massacre of the Innocents: Infanticide in Great Britain, 1800–1939*, London: Routledge & Kegan Paul, 1986.

Rose, Lionel, *The Erosion of Childhood: Child Oppression in Britain, 1860–1918*, London: Routledge, 1991.

Rose, Nikolas, *The Psychological Complex: Psychology, Politics and Society in England, 1869–1939*, London: Routledge & Kegan Paul, 1985.

Rose, Nikolas, *Governing the Soul: The Shaping of the Private Self*, London: Routledge, 1990.

Rosman, D., *Evangelicals and Culture*, London: Croom Helm, 1984.

Rowe. J., and Lambert, Lydia, *Children Who Wait*, London: Association of British Adoption Agencies, 1973.

Rutter, M., and Madge, N., *Cycles of Disadvantage: A Review of Research*, London: Heinemann, 1976.

Rutter, M., Tizard, J., and Whitmore, K., *Educational Health and Behaviour*, London: Longman, 1970.

Sampson, Olive, *Child Guidance: Its History, Provenance and Future*, London: British Psychological Society, Occasional Papers No. 3, 1980.

Selleck, R. J. W., *English Primary Education and the Progressives*, London: Routledge & Kegan Paul, 1972.

Simon, Brian, *Education and the Labour Movement, 1870–1920*, London: Lawrence & Wishart, 1965.

Simon, Brian, *The Politics of Educational Reform, 1920–1940*, London: Lawrence & Wishart, 1974.

Sinclair, Lucy, *The Bridgburn Days*, London: Victor Gollancz, 1956.

Smith, F. B., *The People's Health, 1830–1910*, London: Croom Helm, 1979.

Somerville, John, *The Rise and Fall of Childhood*, London: Sage, 1982.

Springhall, John, *Coming of Age: Adolescence in Britain, 1860–1960*, Dublin: Gill & Macmillan, 1986.

Stacey, M., *et al.*, *Hospitals, Children and Their Families: A Pilot Study*, London: Routledge & Kegan Paul, 1970.

Steedman, Carolyn, *Childhood, Culture and Class in Britain: Margaret McMillan, 1860–1931*, London: Virago Press, 1990.

Stephens, Tom (ed.), *Problem Families*, Liverpool: Pacifist Service Units, 1947.

Stevenson, John, *British Society, 1914–45*, Harmondsworth: Penguin, 1984.

Stroud, John, *The Shorn Lamb*, London: Longmans, 1960.

Stroud, John, *Thirteen Penny Stamps: The Story of the Church of England*

Children's Society from 1881–1970, London: Church of England Children's Society, 1971.

Sutherland, Gillian, *Ability, Merit and Measurement: Mental Testing and English Education, 1880–1940*, Oxford: Clarendon Press, 1984.

Thomas, K., *Man and the Natural World: Changing Attitudes in England, 1500–1800*, Harmondsworth: Penguin, 1983.

Titmuss, R. M., *Poverty and Population: A Factual Study of Social Waste*, London: Macmillan, 1938.

Titmuss, R. M., *Birth, Poverty and Wealth: A Study of infant mortality*, London: Macmillan, 1943.

Titmuss, R. M., *Problems of Social Policy*, London: HMSO/Longmans, 1950.

Townsend, Peter (ed.), *The Fifth Social Service: A Critical Analysis of the Seebohm Proposals*, London: the Fabian Society, 1970.

Tredgold, Alfred, F., *Mental Deficiency*, London: Baillière, Tindall & Cox, 1908.

Turner, B. S., *The Body and Society*, Oxford: Basil Blackwell, 1984.

Urwin, Cathy, and Hood-Williams, John (eds), *Child Psychotherapy, War and the Normal Child: Selected Papers of Margaret Lowenfeld*, London: Free Association Books, 1989.

Vincent, Andrew, and Plant, Raymond, *Philosophy, Politics and Citizenship*, Oxford: Basil Blackwell, 1984.

Wagner, Gillian, *Barnardo*, London: Eyre & Spottiswoode, 1979.

Wagner, Gillian, *Children of the Empire*, London: Weidenfeld & Nicolson, 1982.

Walvin, James, *A Child's World. A Social History of English Childhood, 1800–1914*, Harmondsworth: Penguin, 1982.

Warner, Francis, *Report on the Scientific Study of the Mental and Physical Conditions of Childhood, with Particular Reference to Children of Defective Constitution and with Recommendations as to Education and Training*, London: Royal Sanitary Institute, 1895.

Waugh, B., *The Gaol Cradle: Who Rocks It?*, London: Daldy, Isbister, 1876.

Waugh, W., *These My Little Ones*, London: 1911.

Webb, B., *My Apprenticeship*, London: Longmans, Green, 2nd edn, n.d.

Webb, S. and B., *English Poor Law Policy*, 2 vols, London: Cass Reprint, 1963.

Webster, Charles (ed.), *Biology, Medicine and Society, 1840–1940*, Cambridge: Cambridge University Press, 1981.

Weeks, Jeffrey, *Sex, Politics and Society: The Regulation of Sexuality since 1800*, London: Longman, 1981.

Whyte, L. L., *The Unconscious before Freud*, London: J. Friedman, 1979.

Winter, J. M., *The Great War and the British People*, London: Macmillan, 1986.

Wohl, A. S. (ed.), Andrew Mearns, *The Bitter Cry of Outcast London*, Leicester: Leicester University Press, 1970 edn.

Women's Group on Public Welfare, *Our Towns: A Close-Up*, London: Oxford University Press, 1943.

Women's Group on Public Welfare, *The Neglected Child and His Family*, London: Oxford University Press, 1948.

Worsley, H., *Juvenile Delinquency*, London: Gilpin, 1849.

Younghusband, Eileen, *Social Work in Britain, 1950–1975*, London: George Allen & Unwin, 1978.

Zelizer, Viviana, *Pricing the Priceless Child: The Changing Social Value of Children*, New York: Basic Books, 1985.

ARTICLES AND ESSAYS IN SYMPOSIA

Bottoms, A. E., 'On the Decriminalization of English Juvenile Courts', in Hood, R. G. (ed.), *Crime, Criminology and Public Policy*, London: Heinemann, 1974.

Bowlby, J., 'Forty-Four Juvenile Thieves: Their Characters and Home Lives', *International Journal of Psychoanalysis*, 25, 1944.

Bruin, E. de, 'The Correlation of Hygiene and Civics', *School Hygiene*, 1, February 1913.

Bryder, Linda, ' "Wonderlands of Buttercup, Clover and Daisies": Tuberculosis and the Open-Air School Movement in Britain, 1907–39', in Cooter, Roger (ed.), *In the Name of the Child: Health and Welfare, 1880–1940*, London: Routledge, 1992.

Burke, H., and Miller, Emmanuel, 'Child Mental Hygiene', *British Journal of Medical Psychology*, 9, 3, 1929.

Burt, Cyril, 'The Causal Factors of Juvenile Crime', *British Journal of Medical Psychology*, 3, 1923.

Burt, Cyril, 'Symposium on Psychologists and Psychiatrists in the Child Guidance Service', *British Journal of Educational Psychology*, 23, 1953.

Burt, Cyril, 'The Permanent Contribution to Psychology of McDougall', *British Journal of Educational Psychology*, 25, 1955.

Burt, Cyril, 'Intelligence and Social Mobility', *British Journal of Statistical Psychology*, 14, 1961.

Caffey, J., 'Some Traumatic Lesions in Growing Bones other than Fractures and Dislocations: Clinical and Radiological Features', *British Journal of Radiology*, 30, 1967.

Clark, Barrie, Parkin, Wendy, and Richards, Martin, 'Dangerousness: A Complex Practice Issue', in Violence Against Children Study Group, *Taking Child Abuse Seriously*, London: Unwin Hyman, 1990.

Clarke, John, 'Social Democratic Delinquents and Fabian Families', in National Deviancy Conference (ed.), *Permissiveness and Control: The Fate of the Sixties Legislation*, London: Macmillan, 1980.

Clarke, John, Langan, Mary, and Lee, Phil, 'Social Work: The Conditions of Crisis', in Carlen, P., and Collinson, M. (eds), *Radical Issues in Criminology*, Oxford: Martin Robertson, 1980.

Clarke, John, 'Managing the Delinquent: The Children's Branch of the Home Office, 1913–30', in Mangan, Mary, and Schwarz, Bill (eds), *Crises in the British State, 1880–1930*, London: Hutchinson, 1985.

Collison, Mike, 'Questions of Juvenile Justice', in Carlen, P., and Collinson, M. (eds), *Radical Issues in Criminology*, Oxford: Martin Robertson, 1980.

Colls, Robert, ' "Oh Happy English Children!": Coal, Class and Education in the North-East', *Past and Present*, 73, 1976.

Colvin, Madeleine, 'Children, Care and the Local State', in Freeman, Michael (ed.), *State, Law, and the Family: Critical Perspectives*, London: Tavistock/Sweet & Maxwell, 1984.

Court, Donald, and Alberman, Eva, 'Worlds Apart', in Forfar, John, O. (ed.), *Child Health in a Changing Society*, Oxford: Oxford University Press, 1988.

Daglish, N. P., 'Robert Morant's Hidden Agenda? The Origins of the Medical Treatment of Children', *History of Education*, 19, 2, 1990.

Davin, Anna, 'Imperialism and the Cult of Motherhood', *History Workshop Journal*, Spring 1978.

Davin, Anna, 'Child Labour, the Working-Class Family, and the Domestic Ideology in 19th Century Britain', *Development and Change*, 13, 1982.

Dennis, Wayne, 'Historical Beginnings of Child Psychology', *Psychological Bulletin*, 46, 1949.

Dingwall, Robert, 'Some Problems about Predicting Child Abuse and Neglect', in Stevenson, Olive. (ed.), *Child Abuse, Public Policy and Professional Practice*, London: Harvester Wheatsheaf, 1989.

Dingwall, Robert, and Eekelaar, J. M., 'Rethinking Child Protection', in Freeman, Michael (ed.), *State, Law and the Family: Critical Perspectives*, London: Tavistock/Sweet & Maxwell, 1984.

Dingwall, Robert, Eekelaar, J. M., and Murray, Topsy, 'Childhood as a Social Problem: A Survey of the History of Legal Regulation', *Journal of Law and Society*, 11, 2, 1984.

Dunckley, Henry, 'The Half-Timers', *Contemporary Review*, 306, 1891.

Eekelaar, John, Dingwall, Robert, and Murray, Topsy, 'Victims or Threats? Children in Care Proceedings', *Journal of Social Welfare Law*, March 1982.

Ferguson, Harry, 'Rethinking Child Protection Practices: A Case for History', in Violence Against Children Study Group, *Taking Child Abuse Seriously*, London: Unwin Hyman, 1990.

Ferguson, Harry, 'Cleveland in History: The Abused Child and Child Protection, 1880–1914', in Cooter, Roger (ed.), *In the Name of the Child: Health and Welfare, 1880–1940*, London: Routledge, 1992.

Freeden, Michael, 'Eugenics and Progressive Thought: A Study in Ideological Affinity', *Historical Journal*, 22, 1979.

Freeden, Michael, 'Eugenics and Ideology', *Historical Journal*, 26, 1983.

Frister, Osker, 'Psycho-analysis and Child Study', *School Hygiene*, 7 and 8, 1911.

Frost, Nick, 'Official Intervention and Child Protection: The Relationship between State and Family in Contemporary Britain', in Violence Against Children Study Group, *Taking Child Abuse Seriously*, London: Unwin Hyman, 1990.

Frost, N., and Stein, M., 'Educating Social Workers: A Political Analysis', in Fieldhouse, Roger (ed.), *The Political Education of Servants of the State*, Manchester: Manchester University Press, 1988.

Fry, Margaret, 'A Belgian Psychological Laboratory', *Howard Journal*, 1, 1924.

Fuller, S. D., 'Penny Dinners', *Contemporary Review*, 48, 1885.

Gelles, R. J., 'The Social Construction of Child Abuse', in his *Family Violence*, Beverly Hills, Calif.: Sage, 1979.

Gil, D., and Noble, J. H., 'Public Knowledge, Attitudes and Opinions about Physical Abuse', *Child Welfare*, 49, July 1969.

Gillis, J. R., 'The Evolution of Juvenile Delinquency in England, 1890–1914', *Past and Present*, 67, 1975.

Gorham, Deborah, 'The "Maiden Tribute of Babylon" Re-examined: Child Prostitution and the Idea of Childhood in Late-Victorian England', *Victorian Studies*, 21, 3, 1978: 353–79.

Griffiths, D. L., and Moynihan, F. J., 'Multiple Epiphyseal Injuries in Babies ("Battered Baby Syndrome")', *British Medical Journal*, 21 December 1963.

Hall, C., 'The Early Formation of Victorian Domestic Ideology', in Burman, S. (ed.), *Fit Work for Women*, London: Croom Helm, 1979.

Hall, G. S., 'The Content of Children's Minds', *Princeton Review*, 11, 1883.

Hamilton-Pearson, Edgar, 'The Problem of the Delinquent Child', *Child*, 11, 1921.

Harding, L. Fox, 'The Children Act 1989 in Context: Four Perspectives in Child Care Law and Policy', *Journal of Social Welfare and Family Law*, 1991.

Harris, Robert, 'A Matter of Balance: Power and Resistance in Child Protection Policy', *Journal of Social Welfare and Family Law*, 5, 1990.

Hendrick, Harry, 'Child Labour, Medical Capital, and the School Medical Service, c.1880–1918', in Cooter, Roger (ed.), *In the Name of the Child: Health and Welfare, 1880–1940*, London: Routledge, 1992.

Hill, M., 'Prize Essay on Juvenile Delinquency' in Hill, M., and Cornwallis, C. F., *Two Prize Essays on Juvenile Delinquency*, London: Smith, Elder, 1853.

Hirst, J. David, 'The Growth of Treatment through the School Medical Service, 1908–1918', *Medical History*, 33, 3, 1989.

Hodges, Jill, and Hussain, Athar, 'Review Article: Jacques Donzelot, La police des familles', *Ideology and Consciousness*, 5, 1979.

Hogg, Edith, 'School Children as Wage-Earners', *The Nineteenth Century*, 42, 187.

Horn, Pamela, 'The Employment of Elementary School Children in Agriculture, 1914–1918', *History of Education*, 12, 3, 1983.

Hurt, John, 'Reformatory and Industrial Schools before 1933', *History of Education*, 13, 1, 1984.

Hurt, John, 'Feeding the Hungry Schoolchild in the First Half of the Twentieth Century', in Oddy, D. J., and Miller, Derek, S. (eds), *Diet and Health in Modern Britain*, London: Croom Helm, 1985.

Hutchison, A. M., 'Symptoms in Children: Bad Habits, Sexual Precocity, Thieving', *The Lancet*, 1926.

Iselin, Henry, 'The Story of a Children's Care Committee', *Economic Journal*, 22, 1912.

Johnson, Richard, 'Educational Policy and Social Control in Early Victorian England', *Past and Present*, 49, 1970.

Jones, Ernest, 'Psycho-analysis and Education', *School Hygiene*, 2, 1911.

Jones, Greta, 'Eugenics and Social Policy between the Wars', *Historical Journal*, 25, 1982.

Jones, R. Huws, 'Physical Indices and Clinical Assessments of the Nutrition of Schoolchildren', *Journal of the Royal Statistical Society*, 100, 1938.

Jordanova, Ludmilla, 'Children in History: Concepts of Nature and Society', in Geoffrey Scarre (ed.), *Children, Parents and Politics*, Cambridge: Cambridge University Press, 1989.

Keir, Gertrude, 'A History of Child Guidance', *British Journal of Educational Psychology*, 22, 1952.

Kempe, C. H., Silverman, F. N., Steele, B. F., Droegemueller, W., and Silver, H. K., 'The Battered Child Syndrome', *Journal of the American Medical Association*, 18, 1, 1962.

Lambert, J., 'The Feeding of the School Child', in Kelynack, T. N., (ed.) *Medical Examination of Schools and Scholars*, London: P. S. King, 1910.

Land, Hilary, 'The Introduction of Family Allowances', in Hall, P., *et al.* (eds), *Change, Choice and Conflict in Social Policy*, London: Heinemann, 1975.

Layburn, K., 'The Issue of School Feeding in Bradford, 1904–1907', *Journal of Educational Administration and History*, 14, 2, 1982.

Lewis, Jane, 'Anxieties about the Family and the Relationships between Parents, Children and the State in Twentieth-Century England', in Richards, Martin, and Light, Paul (eds), *Children of Social Worlds*, Cambridge: Polity Press, 1986.

Lowe, R. A., 'Eugenicists, Doctors and the Quest for National Efficiency: An Educational Crusade, 1900–1939', *History of Education*, 7, 1979.

Lowe, R. A., 'The Early Twentieth Century Open-Air Movement: Origins and Implications', in Parry, N., and McNair, D. (eds), *The Fitness of the Nation – Physical and Health Education in the 19th and 20th Centuries*, Leicester: History of Education Society, 1983.

MacCalman, Douglas, R., 'The Present Status and Functions of the Child Guidance

343

Movement in Great Britain, and its Possible Future Developments', *Journal of Mental Science*, 85, 1939.

McCarthy, M., 'The Personal Social Services', in McCarthy, M. (ed.), *The New Politics of Welfare: An Agenda for the 1990s*, London: Macmillan, 1990.

Macnicol, John, 'Family Allowances and Less Eligibility', in Thane, Pat (ed.), *The Origins of British Social Policy*, London: Croom Helm, 1978.

Macnicol, John, 'The Evacuation of Schoolchildren', in Smith, Harold, L. (ed.), *War and Social Change: British Society in the Second World War*, Manchester: Manchester University Press, 1986.

May, Margaret, 'Innocence and Experience: The Evolution of the Concept of Juvenile Delinquency in the Mid-Nineteenth Century', *Victorian Studies*, 18, 1, 1973.

Miller, Emmanuel, 'Early Treatment and Prevention', in his *Modern Psychotherapy*, London: Jonathan Cape, 1930.

Mitchell, Margaret, 'The Effects of Unemployment on the Social Condition of Women and Children in the 1930s', *History Workshop Journal*, 19, 1985.

Moodie, William, 'Child Guidance and the Schools', reprinted from *Educational Research* supplement of the *Head Teachers' Review*, St Albans, 1931.

Norton, Bernard, 'Charles Spearman and the General Factor in Intelligence', *Journal of the History of the Behavioural Sciences*, 15, 1979.

Norton, Bernard, 'Psychologists and Class', in Webster, Charles (ed.), *Biology, Medicine and Society, 1840–1940*, Cambridge: Cambridge University Press, 1981.

Packman, J., and Jordan, B., 'The Children Act: Looking Forward, Looking Back', *British Journal of Social Work*, 21, 1991.

Parker, R. A., 'The Gestation of Reform: The Children Act, 1948', in Bean, P., and McPherson, S. (eds), *Approaches to Welfare*, London: Routledge & Kegan Paul, 1983.

Parton, C. and N., 'Child Protection: The Law and Dangerousness', in Stevenson, Olive (ed.), *Child Abuse: Public Policy and Professional Practice*, London: Harvester Wheatsheaf, 1989.

Parton, N., 'Child Abuse, Social Anxiety and Welfare', *British Journal of Social Work*, 11, 4, 1981.

Parton, N., 'The Contemporary Politics of Child Protection', *Journal of Social Welfare and Family Law*, 1992.

Parton, N., 'Children in Care: Recent Changes and Debates', *Critical Social Policy*, 13, 1985.

Parton, N., 'Taking Child Abuse Seriously', in Violence Against Children Study Group, *Taking Child Abuse Seriously*, London: Unwin Hyman, 1990.

Pfohl, J. S., 'The Discovery of Child Abuse', *Social Problems*, 24, 3, 1977.

Pinsent, Ellen, 'On the Permanent Care of the Feeble-Minded', *The Lancet*, 21 February 1903.

Plumb, J. H., 'The New World of Children in Eighteenth-Century England', *Past and Present*, 67, 1975.

Porter, Roy, 'History of the Body', in Burke, Peter (ed.), *New Reflections on Historical Writing*, Cambridge: Polity Press, 1991.

Power, Michael, *et al.*, 'Delinquency and the Family', *British Journal of Social Work*, 4, 1, 1974.

Pritchard, Eric, 'The Physiology of the Child', *Child-Study*, 11, 1, 1909.

Prout, Alan, and James, Alison, 'A New Paradigm for the Sociology of Childhood? Provenance, Promise and Problems', in Prout and James (eds), *Constructing and Reconstructing Childhood: Contemporary Issues in the Sociological Study of Childhood*, London: Falmer Press, 1990.

344

Ravenhill, Alice, 'Some Results of an Investigation into Hours of Sleep among Children in the Elementary Schools of England', *Child-Study*, 1, 4, 1909.

Renton, G., 'The East London Child Guidance Clinic', *Journal of Child Psychology and Psychiatry*, 19, 1978.

Riverie, Clive, 'Heart Strain in Boys', *School Hygiene*, 3, 1, 1910.

Robertson, Priscilla, 'Home as a Nest: Middle Class Childhood in Nineteenth-Century Europe', in Mause, Lloyd de (ed.), *The History of Childhood*, London: Souvenir Press, 1976.

Rowan, Caroline, 'Child Welfare and the Working-Class Family', in Langan, Mary, and Schwarz, Bill (eds), *Crises in the British State, 1880–1930*, London: Hutchinson, 1985.

Sandiford, Peter, ' The Half-time System in the Textile Trades', in Sadler, M. E. (ed.), *Continuation Schools in England and Elsewhere*, Manchester: Manchester University Press, 1907.

Schnell, R. L., 'Chilhood as Ideology: A Reinterpretation of the Common School', *British Journal of Education Studies*, 27, 1, 1979.

Searle, G. R., 'Psychologists and Class', in Webster, Charles (ed.), *Biology, Medicine and Society, 1840–1940*, Cambridge: Cambridge University Press, 1981.

Slack, J. A., 'The Provision of Reformatory Schools, the Landed Class, and the Myth of the Superiority of Rural Life in Mid-Victorian England', *History of Education*, 8, 1, 1979.

Smith, Samuel, 'Social Reform', *The Nineteenth Century*, 13, 1883.

Steedman, Carolyn, 'Bodies, Figures and Physiology: Margaret McMillan and the Late Nineteenth Century Remaking of Working-Class Childhood', in Cooter, Roger (ed.), *In the Name of the Child: Health and Welfare, 1880–1940*, London: Routledge, 1992.

Sully, James, 'Babies and Science', *Cornhill Magazine*, 43, 1881.

Sutherland, Gillian, 'Measuring Intelligence: English Local Education Authorities and Mental Testing, 1919–1939', in Webster, Charles (ed), *Biology, Medicine and Society, 1840–1940*, Cambridge: Cambridge University Press, 1981.

Taylor, D. M., 'The School Child Worker', in Kelynack, T. N. (ed.), *School Life*, London: P. S. King, 1911.

Thom, Deborah, 'Wishes, Anxieties, Play and Gestures: Child Guidance in Inter-War England', in Cooter, Roger (ed.), *In the Name of the Child: Health and Welfare, 1880–1940*, London: Routledge, 1992.

Turner, D., 'The Open-Air School Movement in Sheffield', *History of Education*, 1, 1972.

Urwin, Cathy, and Sharland, Elaine, 'From Bodies to Minds in Childcare Literature: Advice to Parents in Inter-War Britain', in Cooter, Roger (ed.), *In the Name of the Child: Health and Welfare, 1880–1940*, London: Routledge, 1992.

Webster, Charles, 'Healthy or Hungry Thirties?', *History Workshop Journal*, 13, 1982.

Webster, Charles, 'The Health of the School Child during the Depression', in Parry, Nicholas, and McNair, David (eds), *The Fitness of the Nation – Physical and Health Education in the Nineteenth and Twentieth Centuries*, Leicester: History of Education Society, 1983.

Webster, Charles, 'Health, Welfare and Unemployment during the Depression', *Past and Present*, 109, 1985.

Winter, J. M., 'Infant Mortality, Maternal Mortality and Public Health in Britain in the 1930s', in *Journal of European Economic History*, 8, 1979.

Winter, Jay, 'Unemployment, Nutrition and Infant Mortality in Britain, 1920–50', in Winter, Jay (ed.), *The Working Class in Modern British History*, Cambridge: Cambridge University Press, 1983.

Wohl, A. S., 'Sex and the Single Room: Incest among the Victorian Working Classes', in his *The Victorian Family*, London: Croom Helm, 1978.

Woodhead, Martin, 'Psychology and the Cultural Construction of Children's Needs', in James, Allison, and Prout, Alan (eds), *Constructing and Reconstructing Childhood: Contemporary Issues in the Sociological Study of Childhood*, London: The Falmer Press, 1990.

JOURNALS

British Medical Journal
Child-Study
The Children's Guardian
The Lancet
School Hygiene

UNPUBLISHED THESES

Harris, Bernard John, 'Medical Inspection and the Nutrition of Schoolchildren in Britain, 1900–1950', University of London PhD thesis, 1988.

Hirst, David J., 'The Origins and Development of the School Medical Service, 1870–1919', University of Wales (Bangor), PhD thesis, 1983.

Riddell, Jennie, 'A Study of the History and Development of the School Medical Service in Liverpool from 1908 to 1939', University of Liverpool MA thesis, 1946.

Ross, A. M., 'Care and Education of Pauper Children', London University PhD thesis, 1955.

Sherrington, C., 'The NSPCC in Transition, 1884–1983: A Study in Organizational Survival', London University PhD thesis, 1985.

Stewart, John, 'Children and Social Policy in Great Britain, 1871–1909', London University MPhil thesis, 1988.

Welshman, John, 'The School Medical Service in England and Wales, 1907–1939', Oxford University DPhil thesis, 1988.

Wooldridge, A., 'Child Study and Educational Psychology in England, c.1850–1950', Oxford University DPhil thesis, 1985.

INDEX

abuse and cruelty 7, 11, 12, 49–60, 182, 225, 241, 251–3; rediscovery of 253–7; *see also* NSPCC, child abuse, and child neglect

Acts of Parliament: Adoption of Children Act (1926) 237; (1958) 239; Bastardy Laws Amendment Act (1872) 47; Birth and Death Registration Act (1874) 47; Children Acts (1908) 55, 121–6, 177, 179, 182–4, 250; (1948) 6, 217–20, 222, 238, 240, 245, 251, 287–8; (1975) 11, 237, 239–41; (1989) 15, 276–84, 287–8; Children and Young Persons Acts (1933) 10, 177–8, 183–8, 191, 206, 227, 250; (1963) 227–9, 235, 277; (1969) 11, 231–5, 240; Contagious Diseases Acts (1864, 1866, 1869) 61; Criminal Justice Act (1948) 229; Criminal Law Amendment Act (1885) 60–4, 67; Education Acts (1902) 113, 154; (1914) 147; (1918) 71, 88, 157; (1921) 142, 154; (1944) 89, 153, 173, 200–1; Education (Administrative Provisions) Act (1907) 111, 116, 119; Education (Defective and Epileptic Children) Act (1914) 92; Education (Provision of meals) Act (1906) 104, 108–10; Elementary Education Acts (1870) 86; (1876) 70; (1880), (1891), (1899) 29; Elementary Education (Blind and Deaf Children) Act (1893) 88; Elementary Education (Defective and Epileptic Children) Act (1899) 90, 92, 146; Employment of Children Act (1903) 71; Factory Acts (1802, 1819, 1833, 1844, 1850, 1853, 1864, 1867) 24–5; (1861) 10; Factory and Workshops Act (1878) 70; Friendly Societies Act (1875) 55; Industrial Schools Act (1857) 189; Infant Life Protection Acts (1872, 1897) 46–9; Infant Life Protection Act (1908) 49; Legitimacy Act (1926) 238; Local Authority Social Services Act (1970) 232, 237; Maternity and Child Welfare Act (1918) 102, 144; Mental Deficiency Act (1913) 90, 92; Milk Act (1934) 140; National Assistance Act (1948) 219; National Health Service Act (1946) 102, 201; National Insurance Act (1911) 100, (1946) 219; Notification of Births Act (1907) 97, 99; (1915) 97, 101; Offences against the Person Act (1861) 54; Poor Law Amendment Acts (1834) 44, 74; (1844) 44–5; (1868) 53; Prevention of Cruelty to Children Act (1889) 7, 53–6; Prevention of Cruelty to Children Amendment Act (1904) 55; Punishment of Incest Act (1908) 65–7; Registration Act (1926) 48; Registration of Births and Deaths Act (1836) 44; Summary Jurisdiction Act (1879) 124; Youthful Offenders Act (1901) 125; Youthful Offenders Act (1854) 27

Adams, Sir John 150, 152
Adler, Alfred, *Guiding the Child* 170
adolescence: and age of consent 63–4
adoption 237, 272; Adoption of Children, Departmental Committee (Houghton Report, 1972) 239–40,

347

248; and poor law guardians 237–8; *see also* fostering
age of consent (sexual) *see* Criminal Law Amendment Act (1885)
ageism xii, 291
Agnew, F. A. Thomas 51
Allen, Marjorie (Lady Allen of Hurtwood) 212; *Whose Children?* 213, 221, 254

Bailey, Victor 177, 180, 188
Ballantyne, Dr John 95
Ballard, P. B. 152, 155
Barnardo, Dr 3, 41, 80–1
Beckford, Jasmine 12
Behlmer, George 47, 49, 55, 57
Bell, Stuart 274, 282
Beveridge, W. H. 220–2
Beveridge Report 232
Binet, Alfred 154, 164
Black, Sir Douglas 267–8
Black Report, The (1980) 267–71; recommendations of 269; *see also* child health and *The Health Divide* (1988)
Blake, William 22
blind, the: 85–7; *see also* legislation for defective child
bodies, of children 1–7, 12–13, 36, 42, 90, 127–8, 131, 153, 188–9, 206, 211, 270, 287–8, 290–1; *see also* minds
Boer war, social and racial anxieties caused by 14, 93, 104, 106, 114
Booth, Charles 58, 68, 105
Booth, William 65
Bowlby, John 6, 11, 173, 259; *Maternal Care and Mental Health* (1951) 219, 235
Boyd, William 152
Boyd-Orr, Sir John 133, 136–7, 205
British Medical Association (BMA) 34–5, 118, 136, *The Adolescent* (1961) 230
British Medical Journal (*BMJ*) 45, 48, 73, 94, 107, 113, 244, 248, 267
British Paediatric Association 5, 6, 245, 270
Burdett-Coutts, Baroness Angela 52
Burt, Cyril 151; and Child Guidance Council 165; and 'difficult children' 163; his *Distribution of Mental Abilities* 155; and hereditability 156;

and juvenile delinquency 174, 178, 206; as LCC psychologist 152; and mental testing 153, 160–1; and political anxieties 161; his *Psychology of the Young Criminal* (1924) 180; and 'treble-track' system 158; his *The Young Delinquent* (1925) 178
Butler-Sloss, Mrs Justice (Cleveland Inquiry) 274

Cadbury, Geraldine 181
Caffey, Dr John 243–4
Calder, Angus 194
Cameron, Hector 5
care orders 234
care proceedings (under 1969 legislation) 232
'care and protection', of children 27–8, 123–4, 186
Carlebach, Julius 191
Carlton Miller, Dr Hugh 164
Carpenter, Mary 28–9, 31, 41, 250
Cattell, James 153
Cattell, Raymond 150
Central Association for Mental Welfare CAMW 165–6, 206
Charity Organisation Society, The: 86, 88, 90–1, 93, 105
Charley, W. T. 47
child abuse 242, 286; and the 'battered baby' 243–6; cases 273–4; and Children Act (1989) 279–80; and Cleveland 275–6; concepts of 254–7; disease model 244; rediscovery of 253–7; sexual 276; state intervention in 246
child care policy: assessment of (1989 Act) 281–4; concepts of (1989 Act) 276–80; criticisms of 272–6
child guidance clinics 5, 163–4; authority of 172; and childhood 'disorders' 167, 172; jurisdiction of 171–2; numbers of 168; patients 168–9; principles of treatment 169–71; psychiatric influence 167
Child Guidance Council 5, 131, 165–6, 170, 172–3, 175, 205
child guidance movement: aims of 176, 205–6; and mental hygiene 211; sources and origins 162–4; wartime

development of 172–6; *see also*
Feversham Committee
child health services 263–7; and Black
Report and *The Health Divide*
267–71; *see also* School Medical
Service and School Dental Service
child labour 24–7, 29–30; critique of
68–9; Employment of School
Children, Interdepartmental
Committee on 69; government
response to 69–71; and medical
opinion 71–3; numbers 69; reform
of 67–74; varieties 69–70
child neglect 10, 56–60, 182–3, 186–7,
252; and Ingleby Report 224; and
Juvenile Offenders Committee 250–1
child poverty 268, 286–7
Child Study movement 4, 33–6, 125,
128, 290; *see also* psychology
childhood, constructions of 19–37: and
Child Study 33–7; 'delinquent' 27–9;
'Factory' 24–7; ' "natural",
Romantic and Evangelical' 21–4;
'school' 29–33
children 5; as investments 14–15, 42, 82,
106, 126, 176, 211, 285; Nation, of
the 41; State, of the 41; and voluntary
societies 78–80
children in care: categories and
numbers of 214, 218; conditions
213–16; system of 212–13; *see also*
corporal punishment; Curtis Report
Children's Committees (Local
Authority) 217–18
Children's Departments (Local
Authority) 217, 222, 228, 236, 245,
251, 254
Children's Minimum Council 138, 205
Children's Officers (Local Authority)
217–19, 235, 245
children's rights 59, 241, 275, 283–4
Churchill, Winston 190
Cleveland inquiry (child abuse scandal)
274–6
Coleridge, S. T. 22–3
Colwell, Maria 11, 240, 242; inquiry
246–9, 253–4
Consultative Committee at the Board
of Education: inter-war inquiries of
152; and *Psychological Tests of
Educable Capacity* (1924) 155; and
Report on the Primary School (1931)

155; and *The Spens Report* (1938)
155
Consumers' Association, survey of
children in hospital 262
corporal punishment: 57, 77–8; in
children's homes 216; in families
256; of juvenile delinquents 181,
188–91; *see also* Curtis Report
Court, Professor Donald 264
Court Committee (on Child Health
Services) 261; Report 'Fit for the
Future' (1977) 264–7, 270
Crichton-Browne, Sir James 34
Crowley, Dr R. H. 165
Cruickshank, George 81
Cunningham, Hugh 26, 33
Curgenven, Dr John 45
Curtis, Dame Myra 213
Curtis Report (1946): 6, 214–17, 220–1,
237, 239, 254, 258, 260;
recommendations 216–17; *see also*
children in care

Darwin, Charles 33
Davenport-Hill, Florence 52
deaf, the 85–8; *see also* legislation for
defective child
Dendy, Mary 91
Department of Health and Social
Security (DHSS) 266–7; *Child
Abuse – Working Together* (1986)
275; *Review of Child Care Law*
(1985) 273–4, 278
Departmental Committee on Defective
and Epileptic Children (1898) 89
Departmental Committee on
Reformatory and Industrial Schools
(1913) 190
Departmental Committee on the
Treatment of Young Offenders
(1927) (Young Offenders
Committee) 10, 178–83, 192, 250
Devlin, Tim 274
Dingwall, Eekelaar and Murray 249
Dingwall and Eekelaar 284
doctors, and 'baby-farmers' 45–6
'Domestic Ideal' 24–5, 58; and incest 65
Donzelot, Jacques 226–7, 232–3, 282,
289
Drever, James 151
Dwork, Deborah 97

East London Child Guidance Clinic
(1927) 165
Eder, David 4
emigration 80–3
eugenics 68, 90, 92–3
evacuees, evacuation 5, 131, 173, 194–9,
211–12, 221
evangelical, evangelicalism 8, 20, 82

family, the: bourgeois 51, 274–5; and
child abuse 246, 282; and child
health 265–71; and Children Acts
(1908) 122; (1948) 220–2; (1989) 277,
280–2; and Cleveland 274–6;
difficulties of 219; discipline 57–8;
and 'family service' 231, 235–7;
intervention 59, 235; and juvenile
delinquency 222–3; and liberal
theory 282–3; 'natural' ('blood-tie')
240–1; the poor 51, 82; and
preventive social work 227–9; as
privatised 287; 'problem' families 11,
206, 222, 251–2; and psychiatric care
166; the 'psychological family' 162;
purity of 60; and respectability 112;
'at risk' 223, 237; and the State 220–2;
and 'therapeutic familialism' 231,
233, 235; see also child guidance and
clinics; Ingleby Report
'feeble-minded', the 42, 85–93
Feversham Committee, The Voluntary
Mental Health Services (1939) 172–6
Fildes, Lucy 173
fostering 217, 239
Foucault, Michel 2, 226
Fox, Dame Evelyn 165
Freeman, Michael 276–7, 279, 281
Freud, Anna 6, 170, 259
Freud, Sigmund 151, 164
Frost, Nick 283
Fyvel, T. R. The Insecure Offenders
(1961) 230

Galton, Francis 34, 153, 163
Gil, David 255, 257
Gilbert, Bentley 14
girls: as drudges 70; and medical
inspection 115; protection of 65;
sexuality of 61–4, 91, 185
Gorham, Deborah 63–4
Gorst, Sir John 9, The Children of the
Nation (1906) 41–2, 84, 105, 107

Hadow Report (1926) 151, 157
Hall, Penelope 252
Hall, Stanley 33, 34
Hall, William Clarke 181
Hamley, H. R. 152
Hart, Ernest 46
Health Divide, The (1988) 268–9
Healy, William 163, 168, 178
Heywood, Jean 76, 188
Higgs, Dr Marietta (and Wyatt, Dr
Geoffrey) 274
Hill, Florence Davenport, Children of
the State (1868, 1889) 41
Hill, M. D. 27
Hill, Micaiah 27–8
Hogg, Edith 69
Holman, Robert 239
Home Office 66
Home and Schools Council, Advances
in Understanding the Child (1935)
171
hospitals 117; welfare of children in
258–63; see also Platt Committee
housing, of the working classes 65
Hug-Hellmuth, Hermione 170
Hughes, A. G. 152
Hutchison, Robert 107

imperialism (and Empire) 68, 81–2,
93–4
incest 14, 65–7; see also Punishment of
Incest Act
industrial schools (and reformatories)
10, 123, 182, 192, 250
Infant Life Protection Movement 43–9
Infant Life Protection Society (ILPS) 3,
46–7
infant mortality rates 94–5, 98, 103, 145,
264–5
infant welfare: 93–103; and health
visitors 96–7; milk depots 95–6;
problem of 93–5; responses to
problem of 95–6; state social service
100–2; and welfare schemes 98–100;
in war years 101–3
infanticide 44–5, 55
infants and pre-school children, welfare
services for 143–5
Ingleby Report (1960) (Committee on
Children and Young Committee):
11, 223–7, 230; and child cruelty 251;

neglect of children's services 223; and 'welfare model' 225–7
Institute for the Scientific Treatment of Delinquency (1931) 165
Intelligence Quotient 155–6
Isaacs, Susan 6, 151

Joseph, Sir Keith (and 'cycle of deprivation' theory) 247, 263
juvenile courts 123–4, 179–80, 187; and Ingleby Report 223, 231–3
juvenile delinquency: 10, 27–9, 31, 174, 235; changing perspectives on 177–8; and depravation and deprivation 222–5; and Juvenile Organisations Committee findings 180; psycho-medical treatment of 181; rate of 178, 229–30; threat from 250
juvenile justice 235

Kahan, Barbara 236
Keeling, Frederic 69
Kelynack, T. N. 42
Kempe, Dr Henry 243–5
Kimmins, Dr C. W. 152
Klein, Melanie 6, 173
Knight, Dame Jill 282

Labour Party White Paper, Children in Trouble (1968) 231
Lancet, The 65, 72, 93, 97, 105
legislation for the 'defective child' 88–90
Liverpool SPCC, founding of 51
Local Education Authorities (LEAs): and child guidance clinics 168, 173; and evacuation 197; and Feversham committee, recommendations 174–6; and handicapped children 146–7, 201; and mental testing 159–60; and payment for medical treatment 119–20; and preventive social work 227; and psychologists 149; and school clinics 117–19; and school dentistry 143; and school meals 108–11, 135, 138, 141, 199–200; and School Medical Service 115, 120–1; and welfare provision 113
London Child Guidance Training Centre and Clinic in Islington (1928) 165

Longford Report, The 231
Lowenfeld, Margaret 165

McCleary, G. F. 96
McDougall, William 151, 163
M'Gonigle, G. C. M. 133, 140
Mackenzie, Dr W. Leslie 113
McMillan, Margaret 3, 4, 151
McNally, C. E. 133
Macnicol, John 133, 205
Macpherson, Annie 80
Madden, Max 282
malnourishment 105–6, 110; see also nutrition; school meals
Manchester Guardian 212
Manning, Cardinal Henry 52
Mansfield, Katherine 264, 292
Masterman, C. F. G. 190
maternal deprivation 218–19, 259; see also Bowlby, John
Maxwell, Alexander 192
May, Margaret 27
Mearns, Reverend Andrew 51, 65
media, the, and discovery of child abuse 253–4
Medical Inspection and School Feeding, Interdepartment Committee on (1905) 107
medicine, medical opinion 2, 127; child labour and 71–3; preventive 127
mental health (see child guidance; Feversham Committee)
mental testing 4, 92, 153–61; see also psychology
meritocratic ideal 161–2
Miller, Emmanuel 15, 170; The Growing Child and Its Problems (1937) 171, 206
Miller, H. C. 170
mind/s: 1, 3–7, 12, 42, 131, 149–50, 153, 211, 287–8, 290–1; see also bodies
Ministry of Health, paper, 'The Break-Up of the Poor Law and the Care of Children and Old People' 212
Monckton, Sir Walter 212
Montessori, Maria 92, 150
Moodie, Dr William 165, 168–9
Moore, Dr G. S. 98
'moral panic' 11, 249, 253
Morant, Sir Robert 204
More, Hannah 8, 24

Morgan, Jane and Zedner, Lucia, *Child Victims* (1992) 291
Morley, John 54
Morton, Reverend Arthur 245, 254
Mundella, A. J. 50, 54

National Association for Promoting the Welfare of the Feeble-Minded (NAPWFM) 89–91
National Association for the Welfare of Children in Hospital (NAWCH) 261
National Children's Bureau 270
National Council for Maternity and Child Welfare 212
National Council for Mental Health (NCMH) 165–6, 173, 206
National Council for the Unmarried Mother and Her Child 238
'national efficiency' 68, 93–4, 126
National Health Service (NHS) 201–2, 263; and child health 266
National Institute of Child Psychology 5
National Society for the Prevention of Cruelty to Children (NSPCC): 3, 41, 49; and abuse and neglect 251, 256; and age of consent legislation 61, 66; and Children Act (1908) 122; founding of 50–2; policy of 52; 'practice and experience' 56–60; and rediscovery of child abuse 244–6
National Vigilance Association 62, 66
'New Right' 11, 235, 247, 253
Newman, Sir George 99, 108–10, 116, 118, 120–1, 126, 127, 133–5, 138–9, 141, 144, 154, 164, 203–4
Newsholme, Dr Arthur 95, 102–3
Norris, Arthur 190
Norwood Report (1943) 153
Nunn, Percy 151
nutrition 110–11; inter-war debate on 133–40, 205; *see also* school meals; malnourishment

O'Neill, Denis 212, 222, 253
Owen, David 240

Packman, Jean 222, 230, 232, 234–5
parents: and child care policy 275; and Children Act (1989) 276–8; and Ingleby Report 225; and NSPCC 52, 80; power 59; responsibility 107, 125; rights, 54, 275; and voluntary societies 79–80; and 'welfare model' 226
Parr, Robert 59
partnership, between parents and State 273; *see also* Children Act (1989)
Parton, Nigel 241–2, 245, 253, 255, 273, 276, 279
Paterson, Alexander 181
Pearson, Geoffrey 229
'permissiveness' 12, 271
philanthropic and philanthropy 41, 52, 82
Physical Deterioration, Interdepartmental Committee on (1904) 107
Pinsent, Ellen 91, 93
Platt Committee (on welfare of children in hospital) 258–9; recommendations 259–60
Poor Law 41; board of guardians 47, 53; Relief (School Children) Order (1905) 108; Unions 49; and voluntary societies 78
poor law children 74–9; experiences of 77–8; numbers of 76; reports on (Macnamara) 1908, 77; (Mundella) 1896, 75–7; (Senior) 1873, 77
poverty 100, 105, 253
Preyer, Wilhelm 33
Priestley, J. B. 228
Pritchard, Dr Eric 100
pronatalism 220–1, 285–6
Provisional National Council for Mental Health 174
psychological, psychology 131, 149–50; of evacuation 198; *see also* Child Study
psychology, educational and mental testing 153–60
psychology and progressive education 150–3

reformatory schools 10
Report of the Care of Children Committee (1946) (Curtis Report) 147–8, 192
Report of the Departmental Committee on Reformatories and Industrial Schools (1913) 182
Report of the Joint Departmental

Committee on Mental Deficiency (1929) (Wood Report) 147, 154
Robertson, James 259, 261
Rose, Lionel 47
Rose, Nikolas 14, 127–8, 162, 164, 167, 231, 235, 283, 291
Rousseau, J.-J. 21–2, 26
Rowntree, Seebohm 68
Royal Commissions: Care and Control of the Feebleminded (1908) 91, 93; Education of the Blind, Deaf and Dumb, and the Feeble Minded (1889) 89; Physical Training (Scotland) (1903) 106; the Population (1949) 15, 220
Russell, Charles 181–2, 190
Rye, Maria 80

Samuel, Herbert 125–6
school and schooling: 29–33; and corporal punishment 50; and health 113; influence of 103–4; 'over-pressure' 34; The Primary School (1931) 152; secondary education, rising demand for 156–7; streaming 158–60; see also psychology, educational and mental testing
school clinics 116–19
School Dental Service 143, 194, 197
school meals: 103–10, 133–41; debate on 105–8, 205; early efforts 104–5; legislation 108–10; and manners 110; milk meals 135, 140–1, 199–200; and Second World War 199–200; and socialists 106; voluntary feeding agencies 104–5
school medical inspection and treatment 111–21, 141–3, 195–6
School Medical Officers (SMOs) 109, 111, 113–15, 134–5, 139, 194
School Medical Service: 111, 133, 141; assessment of 203–5; and First World War 120–1; and handicapped children 145–48; origins of 112–14; and payment 119–20; and Second World War 194–5, 197–8
Seebohm Report (1968) 236, 247
Select Committee on Death Certification (1893) 48
Shaftesbury, Lord 8, 9, 46, 50
Short Report (1984), review of child care law 276

Shuttleworth, G. E. 93
Simon, Brian 158
Simon, Victor 153
Smith, Samuel 51, 59, 66, 81
Social Darwinism 84–5, 90, 92–3
social problems 50–2, 253
Social Services Departments 247
social work, social workers 11, 234, 247
Spearman, C. 153, 155
Staite, Reverend George 50
Stead, W. T. 62, 66
Stern, William 155
Stocks, Mary 212
Strachey, Mrs St Loe 165, 180
Straus, Gelles and Steinmatz 256
Stretton, Hesba 52
Sully, James 33, 163
Sunday Times 248
Sutherland, Gillian, Ability, Merit and Measurement 159–60

Tavistock Clinic 5, 164, 169–70, 259–60
Thompson, Godfrey 152
Times, The 137–8, 229, 248
Times Educational Supplement 155
Titmuss, R. M. 139, 145, 198, 236
Tuckwell, Gertrude, The State and Its Children (1894) 41
'Tunbridge Wells Study Group on Child Abuse' 247
Turner, Bryan 1

victims (and threats) 1, 7–13, 42, 128, 182, 206–7, 211, 228, 249–51, 285–6, 291
Violence in the Home, House of Commons Select Committee on 248–9

Wagner, Gillian 82
Waifs and Strays Society 48
Warner, Francis 34, 89
Watkins, D. 219
Waugh, Bejamin 54, 66
Webb, Beatrice 65
Webster, Charles 133, 144–5, 204
Weeks, Jeffrey 61
welfare ideology: new perspectives on 59, 186, 206; 'welfare model' 226–7; 'welfare' and 'classical justice' 231; welfare orientation, criticism of 272
Welfare State, the 104, 202, 211, 220, 237

INDEX

Wheeler, Olive 151
Winter, J. M. 103
Wohl, A. S. 65
Women's Group on Public Welfare

212; *The Neglected Child and His Family* 252
Wordsworth, William 22
Worsley, Reverend Henry 28

Printed in Great Britain
by Amazon